S0-AZV-479

CRIME AND JUSTICE
in New York City
1998-1999 Edition

Written by the Faculty of JOHN JAY COLLEGE
of Criminal Justice of the City University of New York

Edited by Andrew Karmen

The McGraw-Hill Companies, Inc.
Primis Custom Publishing

New York St. Louis San Francisco Auckland Bogotá
Caracas Lisbon London Madrid Mexico Milan Montreal
New Delhi Paris San Juan Singapore Sydney Tokyo Toronto

McGraw·Hill

A Division of The McGraw·Hill Companies

CRIME AND JUSTICE in New York City
1998-1999 Edition

Copyright © 1998 by The McGraw-Hill Companies, Inc. All rights reserved. Printed in the United States of America. Except as permitted under the United States Copyright Act of 1976, no part of this publication may be reproduced or distributed in any form or by any means, or stored in a data base retrieval system, without prior written permission of the publisher.

pp. 82-93 is excerpted from "The Improbable Transformation of Inner-City Neighborhoods: Crimes, Violence, Drugs, and Youth in the 1990's" by Richard Curtis appearing in *The Journal of Criminal Law and Criminology*, volume 88, issue 4. Copyright Northwestern University.

McGraw-Hill's Primis Custom Publishing consists of products that are produced from camera-ready copy. Peer review, class testing, and accuracy are primarily the responsibility of the author(s).

1 2 3 4 5 6 7 8 9 0 BBC BBC 9 0 9 8

ISBN 0-07-289724-4

Editor: Adam Knepper
Cover Concept: Gary Zaragovitch
Printer/Binder: Braceland Brothers, Inc.

DEDICATION

This collection of articles is dedicated to the many students at John Jay College who must struggle to overcome severe economic disadvantages in their quest to fulfill their own potentials as well as to make their contributions to furthering social and criminal justice. The proceeds from the sale of this book will be set aside for the most hardpressed students in the form of a scholarship fund.

Crime And Justice In New York City

1998-1999 Edition

TABLE OF CONTENTS

PART TWO:
NEW YORK CITY'S CRIMINAL JUSTICE SYSTEM

FORWARD TO THE 1998-1999 EDITION

BY

GERALD W. LYNCH

PRESIDENT

JOHN JAY COLLEGE OF CRIMINAL JUSTICE

CITY UNIVERSITY OF NEW YORK

After racial tragedies struck America in the 1960s, most notably in Watts, Detroit, and Newark, several presidential commissions called for the professional development of the police. They also recommended the further refinement of criminal justice as a body of knowledge. In response, New York City's Mayor, the City University Of New York's Chancellor, and the Police Commissioner worked to set up a College of Police Science (C.O.P.S.) in 1964 to serve the needs of police officers and to address public concerns over perceived shortcomings in the criminal justice system and the inadequate training of police personnel. In an early document, the founders envisioned an institution which would become "a well known regional and international facility of higher education for the training of law enforcement officers from here and abroad." In 1966, it was renamed John Jay College of Criminal Justice to indicate the broader scope of its mission.

John Jay College is currently the only college entirely devoted to the study of criminal justice and has become the locus where theory and practice converge. The mission of the College addresses the core issues which shape American society -- social justice, public order, and right versus wrong. The College has won wide acclaim and earned a reputation for excellence in criminal justice and public service education, research, and training. It has further developed the field of criminal justice and improved its standing.

John Jay College has been at the center of the effort to professionalize policing. Indeed, it has become a leading voice for the recognition of higher education as a fundamental component for the training of police personnel and other public safety and criminal justice professionals. In the global arena, it has fostered a new dialogue between practitioners and scholars, in order to create a more collaborative environment for addressing public safety problems which now transcend geographic borders and jurisdictional boundaries.

The College has an ethnically and culturally diverse student body in excess of 11,200. Many of these students are members of uniformed criminal justice and fire service agencies. The majority of the students are civilian professionals who plan careers in public service. An impressive proportion of the College's 25,000 alumni have assumed leadership roles in public and private organizations around the world. The Ph.D. program in Criminal Justice is now the largest such program in the country.

The Lloyd George Sealy Library is the leading criminal justice research library in the United States and serves to support the needs of students and faculty at the College, and scholars, researchers and journalists from around the world.

Indeed the strength, reputation and vitality of John Jay College is embodied in the commitment to excellence maintained by its faculty. They are leading experts in their respective fields. Many professors embody a combination of academic achievement and extensive practical experience in agencies throughout the criminal justice system. This collection of intellectual talent is diverse and covers a broad spectrum of interests. There is a strong commitment to share this intellectual resource not only in the classroom but in the world of scholarship. Faculty are active in publishing their work through major texts, scholarly journals, making presentations at academic conferences, and providing expert commentary in the media. They also make valuable contributions through their affiliation with and leadership roles in numerous professional organizations. The curriculum is constantly renewed and re-invigorated by the emerging interests and innovative scholarly work of the faculty. The College's commitment is to continue to question conventional methods and ideas, reassess traditional approaches, and identify best practices worldwide.

The College is in a unique position by virtue of its special mission to assemble an area handbook about New York City's crime problem and its criminal justice system (the first collection of its kind for any major city.) Contributions were drawn from the faculty of a number of departments at the College and represent a wide variety of professional experiences and areas of academic expertise. With the talent, knowledge, and insight available at John Jay, it was possible to cover all the major issues necessary for this ambitious undertaking from within the ranks of the College's faculty.

Although this is not an official publication of John Jay College, and the views expressed in these chapters are strictly those of the authors, this collection of articles is indicative of the high caliber of scholarly work that takes place at the College. This publication demonstrates the kind of research, scholarship, and policy analysis which led to the number one ranking in 1998 by *US News & World Report* received by the College's graduate program in Public Management: Criminal Justice Policy.

Readers hopefully will find "Crime and Justice in New York City" to be informative, insightful, comprehensive and thought-provoking.

INTRODUCTION TO THE 1998-1999 EDITION,

BY THE EDITOR

This *area handbook* is the first of its kind and fills an important void in the professional literature. Many newspaper, magazine, and journal articles have been written about New York City's crime problem and its legal system. Indeed, whole books have been written about one aspect or another of lawbreaking in the City (especially its drug scene and mob activities) or some component of it's justice system (particularly the police, or the courts). But no single volume has stitched together a general overview of the major aspects of New York's crime problem and its entire criminal justice apparatus. The City's crime problem is so serious and multi-faceted, and its justice system is so complex and extensive that no one individual can be simultaneously a knowledgeable-enough generalist as well as an expert specialist to "do justice" to the entire subject. Dr. James Davis (who has taught courses at John Jay College) deserves credit for single-handedly undertaking the tasks of describing law enforcement, adjudication, and corrections in his 1990 book entitled "Criminal Justice in New York City" (McFarland Press). In assembling this reader, I had the advantage of "calling for back-up" and got a quick and supportive response from my highly-qualified colleagues at John Jay College.

The first half of this collection fits under the heading of "criminology." Criminologists want to find out about illegal activities (like mob rackets), understand the motivations of offenders (such as members of street gangs), examine the plight of crime victims (including persons who get murdered), uncover the immediate and root causes of involvement in crime (such as the underlying economic transformation of the job market), review the historical development of illicit activities (especially drug selling), and explore the social reaction to lawbreaking (including the spread and entrenchment of fearfulness).

The second half of this book of readings covers the components of the City's legal system. The discipline of criminal justice is devoted to the study of law enforcement (especially innovative police strategies); adjudication (particularly the prosecution of cases in court); and punishment (primarily imprisonment, and even execution; but also alternatives to incarceration like probation).

Specifically, in the opening chapter of the set of criminological articles in Part One, Charles Bahn and Marvie Brooks expose the myth that New York City is the crime capital of the country. The level of criminal activities in some neighborhoods may be very threatening, but other large cities with better reputations have much more serious problems with lawless behavior. If New York is number one, it is first in terms of the size and complexity of its criminal justice apparatus, and it currently leads all other urban areas in the rate of improvement of public safety during the 1990s.

Robert McCrie examines the historical record to reconstruct the earliest conflicts leading to bloodshed that broke out between explorers and colonists versus the native American tribes inhabiting what is now the metropolitan area.

Andrew Karmen derives some statistics from the databases he has collected to summarize the murders that have taken place in recent years. He makes clear who the killers are, who their victims were, what the reasons were for the slayings, where the crimes took place, and the possible explanations that try to account for the remarkable "crime crash" of the 1990s.

David Brotherton reports his observations drawn from field notes and interviews about how street gangs, especially the Latin Kings, may be transforming into vehicles for grass-roots social and political activism in the City's poverty-stricken neighborhoods.

Daniel Vona traces the evolution of organized crime syndicates from the days of pirates and robber barons right up to present times, showing how the process of ethnic succession has enabled new immigrant groups to muscle in on the rackets formerly dominated by five New York based Mafia families.

Mangai Natarajian analyzes cocaine and heroin trafficking and identifies the smuggling routes that have been established to bring these products into New York, the hub of national distribution networks.

Ethnographer Richard Curtis tells about the changes in the street drug scene he has witnessed in Bushwick, Brooklyn during the 1980s and 1990s.

Delores Jones-Brown describes the mood in Brownsville, Brooklyn, where the impressive improvement -- on paper -- in crime statistics has not yet changed perceptions of safety vs. danger among neighborhood residents.

Economist Joan Hoffman dissects the local economy and links deteriorating job opportunities for poor, unskilled women to their growing involvement in thievery and the lowest levels of the drug trade.

Andrew Karmen examines tragic and infuriating line-of-duty deaths in which police officers are murder victims, and analyzes the dangers members of the service face of getting killed on the job. He then explores the deaths of suspects at the hands of NYPD officers, and the recurring controversies that surround a small number of these justifiable homicides each year. This last chapter in the criminological section makes the transition to the focus on criminal justice operations that runs through the chapters in Part Two.

Eli Silverman and Paul O'Connell draw on NYPD documents to describe how the Department has been re-engineered into a much more effective crime fighting force. He explains the new strategies that have been devised to prevent crime, to catch criminals, and to make the City's streets even safer.

Vincent Del Castillo draws upon his experience as a former Transit Chief to describe the tactics that were used to protect subway riders and stem fare-beating and graffiti vandalism.

Robert Louden chronicles the emergence and refinement of NYPD crisis negotiation techniques he helped to develop which are designed to persuade hostage takers to avoid bloodshed, surrender peacefully, and release their captives unharmed.

Martin Wallenstein relies upon his legal training and experiences as an assistant district attorney to explain the responsibilities of prosecutors and the challenges they face.

Dan Pinello applies his expertise in legal matters to help make sense of New York's unusually complicated court system.

James Levine shares some data he has collected and analyzed to illustrate how New Yorkers serving on juries are influenced by their political leanings when they render verdicts.

Charles Lindner draws upon his years of experience in the Department of Probation to recount the agency's origins and early difficulties, and then fast-forwards to the present to critically examine its current operations and programs.

Andrew Karmen summarizes information provided by the Department of Correction about the City's jails.

Barry Latzer utilizes his legal training and experience as an assistant district attorney to dissect the provisions of New York's 1995 capital punishment statute that will slowly fill the cells on death row in upstate prisons with convicts awaiting execution.

Maria Volpe provides a reminder that there is a viable challenge to the hegemony of the punitive approach within criminal justice, and that community-based mediation and dispute resolution programs have been an overlooked alternative to adjudication and incarceration in the five boroughs for a number of years.

Michael Jacobson brings this collection of articles to a close by drawing upon his expertise in fiscal matters and his experiences as the Commissioner of Probation (in the administrations of both Mayor Dinkins and Mayor Giuliani) and also of Correction. He assembles otherwise inaccessible data about the actual amount of taxpayer money spent on government functions, as well as the expanding and contracting employment opportunities in municipal agencies over the past two decades, in order to trace how the allocation of financial and human resources by different mayors affected public safety.

Clearly, this collection of articles should prove indispensable to those who want to find out -- or need to know -- what the true dimensions of New York's crime problem actually are, and how the City's justice machinery really works.

An area handbook is needed because standard textbooks that provide an "Introduction To Criminal Justice" describe a generalized legal system that is invariably modified in every jurisdiction. Although the institutions (state criminal statutes, municipal law enforcement agencies, local courts, and county probation departments and jails) might be comparable, there are always variations on a theme. To give but one example, in New York City, the jails are not run by an elected county sheriff but by an appointed Commissioner of the Department of Correction.

An area handbook should be as comprehensive as possible, since it is intended to save the reader hours of library research. It ought to be packed with useful insights, accurate descriptions, handy facts, policy analyses, evaluations of effectiveness, exposes of widely held myths, and critiques of hidden assumptions and proclaimed intentions. It should not serve as an extension of the public relations offices of City agencies or business interests. The contributors should be alert to the latest trends, emerging issues, new developments, and longstanding controversies. Custom publishing will enable the chapter authors in this easily revised volume to be held accountable for their ideas as they receive comments and constructive criticisms. With each passing year, this reader will grow, become more comprehensive, and strive to remain up-to-date. It is anticipated that future editions will include additional chapters about a number of subjects, including white collar crime in New York's business world; the problem of automobile theft; the handling of domestic violence; juvenile delinquency and juvenile justice; police training and professionalism; charges of police brutality; investigations of police corruption; the process of making bail; the treatment of crime victims; civil liberties concerns; crime reporting; and the application of forensic science to crime solving.

xii

Acknowledgements:

At McGraw-Hill and Primis Custom Publishing, I want to thank Betty Whitford and Adam Knepper for their encouragement and enthusiasm. At John Jay College, I appreciate the endorsement of this project by President Gerald Lynch and the oversight provided by this volume's Editorial Board: Provost Basil Wilson, Associate Provost Larry Kobilinsky, Graduate Dean James Levine, and Chief Librarian Larry Sullivan. In proofreading and preparing the camera-ready copy of this collection of articles, I was assisted by a graduating senior, Tracy Ann Brown, and my wife Jessica Karmen.

Dr. Andrew Karmen
New York City
July, 1998

ABOUT THE CHAPTER AUTHORS:

Dr. Charles Bahn is professor emeritus of forensic psychology and was formerly the dean of the social sciences division. He has served as a consultant for local, federal, and international law enforcement agencies.

Prof. Marvie Brooks is a librarian specializing in security management materials who is currently studying minority women in administrative positions in criminal justice agencies.

Dr. David Brotherton teaches undergraduate and graduate courses about juvenile delinquency. He is studying the evolution of street gangs like the Latin Kings under a grant from the Spencer Foundation and will write up his findings in a book for Columbia University Press.

Dr. Richard Curtis has carried out ethnographic research for NDRI for many years, and is currently studying the resurgence of heroin use in the New York area. He teaches courses about drug abuse in the Anthropology Department.

Dr. Vincent Del Castillo was the Chief of the Transit Police Department during the late 1980s, and wrote a Ph.D. thesis about the public's fear of crime in the subways. He also was the Acting Dean in charge of John Jay College's branch campus for police officers in Puerto Rico.

Dr. Joan Hoffman is an economist in the Department of Public Management who teaches courses about fiscal policy and governmental regulations. She is studying female drug offenders and has written about New York City's economy.

Dr. Delores Jones-Brown has a law degree and has served as an assistant district attorney in New Jersey. She is carrying out a study of the crime problem and fear levels in Brownsville, Brooklyn. Recently, she completed post-doctoral fellowship research about the socialization of adolescent boys into law-abiding vs. lawbreaking behavior at Columbia University's Teachers College.

Dr. Andrew Karmen has served as one of the graduate coordinators of the Masters Program, and is currently the coordinator of the Criminal Justice major as well as the Criminology major. He is the author of a textbook, "Crime Victims: An Introduction to Victimology" (Third edition, Brooks/Cole-Wadsworth, 1996) and is currently writing "New York Murder Mystery" (N.Y.U. Press, forthcoming) about the remarkable "crime crash" of the 1990s.

Dr. Barry Latzer teaches a course on capital punishment in the Masters Program and is the author of Death Penalty Cases: Leading U.S. Supreme Court Cases On Capital Punishment (Butterworth-Heinemann Publishers, 1998). He also has a law degree and was an ADA in the Kings County District Attorney's office.

Dr. James Levine is the Dean of Graduate Studies and also the Executive Officer of the City University's Ph.D. program in criminal justice housed at John Jay College. He is the author of "Juries and Politics" (Brooks/Cole-Wadsworth, 1992).

Prof. Charles Lindner has a law degree as well as a masters in social work degree and formerly was the Director of Training and also of Public Relations for the New York City Department of Probation. He has written about the history of probation, the role of technology in probation, and about the threat of probation officer victimization. Currently he designs training programs and is the coordinator of the Corrections major.

Director Robert Louden of John Jay College's Criminal Justice Center was a Detective Lieutenant and the Commanding Officer as well as the chief negotiator of the NYPD's Hostage Negotiation Team. He is writing a Ph.D. thesis in the City University's doctoral program about the adoption of crisis negotiation techniques by law enforcement agencies across the country.

Dr. Gerald Lynch has served as the President of John Jay College since the CUNY fiscal crisis that threatened the institution's existence in 1976. He holds a doctorate in clinical psychology and is an internationally recognized expert in behalf of police professionalism. He is Vice Chairman of the New York City Police Foundation, a member of the National Council on Crime and Delinquency, and a member of the Independent Commission on Policing In Northern Ireland.

Dr. Robert McCrie is the chairman of the Department of Law and Police Science. He is the editor of a security journal and is completing a book about the history of murders in New York City.

Dr. Mangai Natarajian has studied the role of women in policing as well as international aspects of the drug problem as a researcher for NDRI in New York City. She is currently analyzing trial transcripts from the Pizza Connection case that exposed organized crime's role in drug smuggling.

Paul O'Connell was formerly an officer in the NYPD and currently teaches criminal justice courses at Iona College. He is a candidate in City University's Ph.D. program in criminal justice at John Jay College.

Dr. Daniel Pinello wrote the book, "The Importance of Judicial Selection Method On State Supreme Court Policies" (Greenwood Press, 1995). He has a law degree and was an attorney, and now serves as the coordinator of the Legal Studies Major.

Dr. Eli Silverman teaches a course on community policing and is writing a book about the re-organization of the NYPD entitled, "Revolution In Blue" (Northeastern University Press, forthcoming in 1999). He was an associate dean and also has served as a Special Assistant in the U.S. Department of Justice and a research associate at the National Academy of Public Administration.

Dr. Maria Volpe is the Director of John Jay College's Dispute Resolution Program. She teaches undergraduate and graduate courses and training sessions in dispute resolution, and serves as a mediator in educational settings. She is the past president of the International Society Of Professionals In Dispute Resolution and serves on the editorial board of several journals in the field.

Dr. Daniel Vona teaches the senior seminar about organized crime. He served as a Special Assistant Police Commissioner of the NYPD for Organized Crime Control, Internal Affairs, and Intelligence in the wake of the Knapp Commission investigation into corruption and wrote the legal guidelines governing eavesdropping in 1973.

Dr. Martin Wallenstein was the Dean Of Undergraduate Studies and chairman of the Speech and Theater Department. He also has a law degree and served as an ADA in the Kings County District Attorney's office.

Chapter 1

New York City's Crime Problem and Justice System in Perspective

By Prof. Charles Bahn

Department of Psychology

and

Prof. Marvie Brooks

John Jay College Library

When considering an issue as vital to all Americans as crime and justice, why should any single city be the sole focus of attention? The answer is that studying New York City is not parochial or narrow, but highly instructive. When it comes to problems and solutions, if it happens anywhere in the world, it shows up in New York City as well. New York has it all: terrorist bombings, drug trafficking, sieges requiring negotiations to free hostages, clashing street gangs, cold-blooded killings of police officers, outrageous acts of police brutality, overcrowded jails, even experimental programs to resolve conflicts without bloodshed.

New York often plays a central role in setting trends that affect every state of the union as well as foreign countries. In the post-Cold War economic order, it is one of three world or "global" cities (along with London and Tokyo). New York City houses the United Nations, major radio and television broadcast networks, magazine and book publishing headquarters, and three of the ten largest airports in the United States. New York City is the home of international business services, corporate headquarters for national and foreign businesses, the main offices for numerous professional and trade associations, government agencies and their affiliate organizations, and prominent cultural and educational institutions (Knox, 1977: 22-23). The city's claim to preeminence in national and international affairs appears to be well founded for the foreseeable future.

NEW YORK CITY'S UNDESERVED "BAD REPUTATION"

New York City suffers from the negative stereotype that it is the crime capital of the country. This false image can be traced back over many years. The novelist who wrote "Treasure Island," Robert Louis Stevenson, described this viewpoint very well in some passages he penned in 1895:

> *As we drew near to New York I was at first amused and then somewhat staggered, by the cautious and grisly tales that went around. You would have thought we were to land upon a cannibal island. You must speak to no one in the streets, as they would not leave you till you were rooked and beaten.*
>
> *You must enter a hotel with military precautions: for the least you had to apprehend was to awake next morning without money or baggage, or necessary raiment, a lone forked radish in a bed; and if the worst befell, you would instantly and mysteriously disappear from the ranks of mankind* (Quoted in Clapp, 1984, no. S207).

Many people assume that New York City has the highest rate of violent crime in the country, possibly in the world. This belief is patently not true. In fact, New York City has never had the highest crime rate in the nation since those rates have been gathered and published by the federal authorities. *The Uniform Crime Report* (UCR) is the product of a national system for statistical collection that began in 1930 (Bailey, 1988: 535). Other cities have always had higher crime rates that posed graver dangers to the hapless visitor. Nevertheless, New York City has been seen by tourists, particularly from smaller cities, towns, and rural areas, as crime-ridden. The media pictured it as a "city of sin," or at least of adventure and risk. When tourists say "it is a great place to visit, but I would not want to live there," what they are really saying is that the fear of crime that pervades everyday life outweighs the pleasures to be found in New York's strikingly different neighborhoods.

THE TRUE DIMENSIONS OF NEW YORK CITY'S CRIME PROBLEM

Just how dangerous is New York City? There are many answers to this question. Should the city today be compared to a simpler, quieter time like the 1940's and 1950's, when urban life was much more sedate and orderly? Would it be instructive to see how New York stands vis-a-vis other large cities in the country? Should the five boroughs be compared to the surrounding counties that are included in the greater metropolitan area, or to other nearby metropolitan areas in the Northeast? Should the city of New York be compared to the rest of the state of New York? What is the appropriate unit of analysis and standard for comparison?

How Dangerous Is New York Compared to Other Major Cities?

Statistics compiled by the FBI in its annual *Uniform Crime Report* can be assembled in order to determine how serious New York's crime problem is relative to other large U.S. cities. The UCR provides data on crime rates: the number of reported crimes per 100,000 residents. (The yearly *National Crime Victimization Survey* has established that reporting rates vary substantially by type of crime and type of victim. If reporting rates also differ dramatically from city to city, then the following rankings would not accurately reflect the real crime risks faced by residents in American cities).

When it comes to violent crimes, New York City tends to fall somewhere in the middle in a ranking of the 75 major cities in the United States (Garoogian & Garoogian, 1997). For some of the property crimes, its rankings are even lower, toward the very bottom of the list (which is very favorable, indicating a low incidence per 100,000 residents)

Specifically, in 1996, the cities with the highest murder rates were (in descending order) Washington, D.C., New Orleans, Richmond (Virginia), Atlanta, Baltimore, St. Louis, Detroit, Miami, Flint (Michigan), and Chicago. New York ranked 33rd, far safer than most other large cities. Minneapolis had the highest rate for forcible rapes that were reported to the police. The other nine cities with very high rape rates were Lansing (Michigan), Flint, Cleveland, Detroit, Jacksonville (Florida), Orlando, Atlanta, Kansas City, Nashville, and Tampa. New York ranked a distant 71st of the 75 cities. But when it comes to robbery, New York placed 18th. Still, the chances of being robbed were much greater in Baltimore, followed by Miami, Washington, D.C., New Orleans, Atlanta, St. Louis, Philadelphia, Oakland, Detroit, Tampa, Minneapolis, and seven other big cities. As for aggravated assault, the risks of being attacked by an assailant intending serious bodily injury were highest in Atlanta, and then in Tampa, Flint, St. Louis, Chicago, Detroit, Kansas City, Washington, Baltimore, Portland, Charlotte, and Tacoma. New York ranked 34th, tied with Worcester, Massachusetts (FBI, 1996; Garoogian & Garoogian, 1997).

As for reported crimes against property, burglaries were committed much more often per capita in Flint, Topeka, Durham, Ft. Lauderdale, St. Louis, Atlanta, Miami, Tampa, Orlando, Albuquerque, Detroit, Minneapolis, and Mobile. New York ranked near the bottom, in 69th place. Motor vehicle thefts were much more common in Detroit, Atlanta, New Orleans, Tampa, Miami, St. Louis, Washington, Ft. Lauderdale, Cleveland, and Boston than in New York, which placed 45th. As for larcenies, reports of thefts were recorded by the police much more often in Atlanta, Ft. Lauderdale, Salt Lake City, St. Louis, Topeka, Eugene (Oregon), Orlando, Tampa, Seattle, and Tallahassee. New York's reported larceny rate was next to the lowest (Garoogian & Garoogian, 1997).

Table 1-1 presents the actual number of offenses reported to the NYPD, the victimization rate for every 100,000 New Yorkers per year, the odds of becoming a victim during 1996, and the city's rank vis-a-vis the other 74 large cities in the country.

To summarize the data in Table 1-1, the first column shows that the most common crime committed within the five boroughs is the category of assorted thefts (grand and petit larceny), and the least frequent, fortunately, is murder. The second column indicates that New York's murder rate was 13 killings for every 100,000 residents in 1996, and so on. The third column demonstrates that the odds of being robbed are 1 in 148, or one person robbed out of every 148 New Yorkers per annum, and so on. The last column displays the rankings that were cited above.

The principal conclusion to be drawn from this analysis of FBI statistics is that New York

City is far from the most dangerous city in the United States, no matter which crime is measured. As long as its huge population is taken into account, New York is not the "crime capital" of the nation. When the evidence is carefully examined, its bad reputation is without merit: its streets are relatively safe. Ironically, in many other cities whose reputations are better, the odds of being victimized are much worse.

NEW YORK CITY AS PART OF THE MEGALOPOLIS AND CONURBATION

A "megalopolis" has developed within the northeastern part of the United States, because the metropolitan areas and cities in this area have grown together to form one virtually continuous urban corridor (Whittick, 1974:676-677; Abrams, 1971:187). The phrase

Table 1-1:

Ranking of New York City's 1996 Reported Crime Rates Among the 75 Major U.S. Cities

Crime	Number of Reported Offenses	Crime Rate per 100,000	Victimization Odds	National Rank
Any Violent Crime	98,428	1,341	1:74	29th
Murder	983	13	1:7,467	34th
Forcible Rape	2,331	32	1:1,673	72 nd
Robbery	49,693	677	1:148	18th
Aggravated Assault	45,721	622	1:161	34th
Any Property Crime	285,175	3,855	1:26	72nd
Burglary	61,398	837	1:120	69th
Larceny/Theft	163,096	2,222	1:45	74th
Motor Vehicle Theft	60,381	823	1:122	45th

Sources: Data derived from the FBI's UCR, the DCJS's annual report, Crime and Justice in New York State, and Garoogian & Garoogian, 1997.

"conurbation" denotes a polynucleated metropolitan area that includes a number of identifiable municipalities that have merged (Schultz & Kasen, 1984:86). The term megalopolis is now used when an entire metropolitan area, not just communities, have grown together" (Schultz& Kasen, 1978: 86). It also indicates a blending of the areas, leading to a loss of open space and farms, and the necessity of cooperation between elected officials and criminal justice agencies (Schultz & Kasen, 1984:239). As part of this "northeastern corridor"/megalopolis ranging from Boston to Washington, it seems that criminal activities in New York City could have consequences elsewhere in the megalopolis.

But an examination of 1996 violent crime rates shows that there are other cities in the megalopolis which have more serious crime problems than New York. The six cities in the northeast corridor with the highest crime rates appear in Table 1-2.

It is interesting to note that New York City, the heart of this megalopolis, has a lower violent crime rate than the other five large cities. And, of the six northeastern megalopolis cities, only Newark and Washington, D.C. have rates of criminal violence that place them in the top ten worst cities in the country.

Table 2:

Violent Crime Rates for Cities in the Northeast Corridor, 1996

#1 Newark (NJ)   3,345   reported incidents per 100,000 residents

#2 Washington (DC)   2,470   reported incidents per 100,000 residents

#3 Jersey City (NJ)   1,660   reported incidents per 100,000 residents

#4 Boston (MA)   1,657   reported incidents per 100,000 residents

#5 Philadelphia (PA)   1,529   reported incidents per 100,000 residents

#6 New York City (NY) 1,344   reported incidents per 100,000 residents

Note: Violent crimes include all reported murders, rapes, robberies, and aggravated assaults.

Source: (FBI's Uniform Crime Reporting Program, 1998; Selected cities reported in 1996 UCR, Table 8, 121-145).

NEW YORK CITY'S RELATIONSHIP TO THE METROPOLITAN AREA

The question arises, does New York City serve as an exporter of crime to the "burbs" and the surrounding countryside? Or does the city attract out-of-town criminals? One way to frame the issue is to wonder to what extent offenders are mobile, and travel far from home before committing their crimes.

In order to test the notion of the crime risk spreading from the center city out to its suburbs in the greater metropolitan area, figures were sought on the percentage of arrestees in the abutting suburbs who had New York City addresses. Similarly, the percentage of arrestees in the precincts on New York City's borders who gave out-of-city addresses was sought. Unfortunately, none of the local police departments, including the NYPD, were able to furnish an analysis of arrestees' addresses by zipcode. However, telephone inquiries made to NYPD precinct commanders and out-of-town police chiefs produced the following rough estimates given below. This is an area of study that requires further and better research to update the comments given.

1) Police chiefs in three abutting counties estimated that about twenty percent of those arrested in their towns had New York City addresses.

2) All but one precinct commander (of the four queried) estimated that about five percent of those arrested in their areas had out-of-city addresses.

3) One commander of a precinct near the George Washington Bridge estimated that between 15% and 20% of all arrestees were from out-of-town, especially New Jersey residents caught purchasing illegal drugs in Upper Manhattan.

NEW YORK COMPARED TO THE REST OF THE STATE

Under the federal system, the 50 states have the authority and responsibility to make and enforce their own criminal laws. The laws governing behavior in New York City are debated and passed by the state legislature in Albany. New York City offenders charged with felonies are put on trial in state supreme courts. If convicted, they serve time "upstate" in state prisons. If released before their maximum sentences expire, they are supervised by the state Division of Parole. The question arises, how much of the burden imposed by the crime problem in New York State is due to the illegal activities of city residents?

The comparisons can be best examined according to the type of crime. Across New York State in 1996, 1,330 people were murdered. New York City (with 983 killings) accounted for 74% of the state's body count. More than half (56%) of the state's number of reported rapes took place within the five boroughs. Eighty percent (nearly 50,000) of the state's total number of reported robberies occurred within NYC. More than 70% (more than 45,000) of the state's aggravated assaults were committed within New York City. About two-thirds of the state's motor vehicle thefts were carried out within the five boroughs. However, less than half (only 47%) of the total burglaries reported throughout the state were committed within City limits. Similarly, only 41% of the total number of larcenies committed within the state occurred within New York City (DCJS, 1996).

Clearly, most of New York State's crime problem, with the exception of burglaries and larcenies (which are not well reported to the police) is concentrated within the five boroughs.

NEW YORK STATE'S CRIME PROBLEM IN COMPARISON TO OTHER POPULOUS STATES

New York State's crime statistics are profoundly shaped by what happens in New York City. After unfortunately setting new records in 1990, crime rates have been falling in New York City, slowly at first, and then rapidly since 1993.

Crime rates have been subsiding in the rest of the country as well, especially in the big cities and the most populous states. Table 3-1 shows that out of selected high population states (California, Florida, Illinois, and Texas), the state of New York experienced the largest decreases in each of the violent and property crime categories in the 1990's, with the exception of rape (which dropped faster in California) and burglary (which declined more impressively in Texas).

Table 1-3:

Changes in Crime Rates in Populous States 1990 - 1996

	All Violent Offenses	All Property Offenses	Murder	Rape	Robbery	Assault	Burglary	Larceny	Vehicle Theft
New York	-39%	-34	-50	-23	-46	-31	-38	-26	-53
California	-18	-22	-24	-28	-22	-14	-27	-19	-25
Florida	-16	-15	-30	-1	-31	-8	-30	-8	-13
Illinois	-8	-11	-3	-13	-29	+7	-14	-7	-24
Texas	-15	-28	-45	-15	-34	-3	-42	-20	-40
U.S.	-13	-13	-21	-12	-21	-9	-24	-7	-20

Source: FBI Uniform Crime Report 1996; Kruger, 1997

In sum, it should be clear that neither New York City alone, nor the New York metropolitan area, nor the state of New York, is really the crime center of the country. It is true that New York City's crime problem was much worse in the recent past, and hit all-time highs in 1990. But today, if New York City is Number One in anything, it stands out as the place that has achieved the most impressive rate of crime reduction since 1990. And this is not the result of some statistical manipulation or change in crime reporting methods, as some cynics and skeptics might argue. The sharp drop in the murder rate (which is a reliable indicator), proves that the dramatic improvement in New York City's crime problem is real.

NEW YORK CITY'S CRIMINAL JUSTICE SYSTEM: ITS SIZE AND COMPLEXITY

Although all states were obligated by federal law to set up agencies to coordinate their criminal justice operations, only a few cities have found it necessary to do so. New York is one of those cities that needs to coordinate its activities because its criminal justice machinery is so comprehensive and complex, and its crime problem is so serious and complicated. New York City has had, successively, a Deputy Mayor for Public Safety, whose title was then changed to Criminal Justice Coordinator, and, currently, is called the Mayor's Advisor on Criminal Justice. This office directly supervises four agencies that are among the largest parts of any crime control apparatus in the world (see Box 1-1 to get some impression of the massive scale of the City's operations).

In addition, the Mayor's Advisor on Criminal Justice is the liaison to the five district attorneys in New York City's five boroughs, and to the state Office of Court Administration, the state parole division, as well as a number of state and federal law enforcement agencies, including the FBI, DEA, BATF, and others, some participating in joint task force activities.

Box 1-1:
How Big New York's Criminal Justice System Was During 1996

The New York City Police Department employed a total of close to 47,000 people. It had an average uniform headcount of nearly 38,000 officers, who patrolled more than 6,000 miles of city streets and nearly 580 miles of waterfront. In 1996, officers of the NYPD made nearly 140,000 felony arrests and over 205,000 misdemeanor arrests.

The New York City Department of Correction operated 16 jails, including 10 on Riker's Island, the largest penal colony in the world, as well as 15 court detention pens and four prison wards in city hospitals. The jail system was run by more than 11,300 correction officers, assisted by about 1,600 civilians. The Department supervised an average of 19,000 inmates on any given day, which is more than the entire population behind bars in 40 of the 50 states. Its fleet of buses transported about 1,700 detainees to court daily. Over the course of a year, about 133,000 people were processed through the court holding pens, houses of detention, and jails run by the DOC.

The Department of Probation employed a full-time staff of more than 1,500 officers and civilians. The Department's average daily caseload of adult pobationers numbers approximately 60,000. Annually, the Department of Probation processed approximately 90,000 adult probationers and 23,000 juvenile delinquents. Probation officers prepared more than 50,000 pre-sentence investigations reports each year to help judges hand down appropriate sentences.

The Department of Juvenile Justice had more than 500 staff members working for it. The agency provided detention (secure and non-secure), aftercare, and prevention services for troubled youths through the age of 15 who were awaiting trial, sentencing, court appearances, or transfer to a state facility. The Department was responsible for juvenile delinquents (JDs) and juvenile offenders (JOs). Juvenile delinquents, age 7-15 are charged with committing acts which would be crime if done by adults. Their cases are handled in family court. Juvenile offenders, age 13-15, are charged with committing one of a list of 15 enumerated serious felonies (including murder) that can be prosecuted in adult courts.

During fiscal 1997, the Department received 4,810 juveniles for secure detention and housed over 1,450 youths in non-secure facilities. Hence, over 6,250 youths were under supervision. In 1996, the average daily population reached almost 270 young people, mostly boys.

Source: *The Mayor's Management Report*, Fiscal 1997; v. II, Agency and.Citywide Indicators

---

The office of the Mayor's Advisor also contracts with eight organizations that provide legal services to the indigent; the largest and best known is the Legal Aid Society. The Mayor's Advisor on Criminal Justice supervises the Office of Assigned Counsel, which certifies and assigns lawyers who represent defendants too poor to hire private attorneys.

Indirectly, coordination also extends to the operations of the Office of the Corporation Counsel, where a unit of attorneys represent the City in Family Court, and the Department of Finance, in which is found both the Sheriff's office and a unit which handles Bail Collection.

The only agency whose activities are not coordinated and supervised by the Mayor's Advisor is the Department of Investigation. Its special role requires independence and even secrecy as it works with the Inspectors General in all of the city's agencies to uncover white collar crime and corruption.

One more comparison should clinch the point that New York City is in a class by itself when it comes to the magnitude of its criminal justice apparatus. Table 1-4 demonstrates that the NYPD is many times larger than any federal law enforcement agency that arms sworn officers and grants them the authority to make arrests.

Table 1-4:
Number of Full-time Law Enforcement Officials, NYPD and Federal Agencies 1996

Agency	Number of Officers
New York City Police Department	38,000
U.S. Immigration and Naturalization Service	12,403
Federal Bureau of Prisons	11,329
Federal Bureau of Investigation	10,389
U.S. Customs Service	9,749
Internal Revenue Service	3,784
U.S. Postal Inspections Service	3,576
U.S. Secret Service	3,185
Drug Enforcement Administration	2,946
Administrative Office of the U.S. Courts	2,777
U.S. Marshal's Service	2,650
National Park Service	2,148
Bureau of Alcohol, Tobacco and Firearms	1,869
U.S. Capitol Police	1,031
U.S. Fish and Wildlife Service	869
GSA-Federal Protective Service	643
U.S. Forest Services	410

Source: Reaves, 1997: Federal Law Enforcement Agencies Employment, 1996

The NYPD is, of course, the largest municipal police department, almost three times bigger than Chicago's force, and more than four times the size of the LAPD. However, when each city's population is taken into account, New York is not the most heavily patrolled city. The ratios of city residents to the number of officers protecting that metropolis' inhabitants is assembled in Table 1-5. The data indicates that the District of Columbia is the most heavily policed city in the country, with one officer for every 150 residents. New York comes in second, with about 200 residents for every one officer of the NYPD. In contrast, in Phoenix, residents outnumber officers by more than 500 to 1.

Table 1-5

Residents per Officer, Large Cities, 1996

Rank	City	Population	Officers	Residents per Officer
#1	Washington, DC	543,200	3,611	150
#2	New York City, NY	7,380,900	38,000	194
#3	Chicago, IL	2,721,500	13,032	209
#4	Baltimore, MD	675,400	3,081	219
#5	Philadelphia, PA	1,478,000	6,455	229
#6	Detroit , MI	1,000,300	3,917	255
#7	Houston, TX	1,744,100	5,252	332
#8	Dallas, TX	1,053,300	2,822	373
#9	Los Angeles, CA	3,553,600	9,148	389
#10	Phoenix, AZ	1,159,000	2,255	514

Note: Population figures are rounded off to the nearest 100.

Source: FBI Uniform Crime Reports, 1996, Table 78. Number of Full-time Law Enforcement Employees, Cities, on October 31; p. 295-354.

New York Is Number One

One way to deal with an unpleasant reality, like the crime problem, has always been to portray it as part and parcel of urban living. The bigger the city, the larger is its symbolic role as a center of presumed criminal activity and as a place of intense fear of crime. The negative stereotypes of New York have a life of their own, and linger on in the public mind, even though New York never had the worst crime rates, and has enjoyed tremendous relief in the 1990s from the oppressive burden imposed by predatory behavior and unrealistic fears about strangers. There certainly is no longer any factual basis for the City's bad reputation, but the sheer size of its death toll due to murder, its casualties due to assaults and robberies, and the large number of cars that disappear from their parking spots continues to instill alarm in residents and visitors alike. The only continuing reality is that everything about New York is massive, including its complex criminal justice sysytem. New York's prominent role in the global economy guarantees that its problems with lawbreaking and its law enforcement solutions will remain the focus of worldwide attention in the years to come

References

Bailey, W.G. (Ed.). (1988). *The encyclopedia of police science*. New York: Garland.

Clapp, J.A. (1984). *The city, a dictionary of quotable thought on cities and urban life*. New Brunswick, NJ: Center for Urban Policy research, Rutgers University.

Criminal victimization in the United States changes 1995-96 with trends 1993-96. (1997). Washington, DC: U.S. Department of Justice, Bureau of Justice Statistics.

Federal Bureau of Investigation. (1996). *Uniform crime reports for the United States*. Washington, DC: U.S. Government Printing Office.

Garoogian, R., and Garoogian A. (Eds.). (1997). *Crime in America's top rated cities: a statistical profile*. (1997-1998 2nd. ed.). Boca Raton, Fl: Universal Reference Publications.

Knox, P. (1997). "Globalization and urban economic change." In D. Wilson (Ed.), Globalization and the changing U.S. City [special issue]. *The Annals of the American Academy of Political and Social Science* (551 :17-27).

Krueger, Jami. (December, 1997). *Criminal Justice Indicators, Trends in Reported Crime 1990-1996*. (Issue No. 3, December) Albany, NY: Bureau of Statistical Services, New York State Division of Criminal Justice Services

Maguire, K. and Pastore, A.L. (Eds.). (1996). *Sourcebook of criminal justice statistics 1996*. Washington, DC: U.S. Department of Justice, Bureau of Justice Statistics.

The mayor's management report. (1997). New York: Mayor's Office of Operations.

Messages from the Commissioner [Online]. Available:
  http://www.ci.nyc.ny.us/html/doc/html/message.html [1997, May 4].
(Rev. - Wk. 5/18/98: 1-39)

*Preface for Publication of Katharine Bement Davis Mini-History during NYC's 5-Boro Centennia*l [Online]. Available: http://www.ci.nyc.ny.us/html/doc.html/kbd_brnx.html [1997, May 4].

Statistics and Charts [Online]. Available: http://www.ci.nyc.ny.us/html/doc/html/docstats.html

12

[1997, Apr. 25].

Tobin, T.C., Sgt. (1997). *Patrol Services Bureau* [Online]. Available:
    http://www.ci.nyc.ny.us/nyclink/html/nypd/html/3100/psb.html [1997, May 4].

U.S. Bureau of the Census. (1996). *Statistical abstract of the United States*. (116th ed.).
Washington, DC: U.S. Department of Commerce, Social and Economics Statistics Administration.

U.S. Bureau of the Census. (1997). *Statistical Abstract of the United States*. (117th ed.).
Washington, DC: U.S. Department of Commerce, Social and Economic Statistics Administration.

Whittick, A. (Ed.). (1974). *Encyclopedia of urban planning*. New York: McGraw-Hill.

Chapter 2

THE FIRST MURDERS IN NEW AMSTERDAM/NEW YORK: ORIGINS AND CONSEQUENCES

by

Prof. Robert D. McCrie

Department of Law & Police Science

What were the reasons for the earliest "murders" in the region that eventually would become the City of New York? What were their consequences? And how might these earliest incidents inform the thinking about violent crime in later centuries? This chapter identifies the earliest homicides, provides the context for their occurrences, briefly examines the origins of the judicial system for handling crimes, and offers some generalizations about violent crime over the centuries in one urban area.

The First Murder in New Amsterdam

Violence broke out in the region that would be called New Amsterdam, and later New York, as soon as contact occurred between Europeans and the native American Indians. Henry Hudson, an English captain commanding officers and a crew of 18 men, led the pivotal voyage of exploration to the region which was financed by investors in the Dutch East India Company (Jameson, 1909). The excursion led to several encounters-peaceful and otherwise-with the natives.

The natives that Hudson and his crew met first were members of the Algonquian linguistic family. Two Algonquian tribes in the region were predominant during the early years of exploration and settlement: The Wappinger (meaning "Easterners") were located on the east bank of the Hudson River from Manhattan Island to Poughkeepsie and the territory eastward to the Connecticut Valley and the Delaware (derived from Lord Delaware, second governor of Virginia, but also called Len<pe or Leni-len<pe) occupied territory including all of the state of New Jersey, the western end of Long Island, all of Manhattan and Staten Island, and portions of the mainland west of the Hudson (Swanton, 1968).

Robert Juet of Lime-house, an officer on Hudson's Half Moon (de Halve Maen), provided documentation of these explorations. The Anglo-Dutch and aboriginal contacts initially began on a positive note. On September 4, 1609, while sailing near the entrance of what first would

14

be called the Groote Rivier, and later the Hudson River, Juet wrote:

> *This day the people of the Countrey came aboord of us, seeming very glad of our comming, and brought greene tobacco, and gave us of it for Knives and Beets....They desire Cloathe, and are very civll. They have great store of Maiz, or Indian Wheate, whereof they make good Bread* (Jameson, 1909:18).

The <u>Half Moon</u> sailed on, and the next day natives again boarded the craft: *"At night they went on Land againe, so wee rode very quiet, but durst not trust them."* The day after that, September 6, the sailors' distrust of the natives accurately reflected the potential for violence: a sailor from the vessel was killed in a clash with belligerent Indians. Juet reported:

> *Our Master sent John Colman, with foure other men in our Boate, over to the North-side to sound out the other River [probably the Narrows near Sandy Hook], being foure leagues from us....As they came backe, they were set upon by two Canoes, the one having twelve, the other fourteene men. The night came on, and it began to rayne, so that their Match went out; and they had one man slaine in the fight, which was an Englishman, named John Colman, with an Arrow shot into his throat, and two more hurt.*
> (Jameson, 1909:18-19).

This was the first fatal attack-augmented by two aggravated assaults-in the future colony. An English sailor was a homicide victim without any evidence of provocation on his part or that of his mates against the natives, though details of the incident are limited to one participant's diary.

The next morning Colman's body was buried and the <u>Half Moon</u> continued sailing in a northerly direction along the shoreline, with the crew alert to any further possibly unfriendly Indian encounters. From that point on when apparently friendly natives appeared, they were met for trading purposes, but were discouraged from boarding the vessel or were not allowed aboard in any great number.

The sense of foreboding and personal danger must have been great because Juet related a rash move taken by the crew. As the <u>Half Moon</u> continued the voyage upriver, two Indian hostages were seized and held prisoners as a presumed means of coercing future cooperation from natives who might be encountered. These were the first documented kidnap victims in the European exploration of the "new territory." Soon one hostage escaped by leaping overboard, and a few days later the other also slipped away. The voyage continued northward, when on September 12, Juet noted a presumably threatening near confrontation: *"There came eight and twelve Canoes full of men, women and children to betray us: but we saw their intent, and suffered none of them to come abooard of us."*

Continuing their voyage of discovery up the commodious river, the crew encountered friendlier Indians with whom they traded "trifles" for food and tobacco, after plying them with wine and aqua vitae to the point of stupefaction. As the voyage advanced, contacts with the natives were frequent. The two groups often celebrated with communal meals on shore, which provided Juet with the opportunity to observe the "modesty" of the Indian women and the natives' "reverence" for their elders. During such encounters, the sailors of the Half Moon traded with the natives to obtain animal skins and cutting stones as well as food and tobacco. On October 1, 1609, near the present city of Albany, the Half Moon voyagers had just completed trades for animal skins with a group of natives when a simple incident quickly escalated into a deadly shooting spree initiated by a crew member. Juet noted:

> *This after-noon, one Canoe kept hanging under our sterne with one man in it, which we could not keepe from thence, who got up by our Rudder to the Cabin window, and stole out my Pillow, and two Shirts, and two Bandeleeres. Our Masters Mate shot at him, and strooke him on the breast and killed him. Whereupon all the rest fled away, some in their Canoes, and so leapt out of them into the water* (Jameson, 1909: 26).

Following the killing of one of their own for theft of a pillow, two shirts, and two scarves, the natives mobilized the next day apparently ready to exact retributive justice. Two canoes carrying warriors drew near and began to shoot arrows toward the Half Moon. Sailors on the ship were supplied with the best firearms of the time and discharged their muskets in self-defense, killing two or three natives immediately. The Indian offensive persisted and before it was over, the sailors additionally killed between seven and eleven natives more, by Juet's reckoning. Hudson and his crew then determined that it was a propitious moment to conclude their period of exploration in those waters. They quickly sailed down-river to the mouth of the Hudson, then east across the Atlantic Ocean, and arrived at Dartmouth, England, on November 7. Thus, in a span of twenty-eight days of exploring the harbor near the future site of New Amsterdam and the river as far north as the site of the present state capital, Hudson's band experienced one fatality. By contrast, in Juet's estimation, up to fourteen natives died.

Violence Under Dutch Rule

The death of sailor John Colman in 1609, was surely not the first homicide in the region which within four score years would be the site of the town of New York. Colman's demise is merely the first recorded untoward death of a European. The region first was peopled by Paleo-Indians, at least 11,000 years earlier. Evidence of these early residents is found in Staten Island from clovis points, which are distinctive lance-shaped chipped-stone projectile points with a long, channel flake-called a "flute"-removed from the center. Clovis points were parts of weapons used by these hunter-gatherers to kill animals. Whether any of the earliest dwellers used this weapon against other humans would be unsupported conjecture. But the possibilities for homicide existed between people living in close proximity, all competing simultaneously for limited resources, and possessing lethal weapons with the experience and the motivation to use them.

By the time Europeans arrived to explore the pristine land, Indians were living in bark- or grass-covered longhouses, as recorded by Giovanni da Verazzano, the Florentine navigator who made the first recorded landfall by a European in the region in 1524.The natives, mainly the Delaware and Wappinger, shared linguistic similarities within the Algonquin family in the region. A widespread social network existed among the tribes; yet, ethnologists point to evidence of conflict among various clans of the Delawares. Clans warred periodically with each other and sometimes a tribe would be forced to relocate because of tensions with another.

No evidence exists of an earlier incident among the natives that might be equated to the killing of John Colman; that is, the murder of one native by another out of hatred, jealousy, greed, or fear. But the efficiency and deliberateness with which native Americans attacked the Englishmen suggest that this apparently unjustified killing of another-frightening as the presence of Colman and his mates might have been to them-was probably not an unprecedented type of response for the natives and might be expected to reflect earlier violent behavior among them.

The results from Hudson's voyage initially disappointed his Dutch patrons: no direct passageway to the Spice Islands with its enticing opportunities for profit was discovered. Yet, eventually sponsors for another chartered venture were enlisted when investors realized that profits could be derived, if not in trading for spices and other products with the unattainable East, then for other goods. A lucrative commercial enterprise developed with the inhabitants of New Netherland: trading trinkets for furs. Animal skins were in great demand in Europe both for their fashion style and because of their superior means of keeping wearers dry and warm during inclement conditions.

In 1621, the Dutch States General charted the West India Company, a successor company to Hudson's patrons, with a monopolistic trading opportunity for twenty-four years in the new land. Soon it was determined that a permanent settlement was a necessity to protect the trading posts and to enhance the value of the perilous Dutch territorial claim wedged, as it was, between major English settlements to the north and south, and a further potential risk to their security from a distant French presence in the far north.

A few years later, Sweden also was to pose a threat. Ironically, the inspiration for the Swedish colony was the Dutch colonial leader Peter Minuit who established Fort Christina near what is now Wilmington, Delaware. After years of intermittent Dutch-Swedish hostilities, the Dutch suppressed the Swedes under Stuyvesant's military leadership in September 1655.

However, a decision, in about 1610, had been made to establish a fort on a southern tip of the Island of the Mannahates. By a decade later, scattered private houses were clustered near it (O'Callaghan, 1849:600-602).

The Dutch West India Company appointed a series of directors general to manage their investment in New Amsterdam with terms initially lasting about a year. Peter Minuit became director general in 1626 (Weslager, 1968). An event occurred during Minuit's tenure that was to have destabilizing ramifications more than two decades later, during the governorship of Willem Kieft. It was a manslaughter that would create, in time, near catastrophic effects for the region. A Wecquaesgeek Indian, a tribe of the Wappinger confederacy, approached New Amsterdam loaded with furs and with his young nephew in tow: the older Indian hoped to sell his pelts to settlers. Near Fresh Water Pond, three of Minuit's farm servants brutally attacked, then robbed and murdered the Indian, leaving his nephew as a witness. News of this incident apparently never reached Minuit or others in the village. The young nephew escaped, swearing revenge for the cold-blooded killing (which would take him years to attain). This was the second recorded homicide in the early life of the region since the arrival of the Europeans.

When the Dutch West India Company decided to encourage permanent settlement, conditions emerged that would help shape future approaches to crime and justice. In 1629, the States General ratified a proposal granting large tracts of land and the title "patroon" to any member of the Dutch West India Company who would found a colony of fifty adult persons within a four-year period. The patroon's authority would include holding jurisdiction not only over misdemeanors and minor felonies, but also implied the right to try defendants for capital offenses within this fief, though defendants found guilty of such offenses would be returned to Holland for case-review and presumably eventual punishment. While the patroon held territorial judicial and economic powers, the company expected to receive a five percent duty on all trade, excepting furs, for which it hoped to retain exclusive commercial control. Before his term ended, Minuit further added to the security of the community by constructing Fort Amsterdam near the southern tip of the island (Rink, 1986).

Minuit was replaced by Wouter Van Twiller, who tightened societal control measures further in New Amsterdam. These law and order measures included: the confiscation of all furs taken in illegal trades with the natives; the imposition of capital punishment (never enforced) against anyone selling arms to Indians; the requirement of sailors to remain on their ships after nightfall; the reorganization of judicial activities enabling civil and criminal court to meet on Thursdays; and strict rules against vice and profanity. Still immigration was slow and the regulations were burdensome, so inducements to prospective patroons and in turn, incentives to other colonists, had to be made more attractive to entice adequate settlers.

Van Twiller's successor, Willem Kieft, possessed a keen commercial sense and established a company-owned tavern. He sought to increase commerce by starting two annual fairs, and enforced more vigorously the company's regulations already issued during his predecessor's term. However, Kieft provoked contentious relations with the Indians in the Province of New Netherland during his governorship. The director general had forbidden the selling of arms to all Indians under punishment of death. But some tribes, particularly the Iroquois in the northwestern region of the Hudson Valley, and the Mohegans in the Connecticut Valley were able to obtain weapons despite the ban. The Iroquois, therefore, were able to launch aggressive forays into Algonquin territory. This left Indians forced to camp near New Amsterdam feeling agitated, vulnerable, and angry with Kieft for leaving them at a strategic disadvantage. Further, the governor general had tried unsuccessfully to levy a tribute of corn, furs, and wampum upon the Indians which they resented and refused to pay. Dutch-Indian tensions rose sharply.

After the theft from settlers of some hogs, blamed on the Raritan, a Delaware division, in July 1640, Kieft agreed with settlers who had demanded that he exercise a tougher hand in dealing with the natives. He sent Koopman Van Tienhoven to exact summary justice from the suspects. The Raritan proclaimed innocence of any involvement in stealing the swine, but Van Tienhoven's revengeful militia attacked anyway. In the skirmish, ten Indian defenders and one Dutch attacker died. Hours later, the Raritan retaliated by killing four planters and burning some farm storage buildings. Kieft escalated the tensions by placing a high bounty on the heads of all dead Raritans: this was a threat with dire potential repercussions for the tribe as the bounty certainly would be pursued by the enemies of the Raritan who included other tribes as well as Dutch settlers. This forced the Raritan to sue for peace, but it only lasted about six weeks.

The following month, the Indian who was traumatized as a boy years earlier when Minuit's farm servants killed his uncle before his eyes, finally took revenge by bludgeoning to death an innocent wheelwright. Without knowing the attacker's history, Kieft called twelve burghers to a council, August 28, 1641, to consider further retaliatory action. This is considered as the first deliberative assembly ever convened in New Amsterdam; it was called in response to the Indian's homicide, specifically, and due to ominous threats from disaffected natives, generally. Eventually, the council sanctioned what Kieft wanted: a plan for extermination of certain local tribes, including a Wappinger subdivision, the Tankiteke, a thousand of whom had recently been forced to flee their ancestral foes, the Mohawks, and, who were then unarmed, vulnerable, and encamped in two divisions nearby at Pavonia and Corlear's Hook.

The decision on how to annihilate the omnipresent, hostile native threat was delayed for months. But after consuming much alcohol at a Shrovetide feast, Kieft easily was induced by his revengeful co-settlers to sign, on February 25, 1643, an order authorizing an attack on Indians camped at both locations. Perhaps eighty were slaughtered in the ensuing surprise nighttime assaults. But massive retaliation from the natives soon would follow. Eleven Algonquin tribes united to attack settlers throughout the entire Dutch colony, (excluding Rensselaerswyck, where relations between the Hollanders and natives remained friendly). Most settlements outside of New Amsterdam were decimated. "(L)ittle remained to the Dutch save the little colony at Manhattan" (Booth, 1859:119). The conflict between the Dutch colonists and the natives-occasioned by an inflexible European leader and his revengeful confidants who chose not to negotiate a peaceful settlement-led to a rapid depopulation of one-third of the Colonists in the region through death, disappearance, or migration. It was not clear whether New Amsterdam could survive under the circumstances.

Relying on the superiority of European weaponry and the use of surprise tactics to attack Indians, Kieft next dispatched his troops in 1644 against two quasi-belligerent Indian colonies: the Canarsees on Long Island and the western bands of Wappinger encamped near Greenwich. Thousands of Indian fatalities and injuries resulted, almost eliminating the two Tribes. Yet the bloodshed had made the director general a pariah on his own island. Because he was frequently denounced during sermons by the resident Dutch religious leader, the Domine Everardus Bogardus, Kieft refused to attend such church services and ordered cannons to be fired and drums beaten nearby during the minister's sermons. When Bogardus continued railing against the director general nonetheless, Kieft unsuccessfully sought to charge the minister with sedition (Shepherd, 1970). The Dutch West India Company replaced Kieft two years later with Peter Stuyvesant who arrived in May 1647.The new director general formalized judicial procedures by introducing criminal justice measures followed in the Netherlands. In addition, Stuyvesant sought to rebuild the physical security of the town, to make it safer for settlers. A rickety fence that had demarcated the northern limit of the town was rebuilt according to exacting standards and completed in only three months' time. The fence primarily served to keep rummaging animals from straying into the populated streets. Native Indians were hardly deterred by this barrier from entering the town. When it was removed years later by the British, the only reminder was its name, Wall Street (Fern, 1976).

Hostilities between settlers and Native Americans flared up unexpectedly on September 5, 1655. Peter Stuyvesant sailed with seven vessels and 160 men to attack the Swedish colony at Fort Christina. This left New Amsterdam with attenuated defenses and resulted in another precipitous crisis for the colony. A short time before Stuyvesant's departure, Hendrick Van Dyck, had shot dead a squaw whom he had found stealing peaches from his orchard. On September 15, two thousand armed warriors seeking vengeance entered New Amsterdam. They were dissuaded from remaining overnight, but stayed long enough to kill Van Dyck and another colonist. The havoc, later called the Peach War, moved then to Hoboken, Pavonia, and Staten Island, where one hundred settlers were killed over a three-day period. Stuyvesant quickly returned to the endangered community and achieved a quick peace with a mighty show of force coupled with an offering of conciliatory gifts to the Indians. Harmony, precarious as it was, was achieved and Stuyvesant's mollifying style of governorship initiated a period of diminished conflicts between colonists and native Indians.

Yet Stuyvesant remained suspicious and hostile toward the natives for most of his tenure. In an effort to control Indian threats to the colony, he seized Indian children and women as hostages and sold some of them and adult male Indians as well, into slavery in the Caribbean (Waldman, 1995: 96).

The murder rate during these early years cannot be documented; however, homicide was one of many capital crimes recognized by the Dutch colony and a sketch of New Amsterdam, published in 1656, shows a prominent gallows with a body hanging by the shore (Van Der Donck, 1968).

New Amsterdam Becomes New York

With English settlements to the north and south, the Dutch community became an irritant over boundaries and trade. The dream of consolidation, eliminating the Dutch hegemony, led Charles II to grant the colony to his brother for supporting him in various battles. Charles assumed sovereignty over the Dutch property deriving from the right of discovery by John Cabot, who claimed the area for Henry VII in June 1497, and by other explorers in the name of the English monarch.

In 1664, the English took possession of New Netherland, renaming the principal town New York after James, Duke of York, the brother of the English sovereign, Charles II. English legal practices supplanted those of the Dutch, though many similarities existed between the two. A principle in common was that the unjustifiable taking of another's life could lead to a charge of murder and an execution. In 1669, a special higher criminal court of "oyer and terminer" was held to try a defendant on a murder charge. It was the beginning of criminal court practices in the new English colony. A crier made a proclamation; a commission was read; the sheriff convened a jury. The prisoner was brought to the bar and told that he might challenge any of the jurors. The crier then summoned the prosecutor; witnesses were called; the prisoner raised his hand and had the indictment read to him; and the trial proceeded. The minutes of the early courts are fragmented; therefore, the verdict in this first murder trial is unknown.

Again, in 1675, at the Court of Assizes, a defendant named Scudamore was prosecuted for homicide. The prisoner was brought to the bar and the jury sworn. His children were not put on oath, as the common law rule of not swearing defendants' witnesses was explicitly recognized. The jury was charged and returned a verdict of chance medley (an unpremeditated fight), whereupon the prisoner was discharged. In 1697, New York executed its first capital offender for murder: his name and details of the crime have been lost.

English legal procedures dominated cases that came to trial in the community. The court established the guideline that in a charge of murder, commitment to jail pending indictment, trial, and sentence was to be observed. An exception existed in 1698; John Fisher was indicted for murder. He was granted bail and subsequently acquitted of murder, but found guilty of homicide by misadventure (mischance or accident). The weakness of the charge against the accused apparently permitted bail to be granted in this case.

Criminal Violence: Then and Now

What generalization can be made about disorder in New Amsterdam and early New York? How high was the level of violence during this time relative to the late 20th century? Can specific conclusions be drawn about the nature of homicide in the early community?

1. The threat of violent crime per se was not a preoccupation among the Dutch and English settlers during the first two centuries of the colony. The colonists' daily fears and concerns were about other problems. Washington Irving's <u>History of New York</u>, first published in 1809, painted a picture of domestic tranquility in the Dutch colony that influenced the views of later writers. A modern historian similarly played down the extent of the crime problem in those early years:

> (T)he majority of offenses were of such a trifling nature that their commission today would be winked at by the authorities. The explanation of this absorption of New Netherland justice in matters of minor consequence may be attributed to the smallness of the communities, to the nervous tension that always prevailed in frontier outposts, to the dependence of much of European jurisprudence upon religious taboos rather than upon a scientific study of human behavior, and finally to the impossibility of adopting some Old World laws to New World conditions (Raesly, 1965:137).

Other matters preoccupied settlers more than the crime and violence which underscored daily existence in the seventeenth century. The pacific and bucolic views of Irving, Raesly, and others who wrote about the early settlement ignored the perilousness of a fragile, frontier existence. What colonists feared more than disorder from crime was attacks by Indians in the seventeenth century and by slaves in the eighteenth. Further, they dreaded diseases which swept across the region periodically, decimating large fractions of the populace. Finally, as the town grew, residents worried about fires which could race from street to street in minutes, consuming homes and shops which were largely constructed of wood and built close to each other.

2. How high was the level of criminal violence during this time relative to the late 20th century? It is not possible to determine with precision the levels of homicide in the first two

centuries of Anglo-Dutch settlement and compare them with contemporary time. However, the extant court and municipal records, diaries, pamphlets, newspapers, as well as secondary sources, (like . . .) suggest that life in New Amsterdam and early New York was manifestly more violent than in the late twentieth century, when population size is taken into account.

Some murders went unrecorded and unpunished, particularly by colonists against natives. Someone suspected of a crime could flee the community and could not be tracked down by a primitive law enforcement system. Often juries found it hard to convict the accused even when the evidence was compelling. Executions were rare in early New York, and when the first hanging occurred in 1697, the population was less than 1,500. Two executions for murder occurred in 1717 when the population had grown to 5,000.

From 1744 to 1773, some evidence of additional executions can be found in documents describing judicial proceedings (Ritz, 1984). Between 1744 and the end of that century, a total of four executions for murder occurred in New York City. Two more took place for counterfeiting. By 1790, the population was 49,000. Assuming that some murderers were not apprehended and others did not receive judicial attention, it is reasonable to conclude that the level of homicide in early New Amsterdam and New York was higher than in contemporary times on a population-adjusted basis.

3. What specific conclusions can be drawn about the nature of homicide in the early community? Murder is a crime that has existed in all times, under all circumstances, and in all cultures. While theft is by far the most frequent criminal offense, violent crime evokes greater fear within the community. The ultimate result from unrestrained violence is loss of life. Murder is the unlawful killing of a human being with malice aforethought, either expressed or implied. Killing another human is not necessarily a crime since it may be committed in self-defense, in execution of a judicial sentence, or in other circumstances which justify or excuse it, such as defending oneself or one's community from the perception or reality of hostile attackers. Homicide is the unjustifiable, inexcusable, and intentional killing of another without deliberation and malice. Non-negligent homicide specifically refers to criminal homicide committed with deliberation and not as an accidental consequence. Relative to other offenses, homicide has been an infrequent offense, making it difficult to analyze as a factor of societal behavior.

In those days, as now, the reasons why murderers acted as they did generally were because of petty, personal disputes that escalated in magnitude, due to robberies that were compounded by killings, and sexual attacks that claimed their victims' lives. Of the 186 murderers executed in the City of New York between 1717 and 1900, 112 (60 percent) apparently were related or otherwise knew their victims. Of the remainder, 57 (31 percent) were charged with murders during the commission of robbery. Six persons executed were guilty of conspiracy to commit murder including murder for hire. Four were executed for rape and murder, and a fifth for rape, murder, and burglary. Two were executed for kidnaping and murder and another two were executed for murder arising out of burglary.

Hence, most executions in New York were for crimes not by strangers, and not for direct financial gain. The killings were carried out by husbands, wives or other relatives or friends or acquaintances who expressed uncontrollable rage against another, or otherwise acted so brutally to merit this most severe sanction by the state. In these respects, the seventeenth and eighteenth centuries were no different from present times.

References

Booth, M.L. (1859). <u>History of the City of New York from its Earliest Settlement to the Present Time</u>, New York: W.R.C. Clark & Meeker.

Fernaw, B., ed. <u>Records of New Amsterdam from 1653 to 1674</u>, Baltimore: Genealogical Publishing Co., 1976.

Gehring, C.T. trans. & ed. (1995). <u>Council minutes: 1655-1656</u>, Syracuse: Syracuse University Press.

Hodge, F.W. ed. (1971). <u>Handbook of American Indians North of Mexico</u>, New York: Rowman and Littlefield.

Jameson, J.F., ed., (1909). <u>Narratives of New Netherland, 1609-1664</u>, New York: Charles Scribner's Sons.

O'Callaghan, E.B. comp. & ed. (1849). <u>Documentary history of the State of New-York</u>, Albany: Weed, Parsons & Co.

Phelps-Stokes, I.N. (1967). <u>Iconography of Manhattan Island</u>, New York: Arno Press.

Raesly, E.L. (1965). <u>Portrait of New Netherland</u>, Port Washington, NY: Ira J. Friedman.

Rink, O.A. (1986). <u>Holland on the Hudson: An economical and social history of Dutch New York</u>, Ithaca: Cornell University Press.

Ritz, W.J. (1984).<u>American Judicial Proceedings First Printed before 1801</u>, Westport, CT: Greenwood Press.

Rosenwaike, I. (1972). <u>Population History of New York City</u>, Syracuse: Syracuse University Press.

Shepherd, W.R. (1970). <u>The Story of New Amsterdam</u>, Port Washington, NY: Kennikat Press.

Swanton, J.R. (1968). <u>The IndianTribes of North America</u>, Washington, D.C.: Smithsonian Institution Press, Bulletin of American Ethnology, Bulletin 145.

Van Der Donck, A. (1968). <u>A Description of the New Netherlands</u>, Syracuse: Syracuse University Press.

Violence Research Data, 2nd ed. (1996, October). Ann Arbor, MI: National Archive of Criminal Justice Data.

Waldman, C. (1985). <u>Atlas of the North American Indian</u>, New York: Facts on File.

Weslager, C.A. (1968, Oct.). Did Minuit buy Manhattan Island from the Indians ?, <u>The Halve Maen</u>, xlii.

Chapter 3

MURDERS IN NEW YORK CITY

by Prof. Andrew Karmen

Department of Sociology

This chapter explores the reasons why New Yorkers get murdered, where most of the killings take place, who the perpetrators are, who their victims were, and how the homicide problem has changed over the past few decades. In the process of examining these issues, this chapter also uncovers which neighborhoods are the safest and the most dangerous, which precincts are busiest, how often homicide detectives solve murders, and what might be driving recent trends.

STUDYING MURDERS

Murders are the most terrible of all crimes because nothing can be done to undo the harm inflicted by offenders. For this reason, the penalties meted out to murderers by the criminal law are the most severe of all. Some killers face the possibility of execution under New York State's 1995 capital punishment law.

For criminologists pledged to objectivity, killings are a difficult subject for research because these vicious and unsettling crimes arouse strong emotions and stimulate pro-victim, anti-offender, pro-police, pro-punishment biases. Yet, homicide is the best street crime to study for a number of reasons. The records kept about murders - who died, who did it, with what weapon, where, when, and why - are more accurate, complete, and detailed than for any other criminal act (the FBI receives Supplementary Homicide Reports {SHRs} recounting most of these details - if they are known - about each murder from every police department in the country). Besides police department records, there is always a second source of data: the files maintained by the coroner's or medical examiner's office. In New York, researchers can "double check" NYPD records against the files of the Office of the Chief Medical Examiner to make sure the numbers and victim characteristics correspond. Low reporting rates undermine the accuracy of attempts to measure trends in most street crimes, but the unwillingness of some victims to report crimes to the police is not a problem in homicides; most corpses eventually turn up. Detectives assigned to solve these cases are the department's best, so solution rates for homicides are the highest of any crime. Since so many killers are brought to justice, more comprehensive information can be found out about murderers than about any other types of street criminals, such as burglars, car thieves, rapists, or robbers.

To criminologists, the contention that "Anyone is capable of carrying out a homicide; everyone is a potential murderer" is not a satisfactory statement of the problem. Clearly, some people are more prone than others to resort to violence, and are more inclined, willing, or prepared to kill. That is why criminologists study homicide statistics describing the characteristics of the typical perpetrators. The goal is to examine the phenomenon of differential rates of offending: the greater likelihood of involvement in criminal activity of certain groups of people (for example, males and youths) than other groups (such as females and the elderly).

When it comes to being murdered, technically, everyone is "at risk," and "anyone can lose his or her life at any moment." But to victimologists, this is not a satisfactory statement of the problem either. Victimologists do not put forward formulations that emphasize randomness, destiny, fate, or the bad luck of being at the wrong place at the wrong time. There are, of course, senseless killings that take place without rhyme or reason, as when an unsuspecting person gets struck down by a stray bullet intended for someone else. But the way victimology enriches criminology and contributes to a greater understanding of the etiology of violent crime is by raising and exploring the possibility of "differential risks." Victimology's concept of differential risks of being harmed by illegal acts parallels criminology's concept of differential rates of offending. Victimologists emphasize the non-random distribution of the burden of becoming targeted by offenders on the prowl. By studying the characteristics of deceased persons, victimologists can discover which groups of people are disproportionately involved and uninvolved in deadly physical confrontations, and can then derive estimates of the level of the threat faced by these different "types," or "kinds," or "categories" of people.

The expression "types of people" has a psychological ring to it, as in personality types. At one extreme might be homicide victims who could be described as having been shy, retiring, mild-mannered, cautious and prudent, and at the other end of the spectrum are those who were confrontational, aggressive, argumentative, volatile, reckless, thrill-seeking, even foolhardy. Some casualties in fatal confrontations may have acted out-of-character, and were irritable, hostile, paranoid, and impulsive because they were disinhibited by alcohol or other drugs like cocaine. It seems logical to hypothesize that one's personality type in a number of ways and for various reasons might directly influence an individual's odds of getting killed, by former friends or longstanding enemies, in spontaneous quarrels or smoldering conflicts. A victim could have been slain by a brutal spouse or a jealous lover, or even by an abusive parent or an embittered child. Some homicide victims, however, were antisocial troublemakers themselves when they entered into the final showdowns that cost them their lives. But personality data about deceased victims is hard to come by or reconstruct, unless these unfortunate souls were observed and analyzed right before their demise.

Victimologists adopting an approach that is more sociological than psychological tend to focus upon the social "categories" or groupings into which murder victims fall. Like personality traits, these groupings might be clues to such important risk-determining factors as social contacts, willingness to enter into physical confrontations, routine activities, lifestyle choices, and leisure-time pursuits. Social constructs that might be relevant determinants of behavior include such obvious groupings as sex and age, as well as indicators reflecting social position or social class and status, such as education, occupation, area of residence, and even race/ethnicity.

CIRCUMSTANCES SURROUNDING KILLINGS

The first question criminologists might ask about murders in New York City concerns the reasons for the bloodshed. What were the circumstances surrounding the killings? In other words, why did the perpetrators slay their victims?

When it comes to different kinds of murders, New York has them all, not just the common "everyday" kinds of tragic or infuriating or frightening killings, but also the unusual headline-making cases too: mob hits (as of Mafia boss Paul Castellano, apparently on orders from John Gotti in 1986); sprees by serial killers ("Son of Sam, the 44 Caliber Killer" in the late 1970's; and the Zodiac Killer in the early 1990's); celebrity stalkings (the shooting of Beatle John Lennon in 1981); assassinations of political figures (of Malcolm X in 1965; and Rabbi Meir Kehane in 1993); deaths of innocent people from terrorist bombings (the explosion at the World Trade Center killed six people in 1993); and eruptions of ethnic antagonisms (such as the hate crimes that claimed the lives of Michael Griffith in Howard Beach in 1986; Yusuf Hawkins in Bensonhurst in 1989; Yankel Rosenbaum in Crown Heights in 1991).

But the major reasons behind most New York murders are much more mundane, according to the data appearing in Table 3-1 (for 1995, the most recent year for which there is available a relatively complete breakdown of motives). The data in Table 3-1 indicates that in 1995 the circumstances surrounding about a quarter of all slayings could not be determined by homicide detectives. But of those cases that were solved, many lives were lost due to arguments over all sorts of contentious issues which seemed so important at the time (but may simply have been about minor matters like money owed by former friends or acts by complete strangers that were perceived to be insults or challenges). Aside from this catchall category of "all other disputes" (that claimed more than one quarter of all lives lost during 1995), intense struggles within the drug scene added significantly to the body count (causing one sixth of all deaths). Vicious robbers also contributed substantially (one ninth) to the death toll that year. Violent quarrels within families accounted for a smaller proportion of all killings (around one twelfth). Stray bullets meant for someone else robbed almost as many people of their lives. But the depredations of mobsters, street gang members, kidnappers, rapists, and burglars did not result in many fatal encounters.

WHERE KILLINGS TOOK PLACE

The location of the crime scenes can be described along two dimensions. The first way to examine where the victims died is to make note of the number of slayings at different types of location; the second way is to identify geographical areas like precincts or neighborhoods that have high murder rates from precincts or neighborhoods that have moderate or low ones.

The types of locations in which murders took place during the first six months of 1997 (the most recent year for which complete data is available, extracted from the Office of the Chief Medical Examiner) appears in Table 3-2. The breakdown of specific settings indicates that the most common crime scene was someone's residence (43%), most often the home of the deceased (25%). Other indoor locations included stores, clubs, and bars. Taken together, about half of all the murders committed in 1997 were carried out in locations that were "not visible" to officers who might have passed by on routine patrol. Of the remaining slayings that were committed outdoors, most of them were committed right out in the open, on the street (37%). Others took place in parked cars or parks.

Table 3-1:

"Circumstances" Surrounding the Murders Committed in New York City in 1995

Reason, Type	Number	Percent
Killings related to the drug scene	204	17%
Killings of robbery victims	131	11%
Killings of burglary victims	6	0%
Killings of sexual assault victims	5	0%
Killings of kidnap victims	2	0%
Killings within families	72	6%
Fatalities from child abuse and neglect	28	2%
Killings of innocent bystanders	13	1%
Killings related to youthful street gangs	2	0%
Killings related to organized crime	2	0%
Killings of police in the line of duty	0	0%
Killings from all other disputes	343	28%
Killings for unknown reasons	323	27%

Notes:
-All categories are mutually exclusive; no murder is counted twice.
-"All other disputes" is a residual category; altercations that are not between members of the same family, or over drugs, or between gang members or mobsters.
-Robberies of drug sellers and users are scored as "drug related "
-Burglars and other intruders who invade homes technically are robbers, but are counted separately here.
-"Family" includes live-in lovers but not boyfriend/girlfriend dating relationships.
-Child abuse deaths caused mostly by parents but also by babysitters were not included under the heading "within families."
-Most innocent bystanders were killed by indiscriminate gunfire.

Source: NYPD Chief of Detective's Homicide Log for 1995, made available by Newsday

Table 3-2:
Crime Scenes - New York City, 1997

Location	Number of Victims	Percent of Cases
Victim's home	93	25
Victim's apartment building	19	5
Someone else's home	12	3
Inside someone else's building	31	9
Hotel, motel room	4	1
Total "Residence"	**159**	**43**
Abandoned Building	2	1
Office	1	0
Store	15	4
Bar, Club	9	3
Total "**Not Visible**" Murders	**186**	**51**
Street	137	37
Car	16	4
Highway	1	1
Parking Lot	5	1
Park	15	4
Empty Lot, Field, Woods	3	1
Total "**Visible**" Murders	**178**	**49**

Note:
In 10 cases, the place where the body was found was not considered to be the scene of the crime by the police.
Source: NYC Medical Examiner's files, first six months of 1997

Another way to map the geographical distribution of crime scenes is to make note of the precincts within which they took place. New York City's 76 precinct boundaries often correspond to neighborhoods or community boards. In order to determine which precincts have the highest and the lowest murder rates, it is necessary to take their different sized populations into account. The number of murders, the number of people living within the precinct's boundaries, and the precinct's murder rate (per 100,000 people) is presented for 1996 (the latest year for which complete data is available) in Table 3-3.

The analysis of this data reveals that six precincts stood out as having the highest murder rates, more than three times higher than the average for the entire city (which was about 13 victims for every 100,000 New Yorkers). The precincts and their corresponding neighborhoods that were the most dangerous to reside in during 1996 were the 79th (Bedford-Stuyvesant); the 28th (Central Harlem); the 32nd (Harlem); the 41st (Hunts Point); the 73rd (Brownsville); and the 14th (Midtown South, which has many tourists, commuters, shoppers, and idlers but not so many residents). Four precincts had no murders to investigate in 1996: the 1st (Tribeca/Wall Street); the 6th (Greenwich Village), 18th (Midtown North); and the 22nd (Central Park). Other precincts with the lowest murder rates, due to just one or two killings within their boundaries, were the 17th (Midtown), the 123rd (Totenville); the 111th (Bayside); and the 112th (Forest Hills). Clearly, some parts of town can be considered virtual "killing fields" while other communities not far away were quite safe, statistically speaking, at least in terms of being murdered. A correlation and regression analysis of murder rates and precinct social conditions indicated that the neighborhoods where residents faced the gravest risks in the 1990's tended to be the poorest, most racially and financially segregated sections of the city, inhabited by many female headed households receiving public assistance and by unemployed persons; conversely, the safest communities in the City were the most affluent ones (Karmen, 1996a).

Table 3-3:

Murder Rates by Precinct - New York City, 1996

Precinct	Neighborhood	Population	Murders	Murder Rate
Manhattan				
1	Tribeca, Wall Street	32,980	0	0
5	Chinatown, Little Italy	54,990	2	4 per 100,000
6	Greenwich Village	65,670	0	0
7	Lower East Side	59,100	4	7
9	East Village	68,000	13	19
10	Chelsea	42,250	3	7
13	Gramercy	83,500	3	4

Precinct	Neighborhood	Population	Murders	Murder Rate
14	Midtown South	17,200	8	47
17	Midtown	71,000	1	1
18	Midtown North	48,200	0	0
19	East Side	202,700	7	4
20	West Side	96,900	5	5
22	Central Park	0	0	0
23	Upper East Side	69,400	19	27
24	Upper West Side	114,100	7	7
25	East Harlem	41,100	16	39
26	Morningside Heights	46,000	8	17
28	Central Harlem	36,400	18	49
30	Harlem	61,400	22	36
32	Harlem	62,700	29	46
33-34	Washington Heights	198,200	38	19
Bronx				
40	South Bronx	77,200	29	38
41	Hunts Point	39,400	16	41
42	Tremont	57,200	20	35
43	Soundview	165,600	28	17
44	Morris Heights	120,000	19	16
45	Schuylerville	98,000	6	6
46	University Heights	118,400	37	31
47	Eastchester	130,000	24	18
48	Fordham	68,000	25	37
49	Baychester	98,500	8	8
50	Riverdale	97,000	8	8

Precinct	Neighborhood	Population	Murders	Murder Rate
52	Bedford Park	128,600	28	28
60	Coney Island	102,600	16	16
61	Sheepshead Bay	143,500	9	6
62	Bensonhurst	150,000	10	7
63	Flatlands, Mill Basin	95,500	9	9
66	Borough Park	160,000	6	4
67	East Flatbush	161,300	30	19
68	Bay Ridge	110,600	3	3
69	Canarsie	67,000	7	10
70	Kensington	160,000	19	12
71	Flatbush	110,700	8	7
72	Sunset Park	102,600	12	12
73	Brownsville	84,900	34	40
75	East New York	161,400	40	25
76	Carroll Gdns, Red Hook	42,600	7	16
77	Crown Heights	96,900	28	29
78	Park Slope	59,600	4	7
79	Bedford Stuyvesant	76,700	37	48
81	Bed-Stuy/Brownsville	61,700	16	26
83	Bushwick	102,600	16	16
84	Brooklyn Heights	40,000	3	8
88	Fort Greene	54,500	10	18
90	Williamsburg	101,900	15	15
94	Greenpoint	54,000	4	7

Precinct	Neighborhood	Population	Murders	Murder Rate
Queens				
100	Rockaway	40,500	4	10
101	Far Rockaway	60,100	8	13
102	Richmond Hill	112,200	13	12
103	Jamaica	92,600	20	22
104	Woodside	150,300	5	3
105	Queens Village	177,500	23	13
106	Ozone Park	107,800	7	6
107	Fresh Meadows	130,800	4	3
108	Long Island City	94,800	9	9
109	Flushing	221,800	5	2
110	Elmhurst	137,100	9	7
111	Bayside	108,100	2	2
112	Forest Hills	105,800	2	2
113	South Jamaica	108,700	21	19
114	Astoria	196,700	18	9
115	Jackson Heights	129,000	15	12
Staten Island				
120	St. George	137,900	19	14
122	New Dorp	172,000	8	5
123	Totenville	69,100	1	1
All of New York City		**7,400,000**	**984**	13

Notes: All precinct populations are rounded off to the nearest 100.

All murder rates are rounded off to the nearest integer.

All murder rates are calculated as per 100,000 residents even though many neighborhoods have far less than 100,000 inhabitants.

Sources: NYPD Complaints and Arrests Statistical Report, 1996;
    NYPD Selected 1990 Census Indicators by Precinct

THE CHARACTERISTICS OF NEW YORK CITY'S MURDER VICTIMS

A profile of the typical New York City homicide victim can be drawn from the data describing the nearly 1,000 slayings that took place in 1996. Table 3-4 confirms the insight derived from victimology that different demographic groups of people face dramatically different risks of being murdered.

Boys and men, who make up almost half of the city's residents, comprise more than four-fifths of its homicide victims. Even though there are slightly more females living in New York City, the people dying violently in New York City are disproportionally male, by a ratio of about four to one.

As for race and ethnicity, black New Yorkers make up about one-quarter of the city's population but a little more than half of all victims. Hispanic New Yorkers also make up about one quarter of the population and about the same proportion of the body count. White and Asian New Yorkers are victimized at disproportionally low rates.

When it comes to age, most of the people who were killed could be categorized as "young" as opposed to children, middle aged or elderly. Teenagers and young adults between the ages of 16 and 24 made up almost a third of all victims, as did persons aged 25 to 34. Substantial numbers of people between the ages of 35 and 44 were also killed. Children younger than 16 and adults older than 45 faced lesser risks.

As for educational attainment, most (seven out of ten) of the New Yorkers who died in 1996 had never made it to college, according to their relatives who helped fill out death certificates, from which this "Vital Statistics" database was drawn.

In sum, the statistical portrait of the typical victim that emerges from the data assembled in Table 3-4 is that of a black teenage boy or young man who never attended college.

Table 3-4:
A Statistical Profile of Homicide Victims - New York City, 1996

Attribute	Number	Percent of All Victims
Sex:		
Male	822	82
Female	183	18
Race and Ethnicity:		
Black	512	51
Hispanic	265	27
White (Non-Hispanic)	182	18
Asian and Others	32	3
Unknown	12	1

Attribute	Number	Percent of All Victims
Age:		
0-11	39	4
12-15	15	2
16-19	122	12
20-24	182	18
25-34	301	30
35-44	187	19
45+	157	16
Educational Attainment:		
Didn't Finish High School	189	19
Graduated High School	508	51
Some College	80	8
Graduated College	31	3
Graduate Student or Above	7	1
Unknown to next of Kin	188	19
All Homicide Victims	**1005**	**100**

Notes:
Justifiable homicides (persons killed by the police) are included in this victim file; without them, the total would be 984.
Source:
    Vital Statistics database derived from death certificates, provided by the New York City Department of Health.

THE CHARACTERISTICS OF NEW YORK CITY'S MURDER ARRESTEES

    The profile of the typical homicide arrestee during 1996 can be derived from Table 3-5 below. First of all, the typical arrestee, like the typical victim, is a boy or man. This disproportional male involvement in lethal violence means that boys and men are nineteen times more likely than girls and women to kill.

    Teenagers and young adults were over-represented among the ranks of homicide arrestees. Nearly six out of every ten arrestees were between the ages of 16 and 25, and an additional one out of four fell in-between the ages of 26 and 35. Therefore, more than eight out of every ten arrestees were less than 36 years old. Calculating average ages, the mean and median ages of all homicide arrestees turned out to be in the mid-20s.

Black New Yorkers made up over half of all arrestees, even though the proportion of residents who identified themselves as "black" on the U.S. Census in 1990 was only about one quarter. The involvement of Hispanic New Yorkers in lethal violence also was disproportionally higher than their share of the population, but by a small disparity (more than one third of all accused killers, compared to one quarter of all residents). White and Asian New Yorkers were arrested far less often than their numbers in the city's population.

Most of the suspects (about seven out of ten) taken into custody for committing murder had been arrested before. They previously had been in trouble with the law for allegedly committing felonies, or both felonies and misdemeanors, but not just for misdemeanors, in most cases. Almost half of all arrestees had been convicted before, and in most cases they were guilty of serious crimes, not just minor ones, according to the database of the criminal histories of the roughly one thousand murder arrestees in 1996 that was supplied by the New York State Division of Criminal Justice Services (DCJS).

In sum, statistically speaking, the typical profile of a person accused of murder in New York City is a black teenager or young man who has been arrested before for a serious crime (see Table 3-6 below). That offender profile resembles the victim profile (in terms of sex, age, and race/ethnicity) that was derived from Table 3-5 above.

TRENDS IN NEW YORK CITY MURDERS

There are three striking trends that stand out in any analysis of New York City's violent crime problem. The first is the very positive development that materialized during the 1990's. After years of rising death tolls, which peaked in 1990 when the bloodshed reached a record high of 2,262 victims, the level of violence subsided dramatically, dropping back in 1997 to a body count of 767 unfortunate souls, the "best" it has been in thirty years. This dramatic improvement was made possible by the second trend, a plunge in the number of people killed by gunfire. Gun deaths comprised a small proportion of all slayings until the mid 1960's. The explosion of violence in the city since then was fueled by an arms race which intensified in the late 1980's among crack sellers but spread to other young men. Ever since handguns caught on as the weapon of choice, other modes of killing, (especially stabbing, clubbing with blunt instruments, and strangling) have been "going out of style"(see Karmen, 1996b).

These two trends are depicted in Graph 3-1, which also reveals that during the 1990's, the gun-toting fad that caused devastating losses of life for poor young male minority New Yorkers has been dying out.

The third sharp trend that is worthy of note, also quite positive, is the vast improvement in the ability of the police to solve murders. Until the mid 1990's, around one third of all killers were literally getting away with murder. The NYPD's clearance rate was below the national average (which has hovered around 67% in recent years, according to the FBI's Uniform Crime Report). But since 1994, the solution rate has soared well above the national average, as homicide detectives in the City have been bringing many more killers to justice. As Table 3-7 shows, the clearance rate for other types of street crimes has not improved as much as for murders.

Table 3-6:
A Statistical Profile of Homicide Arrestees - New York City, 1996

Attribute	Number	Percent of All Arrestees
Sex:		
Males	952	95
Females	51	5
Race and Ethnicity:		
Whites	60	6
Blacks	555	55
Hispanics	356	36
Asians	32	3
Age Groups:		
1-15	31	3
16-20	320	32
21-25	262	26
26-30	140	14
31-35	110	11
36-40	64	6
41+	76	8
Median Age	23	
Mean Age	26	
Past Criminal Record:		
Never Arrested	280	28
Only Misd. Arr.	64	6
Only Fel. Arr.	260	26
Both M & F. Arr.	399	40

Attribute	Number	Percent of All Arrestees
Never Convicted	508	51
Only Misd. Conv.	88	9
Only Fel. Conv.	212	21
Both M. & F. Arr.	195	19
All Arrestees	1,003	100

Source: NYC homicide arrestee database, provided by the DCJS, Albany.

Table 3-7:
Trends in the Percentage of Crimes Reported to the NYPD
That Are "Cleared by an Arrest"
New York City, 1990 - 1996

Type of Crime	1990	1991	1992	1993	1994	1995	1996
Murder	62%	59	59	62	64	73	87
Rape	49	57	49	44	51	61	52
Robbery	22	22	21	21	25	29	30
Felonious Assault	50	51	50	47	53	56	55
Burglary	9	9	8	8	9	12	13
Grand Larceny	7	7	6	6	7	9	9
Motor Vehicle Theft	7	7	6	5	5	7	7

Notes:
All clearance rates are rounded off to the nearest integer.
 A case is cleared when an arrest is made, whether or not the defendant is ultimately convicted of the crime.

Source: NYPD Complaints and Arrests Annual Reports, 1990-1996

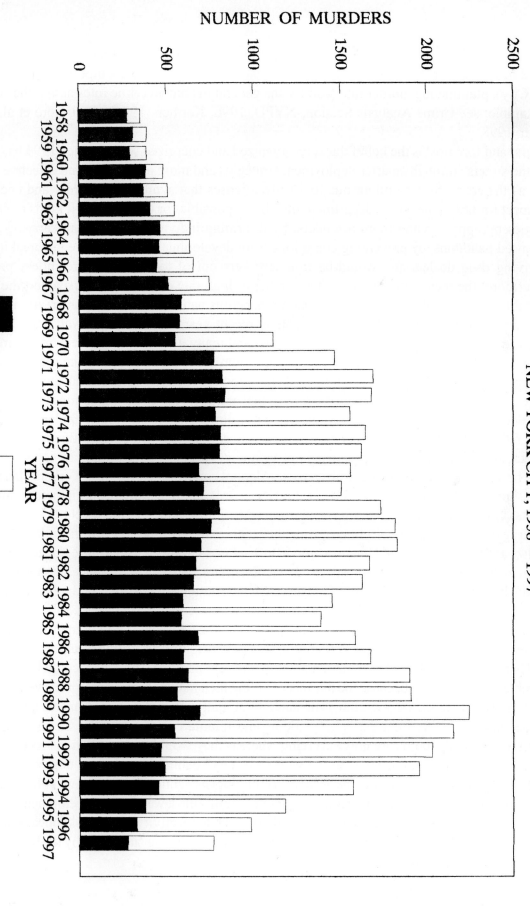

TRENDS IN MURDERS, BY TYPE OF WEAPON
NEW YORK CITY, 1958 – 1997

NUMBER OF MURDERS

2500 2000 1500 1000 500 0

YEAR

1958 1960 1962 1964 1966 1968 1970 1972 1974 1976 1978 1980 1982 1984 1986 1988 1990 1992 1994 1996
1959 1961 1963 1965 1967 1969 1971 1973 1975 1977 1979 1981 1983 1985 1987 1989 1991 1993 1995 1997

■ other weapons □ guns

Source: NYPD's 1991 Homicide Analysis Report; 1992 – 1996: NYPD SHRs; 1997: Estimated from M.E. files
Note: Gun = any kind of firearm; Non−Gun = any other kind of weapon, plus sheer physical force.

A number of hypotheses have been put forward by criminologists, criminal justice professionals, elected officials, journalists, and other knowledgeable observers in an attempt to account for New York City's plummeting murder rate (and for the general decline in crime rates across the country; for example, see Crime Analysis Section, NYPD, 1996; Karmen, 1996b; Lattimore et al, 1997; Witkin, 1998).

First and foremost is the belief that a re-organized and energized NYPD since 1994 has "taken back the streets" through smarter deployment strategies and more aggressive and effective tactics (such as the crackdown on minor quality of life offenses that symbolize disorder and encourage disrespect for law). The police department may be responsible for the drop in all kinds of criminal activities by apprehending more offenders, by disarming individuals who were carrying around unlicensed handguns, by preventing conditions from developing that encourage lawbreaking, and by driving drug dealers and would-be troublemakers out of town through relentless pressure. Furthermore, the incareration of a greater number of high rate offenders may have left the streets noticeably safer. Another hypothesis is that a prosperous national economy has greatly improved local employment prospects for city residents in recent years. Even though well paid, full-time, unionized jobs in manufacturing are disappearing, and many white collar office workers are being laid off as well, the number of part-time and minimum wage jobs in the service sector may have increased. These less-than-desirable jobs could be attractive enough to serve as an alternative source of income to individuals being driven out of criminal activity. Another explanation is that the extent of hardcore drug abuse among poor young men has diminished as the crack epidemic of the late 1980s fades away. (Crimes of violence are frequently committed "under the influence" by abusers who act "out of character," or are carried out by addicts desperate for money to pay for cocaine, crack, heroin, and other controlled substances.) Alcohol consumption by New Yorkers also may be down significantly (either the offender or the victim or both often were drinking before outbreaks of lethal violence). Connected to this contention is the impression that the level of conflict among rival drug dealing groups has declined during the 1990s as the cocaine and heroin markets "mature," stabilize and move indoors, leading to a drop in turf-related killings. Furthermore, "peace" may have broken out between rival organized crime factions, and between the City's street gangs, who previously went to war over control of lucrative rackets, notions of territory, and other disputes that motivated them to slay each other's members at a higher rate in the recent past. Most important of all, it is possible that in the 1990s the cultural values of the City's poor young men are undergoing profound changes, in the direction of rejecting gang membership, gun-toting, drug-taking, and other self-destructive expressions of alienation and rebellion. In addition, the 1990s could be a period of favorable demographics, because the number of young men in their high crime-prone years residing in New York City might have declined substantially. Finally, dramatic improvements in emergency medical care at city hospital emergency rooms and trauma centers might be so substantial that seriously wounded victims are now surviving whereas they would have died in the recent past.

The task for criminologists is to "solve the mystery" behind New York's unprecedented and unpredicted "crime crash" during the 1990s. Criminologists cannot simply accept at face value the claims of self-interested parties that are taking credit for this most welcomed development. As social scientists, they must maintain an approach of disinterested objectivity, adopt a skeptical stance, and demand proof before accepting any of the above hypotheses as being supported by the best available statistical evidence.

Acknowledgements

The author appreciates the assistance of Anthony Destefano, the Assistant City Editor of Newsday, Queens bureau, who made available a photocopy of the 1995 Homicide Log maintained in the office of the NYPD's Chief Of Detectives, which was obtained by that newspaper from the Police Department under the Freedom of Information law; and the financial support from the Reisenbach Foundation to collect data about 1997 homicide victims from the files maintained at the Office of the Chief Medical Examiner, Dr. Charles Hirsch.

References

Karmen, A. (1996a). Crime rates and precinct social conditions. An unpublished paper delivered at the American Criminology Society meeting in Chicago, November 9th.

----------- (1996b). "What's driving New York's crime rate down?" Law Enforcement News, November 30, pp. 8-10.

Lattimore, P., Trudeau, J., Riley, K., Leiter, J., and Edwards, S. (1997). Homicide in Eight U.S. Cities: Trends, Context, and Policy Implications. NIJ Research Report. Washington, D.C.: U.S. Department of Justice.

NYPD Crime Analysis And Program Planning Section (1996). New York City Crime Control Indicators and Strategy Assessment. New York: Office of Management Analysis and Planning.

Witkin, G. (1998). "The crime bust." U.S. News and World Report, May 25, pp. 28-37.

Sources of Data:

Division of Criminal Justice Services (DCJS), Albany.

Database of New York City Murder and Manslaughter Arrestees, 1978-1997.

Office of the Chief Medical Examiner, New York City: Homicide files, 1997.

New York City Department of Health: Vital Statistics of Homicide Victims database.

New York City Police Department, Crime Analysis Unit, Office Of Management Analysis and Planning: Complaints and Arrests Annual Report, 1990-1996.

New York City Police Department, Crime Analysis Unit, Office of Management Analysis And Planning: Homicide Analysis: selected years, 1970s, 1980s, 1991 (latest).

New York City Police Department, Crime Analysis Unit, Office of Management Analysis And Planning: Selected 1990 Census Socio-economic Indicators By Precinct.

Chapter 4

THE EVOLUTION OF NEW YORK CITY'S STREET GANGS

by

Professor David C. Brotherton

Department of Sociology

During the last two decades, street gangs in New York City have gone through several stages of development. In the sixties and seventies, most gangs were largely traditional or cultural (Skolnick, 1991), based on territory and the defense of parochial neighborhood spaces (Thrasher, 1927; Suttles, 1968). In the 1990's, street organizations have emerged that are strikingly different from the previous two gang types.

This chapter is based on data compiled from qualitative life history interviews (each taped and transcribed) with twenty "old heads" who are or have been members of gangs and street organizations in New York City dating back to the 1970's.

From fighting gangs to politically oriented street organizations

Street gangs, as opposed to organized crime syndicates such as the Mafia, have found a home among impoverished males and females in New York City for more than a hundred and fifty years. In the early 1800's (Sante, 1993) the slums of the Five Points District in lower Manhattan were the site of the first urban gang recorded in the United States. This Irish immigrant group, calling themselves the Forty Thieves, specialized in robbery and claimed the area as their territory (Collins, 1979). Throughout the ensuing eras of capitalist industrialization and urbanization, gangs (Asbury, 1927) such as the Shirt Tails, the Plug Uglies and the Dead Rabbits fought massive territorial gang wars and were engaged in a variety of thuggery, often manipulated by the corrupt politicians of Tammany Hall. Notably, however, all the gangs consisted primarily of lower class males from communities mired in "conditions of poverty and alienation common to those at the lowest levels of urban life" (Campbell, 1984:33).

While the marginalizing and socially destabilizing economic conditions under which New York City gangs emerged were similar to the social ecological characteristics of gangs in other cities, so too were the activities of their members. According to the early literature, gang members were largely split between *"those who were fighters and those whose motivation was primarily financial gain"* (Campbell, 1984:10). Ironically, Campbell adds, *"street gangs may not have been so prevalent in the United States without the role model of the social clubs with their use of names, emblems, rules, initiations, and dues"* (1984:12).

New York City street gangs continued to emerge and decline throughout the 20th century, their ideals typically ranging across a continuum of conflict, retreatist and criminal subcultures (Cloward & Ohlin, 1959), each conditioned by neighborhood opportunity structures. By the 1950's, however, gangs in Harlem were moving away from their social or delinquent orientations and were mainly concerned with irrational violence. *"This type of gang-banger or warfare-oriented gang was the primary gang of the 1950's . . . In contrast with other gang types, the violent gang was primarily organized for emotional gratification and violent activities"* (Yablonsky, 1997:41). This New York City street gang type was so lacking in social cohesiveness it could only be called a "near-group" (Yablonsky, 1962).

During the 1960's, the gang presence in New York City seemed to wane as youth became more involved in the ghetto and barrio politics of the Young Lords Party and the Black Panthers. By the 1970's, this situation had again changed, and there was some evidence of a gang cycle (Galea, 1997). By the mid-1970's the police estimated that there were more than 400 street gangs in New York City with more than 40,000 members, mostly in the Bronx, Brooklyn and Manhattan (Collins, 1979).During the 1980's, these street subcultures once more declined in number and almost disappeared from many of the neighborhoods with the exception of a few residual units in the poorest areas. A Department of Justice Report in 1983 stated that "gang membership . . . numbers have declined to 4,300 members in 86 gangs."

However, while the "jacket gangs" faded into the background as a major street subculture among the city's most marginalized youth, they were replaced by crews, some of which were organized around tagging (Chalfant & Silver, 1984), but mostly they derived from the opportunity structures of the ever mutating drug trade. These crews contained many members from the former jacket gangs although they also drew on a new generation of the marginalized working-class in the City (Curtis, 1997; Sullivan, 1989). The crews were different in both appearance and substance to the jacket gangs, and reflected the changed economic and social conditions of the now thoroughly de-industrialized inner-city (see Kasarda, 1989; Bluestone and Harrison, 1982; Vergara, 1995).

In the 1990's, many of the youth's street subcultures of New York City again qualitatively transformed, this time emerging as "street organizations" filled with members seeking to break with their gang and/or posse pasts and proactively come to terms with ghetto life. Table 4-1 below provides an overview that compares the characteristics of these three sub-cultural types.

Combining both American and British theoretical approaches, a comparative interpretation of each of these sub-cultural characteristics is offered in following section. In the comparison over time between these three group types, what is striking is how demarcated the contemporary street organizations are from the previous two subcultures on issues of delinquency, territory and ideology.

From Fighting Sub-Cultures to Street Organizations
Group Types

The jacket gangs of New York City, consisting primarily of Puerto Rican and African-American working-class youth, emerged in Manhattan, the South Bronx and Brooklyn during the late 1960's and early 1970's.

Table 4-1:

Overview of Three Types of Youth Organizations

Period	1970's	1980's	1990's
Types	jacket gangs	street crews	street organizations
Structure	vertical	loose/situational	vertical/contingent
Territory	local turfs	drug spots	extraterritorial
Ideology	street lore/some radicalism	street entrepreneurial	communitarian/utopian
Delinquency	"cafeteria-type"	drug focused	anti-delinquent
Conflict Management	negotiated terrains	market competitive	conflict mediation/ arbitration
Symbolism	clothing/names/graffiti	conspicuous consumption	beads/colors/meetings/ banners
Integration	relatively well integrated	situational	well integrated/ high solidarity
Duration	10 years	temporary	long term commitment

According to the "old heads," gang members grew up within a lower class cultural milieu (Miller 1958) of dozens of youth subcultures in their respective neighborhoods. Their outlaw-type names like the Tomahawks, the Black Peacestone, the Saigon, the Vanguards, Crazy Homicides, the Jolly Stompers, were part of the complex signification process embedded in young working-class identity construction, and embodied symbolic reactions to the alienating environment within which these youth were raised.

These jacket gangs had many of the characteristics found in the traditional U.S. gang literature. Their adherents lived throughout the five boroughs of New York City. The gangs possessed defined rules and roles of membership, and succeeded in creating a powerful subsystem of values, rituals and communication styles that attracted many of the city's most marginalized young people. At the end of the 1970's, these groups began to disappear, their social and physical spaces destroyed by landlord-inspired arson (Vergara, 1995), and their numbers, particularly their leaderships, depleted by the arrival of heroin and its self-destructive properties.

The 1980's, however, saw the appearance of a different type of street grouping that was built on the illegal opportunity structures (Cloward and Ohlin, 1960) offered by the mushrooming marijuana, heroin, and (by the late 1980's) crack cocaine drug trade. Some members of these groups combined their drug selling with other low level criminal activity.

These crews or posses proliferated throughout New York City's poorest neighborhoods (Sullivan, 1989) at a time when manufacturing jobs were lost at a rate greater than in any other large American city (Fitch, 1993) and services to the least affluent were dramatically pared as part of the city's "planned shrinkage" response to the fiscal crisis of the early seventies.

In the late 1980's, the dominant youth subcultures in the city again changed their form, as large organized gangs came back. At first, they were not so different from the old jacket gangs. However, in the early 1990's, with the emergence of a new leadership and a more heterogeneous membership, these gangs began to transform themselves into street organizations or cultural associations for self and community empowerment.

Structure

The organizational structure of the jacket gangs was always vertical (Jankowski, 1991), based on the pyramidal design of a corporation or the traditional hierarchy of a social club. The groups' members socially hung out together on a daily basis, either in their club houses or on street corners and assembled weekly to discuss their business. A great deal of emphasis was placed on the role of leadership and the position of the President was a prized one. Under him in the hierarchy was the Vice-President, the War Lord and the Sergeant-at-Arms, all of whom met to decide on group policy before putting it to the members - although it was the President that made the final decisions. As their numbers grew and their activities took hold, not only in many of New York City's poorest neighborhoods but in other states and the commonwealth of Puerto Rico, they divided up into semi-autonomous units.

In comparison, the drug crews of the 1980's were much less structured with none of the formal titles described above; nor did they remain in existence for long periods of time. Consequently, they did not build up the sub-cultural histories and traditions of the jacket gangs. Rather, they were short-lived, locally organized small groups, made up of neighborhood friends and associates. They primarily concentrated their activities on the execution of criminal tasks, adapting their organization to a fast moving, drug-oriented environment (Fagan, 1989).

The street organizations are different from the drug-dealing crews and place great store in their ability to organize, multiply their ranks and maintain their inner solidarity. They have written organizational guidelines which are followed assiduously. Like the jacket gangs, these groups divided into semi-autonomous units as they grew. In the case of the Latin Kings, these subdivisions are called "tribes." Each tribe is led by a group of "five crowns" with a "supreme crown" in overall charge of the tribe. As with the jacket gangs, there is one President, or "Inca," who heads a "Supreme Team" which makes policy decisions for the entire organization.

Similar to the jacket gangs, there is a strict division of labor in these organizations, with members nominated to positions called a Secretary of State, Public Relations Officer, Political Advisor, and Santo (essentially Spiritual Advisor). These positions change as the needs of the organization change but the duties are taken very seriously; unlike the jacket gangs, the members are more accountable for their actions and group responsibilities. As these street organizations have evolved out of their gang stage, they have had to change a number of their old practices, particularly the severe, physical punishments for rule transgressions and initiations.

The "universals" (general meetings), which often resemble a religious revival, take on a special significance for the discipline and maintenance of the organization's local and state structure, now that the use of physical punishment has been renounced. The three largest street organizations in New York City hold monthly or bimonthly all-inclusive universals, at which internal business is discussed and the various leaders from the different subdivisions confer with one another. It is at these meetings that the main leaders get to rally the membership, providing them with information on future activities, an analysis of the organization's progress, the obstacles facing the movement, and recount an oral history of the group.

Territory

"Hanging out" by working class youth is not simply an example of idleness but is a forced outgrowth and reaction to industrial society's authority over time and space (see Stark, 1993; Corrigan, 1979; Harvey, 1996; Lefebvre, 1991) and its segregation by age (Greenberg, 1993). Hence, "hanging out" can be seen as an expression of resistance to the needs of the business world and the school systems it helps to shape (Bowles & Gintis, 1977).

Over time, it was out of this activity of "hanging out" among friends, that the jacket gangs were formed. Just as they constructed a nominal identity for themselves, they also "imagined" (Anderson, 1990) themselves to be within intricate borders that overlay the racial and ethnic residential zones of the members. These borders became their territories or psycho-social spheres of control (Vigil, 1988) whose real and symbolic properties (i.e., marked by early examples of graffiti) frequently led to inter-gang conflict. However, since these zones of gang influence were within densely populated, ethnically mixed residential areas of public and private housing, it did not produce the "no-go zones" in New York often mentioned in accounts of Los Angeles and Chicago gang wars.

Rather, the gang territories were negotiated domains, with members able to wear their jackets in some zones and not in others. Thus, these gangs were constantly involved in generating and regenerating feuds and alliances with and against other gangs, which became a precondition of their existence.

In comparison, the closest that the drug-dealing crews came to expressions of territory was in the boundary maintenance of selling spots which were centered on market domains. Like capitalist enterprises, crew members wanted to keep competition down to a minimum, which they could only do physically by protecting their own selling areas or muscling in on others, or through marketing strategies that undercut rival dealers. The struggle for and defense of drug turfs could be very intense and sometimes it mushroomed into an expression of inter-ethnic rivalry.

In terms of territory, the new street organizations are markedly different from either the jacket gangs or the crews. As they build their organizations into "nations," parochial boundaries become obstacles. As a result, the members and leadership tend to have a much broader vision of their organization's aims, which dramatically reduces the potential for inter-gang feuding.

Ideology and Politics

It is often asserted in the gang literature that any conscious attempt to develop an ideology, or a set of beliefs that defend and reflect the interests of a certain class (Robertson, 1987), are absent among gang members. Certainly, for many members of the jacket gangs, there was a limited concern for political matters of the neighborhood (let alone the entire nation state).Most of what was discussed when gang members interacted was restricted to the immediate concerns of the gang, such as whom the group was now aligned with, what threats other gangs posed, whether to induct new members, if criminal proceedings would be initiated against them, and so on.

Most of the jacket gangs of the 1960's and 1970's did not take up the radical political causes of the time, and therefore did not develop a counter-cultural or anti-Establishment ideology. Rather, they remained within their own subterranean gang value system that was culturally oppositional but undeveloped in terms of a cohesive system of thought and action. Similarly, the 1980's crews did not advance an oppositional ideological line and, in fact, adopted many of the shibboleths of the dominant materialistic culture in pursuing their entrepreneurial aims. However, the contemporary street organizations are quite different from both these prior types. For example, the Ñetas, formed in the Puerto Rican prison system by a member of the Puerto Rican Socialist Party, are strongly motivated by their commitment to unite, defend and empower the Latino community, fight racism, agitate against the colonialist subjugation of Puerto Rico and advocate for prisoners' rights. Similarly, the Latin Kings are wedded to the doctrine of Kingism from which many of the group's lessons are drawn. This belief system, an eclectic mix of spiritualism, self-help prisoner guidance and community/nationalist empowerment themes, is thoroughly infused with the politics of social justice. Like the Netas and Zulu Nation, the Latin Kings have been active in opposing police brutality and the racism within the public education and criminal justice systems.

Delinquency

In the literature of orthodox criminology, delinquency is a major vehicle for proclaiming a gang's existence. Indeed, a significant amount of "cafeteria-type" delinquency (Klein, 1971) was engaged in by members of the jacket gangs. This included truancy, fighting, petty larceny, car theft and even serious assault.

However, the context in which this delinquency is taken, is relevant. The youth in these jacket gangs were from the lowest social strata, and experienced many of the pathologies that conditions of poverty induce, such as disengagement from legitimate adult authority, rejection of (and being rejected by) public and parochial schools, a paucity of meaningful employment and job training opportunities, cultural invisibility, and the constant threat of police harassment. At the same time, many of these youth were in the throes of adjusting to two worlds, either having been brought north by Southern black families or having immigrated with their families from Puerto Rico. One consequence of this dynamic of social displacement and inadequate socialization was the norm of living on the street from a young age. Thus, by their early teens, these youth had already become immersed in the streets' survivalist, "living off your wits" codes of conduct.

The drug-dealing crews, active within the illegal economy, attracted mostly high school truants and dropouts who were well on their way to developing "moral careers" (Becker, 1963) based on crime. Shaped by the deepening poverty of New York's dual society (Castells & Mollenkopf, 1991), these youth saw their membership in the crews as a realistic means to "get paid" and have an active social life.

As for these street organizations, some of their members are still selling drugs and are involved in crime, but most are eager to develop an alternative mind set to the fatalism inspired by the bleak ghetto economy. With so many members already incarcerated, and others who have experienced prison, physical violence, drug use and abuse, they are attempting to help their members reconstruct their lives through networks of mutual support and consistent messages of self- and cultural affirmation.

Conflict

Among the jacket gangs, nearly all of the fighting was "expressive" (Block and Block, 1993), typically arising from disputes around perceived malicious intentions, disrespect for local turf boundaries, and transgressions of personal honor (Horowitz, 1983). The 1980's crews mainly fought over drug turfs and related interpersonal disputes. Contemporary street organizations, however, have learned many bloody lessons from the fratricidal conflicts of the past and have instituted their own forms of conflict resolution and peacemaking.

This commitment to a peaceful process of dispute resolution within the ranks has led to a sharp reduction in the deaths and injuries among their members (for example, in the trial against King Blood, the Manhattan District Attorney's Office produced evidence of at least 20 murders by the Latin Kings during the period from 1986-1991). This does not mean that gangs that have not ascended to a new "stage" in their development, are going to cease intergroup rivalry. An important test, therefore, for the street organizations is whether they can hold their members in check when provoked and forestall a destructive and potentially disastrous spiral of escalating conflict (Hocker & Wilmot, 1995). Contrary to law enforcement predictions, the likelihood of the organization returning to its gang mentality is not inevitable (the Latin Kings say that they are at the third stage as they move toward becoming a fully integrated "nation").

Symbolism

The names of jacket gangs connoted evil and the audaciousness of outsiders, and symbolically inverted the powerlessness that was being experienced in their members' daily lives (Brake, 1985). Hence, many of their cultural symbols, i.e., clothing, group monikers and function titles, were borrowed from the middle and upper classes. Once appropriated, these symbols became, literally, the property of the new subcultures and subject to their own myriad, "from below" interpretations. This transgressive act is akin to "performance rhetoric" (Conquergood, 1992) and embodies the tension between two discursive systems: that of official society (or high culture) complemented by its fetishistic processes of commodification and that of the street (or low culture) and its underground "naming and renaming, symbolizing and re-symbolizing, empowering and dis-empowering."

This "slippage" (Conquergood, 1992:3) between the two cultures, with so much emphasis placed on symbolic representation, was not present in the style of the drug-dealing crews, except for those who were fully immersed in the subculture of graffiti art. The drug crews, whose raison d'etre was the acquisition of status, wealth and power, had little time for such symbolic playfulness. For them, it was enough to brandish artifacts of conspicuous consumption such as prestigious cars, gold jewelry and trophy women.

The contemporary street organizations, however, place great importance on their symbolic displays, since crafting a new identity is a critical element of self discovery and group self-determination. Table 4-2 highlights some of the current symbolic artifacts and gestures of the street organizations and their complex set of interpretive meanings.

Table 4-2:

Symbols Used By Street Organizations

Symbols/Artifacts/Gestures	Interpretive Meanings
Multicolored beads worn as necklace, similar to rosary	group affiliation, position in hierarchy, length of membership, sacrifice for group, initiation blessing
hand signs	interactional greeting, mutual and self-recognition, gesture of group and self-defiance
greeting (grito), eg., "amor de rey" (Latin Kings), "de corazon" (Netas)	personal membership claim, micro-ritual of commitment & respect for group, claim of independence, autonomy and self-determination, Latino self- and cultural affirmation
universals (monthly meetings)	organizational necessity, informational forum, time for active dialogue and analysis, connection to history, friendship renewal, solidarity reinforcement, macro-ritual of group integration

Although the items in Table 4-2 require a more detailed exposition, it should suffice to indicate the extraordinary weight attached to symbolism within these contemporary groups. Much of the enactment and construction of everyday life comes in the form of micro- and macro-rituals which are crucial to the production and reproduction of current power relations (McLaren, 1993). These street organizations are no exception to this rule. With their increasingly conscious opposition to internal and external colonization, and their origins in the symbolically saturated and contested world of the prison system, they struggle openly for a "third space" (Bhaba, 1994) between the oppressor and the oppressed.

Understanding Gangs

The above comparative interpretations offer some important reminders of the limitations in the dominant paradigms of gang theory. Part of the problem has been that since the 1960's, instead of viewing gang subcultures through their interface with conditions of poverty, changing market relations and increasing state controls over working-class and poor youth, it was their involvement in delinquency and crime that became the main focus of inquiry. Today, this preoccupation with lawbreaking is still part of the "root paradigm" (McLaren, 1992.) used to conceptually distinguish whether a group is a clique, a gang or part of a street corner society. Two prominent researchers and their associates put it this way:

> *Some gangs are more violent than others, some are more instrumental than others, some are more involved in drug use than others and so on. Although this variation across gangs exists, it does not detract from the virtually universal finding that gang members are much more heavily involved in delinquency and drug use than non gang members.*

(Thornberry, Krohn, Lizotte, Chard-Wierschem, 1993).

Another researcher (Klein, 1995:30), exhibiting a little more caution, states:

> *"Where is the tipping point beyond which we say, "Aha - that sure sounds like a street gang to me? I suggest two useful signposts. The first . . . is a commitment to a criminal orientation . . . Note carefully, however, that I specify orientation, not a pattern of serious criminal activity, as many in the enforcement world might require . . . My second signpost, admittedly difficult to judge from outside the group: the group's self-recognition of its gang status."*

For most gang-focused social scientists, therefore, the pursuit of illegal goals remains the marker that signifies a gang's presence and that accentuates its "difference" from other normative social groups. These empiricist foci, however, contain at least four central flaws that limit their explanatory power.

First, they leave little room for longitudinal considerations of gang subcultures. Second, they overlook the gang as a historically-emergent phenomenon. Third, they are non-reflexive and rarely question the underlying "domain of assumptions" (Gouldner, 1970) that constitute social science discourse. Fourth, they overlook the contradictoriness (or dialectics) of agency within gang membership, e.g., the notion that youth may be joining gangs as much to shape them as to be shaped by them. Rarely do researchers ask whether gangs have the possibility of becoming more than the criminal sum of their parts, or whether membership in groups with strong internal bonds, community ties, long sub-cultural histories, can be the basis of social innovation rather than social destruction and mal-adaptation!

The need for a more critical approach to the study of these subcultures seems to be especially borne out with groups as complex and contradictory as the Latin Kings and the Netas. Based on the above data, it is simply not possible to understand these emergent social movements of ghetto and barrio youth from the traditional criminological empiricist standpoint. To this extent, the British tradition of critical cultural studies, although usually overlooked, offers an alternative to the mainstream tautology (Morash, 1983) of gangs, drugs, crime and violence that dominates the American literature on the subject.

New York's Gang Scene - Some Explanatory Factors

A combination of social, economic, political, and criminological factors have contributed to the qualitative changes in the New York City gang scene described above. Below, several of the leading influences are briefly discussed.

(i)"Going straight" and leaving the gang:

The mushrooming rates of incarceration among ghetto and barrio residents[1], and the lengthening of prison sentences (i.e., the introduction of determinate sentencing) for all types of offenders has made "going straight" and disassociating with gang acquaintances an urgent option for recently released inmates. But leaving gang life "on the outside" is not a simple task, especially when membership in a prison gang once offered an important source of social support, self-defense and access to the scarce resources of the prison economy. Former prison gang members find the reform of the organization a perfect solution to their dilemma.

(ii) The absence of territoriality and the "nation-building" of New York City street gangs:

Dating back to the 1970's, New York City street gangs were already breaking away from the violence of the turf-bound territorialism of previous gang generations. The nation-building ideology of the Latin Kings among others has further encouraged this local sub-cultural evolution, moving these groups toward a form of pan-territorialism and away from turf-driven conflicts.

(iii) From prison gangs to street organizations:

Most New York City street organizations in the recent period have followed a prison-to-street development. This path of development meant that these groups have never viewed themselves as particularly tied to neighborhood turf boundaries, unlike so many Latino and Black gangs in the segregated terrains of the West Coast and Chicago. This further lack of a "turf consciousness" mitigates against the likelihood of the highly self-destructive, violent syndrome of "gang-banging."

(iv) Anti-colonial consciousness and the continued repression of barrio/ghetto youth:

Although it is not popular to think that working-class youth and adults can develop more than a rudimentary sense of their subjugation, street organization members consistently engage in social and political discourses about their colonized condition. Increasing incidents of police brutality in minority areas, the authoritarian policies adopted in New York City, and the blatant disinvestment in the City's public schools and City University have allowed street organization members to concentrate their anger on those who are hostile to their community instead of dissipating their energies on fighting each other in internal or external feuds.

---

[1]About 70% of the 70,000 New York State prisoners come from New York City; 92% of the inmates in New York City's jails and 85% of New York State's prisoners are Black and Latino; between 1983-1993 the rate of increase among Black, Latino and White inmates for New York State was 95%, 146% and 35% respectively.

(v) The timely intersection of "maturing-out" gang leaders, ex-gang organic intellectuals and long time political radicals:

Many of the current leaders, now in their late 20's, have entered a "maturing-out" stage in their gang career life-course. Precisely at this point, veteran Puerto Rican and Black radicals in the community (many of whom are former members of the Young Lords Party and the Black Panthers), established strong advisory relationships with the groups' leaders. These relations have developed to the point that a range of trusted "outsiders" now help the groups' leadership to: (i) strategize on community interventions, (ii) critically analyze internal membership dynamics, (iii) constantly review relations with the media, and (iv) institute processes of conflict mediation to avoid violent disputes.

(v) The changing nature and organization of the illicit economy and its capacities for self-regulation:

As recent studies on the New York City drug economy have shown, the increased organization and consolidation of the crack cocaine trade, the waning of the crack epidemic and the stigmatization of the "crack-head" has limited the opportunities for young people to become involved in drug selling (Curtis and Maher, 1992, Johnson and Golub, 1997). In addition, changes in the demographic configuration of the drug trade hierarchy, as Dominicans replaced Puerto Ricans in key positions of power within the cocaine economy (Curtis, 1997), have led Puerto Rican youth to seek social and cultural power through their reformed street organizations.

(vi) The resistance of barrio and ghetto youth to the culture of violence and the punitive social control of the police:

The new generations of barrio and ghetto youth come with bitter memories of the drug-related violence of the past (Bourgois, 1995). This has produced a collective experience that might be called a "critical mass of suffering" which means that today, these youth are less likely to place themselves in "high risk," violence-prone situations. The street organizations, in turn, argue that youths are joining their ranks precisely to take back their neighborhoods both from the drug-dealers and the predations of the police [2].

(vii) The influence and changing role of women within these new subcultures:

As females have joined the street organizations in increasing numbers, the more progressive members among them have challenged a range of male sexist practices, such as the prerogative of having both a wife and a mistress. While pushing for a more socially responsible development of the organizations, female members have been particularly successful in keeping the groups focused on the issues of prisoners' welfare, family survival, domestic violence, community projects on behalf of the poor, and recovery from drugs and alcohol.

---

[2] The argument regarding the latter has been particularly strengthened after the highly publicized cases of the Louima police torture case in Brooklyn and the police killing of Antonio Baez in the South Bronx.

Towards the Future

In response to the massive increase in the criminalization of Latino and Black youth and the ongoing economic, social and political marginalization of poor barrio and ghetto communities, formerly notorious gangs are now engaged in what might be described as a war of resistance. As they evolve, these groups, described above as street organizations, are forming socio-political and cultural associations, recruiting both those on the outside as well as among the incarcerated. These highly innovative, contemporary organizations of the dispossessed are much more sophisticated than any of the previous sub-cultural youth groups. Expressing distinct goals of self-determination and self-help, they are rapidly developing into a grassroots social movement guided by an eclectic political ideology that melds spiritualistic, communitarian, and utopian themes.

Two questions remain: (i) What is the future for these street organizations? and, (ii) What about the development of other youth groups that are more like traditional gangs? In answer to the first question, it is likely that the more political youth configurations will grow, perhaps even becoming more mainstream as their status in the community increases. In fact, the political repression that they are currently subjected to may help to expand and unite their ranks rather than to shrink and fragment them. This is because the constant demonization and harassment of their members have the "unintented consequence" of increasing the groups' street credibility, reinforcing their group cohesiveness, and encouraging an even wider range of community activists to work in their political defense.

As for the other "gangs," these formations probably will come and go in the typical 10-year cycle of sub-cultural evolution that has characterized New York City's youth and street cultures. Such groups as the Bloods and the Crips that are both active in the prison system and on the streets do not have the membership solidarity, the organizational discipline, nor the political purpose of the street organizations. According to police reports, these more prototypical gangs are now responsible for the lion's share of gang-related incidents in the city which makes them particularly vulnerable to a combination of law enforcement sanctions and community social controls. While these "gangs" are certainly symptomatic of high rates of system-induced poverty and social isolation, their self-destructive and predatory practices only reproduce the race-class imbalances of the status quo and serve to de-legitimize the reform movement of street organizations.

As the 1990's draw to a close, the political transition of the street organizations in New York City goes on apace. Despite this seemingly welcome development, the enemies in law enforcement and politics remain adamant that such a transformation is impossible. Is this simply a conflict of perception or one of vested interests? As the United States political economy enters into greater levels of race and class disequilibrium, albeit in the midst of an officially declared economic boom, the dominant society constantly requires imagined enemies to eradicate. Rather than wage war on the glaring social ills that emerge from a growing imbalance in the ownership of wealth and the distribution of power, the focus of concern is consistently shifted to deviant groups that the public has been conditioned to hate and condemn.

POSTSCRIPT

Recently, a series of events occurred that brought this latter point home. On Thursday May 14, 1998 at around 5:00 a.m., 1,000 officers of the New York City Police Department and the Federal Bureau of Investigation were mobilized to carry out a grand jury indictment against 90 alleged members of the Almighty Latin King and Queen Nation. The New York Times described the raid as the biggest police sweep since Prohibition; however it also noted that almost half of those arrested were only charged with misdemeanors. The cost of the raid was more than $1 million. To justify this action, the Commissioner of the New York City Police Department declared how they had beheaded the organization and removed its essential power structure. Yet, within three days of the arrests, the Latin Kings youth section turned out 100 members for the New York City "AIDS Walk," and the following weekend 250 members met in a church to show their solidarity with their incarcerated brothers, half of whom already had been released. In fact, of those arrested, less than 50 were actually members of the organization.

Acknowledgments

The data for this article was made possible with support from the Spencer Foundation's Small Grants Program, a PSC-CUNY Research Award and the CUNY-Dispute Resolution Consortium housed at John Jay College of Criminal Justice in New York City. In addition, I am also indebted to my colleagues in the field, Luis Barrios, Ric Curtis, Lorine Padilla, Marcia Esparza, Rose Santos, Angela Lucharsky, Rita Fecher, and Henry Chalfant. Finally, without the collaboration of the many members of the above- mentioned street organizations this study would not have been possible.

References

Anderson, E. 1990.Street Wise: Race, Class and Change in an Urban Community. Chicago: University of Chicago Press.

Asbury, H. 1970 (orig. 1927).The Gangs of New York. New York: Capricorn Books.

Batten, A. 1973. "Ain't Gonna Eat My Mind." New York: CBS.

Beck, U. 1994."The Reinvention of Politics: Towards a Theory of Reflexive Modernization" in Reflexive Modernization, Beck, U., Giddens, A. and Lash, S. Stanford: Stanford University Press.

Becker, H. 1963.Outsiders: Studies in the Sociology of Deviance. New York: The Free Press.

Bhabha, H. 1994. The Location of Culture. New York: Routledge.

Block, C.R. and R. Block. 1995."Street Gang Crime in Chicago" in The Modern Gang Reader, edited by MW Klein, C.L. Maxson and J. Miller. Los Angeles, Ca. : Roxbury Publishing Co.

Bluestone, B. and Harrison, B. 1982. The Deindustrialization of America: Plant Closings, Community Abandonment, and the Dismantling of Basic Industry. New York: Basic Books.

Bourdieu, 1984. Distinction. A Social Critique of the Judgment of Taste. Trans. R. Nice. Cambridge,

MA: Harvard University Press.

Bourgois, 1995. In Search of Respect: Selling Crack in El Barrio. New York: Cambridge University Press.

Bowles, S. & Gintis, H. 1977. "I.Q. in the U.S. Class Structure" in Power and Ideology in Education edited by J. Karabel and A.H. Halsey. New York: Oxford University Press.

Brake, M. 1985. Comparative Youth Subculture. London: Routledge and Kegan Paul.

Brotherton, D. 1994."Who do you claim?: Gang Formations and Rivalry in an Inner City High School," Perspectives on Social Problems, vol 5: 147-171, 1994, eds. J. Holstein and G. Miller. Connecticut: JAI Press.

Brotherton, D. 1996a."The Contradictions of Suppression: Notes from a Study of Approaches to Gangs in Three Public High Schools," Urban Review, 28(2): 95-120, 1996.

Brotherton, D. 1996b."Smartness, Toughness and Autonomy: Drug Use in the Contexts of Gang Female Delinquency." Journal of Drug Issues, 26(1): 261-277, 1996.

Bursik, R. 1993. Neighborhoods and Crime: The Dimensions of Effective Community Control. New York: Lexington Books.

Campbell, A. 1991 (2nd edition). Girls in the Gang. Cambridge, Mass: Basil Blackwell.

Castells, M. and Mollenkopf, JH 1991. Dual City: Restructuring New York. New York: Russel Sage Foundation.

Chambliss, W. 1994."Policing the Ghetto Underclass: The Politics of Law and Law Enforcement." Social Problems 41,2: 177-194.

Chalfant, H. and T. Silver.1984."Style Wars," Video Documentary. New York: Public Broadcasting Service.

Chalfant, H. and R. Fecher. 1989."Flying Cut Sleeves." New York: Cinema Guild.

Christie, N. 1993.
Crime Control as Industry. London: Routledge.

Cloward, R.A. and L. Ohlin. 1960.Delinquency and Opportunity. New York: Free Press.

Collins, H.C. 1979. Street Gangs: Profiles for Police. New York: New York City Police Department.

Cohen, P. 1972. "Subcultural Conflict and Working Class Community," Working Papers in Cultural Studies 2 (Univeristy of Birmingham: Center for Contemporary Cultural Studies).

Conquergood, D. 1992. "On Reppin' and Rhetoric: Gang Representations." Paper presented at the Philosophy and Rhetoric of Inquiry Seminar, University of Iowa.

Corrigan, P. 1979. Schooling the "Smash Street Kids". London: MacMillan.

Curtis, R. 1997. "Crime Reduction in New York City." Unpublished paper: John Jay College of Criminal Justice, New York.

Fagan, J. 1989. "The Social Organization of Drug Use and Drug Dealing Among Urban Gangs." Criminology, 27(4): 633-670.

Ferrell, J.& Sanders, C.R. (eds). 1995.Cultural Criminology. Boston: Northeastern University Press.

Fitch, R. 1993. The Assassination of New York. New York: Verso.

Garland, D. 1997. "Crime Control and Social Order," Paper given at the American Society of Criminology. San Diego, CA.

Gibbons, D. 1980. "Explaining Juvenile Delinquency: Changing Theoretical Perspectives," in Critical Issues in Juvenile Delinquency, edited by D. Schichor and D.H. Kelly, Lexington, Mass.: Lexington Books.

Gilroy, P. 1987. There Ain't No Black in the Union Jack: The Cultural Politics of Race and Nation.

54

London: Unwin Hyman.

Goldstein, A. 1996. <u>Violence in America</u>. Palo Alto, CA: Davies-Black Publishing.

Golub, A.& Johnson, B.D. 1997."Crack's Decline: Some Surprises Across U.S. Cities." National Institute of Justice, Research in Brief: Washington, D.C.

Gouldner, A. 1970. <u>The Coming Crisis of Western Sociology</u>. New York: Basic Books.

Greenberg, D. 1993."Delinquency and the Age Structure in Society" in Crime and Capitalism, edited by D.F. Greenberg. Philadelphia: Temple University Press.

Hall, S. and T. Jefferson (eds.) 1982. <u>Resistance through Rituals</u>. London: Hutchinson University Library Press.

Hall, S., T. Jefferson, Crichter, C., Clarke, J., Roberts, B. 1978. <u>Policing the Crisis: Mugging, the State and Law and Order.</u> New York: Holmes and Meier.

Harvey, D. 1996. <u>Justice, Nature and the Geography of Difference</u>. New York: Blackwell.

Hocker & Wilmot. 1995 (4th edition). <u>Interpersonal Conflict</u>. Dubuque, Iowa: Brown and Benchmark.

Horowitz, B. & Liebowitz, A. 1968. "Social Deviance and Political Marginality," Social Problems 15(3).

Horowitz, R. 1983. Honor and the American Dream: Culture and identity in a Chicano community. New Brunswick, NJ: Rutgers University Press.

Jackall, A. 1997. Wild Cowboys. Harvard, Mass.: Harvard University Press.

Jankowski, M.S. 1991. Islands in the street: Gangs in American urban society. Berkeley: University of California Press.

Katz, J. 1988. <u>Seductions of Crime: Moral and Sensual Attractions in Doing Evil</u>. New York: Basic Books.

Kasarda, J. 1989. "Urban Industrial Transition and the Underclass." Annals of the American Academy of Political and Social Science 501 (January):26-47.

Klein, M. 1971. <u>Street Gangs and Street Workers.</u> Englewood Cliffs, N.J.: Prentice Hall.

Klein, M. 1995. <u>The American Street Gang: Its Nature, Prevalence and Control</u>. New York: Oxford University Press

Lefebvre, H. 1991. <u>The Production of Space</u>. Oxford, England: Blackwell.

McLaren, P. 1993. (2nd edition). <u>Schooling as a Ritual Performance: Towards a Political Economy of Educational Symbols and Gestures</u>. New York: Routledge.

McRobbie, A. 1978. "The Culture of Working Class Girls," in A. McRobbie (ed.) (1991) <u>Feminism and Youth Culture</u>. London: Macmillan.

McRobbie, A. 1994. <u>Postmodernism and Popular Culture</u>. London: Routledge.

Miller, J. 1997. Search and Destroy. New York: Cambridge University Press.

Miller, W. 1958. "Lower Class Culture as a Generating Milieu of Gang Delinquency." Journal of Social Issues, 14: 5-19.

Morash, M. 1983."Gangs, groups and delinquency." British Journal of Criminology, 23:309-335.

Padilla, F. 1992.The Gangs as an American Enterprise. New Brunswick, NJ: Rutgers University Press.

Robertson, I. 1987.<u>Sociology.</u> (Third Edition). New York: Worth Publishers Inc.

Reissman, C.K. 1993. <u>Narrative Analysis</u>. Newbury Park, Ca.: Sage Publications.

Sante, L. 1992. <u>Low Life</u>. New York: Vintage.

Short, J. 1980. "Political Implications of Juvenile Delinquency: A Comparative Perspective," in

Critical Issues in Juvenile Delinquency, edited by D. Schichor and D.H. Kelly. Lexington, Mass.: Lexington Books.

Skolnick, J.H. 1995. "Gangs and Crime Old as Time; But Drugs Change Gang Culture" in The Modern Gang Reader, edited by MW Klein, C.L. Maxson and J. Miller. Los Angeles, Ca.: Roxbury Publishing Co.

Stark, E. 1993."Gangs and Progress: The Contribution of Delinquency to Progressive Reform," in Marxism and Crime edited by D. Greenberg.

Sullivan, M. 1989. Getting Paid: Youth Crime and Work in the Inner City. Ithaca, NY: Cornell University Press.

Sutherland, E. and Cressey, D. 1966. Principles of Criminology (7th edition). Philadelphia: J.B. Lippincott.

Suttles, G. 1968. The Social Order of the Slum. Chicago: University of Chicago Press.

Taylor, C. S. 1990. Dangerous Society. East Lansing, Michigan: Michigan State University Press.

Thornberry, T.B., M.D. Krohn, A.J. Lizotte, D.C. Chard-Wierschem. 1993."The Role of Juvenile Gangs in Facilitating Delinquent Behavior." Journal of Research in Crime and Delinquency, 30(1):55-87.

Thrasher, F. 1927. The Gang: A study of 1,313 Gangs in Chicago. Chicago: Chicago Press.

Vergara, C.J. 1995.The New American Ghetto. New Brunswitck, NJ: Rutgers University Press.

Vigil, D. 1988. Barrio gangs: Street Life and Identity in Southern California. Austin: University of Texas Press.

Wilson, W.J. 1987.The Truly Disadvantaged. Chicago: University of Chicago Press.

Yablonsky, L. 1962. The Violent Gang. London: MacMillan.

Yablonsky, L. 1997. Gangsters: Fifty Years of Madness, Drugs, and Death on the Streets of America. New York: New York University Press.

Chapter 5

ORGANIZED CRIME IN NEW YORK CITY: ITS HISTORY AND CURRENT RACKETS

by

Professor Daniel O'Neal Vona

Department of Law and Police Science

New York has always been the most heterogeneous and freewheeling city in North America and the paradigm for the "melting pot." It may or may not in fact have been a "melting pot," but it has always been a boiling cauldron of ethnically-based syndicates of criminally-inclined men looking for a fast buck and willing to resort to violence to make and preserve their fortunes. As a result, city neighborhoods have been the home bases for cutting-edge local, national and international moneymaking schemes relying upon corruption, deception, and chicanery. Organized crime syndicates - groups of conspirators who run daily, routinized illegal rackets as if they were regular businesses - have always made New York their headquarters. Gangsters from around the world have been attracted to New York as a wide-open place in which to get rich quick. To this day, mobsters continue to provide the highly profitable forbidden goods and services that enough eager consumers clamor for, and run rackets that victimize individuals, businesses, and government benefit programs.

THE FIRST GANGSTERS: PIRATES, TYCOONS, ROBBER BARONS

Starting back in the days when New York was New Amsterdam, criminal syndicates became a hidden political force to be reckoned with. Smuggling was the basis of nearly all the early New York fortunes (Churchill, 1965). Pirate bands, buccaneers, and privateers roamed the harbor in the early 1700's and shared their plunder with power-brokers on shore in the early colonies(Dafoe, 1972).

As the city developed into a center of commerce, the first business tycoons like John Jacob Astor made huge fortunes in the fur trade by plying Native Americans with alcohol and then defrauding them when they traded their pelts.

In the late 1700's, predatory entrepreneurs, allied with thugs, gunmen and government officials, amassed enormous illegal fortunes. Their shady operations were highly organized and well connected. They were willing to resort to chicanery, deception and even violence to further their own desire for wealth and self-gratification. The most notorious of these upwardly mobile New Yorkers was John Jacob Astor, who was born in Germany, and arrived penniless from London but quickly got rich in the fur trade. His agents plied Native Americans with alcohol before defrauding them of the pelts they wanted to trade. His American Fur Company ultimately monopolized the fur trade. Astor committed many civil and criminal law violations while making his millions, but was never prosecuted because he hired the foremost lawyers and paid off the most powerful politicians. He invested his illicit fortune in New York City real estate, and soon became America's most notorious immigrant tenement "slum lord." When he died in 1848, he was the wealthiest man in America (Myers, 1936; Kammen, 1975).

During the era of "brass knuckles business," commercial buccaneers practiced political corruption, fraud, extortion and blackmail to get to the top of the social ladder. One of the most ruthless of these individuals, Cornelius Vanderbilt, started out as an illiterate New York ferry boatman and ended up as a shipping tycoon. During the Civil War, Vanderbilt turned to war profiteering. As a Union agent, he sold rotting, unfit vessels to the government. Meanwhile Vanderbilt was using his shipping fortune to monopolize railroads. He took over the New York Hudson River and Harlem lines. Then he forced the New York Central to sell out. Finally, he went after the Erie Railroad, but ran afoul of Jay Gould, who was the "most hated man in America" when he died in 1892 leaving a fortune of $70 million to his heirs (Klein, 1986). Vanderbilt, the man who coined the expression, "The public be damned! " left $105 million to his sons upon his death (Myers, 1936).

The ancestries of many of these 18th-century vulture capitalists were English, Scottish, Scandinavian or German. They set an example about how to amass a fortune illegally that was emulated later by Irish gangsters in the 1800's, Italian and Jewish mobsters in the early 1900's, and most recently by criminally-immersed groups whose members are African American, South and Central American, West Indian, East Indian, Russian, Chinese, Southeast Asian, and Middle Eastern.

THE MACHINE POLITICS AND CORRUPTION OF THE TAMMANY SOCIETY AND ITS GANGS

The Tammany Society emerged around the time of the American Revolution, but it soon changed from a fraternal club to a political organization in 1811. Virtually from its inception, members of the Tammany Society held important public posts, but they were frequently removed from office for systematic public corruption in the form of bribery, thievery, embezzlement, and extortion.

In the early 1800's, the Tammany Committee was rabidly anti-Irish. However, in 1817, 200 men of Irish descent brandishing bats crashed one of its meetings, battering heads and wrecking furniture. Before long, Irish Catholics dominated Tammany Hall (Petersen, 1983).

The first ethnic gangs which terrorized New York were composed of young Irish men from the Five Points area of the bloody old Sixth Ward, which formerly was the location of a large fresh water lake called the Collect. The area was reclaimed in 1808, after it had become a stagnant marsh, and was known as the Five Points (where Little Water, Cross, Anthony, Orange and Mulberry Streets met, and where the "Tombs" jail was built. It was a notorious Irish slum replete with "dangerous" dance halls and "bucket-of-blood" saloons especially around Paradise Square. Charles Dickens wrote about the Five Points in his <u>American</u> <u>Notes</u> and De Tocqueville regarded its residents as a threat to the security of the republic (see Asbury, 1928; De Tocqueville, 1945; Petersen, 1983).

At the back of a greengrocery in Paradise Square was the headquarters of the Forty Thieves gang, led by the notorious Ed Coleman, one of America's original gangsters, and the first man ever hanged in the Tombs (for murdering his wife). Robberies and murders went unnoticed because the bodies were successfully buried (Asbury, 1928; Petersen, 1983). The phrase, "No corpus delicti, no investigation," originated in the Five Points. (This was still an operating principle of the Irish-American gang, the "Westies," the descendant of the "Gophers," who operated out of the bars in "Hell's Kitchen," in the Clinton District on Manhattan's Westside, as recently as the 1980's (English, 1990).

The Tammany gangs achieved political power in the 1840's and held it until World War I. They were an important force politically and criminally, especially in the Sixth Ward, Five Points District, where the gangs were controlled by Tammany leaders. Gang members served as election day "repeat" voters, who "came early and voted often" at different polling places. Gangsters also served as election day "sluggers" who beat up people unwilling to vote the right way (Petersen, 1983). The Five Points was the center of organized criminal activity in New York: vice, gambling, prostitution, pickpocket rings, robbery rings, burglary rings, river pirate rings, thievery and the selling of stolen goods. Besides the Forty Thieves, other Five Points gangs of newly arrived Irish immigrants included the Kerrygonians, Roach Guards, Plug Uglies, Shirt Tails, and Dead Rabbits (Black Birds). They all fought one another (Ashbury, 1928). The Bowery also had its native-born gangs: The Bowery Boys, American Guards, O'Connell Guards, Atlantic Guards, and True Blue Americans (who wore stove pipe hats and frock coats). Other gangs included the Chichesters (later, the Whyos), the Gophers (later becoming the Parlor Mob and then the Westies), the Gas House Gang (East 18th to 35th Streets), the Cherry Hill Gang, and the Westside Hudson Dusters (which evolved into the Ramblers by the 1940's and 50's). The gangs played an important role in the fraud and violence during the 1827 and 1834 presidential elections. Following Andrew Jackson's election in 1827, Tammany men were able to fill all the federal jobs in New York City (Ashbury, 1928, Petersen, 1983). In 1836, Tammany leader Martin Van Buren became the 8th President of the United States, and Tammany became synonymous with the Democratic Party. Tammany set up a system of Assembly Districts, each of which had a leader, and captains who got out the vote. The leader and captains dispensed favors and social services financed by extortion from the entrepreneurs of vice (like gamblers) as well as a 6 percent kickback from city employees (there was no Civil Service). From these practices, "machine politics" was born in New York!

Mississippi River gamblers from New Orleans and the other river towns came to New York where they found the pickings good. Many set up well organized gambling houses and sponsored rigged lotteries, such as the Medical Science Lottery which was ended by a scandal in 1818. Gambler-gangster alliances not only corrupted government, but they led to New York becoming perhaps the foremost organized crime stronghold in the United States. In the 1830's, "Captain" Isaiah Rynders, a Mississippi gambler, gun, knife, and red hot poker fighter, who had been arrested in Washington, D.C. for U.S. Treasury Note theft, and whose motto was "never give a sucker a break," arrived in New York (Petersen, 1983). By 1844, Rynders was an underworld kingpin. He had taken over the Five Points gang, founded the notorious Empire Vice Club, was the Tammany boss of the Sixth Ward and a member of the powerful Tammany General Committee. Organized gambling in New York was clearly established. Jack Wallis, with ties to Rynders, controlled a "vice resort" on

Park Place in the 1840's where pugilists, thieves, confidence tricksters, and other underworld characters mixed with clerks, mechanics and merchants at the gaming tables (Petersen, 1983). By 1850, there were 6,000 gambling houses, 200 of which catered to the upper class (Asbury, 1928). Crime spiraled out of control. It was unsafe to walk the streets at night. Armed robbers and prostitutes roamed the streets, openly plying their trade. An estimated 30,000 men in New York City were in league with gang leaders allied with Tammany leaders or the Know-Nothing Party, headed by Bill "the Butcher" Poole.

In 1844, the State legislature had authorized the establishment of a police force patterned after Sir Robert Peel's centralized Metropolitan Police in London. But the New York City Police Department was decentralized in the Tammany wards. Each Ward was controlled by the local Alderman who could hire and fire police officers, and the system continued de facto even after aldermanic appointment was discontinued (Repetto, 1978).

Two gangs, the Bowery Boys and the Dead Rabbits were bitter enemies. On the 4th of July, 1857 a gang war broke out between the Dead Rabbits and the Bowery Boys which turned into a bloody melee of a thousand rioters. A week later, the rioters turned on the police. The murder rate rose. Sometimes there were six murders in one day. Riots were frequent, many people got killed, and property losses were high (Petersen, 1983). The gangs continued their feuds until the Civil War Draft Riots of 1863, after which all the gangs and criminals combined to try to sack and burn the city. When the police could not handle the gang fights, the National Guard or Regular Army had to be called out, sometimes with artillery (Asbury, 1928; Petersen, 1983).

In 1899, the state Assembly appointed the Mazet Committee to investigate corruption in New York City. High officials admitted to making all appointments to City positions, controlling the police department, and taking payoffs from gamblers, prostitutes, robbers, and saloon keepers. It was disclosed that Senator "Big Tim" Sullivan ran a gambling syndicate, and William Devery, the Chief of Police, was his partner in a gambling house (Petersen, 1983).

In 1907, Jimmy Hines, whose father was a Tammany captain, hired Harry "Gyp the Blood" Horowitz and his gang friends, the Gophers, to insure his victory as Alderman. Horowitz was later executed at Sing Sing for murdering Herman Rosenthal in behalf of Police Lieutenant Charles Becker, who was also electrocuted there. In 1912, Hines became a Tammany district leader as well. He made the top floor of his clubhouse a gambling den (Petersen, 1983:125). Hines engaged in political corruption, gambling, extortion and bootlegging.

The legendary Boss Tweed mentored three politicians who served as role models for Five Pointer Paul Kelly and Bowery Boy Monk Eastman. Later, Kelly and Eastman would serve as role models for Arnold "The Brain" Rothstein, the gangster who fixed the 1919 Black Sox World Series. From 1914 to 1928, Rothstein ran the gambling concession in the Democratic Party's district club houses, established the famous "floating" Broadway dice game sentimentalized in the musical play Guys and Dolls, and strong armed Wall Street brokerage firms. Rothstein, who controlled gambling, drugs, bootlegging and other illegal operations, was killed in 1928 (Clarke, 1929; Petersen, 1983). Rothstein had Jewish gangster proteges, including Nicky Arnstein (romanticized in the Hollywood film Funny Girl), Meyer Lansky, "Bugsy" Siegal, "Legs" and Eddie Diamond, "Little" Augie Orgen, "Dopey" Benny Fein, Waxey Gordon, "Lepke" Buchalter, "Gurrah" Shapiro, and Dutch Schultz. Lepke moved on to run Murder Incorporated with Shapiro, "Kid Twist" Reles, and later Albert Anastasia (Petersen, 1983). Schultz would run bootlegging, gambling and drugs in Harlem with Joey

Noe, "Abbadabba" Berman, and Vincent "The Mad Dog Killer" and his brother Peter Coll (Petersen, 1983). Rothstein also had Italian gangster proteges such as Frank Costello and "Lucky" Luciano, who established the five La Cosa Nostra families in New York, and the "National Commission." Costello would go on to conduct bootlegging operations with Cotton Club owner Owen "Owney the Killer" Madden, the Westside Gopher/Parlor Mob leader who succeeded "Eat 'em up" Jack McManus, and Joseph P. Kennedy, who established the Kennedy dynasty. After Rothstein, Noe and the Coll brothers were killed in 1928, Madden retired to Hot Springs, Arkansas, a favorite vacation spot and safe haven for organized crime figures (Fox, 1989). In 1929, the Seabury Investigation into Corruption in New York City began, prompted by Rothstein's murder (Petersen, 1983). The City's flamboyant Tammany mayor, James J. "Jimmy" Walker, was implicated in the corruption surrounding the murder, yet he was re-elected. Walker continued his playboy lifestyle, but resigned from office in 1932, and sailed to Europe with his mistress, the actress Betty Compton (Petersen, 1983).

MAFIA ACTIVITIES IN NEW YORK CITY

In the late 1870's, two Mafia dons arrived in New York from Sicily, don Joseph Esposito and don Vito Ferrer. Esposito went to New Orleans where there had been a secret Neapolitan organized crime presence since the 1840's . This group of immigrants brought a secret crime society called the "Camorra" to America. The Camorra evolved from the secret Spanish organized crime society known as the "Garduna" (Chandler, 1975).

To get established in neighborhoods other than those populated by Italian immigrants, the Sicilian mafia had to confront entrenched Irish gangsters. During the Prohibition Era, mobsters providing alcoholic beverages were able to make a great deal of money, gain considerable political influence, and expand their other rackets. Johnny Torio, Frankie Yale and Al Capone operated in Brooklyn, running a lucrative extortion scheme, mainly on the docks, and engaging in constant gunfights with the established Irish White Hand Gang, led by Denny Meehan and "Wild Bill" Lovett (Balsamo and Caposi, 1995). To cultivate good public relations, Frankie Yale adopted the Tammany ploy of providing social services to the community. In 1922, he had his liquor truckers bring coal from New Jersey to ensure his neighborhood's residents would not freeze during a winter coal strike (Balsamo and Caposi, 1995). In the 1920's Nicholas "The Clutching Hand" Morello was Boss of Bosses of the Castelmarese Sicilians. He was killed in 1930 and succeeded by Salvadore Maranzano, which may have touched off the Castelmarese War (Petersen, 1983). An upstart, Lucky Luciano, was able to gain control over most of the rackets run by the Italian-Sicilian mob in New York. Luciano staked out the territories of the Five La Cosa Nostra "families" in the City and organized the other 21 "families" across the United States as part of a "Commission" (Mass, 1968; Petersen, 1983). In 1936, Lucky Luciano was successfully prosecuted by Thomas E. Dewey and was sent to prison. After aiding the war effort against the Axis powers from his prison cell by enlisting the mob in U.S. covert operations, Luciano was pardoned by Dewey (who by then had been elected Governor of New York State) and deported to Italy, where he later died (Petersen, 1983).

In 1940, Abe "Kid Twist" Reles, a member of Murder Incorporated, was arrested for murder in Brooklyn. Tammany attorney William O'Dwyer had just been elected Brooklyn District Attorney, and as he prepared to prosecute Reles, the gangster offered to turn state's evidence and expose the conspiratorial plans of the nationwide syndicate of ethnically-based mobs called the "Combination." Reles was kept under guard in the <u>Half Moon</u> Hotel on Coney Island, under the supervision of Captain Bals, the head of O'Dwyer's DA's Squad. Somehow Reles, "the canary who could sing but not fly," conveniently managed to fall out a window to his death. O'Dwyer never pursued any important organized crime investigations after that. During World War II, President Roosevelt made O'Dwyer a general in the Army. Right after the war ended, O'Dwyer returned to town and became mayor in 1946, and then promoted Captain Bals to Deputy Police Commissioner. In 1950, an investigation exposed a major gambling ring (headed by Harry Gross) which was protected by systematic police corruption that went up the ladder at least as far as Bals. When the investigation expanded to New Jersey, La Cosa Nostra boss Joe Adonis was implicated. As the expose continued, one NYPD commander committed suicide. Mayor O'Dwyer didn't get in trouble because President Truman made O'Dwyer the U.S. Ambassador to Mexico (Petersen, 1983).

During the 1940's, mob chieftain Frank Costello controlled many Tammany district leaders and was the <u>de facto</u> Tammany Boss. For example, when Magistrate T. A. Aurelio was nominated to the New York State Supreme Court, he called Costello (whose phone was being tapped) at his home, thanked him for the opportunity, and promised undying loyalty. Frank Costello retired from an active leadership role after he survived an assassination attempt carried out by Vincent "The Chin" Gigante (who finally was sent away to federal prison for mob activities in 1998, after years of feigning mental illness).

By the end of the 1940's, Carmine DeSapio emerged as the Tammany Boss, but he turned out to be the last of his kind. During the 1950's, Tammany Boss DeSapio supported Mayor Robert Wagner. But in 1961, DeSapio was defeated as district leader in his Greenwich Village stronghold. DeSapio, therefore, could no longer be the Boss of Tammany Hall. In the next local election DeSapio tried to regain his seat, but he was defeated again, this time by Edward I. Koch, who would later become mayor (in 1978). In 1969, DeSapio was convicted, along with the son-in-law of U.S. Ambassador Henry Cabot Lodge, in the Water Supply, Gas and Electricity scandal. When he was sent to prison in 1971, the 150-year long control by Tammany Hall of Democratic politics, crime and corruption in New York came to an end. Tammany could no longer extort money from The Mob; mobsters no longer could pick candidates for elected office; and their candidates no longer could count on the Tammany "war chest" to finance their campaigns. They would have to find their own financial backers if they wanted to make themselves and their friends rich.

The 1950's were turbulent times for La Cosa Nostra. In 1957, for example, Albert "The High Executioner" Anastasia, then head of Murder Incorporated, was slain in the Park Sheraton Hotel barber shop by "the Barber Shop Quartet" led by "Crazy Joe" Gallo. Gallo later unsuccessfully sought control of the Profaci Family; the Gallo-Profaci Wars resulted in Joseph Colombo's rise to power (Petersen, 1983). Also in 1957, sixty three La Cosa Nostra crime bosses from around the nation gathered at the country estate of Joseph Barbara, then president of the Canada Dry Bottling Company of Endicott, New York. They met to discuss how to end the ongoing warfare and to plan the future of La Cosa Nostra. However, an observant State Police Sergeant and his partner in upstate Appalachian, New York noticed all the unfamiliar automobiles arriving in the town. The officers knew of Barbara's association with known gangsters from earlier incidents, so they notified federal authorities who sent two agents from the Alcohol-Tobacco Tax Unit. When the four law enforcement agents went to Barbara's home, the La Cosa Nostra bosses fled in all directions, but their license plates were noted, and most of the nation's organized crime leaders were identified and exposed.

Since these five New York City Mafia families persist right up to the present, albeit in weakened condition, a listing of their leaders over the years should prove useful. This "scorecard", naming the players and their teams, appears in Chart 5-1, for the sake of completeness and to correct the literature, which is deeply flawed by the misrepresentation of acting bosses as bosses, and by the identification of individuals as bosses who never really were (Pollini, 1998).

Chart 5-1 :

The Heads of The Five La Cosa Nostra Families in New York Over the Years

GENOVESE FAMILY	GAMBINO FAMILY	COLUMBO FAMILY	BONANNO FAMILY	LUCCHESE FAMILY
"Lucky" Luciano	Philip Mangano	Joseph Profaci	Joe Bonanno	Thomas Gagliano
Vito Genovese	Vincent Mangano	Joe Magliocco	Carmine Galante	Gaetano Lucchese
Chee Gusage	Abert Anastasia	Sal Mussachio (a)	Frank Lambuzzo	Stefano LaSalle (1day)
Frank Costello	Frank Scalise	Joe Columbo, Sr.	Gaspar DiGregorio	Carmine Trumante
Vito Genovese	Carlo Gambino	Thomas DiBella (a)	Paul Sciacca	Vincent Rao
Vincent Gigante	Paul Castellano	Joe Yacovelli (a)	Naltale Evola	Vittorio Amuso
	John Gotti	Vincent Aloi (a)	Phil Rastelli	
	John Gotti Jr.	Carmine Persico	Joseph Massino	

THE MODERN WAR ON ORGANIZED CRIME

Effective government action against mob activities began with the Kefauver Committee Hearings in 1950, which were set up in the wake of the investigation of Harry Gross's well protected gambling operations in New York. These U.S. Senate hearings led to the New York Waterfront Hearings that revealed organized crime's penetration and corruption of the International Longshoremen's Union (Petersen, 1983).

In 1963, at the McClellan Congressional Hearings, an important mob defector, Joseph Valachi, gave an insider's account of La Cosa Nostra activities, especially in New York (Maas, 1968; Petersen, 1983). By this time, the Gambino Crime family, for example, had interests in the Brooklyn docks; the garment district; the construction industry; the marketing of pornographic films, books, and magazines; the wholesale distribution of meat, poultry and produce; garbage collection; road building contracts; Italian bread distribution; linen and liquor service to restaurants and nightclubs; and the trucking industry (Maas, 1997).

Roughly every 20 years, organized criminal activities in New York have been investigated. The Tweed (1873), Lexow (1894), Mazet (1899) Seabury (1930), McDonald (1950), Knapp (1970) and Mollen (1992) commissions have exposed some aspects of New York's racketeering problems.

The investigative grand jury is the classic method of uncovering the operations of organized crime. Another approach is to rely on the Internal Revenue Code to catch wealthy mobsters on tax evasion charges. The use of informants (see Mills, 1986), undercover agents (see Pistone, 1987), grants of immunity (Maas, 1997), and witness protection (English, 1995) are also crucial. But electronic surveillance is the best tool for fighting organized crime, as demonstrated by the Gotti Tapes (Blumenthal, 1992). In 1968, Congress passed the Title III Omnibus Crime Control and Safe Streets Act (Pl: 90-351), which authorized electronic surveillance of criminals, when, if, and only if all other investigative techniques have been exhausted and there is reasonable cause to believe that crime has been, is being, or is about to be committed. The statute set forth and specified the terms, conditions and constraints under which such surveillance could be conducted to insure compliance with the Fourth Amendment to the U.S. Constitution, which protects citizens against unlawful search and seizure by law enforcement authorities. New York chose to be more protective of the rights of those under surveillance than the federal statute requires.

In 1970, Congress passed the Organized Crime Control Act of 1970 (PL: 91-452), which contained the Racketeer Influenced and Corrupt Organizations statute (RICO). However, RICO was not put to the test until 1975 because prosecutors did not know how to use it or what it might entail. Even the statute's author, Robert Blakely, acknowledged that RICO focused on large trials and pretrial restraints. The trials are often long and complex, resulting in severe financial burdens and lengthy disruptions of defendants' lives; and the joining together of large numbers of defendants (sometimes hundreds) in one megatrial poses the risk of prejudice and guilt by association. When he was the U.S. Attorney in the Southern District of New York, Rudolph Giuliani (1987) successfully used RICO against the Colombo Family (Cantalupo and Renner, 1990), against Paul Castellano (before John Gotti had him assassinated) (O'Brien and Kurins, 1994), in the Pizza Connection Case (Alexander, 1988), and in the Commission case (Jacobs, 1994). The RICO statute has also been applied to Asian, South American and Russian cartels, motorcycle and prison gangs, and rackets connected to the illegal disposal of toxic wastes. There is also a civil version of RICO which was successfully used to oust gangsters from Local 814 of the Brotherhood of Teamsters in New York (Kenney and Finckenauer, 1995), and from the Fulton Fish Market (Cook, 1982), which had been controlled by organized crime since the days of Joseph "Socks" Lanza (Petersen, 1983). Rudolph Giuliani was also the first prosecutor to take action against white collar criminals in the same way he did with other organized criminals; he conducted successful RICO prosecutions against Ivan Boesky and Michael Milken in the insider trader scandal of 1986 (Bruck, 1989; Kornbluth, 1992; Stern, 1992). (However, RICO, especially civil RICO, has been challenged on legal grounds; moderate critics have argued for its refinement rather than repeal (Editors, New York Times, 1989).

THE FULL SCOPE OF ORGANIZED CRIME'S RACKETS

Over the years, mobsters have dreamed up many illegal money making schemes. Some of the goods and services they provide attract willing customers. Other rackets involve the exploitation and use of violence against unwilling victims. Chart 5-2 displays the full spectrum of organized crime activities.

Chart 5-2:

The Rackets Run by Organized Crime Syndicates

Operating games of chance and illegal gambling casinos
Narcotics smuggling, distribution, and sales
Running houses of prostitution
Labor racketeering and corrupting trade unions
Loan sharking
Hijacking cargoes and fencing stolen goods
Stealing cars for resale, or dismantling them in chop shops and selling their parts
Extortion and protection
Counterfeiting of documents
Insider trading, stock manipulation, and security fraud
Smuggling of illegal immigrants
Money laundering
Tax evasion schemes
Computer, real estate, construction, bank, insurance, and commercial frauds
Monopolizing trucking, tow truck franchises, garbage collection (carting)
Illegal methods of disposing of toxic wastes
Music and video piracy
Scams involving precious stones and metals
Illegal arms sales and gunrunning
Pornographic films and adult entertainment
Arson and murder for hire

At present in New York City, La Cosa Nostra no longer runs rackets without competition. Many other ethnically-based crime syndicates operate their own schemes and scams. While no ethnic crime family engages in all of the activities listed above, certain organized crime groups are more skilled in carrying out specific rackets than others. Furthermore, certain schemes and scams are more popular at various times than others. Today, for example, the most lucrative operations center on narcotics trafficking, smuggling in aliens, illegal technology transfer, credit card and insurance fraud, and telephone calling card fraud. Gambling and prostitution remain in vogue. The rule of thumb is that, given the opportunity, every organized crime group will engage in any activity, legal or illegal, if it will produce large profits quickly or on an ongoing basis.

AFRICAN AMERICAN ORGANIZED CRIME IN NEW YORK

Organized crime activities run by African Americans can be traced back into the last century. The most well known black operator in the 1920's was Madame Stephanie St. Clair, the Policy Queen of Harlem, who exploited the numbers racket (Kleinknecht, 1996). However, the Mob discovered Harlem in the late 1920's, and by the 1930's, Dutch Schultz had taken over. After Schulz was rubbed out in 1935, African American gangsters became agents of the Genovese crime family. "Trigger" Mike Copolla and Anthony (Fat Tony) Salerno from East Harlem took over, and retained control into the 1970's. From the 1940's to the 1960's, Ellsworth "Bumpy" Johnson, called the "first Black Gangster," was the intermediary between the Genovese family and many African American criminals, negotiating drug deals, organizing policy rackets, and settling disputes. By the 1970's, however, 14 of the city's 60 policy operations were independently controlled by African Americans (Kleinknecht, 1996). In the 1960's, Frank "Pee Wee" Mathews started out as a collector-enforcer for a numbers operation. Soon he was buying heroin from the Gambino crime family, and by 1968, he headed a major cocaine and heroin distribution network. He eventually serviced the East Coast and was a key supplier to dealers in 12 cities. In 1971, when he was just 27 years old, he organized a gathering of the 40 biggest African American drug dealers in Atlanta. The following year, at the height of his power, he began challenging and then threatening the Gambinos. The Italian mobsters backed down, but in 1973, Mathews was arrested. After posting bail, he disappeared with $20 million (Kleinknecht, 1996).

Leroy "Nicky" Barnes then emerged as "Mr. Untouchable."Barnes, who had pushed narcotics for La Cosa Nostra, was allowed go to branch off on his own in 1964. But in 1965, he was arrested with $500,000 worth of heroin and sent to prison. There he became a close friend of "Crazy Joe" Gallo. They planned (unsuccessfully) to bring together New York's top African American gangsters into one organized crime family. Out of prison in the 1970's, Barnes made millions in heroin, but in 1977, he was arrested, convicted and sentenced to life in prison. However, he made a deal with the government and testified against other drug dealers in return for a place in the Witness Protection Program (Kleinknecht, 1996).

Other gangsters of African descent have recently appeared on the American scene. Criminals from Nigeria are involved in the importation and distribution of narcotics, especially heroin, illegal financial transactions, telecommunications fraud, and insurance fraud (MSNBC, 1997). The Belizian Rollin' 30's Crips Gang has been involved in narcotics and reckless shootings. Caribbean organized crime factions include Jamaican posses and Haitian insurance fraud rings (MSNBC, 1997).

HISPANIC ORGANIZED CRIME SYNDICATES

There are a number of Hispanic organized crime factions. They include the well-known Columbian drug cartels from Cali and Medellin. Dominican heroin and crack dealers, some with Cuban connections, dominate street distribution rings. Hispanic street gangs have been involved in drug distribution and are now designated as organized crime groups by law enforcement agencies.

The Latin Kings, for example, were active in the Bronx, Brooklyn and Manhattan with branches in other major cities and in Puerto Rico. NETA, another group involved in the drug trade, dominates the prison system in Puerto Rico but accepts individuals from other ethnic groups for membership here.

Mexican organized crime groups are heavily involved in supplying illegal documents, such as passports and green cards, and are also involved in the transportation of heroin.

South American Organized Crime groups are involved in drugs, stolen airline tickets, and telecommunications fraud.

ASIAN ORGANIZED CRIME IN NEW YORK

Chinese organized crime syndicates are connected to tongs and triads. Tongs were invented by Chinese men in the western gold fields and San Francisco in the 1860's. They were originally fraternal organizations, and are as American as Chop Suey because they never existed previously in China. The On Leong - Hip Sing Tong Wars began in 1899 and continued for over 20 years. They were generally fought over gambling interests (Asbury, 1928; Kleinknecht, 1996). The Tongs hired young thugs called boo how doy to patrol their turf and protect their illegal activities. These boo how doy evolved into the Chinatown street gangs, each associated with a Tong. After the Immigration Act of 1965 loosened restrictive entrance requirements, Chinese-American and other Asian organized crime groups began to pose a serious problem. By the late 1980's, the DEA felt compelled to establish the Asian Heroin Group to deal exclusively with narcotics traffickers and illegal alien smugglers (Chin, 1996).

In New York, Uncle Benny Ong (Leong) emerged in the 1970's as the undisputed "God father of Chinatown," and "Advisor for life to the Hip Sing Tong. He controlled gambling, loan sharking, extortion and murder and ran the Flying Dragons Street gang. In 1982, Hip Sing member Herbert Liu challenged Ong by opening a gambling house in alliance with the White Tigers street gang, but in short order, three of his gang members were killed and eight were wounded in a shootout with masked gunmen. Ong told New York Magazine, "Sixty years I build up respect and he think he can knock me down in one day." When Uncle Benny died in 1994, a 120-car funeral procession passed through the streets of Chinatown.

The influx of Hong Kong Chinese in the 1970's led to the formation of the White Eagles that engaged the On Leong Tong supported "Ghost Shadows" in a battle for control of Mott Street. In the early 1980's, Chinese from Fukien Provence in mainland China began to arrive in large numbers, many illegally on smuggling ships such as the Golden Venture, which went aground off Rockaway, New York in 1993 with a cargo of 300 Chinese on board (Kleinknecht, 1996).

In the 1990's, the dai Lo or "Big Brother" practice became popular. Sonny Chan, for example, a former enforcer for the Flying Dragons, became the Dai Lo of Grand Street and established "Sonny's Boys," a youth gang involved in extortion and illegal video games. Traditionally, Chinatown has been dominated by six organizations. The On Leong tong and Ghost Shadows controlled Mott, Bayard and Mulberry Streets; The Hip Sing tong and Flying Dragons controlled Pell and Doyers Streets and the Bowery; The Tung On tong and Tung On gang controlled East Broadway and Division and Catherine Streets. Further east, in the newest and poorest section of Chinatown, the Fukien American Association and the Fuk Ching gang controlled Eldridge Street and part of East

Broadway (Kleinknecht, 1996).

Triads also have been a presence in Chinese-American communities; they are the Chinese equivalent of the Mafia or Cosa Nostra families. Triads are well organized and long established secret societies, capable of engaging in the entire spectrum of criminal activities from extortion to the most complicated financial crimes.

Among the refugees from the war in Vietnam were members of the "Born to Kill" (BTK) gang (which took its name from a popular slogan of U.S. military personnel). Led by Tho Hoang "David" Thai, the BTK gang engaged in wild sprees of extortion, robbery, intimidation and murder from the mid 1980's to 1991, terrorizing residents of New York's Chinatown and several other cities across the country (English, 1995). Other more sophisticated Southeast Asian criminal organizations from Vietnam, Myanmar (Burma), Thailand, Laos, Cambodia operate in and around New York with veritable impunity because they are small and maintain a low profile, avoiding the attention of law enforcement. They engage in extortion, drug smuggling, illegal financial and currency transactions, gambling, prostitution, counterfeiting luxury goods, and telephone calling card fraud (at the expense of the major carriers like Bell Atlantic, ATT, MCI, or Sprint).

The Japanese Yakusa is involved only in money laundering and prostitution in New York. Korean organized crime has a presence in Midtown Manhattan where extortion is a big source of its income.

RUSSIAN ORGANIZED CRIME

Russian organized crime, like the Chinese Triads and the Italian La Cosa Nostra, is capable of engaging in the entire spectrum of criminal activities from the most primitive extortion schemes, through the familiar gambling, narcotics and prostitution operations, to the most complex undertakings such as stealing weapons of mass destruction. There are three million members in over 5,000 criminal gangs operating in Russia and the other Republics of the former Soviet Union; some of these syndicates now are establishing a presence in New York (Sterling, 1995). Russian organized crime is extremely dangerous because its major violators are often well educated, highly experienced professionals who readily resort to violence (Modestov, 1995). Many held key positions in manufacturing, distribution, international trade, the military, or in the KGB in the former Soviet Union (Handelman, 1995). They are masters of multinational crime, notably drug trafficking, arms trafficking, espionage and terrorism (Martin and Romano, 1992). The Russian mob attempted to defraud the United States Government in a $140 million tax scam involving fuel oil (Levy, 1995), and Mob Boss Vyacheslav Kirillovich Ivankov was convicted of extorting $8.5 million from his fellow emigres (Raab, 1995; Richardson, 1996). Lucchese crime family defector, Anthony Casso, testified that the Russian mob has an alliance with other organized crime groups in New York City (Raab, 1996). Currently, Russian organized crime is heavily involved in extortion and prostitution, including the importation of females for that purpose. They are also involved in stock, credit card, and insurance fraud (MSNBC, 1997; Pollini, 1998).

OTHER PLAYERS AMONG NEW YORK'S GANGSTERS

Irish organized crime groups are involved in immigration fraud, illegal financial transactions, and labor racketeering.

Jewish organized crime groups are engaged mainly in medicaid fraud, money laundering, other financial and stock market crimes, gambling, and loansharking.

Israeli organized crime syndicates are involved in multinational crimes such as espionage in the public and private sector, smuggling of precious gems through South Africa and Holland, illegal technology transfers and prostitution.

A major source of income for Islamic organized crime groups comes from setting up bogus charitable, educational and religious organizations which overtly and covertly generate money to support terrorist organizations (Castello, 1997)

Pakistani, Afghani, and East Indian organized crime groups are involved in international trade violations, illegal financial transactions, immigration fraud, and narcotics trafficking from the Golden Crescent of Southwest Asia along the Old Silk Trail. They are also involved in insurance fraud (MSNBC, 1997).

THE FUTURE OF ORGANIZED CRIME IN NEW YORK CITY

A number of successful prosecutions have put many of the Mafia bosses of New York's five families behind bars. But the weakened state of La Cosa Nostra enables other ethnically-based mobs to rise to power.

Politically, organized crime cannot exist without official corruption. Historically, organized criminal activity in New York involved alliances between members of three powerful groups: criminals, politicians and businessmen. Organized crime is analogous to a big business. It seeks to increase its market share until it has a virtual stranglehold over consumers and competitors. Besides achieving a monopoly, it tries to enhance its financial security by diversifying its product line. From a social stand point, organized crime families could not exist if a sector of the public did not actively consume its illicit goods and services.

Even though some people might mistakenly view mobsters and organized crime operations in a positive light, from an economic perspective its depredations contribute heavily to a financial burden shouldered by ordinary citizens: any added expenses or financial losses it incurs are passed on to consumers in the form of higher prices; the victims of its products and services, like drug addicts and gamblers, require costly social welfare, rehabilitation, reeducation, and training programs; and government spending to fund the enormous criminal justice system, is exploding like a supernova but still cannot provide effective protection from the threat caused by these gangsters. Consumers also must pay indirectly for the ever-larger private security industry which has twice the number of employees as municipal law enforcement agencies.

If organized crime is, in fact, the enemy of the people, then putting these ethnically-based syndicates out of business would vastly improve the quality of life in the city. To do this, the citizenry would have to be at least as resolute as their ruthless, entrenched adversaries, to actively petition the Department of Justice to take more action on the federal level, and to support the efforts of local law enforcement in their neighborhoods and work places in New York City and across

America. Otherwise, organized crime will surely remain, like the Old Collect marsh in lower Manhattan in centuries past, "a stagnant lake, a sea of rotting weeds" (see Camus, 1958).

Acknowledgments

The author wishes to acknowledge the assistance of NYPD Lt. Joseph Pollini, who also teaches the senior seminar on Organized Crime for the Department of Law and Police Science.

References

Abadinsky, H. (1990). Organized crime. (3rd ed.). Chicago: Nelson Hall.

Alexander, S. (1988). The Pizza Connection: Lawyers, Money, Drugs, Mafia. New York: Weidenfeld and Nicholson.

Ashbury, H. A. (1928). The Gangs of New York. New York: Paragon. Reprinted in 1990.

Balsamo, W. and Caposi, Jr., J., (1995). Crime Incorporated: The First Hundred Years of the Mafia. Far Hills NJ: New Horizons.

Blumenthal, R. (1992). Forward. In the Gotti Tapes. London: Arrow Books.

Bressler, F. (1981). The Chinese Mafia. New York: Stein and Day.

Bruck, C. (1989). Predators' Ball. New York: Penguin Group.

Camus, A. (1958). Caligula suivi de le malentendu. [Caligula followed by the misunderstanding.] Paris: Librairie Gallimard.

Cantalupo, J. and Renner, T. J. (1990). Body Mike. New York: Villard Books.

Chandler, D. L. (1975). Brothers in Blood: The Rise of the Criminal Brotherhoods. New York: Dutton.

Chin, K.-L. (1996). Chinatown Gangs: Extortion, Enterprise and Ethnicity. New York: Oxford.

Clarke, D. H. (1929) Reign of Rothstein. New York: Grosset & Dunlap.

Cook., J. (1982). Fish Story. Forbes, pp. 61-67.

Defoe, D. (1972). A General History of the Pirates. (M. Schonhorn, Ed.). Columbia, S.C.: University of South Carolina Press.

de Tocqueville, A. (1994). Democracy in America. Vol. I. Henry Reeve (Trans.), Francis Bowen (Rev.) and Phillips Bradley (Ed.). New York: Alfred Knopf. (Original work published 1835 and 1840)

Dickens, C. (1985). American Notes. New York: St. Martin's Press (Originally published New York: Chapman and Hill 1892).

English, T. J. (1991). The Westies: The Irish Mob. New York: St. Martin's.

-------------- (1995). Born to Kill. New York: William Morrow.

Fox, S. (1989). Blood and Power: Organized Crime in the Twentieth Century. New York: Penguin.

Giuliani, R. W. (1987). Legal remedies for attacking organized crime. In Herbert Edelhertz (Ed.), Major Issues in Organized Crime Control (pp. 103-130). Washington, D.C.: U.S. Government Printing Office.

Gugliotti, G. and Leen, J. (1989). <u>Kings of Cocaine</u>. New York: Harper, True Crime.

Handelman, S. (1995). <u>Comrade Criminal</u>. New Haven: Yale University Press.

Jacobs, J. (1994). <u>Busting the Mob</u>. New York: NYU Press.

Kammen, M. (1975). <u>Colonial New York: A History</u>. New York: Oxford.

Kaplan, D. E. and Dubro, A. (1986). <u>Yakuza: The Explosive Account of Japan's Criminal Underworld</u>. Reading, Massachusetts: Addison-Wesley.

Karraker, C. (1953). <u>Piracy was a Business</u>. Rindge, NH: Richard R. Smith.

Kenney, D. J. and Finckenauer, J. O. (1995). <u>Organized Crime in America</u>. Belmont, CA.: Wadsworth

Klein, M. (1986). <u>The Life and Legend of Jay Gould</u>. Baltimore: Johns Hopkins.

Kleinknecht, W. (1996). <u>The New Ethnic Mobs: The changing face of organized crime</u>. New York: The Free Press.

Kornbluth, J. (1992). <u>Highly Confident: The Crime and Punishment of Michael Milken</u>. New York: William Morrow.

Levy, C.J. (1995, August 8). Russian emigres are among 25 named in $140 million tax fraud. <u>New York Times</u>, A, 1:1 NY.

Loth, D. (1938). <u>Public Plunder: A History of Graft in America</u>. New York: Carrick and Evans.

Lowe, J. (1992). <u>Secret Empire</u>. New York: Business One, Irwin.

Maas, P. (1968). <u>The Valachi Papers</u>. New York: G.B. Putnam and Sons.

Maas, P. (1997). <u>Underboss</u>, <u>Sammy the Bull Gravano's Story</u>. New York: Harper's.

Martin, J. and Romano, A. (1992). <u>Multinational Crime</u>. Thousand Oaks CA: Sage.

Mills, J. (1986). <u>The Underground Empire: Where Crime and Governments Embrace</u>. New York: Dell Publishing Co., Inc.

MSNBC (Cable television channel) 1997. Weekend Magazine, December 19th.

Myers, G. (1936 and 1937). <u>Histories of the Great American Fortunes, Vols. I and II</u>. New York: Random House.

Myers, G. (1917). <u>The History of Tammany Hall</u>, 2nd Ed. New York: Boni & Liverwright.

Editors, New York Times (1989). <u>The New York Times</u>, August 27, p. 18.

O'Brien, J. and Kurins, A. (1991). <u>Boss of Bosses: The Fall of the Godfather: The FBI and Paul Castellano</u>. New York: Simon and Schuster.

Petersen, V. W. (1983). <u>The Mob: Two Hundred Years of Organized Crime in New York</u>. Ottawa, IL.: Green Hill.

Pistone, J. D. (1987) <u>Donnie Brasco: My Undercover Life in theMmafia</u>. New York: New American Library.

Pollini, J., Lt. Det. Cmdr., NYCPD Organized Crime Intelligence Unit, (Personal Communication, April 6, 1998)

Raab, S. (1995, June 9). Reputed russian crime chief arrested. <u>New York Times</u>, pp. B, 3:4 NY.

Raab, S. (1996, May 14). Former Lucchese crime boss is to testify on Russian mob. <u>New York Times</u>, pp. B, 7:14 NY.

Rankin, H. (1969). <u>The Golden Age of Piracy</u>. New York: Holt Rinehardt and Winston.

Reid, Ed, (1952). <u>Mafia</u>. New York: Random House.

Repetto, T. A. (1978). <u>The Blue Parade</u>. New York: The Free Press.

Rieber, R. (1997). Terrorism, organized crime and social distress. In <u>Manufacturing Social</u>

Distress: <u>Psycopathy in Everyday Life</u>, R. Rieber (Ed.). New York: Plenum.

Richardson, L. (1996). Russian emigre convicted of extortion. <u>New York Times</u>, July 9, p. B3.

Sherry, F. (1986). <u>Raiders and Rebels</u>. New York: Hearst Marine Books.

Sterling, C. (1994). <u>Thieves World</u>. New York: Simon and Schuster.

Stern, B. J. (1992). <u>License to Steal</u>. New York: Simon and Schuster.

Turkus, B. and Feder, S. (1951). <u>Murder Incorporated</u>. New York: Farrar, Straus and Young.

Vona, D. O. (1973). <u>All About Eavesdropping</u>. A New York City Police Department Report to the United States Senate Select Sub-Committee on Eavesdropping and Electronic Surveillance.

Werner, M. R. (1928). <u>Tammany Hall</u>. Garden City, New York: Double Day, Doran.

Chapter 6

DRUG TRAFFICKING IN NEW YORK CITY

by Prof. Mangai Natarajan

Department of Sociology

New York City is widely recognized as the heroin and cocaine capital of the country, *"with half the nation's estimated 500,000 heroin addicts and almost as many hard-core cocaine users residing in the metropolitan area"* (Silbering, 1994). The city serves as both a marketplace and a transhipment point for drug trafficking organizations (U.S. Department of Justice, 1994).

Drawing upon a variety of information sources, this chapter covers drug trafficking routes for marijuana, heroin and cocaine; the nature of drug dealing enterprises, including the involvement of organized crime groups in smuggling and dealing, the structure of drug dealing organizations, and, finally, law enforcement strategies to curb drug distribution and dealing in New York City.

"Drug trafficking" as commonly defined does not generally encompass retail operations and street level drug dealing, but involves all the earlier stages in the drug distribution chain. These have been identified (Johnson et al, 1991) as follows:

"Growing/Producing": Growing of the plants (coca, opium, marijuana)

"Manufacturing": Preparing heroin, cocaine, and marijuana for sale.

"Importing/Smuggling": Secretly transporting large quantities into the country.

"Wholesale Distribution": Middlemen engaged in moving large quantities of drugs from one seller to the other.

"Regional Distribution": Dealing of pound and ounce quantities, often involving the adulteration of the product before sale.

The raw materials for the most important drugs (heroin and cocaine) sold in New York City are grown abroad, in Central and South America, Southeast and Southwest Asia and the Middle East. These crops provide a dependable source of cash or income for farmers, many of whom are in poor or developing countries. The drugs refined from these agricultural crops are smuggled into the U.S. through a variety of routes involving several nations. The raw materials have to be processed before use. This is often done outside the United States, but sometimes within this country. In fact, most of the chemicals used in processing the illicit drugs are legally produced in the United States. This represents one important link between drug trafficking and the legal economy.

After importation, heroin and cocaine are sold in large quantities -- ten to fifty kilo amounts - to wholesalers and regional distributors. The latter are often involved in the processing or adulteration of drugs into products serving different user markets. Heroin is usually diluted in a variety of ways and cocaine may be converted to powder cocaine or to rock cocaine, which is known as "crack."

Drug Trafficking Methods and Routes

New York City, situated as it is on the North-East coast of America, historically has been an ideal location for trafficking drugs. There are several ways in which drugs are smuggled into the city: by individual couriers, in shipping containers, via boats, and by aircraft and motor vehicles. The methods encountered most often are the concealment of contraband in cargo containers aboard ships, in air freight cargo, through international mail parcels, and on commercial airline flights. The largest heroin shipments are smuggled into New York via cargo containers. Individual couriers may conceal up to a kilogram of heroin in their bodies, and generally use commercial airlines. Drug couriers are quite regularly arrested at JFK International Airport and the other airports serving the New York Metropolitan area (U.S. Department of Justice, 1994).

Heroin

Opium-based drugs consumed in the United States come from Southeast and Southwest Asia and Mexico. Burma (currently known as Myanmar) has the highest opium production in the world. The Southeast Asian location is popularly known as the Golden Triangle (Burma, Laos, and Thailand) and supplies almost three-quarters of estimated world opium. The Southwest Asian region is known as the Golden Crescent and consists of Afghanistan, Iran and Pakistan. Though Mexico produces far less than the Golden Triangle or the Golden Crescent, its proximity to the United States makes the heroin business less difficult to carry out than in the Asian countries.

Most heroin from the Golden Triangle coming into North America is smuggled into California or Western Canada. Some of this heroin is transported overland to New York City. Heroin produced in the Golden Crescent is smuggled into New York City via Europe. Mexican heroin is smuggled through the Mexican border and principally serves markets in the Southwestern United Sates, though some of this is transported overland and by boat to the Northeast. Because of improved border interdiction, some Mexican heroin along with cocaine is now sent to New York via Nigeria and Europe.

Cocaine

The base plant for cocaine, coca, is grown primarily in South America, especially Peru, Bolivia and Colombia. Much of that produced in Peru is sent directly to the Southern and Western United States. Some of it goes to Colombia before it reaches New York. Cocaine produced in Bolivia reaches New York directly as well as being routed through Argentina, Colombia or Uruguay (U.S. Department of Justice, 1992).

Marijuana

Most marijuana consumed in the United States comes from Latin American and domestic sources. Marijuana is transported in bulk, making it more difficult to conceal than cocaine or heroin. Marijuana produced overseas is smuggled into the United States by ocean going vessels, small planes and motor vehicles. Some marijuana also comes in from Jamaica and Southeast Asian countries such as Thailand (U.S. Department of Justice, 1992).

DRUG DEALING ENTERPRISES IN NEW YORK CITY

Organized crime groups' involvement in smuggling and dealing: Mafia days

According to the President's Commission on Organized Crime (1986), La Cosa Nostra (LCN) traffickers were forced to look for other sources when the Italian government banned the manufacture of heroin in the early 1950's. *"A new system was quickly devised, by which [the] Turkish morphine base was refined to heroin in Marseilles, then shipped to Montreal or Sicily. Organized crime groups located in these transhipment points then sent the heroin directly to the United States. This arrangement, popularly known as the "French Connection" allowed La Cosa Nostra to monopolize the heroin trade from the 1950's through the early 1970's. During the peak French Connection years, the LCN controlled an estimated 95 percent of all heroin entering New York City, as well as most of the heroin distributed throughout the United States"* (p.106).

Following Turkey's ban on opium production in the early 1970's, the French connection collapsed. Amsterdam replaced Marseilles but New York became an important distribution center. Ultimately this led to the breakdown of LCN's monopoly of drug trafficking in New York City and the emergence of a number of other trafficking organizations. There are now a wide variety of ethnic groups with links to their countries of origin involved in drug trafficking in New York City:

Italian. In New York City, these groups are still involved in heroin dealing as illustrated by the "Pizza Connection"-- a major heroin distribution case[1] prosecuted in New York City involving a network of pizzerias linked to Sicilian Mafia traffickers (Natarajan and Belanger under review; Schurr, 1989; Pileggi, 1982).

South American. These groups have links to the Medellin and Cali cartels in Colombia, which are said to control close to 90% of the world's cocaine business. Unlike other transnational criminal organizations which tend to engage in a range of illegal activity, the cartels are first and last in the drug business. (Williams, 1995).

Dominican. In the early 1990's Colombian drug barons became impatient with the heavy tariffs by Mexican traffickers, and found new partners in the Dominican Republic to help deliver drugs to New York City and throughout the East Coast by immigrants from the Dominican Republic (Rohter and Krauss, 1998).

Russian. These are principally the Odessa Mafia, based in Brighton Beach, the Chechens, who typically specialize in contract murder and extortion, and the Malina/Organizatsiay, a multi ethnic group in Brighton Beach which maintains extensive international ties and is active in a variety of areas-drug trafficking, credit card fraud, extortion, and tax fraud (Williams, 1995).

Nigerian. Nigerian Criminal Enterprises (NCEs) and other West African groups began to be involved in drug trafficking and fraud in the United States following the collapse of oil prices in the early 80's. As a result, many young and well-educated individuals, were deprived of their source of income and became involved in drug trafficking (Abadinsky, 1997).

---

[1] The case, which was in preparation for more than a year, was eventually brought to trial by the government in 1984. The trial lasted 17 months and produced more than 40,000 pages of court transcripts. Wiretap evidence consisted of 55,000 pages of records and statements were made by 230 witnesses and 22 defendants. The case is a classic example of the involvement of organized crime in New York's drug trafficking (Alexander, 1988; Blumenthal, 1988).

<u>Chinese</u>. Chinese organized crime groups, including Tongs and Triads, dominate the New York City heroin trade. They also supply some of the South American and Caribbean groups trafficking in the City (U.S. Department of Justice, 1994).

<u>Afghanis, Lebanese and Pakistanis.</u> These groups are involved in both the importation and distribution of heroin. Some Pakistani groups, in particular, are said to be stockpiling heroin in the New York City area for future distribution (U.S. Department of Justice, 1994).

Distribution strategies and the structure of drug dealing enterprises

The enormous profits available from drug trafficking attract a wide spectrum of participants. These range from individuals working alone to major organized crime syndicates. Many, if not most, domestic drug trafficking groups have not been highly organized, but this is changing in the face of increased enforcement and vast potential profits.

To be successful, traffickers need to develop routine ways of transacting business, so the distribution systems that have been developed in some cases are highly complex. Large drug networks are organized with a distinct hierarchical structure similar to some business corporations. They may be controlled by "drug czars" who are able to establish networks between suppliers and criminal organizations in different countries. Within the networks, trusted managers oversee the day-to-day operations on behalf of the czars; couriers transport drugs to distribution points in the United States, and wholesalers distribute the drugs to street retailers for sale to users (Abadinsky, 1997).

An example of such a complex distribution system would be that developed by the Colombian cartels, which continue to dominate cocaine trafficking in the United States. These cartels have created wholesale distribution and money laundering networks comprising distinct cells functioning in a number of major metropolitan areas, including New York City. From these major centers, cocaine is distributed more widely throughout the country for distribution in other cities. These cells recruit and employ large numbers of personnel, assign them tasks and monitor performance on a daily basis, punish infractions by their operatives, develop corrupt relationships with local law enforcement, maintain meticulous records of drug transactions and revenues, and keep in continuous communication with key mangers in Colombia. They use all available technology, including personal computers, cell phones, pagers, and facsimile machines in their daily operations. The advent of cell phones, together with the development of illegal cloning procedures, has greatly facilitated communications between drug dealers and their domestic clients, and their suppliers overseas (Natarajan et al., 1996).

A high degree of specialization exists in the tasks performed by a variety of trafficking enterprises. A study of thirty-three trafficking enterprises prosecuted in New York City between 1984-95 revealed that there were four categories of organization, namely, "freelance," "family-based businesses," "communal- businesses" and "corporations." Freelance enterprises generally operated higher up in the drug distribution chain. These were small organizations of older individuals drawn from a variety of ethnic groups. There was little difference between communal and family business organizations in the tasks undertaken, but family businesses were larger and composed of younger individuals. Corporations were not only the largest organizations with the youngest members, but all were also involved in retail sales as well as in trafficking/dealing (Natarajan and Belanger, under review).

LAW ENFORCEMENT EFFORTS: THE LAWS, PROSECUTION STRATEGIES, AND PUNISHMENTS FOR TRAFFICKING IN NEW YORK CITY

Enforcement at the Federal Level

In attempting to stop trafficking, a variety of strategies have been pursued by federal agencies including: (1) crop eradication, (2) control of materials used in manufacturing, (3) interdiction, and (4) investigation, arrest, and prosecution.

In the United States, the DEA's Domestic Cannabis Eradication/Suppression Program coordinates domestic crop eradication activities with the U.S. Forest Service, the Bureau of Land management, the Fish and Wildlife Service, the Bureau of Indian Affairs, and the Department of Defense. The U.S. government has also been involved in extensive crop eradication efforts overseas, with some successes. Extensive marijuana eradication programs in Mexico, Jamaica, Colombia and Belize have been implemented at various times, resulting in the large-scale destruction of marijuana crops. According to the U.S. Department of State, in 1990, nearly 8,100 hectares of coca were eradicated representing 14% of the estimated cultivation in Bolivia. (U.S. Department of Justice, 1992).

Eradication of opium crops has posed special problems because of the many countries involved and the fact that elimination of fields in one place may be soon replaced by cultivation elsewhere. However, Turkey was persuaded to shut down its legitimate production of opium and more recently Mexico and Guatemala implemented an effective program of aerial spraying of poppy fields that eliminated about half their crops. Because the U.S. government has little influence over many of the countries where opium is currently grown -- such as Myanmar (formerly, Burma), Vietnam and Afghanistan -- its crop eradication efforts in these regions are coordinated with the United Nations, which is currently conducting negotiations with the countries of the Golden Crescent of Southwest Asia and the Golden Triangle of Southeast Asia.

The federal government is also working to control trafficking of materials and chemicals necessary for the processing of illegal drugs. The Chemical Diversion and Trafficking Act of 1988 requires U.S. companies that manufacture these chemicals to keep records of the sale and export or import of the chemicals and to submit sales lists to the Drug Enforcement Administration for approval and certification (U.S. Department of Justice, 1992).

Interdiction operations prevent illegal drugs entering the U.S. from foreign sources or transit countries by intercepting and seizing such contraband (U.S. Department of Justice, 1992: 146). While several U.S. departments are involved in interdiction, the U.S. Customs Service is principally responsible for interdicting land border smuggling, the U.S. Coast Guard for interdicting smuggling on the high seas, and the Federal Aviation Administration for interdiction by air.

Land interdiction is centered on the Mexican border and involves a multi-agency effort to prevent trafficking. Thus, under the direction of the INS Border Patrol, groups of Customs inspectors, Border Patrol officers, DEA and INS agents, assistant U.S. attorneys, and state and local law enforcement officers work together to interdict the flow of narcotics across the border with Mexico.

Air interdiction involves detecting, tracking, intercepting and apprehending smugglers' aircraft. It is very difficult to sort out smugglers from the enormous volume of legitimate commercial and private air traffic. If detected, smugglers frequently ignore directions to land, and simply jettison their illegal cargo, and flee (U.S. Department of Justice, 1992:146).

Coastal interdiction relies on radar detection and on inspections of boats suspected to be smuggling. Coastal interdiction is difficult because smugglers can easily conceal illegal drugs. They also use small fast boats which sometimes have to travel only short distances. Smugglers try to blend into ordinary marine traffic and their boats are unlikely to be inspected upon entry if they make a declaration to the U.S. Customs agents about what goods they are bringing into the United States (U.S. Department of Justice, 1992:141-147).

It is difficult to know how successful these various interdiction activities have been, though there is some evidence that interdiction has been effective in interrupting the smooth flow of bulkier products. According to Reuter (1990), marijuana smugglers have turned to smuggling cocaine, which is less bulky and thus harder to detect.

The Drug Enforcement Agency (DEA) has been the principal federal agency responsible for domestic drug enforcement since 1973. Much of its effort has been focused on investigating and prosecuting the major traffickers who manage the networks and organizations. Law enforcement is difficult at these levels for several reasons. Major traffickers are not apt to be found at the scene where money is being exchanged for drugs and "buy and bust" techniques (designed to arrest a suspect in the act of selling drugs) are therefore rarely successful in netting top-level traffickers. Instead, the DEA employs more sophisticated investigative techniques, such as the use of informants, electronic surveillance, undercover operations and financial data analysis (Moore and Kleiman, 1989).

Electronic surveillance, primarily through telephone wiretaps, is a proven investigative technique in conspiracy cases, but it has been used relatively infrequently in the prosecution of top-level traffickers. There are two main reasons for this (General Accounting Office, 1984). First, the DEA has always viewed drug cases as transactional in nature, and has pursued a policy of concentrating on the purchase and seizure of narcotics and the arrest of the traffickers, rather than of pursuing conspiracy prosecutions against the large complex criminal organizations involved; second, the DEA has a shortage of personnel experienced in the use of electronic surveillance. (For example, there is a shortage of agents who speak Chinese and other Asian languages and, hence, few Asian organizations are wiretapped (Natarajan and Belanger, under review). Most wiretapping of traffickers is done on the East Coast, especially in New York. For example, in 1994, 88% of all state wiretap authorizations were located in four states: New York (367 applications), New Jersey (59), Pennsylvania (52) and Florida (49).

Financial investigations constitute another important technique in the prosecution of drug trafficking and some notable successes have been achieved. For example, a New York judge froze millions of dollars held in New York bank accounts by the Hong Kong Bank of Panama on the grounds that the money represented cocaine profits smuggled into the banking system, consolidated in Panama, then shipped back to the United states (Farah and Coll., 1998:136).

Whatever the value of electronic surveillance and financial investigations, use of informants remains the most critical investigative technique, according to the Government Accounting Office. As in most criminal conspiracies, drug trafficking is seldom reported to police agencies. Few of the people involved in the chain of production, manufacturing, distribution, and retailing of drugs are likely to come forward voluntarily and report these activities to law enforcement agencies. The lack of complainants means that the use of paid informants, or those with grudges against the traffickers, are critical in drug cases (General Accounting Office, 1984).

New York State and City Efforts

New York State enacted mandatory sentencing laws in the early 1970's, including the Second Felony Offender Law (which requires a prison term for all repeat felons) and the Rockefeller Drug Laws (which require harsh prison terms for the possession or sale of even small amounts of drugs). After 1985, "crack" use and sales expanded dramatically in the New York metropolitan area and in other cities. The public demanded stronger law enforcement, and the police and courts responded. Statistics released by criminal justice agencies began to reflect dramatic increases in arrests for cocaine and crack possession and sales; re-arrests among crack arrestees; convictions; length of jail and prison sentences; size of jail, prison, and probation populations; and cocaine positive urine samples among arrestees (See Nickerson and Dynia, 1988; Ross and Cohen, 1988; Belenko et al., 1990; DUF, 1990; Fagan, 1990; Johnson et al., 1990; New York City Police Department, 1990; and Johnson et al, 1994). Needless to say, these laws have dramatically increased the workload on the law enforcement and criminal justice systems.

The New York City Special Narcotics Prosecutors Office was also established at the beginning of the 1970's to assist law enforcement's response to the growing drug problem. The Office of Special Narcotics investigates and prosecutes cases that are referred by federal, state, and local law enforcement agencies. It is divided into two main areas of prosecutorial responsibility. The Special Investigations Bureau, established in 1992, investigates and prosecutes cases of national and international significance against major narcotics organizations based in New York City. These investigations frequently extend to the surrounding jurisdictions and increasingly, to other states and across international borders. The Trial Division handles high volume street-level felony cases as well as short-term investigations into low and mid-level drug operations (Silbering, 1994).

THE FUTURE OF TRAFFICKING

In New York and elsewhere, patterns of trafficking and drug use have changed markedly in the past few decades. Before the 1970's the problem centered mainly on heroin and marijuana. By the late 1970's cocaine had become the drug of choice. By the mid-1980's, "crack," a new smokable form of cocaine, appeared on the scene (Johnson et al., 1991) with devastating results in terms of increased crime and other social problems. The drug fueled a large increase in crime in the City, and the resultant increased arrests of drug dealers and users led to serious overcrowding in the State and Federal prisons. There was also a large increase in the number of cocaine-related deaths, in the number of births in which cocaine use by the mother was detected, and in the number of children placed in foster care in New York City. Many other parts of the public health system were placed under serious strain by the chronic problems of crack abusers.

Crack use has waned in recent years, which has helped to reduce crime in the City. However, the public health consequences of crack and cocaine are likely to continue beyond the 1990's because these drugs appear to decrease immune system functioning and to increase rates of death from AIDS (Johnson et al 1994).

While crack use may have declined, the market for cocaine is still quite active (Office of National Drug Control Policy, 1997). Judged by seizures, it is clear that the drug continues to be sold and used at unacceptable levels in the city. The gravity of the drug trafficking situation has been magnified in the 1990's by the introduction of high-quality, smokable heroin to the New York market by Colombian trafficking organizations (Silbering, 1994). The market for marijuana is also growing and there is an increase in poly-drug use, such as combining heroin and cocaine or cocaine and marijuana, and so on.

These changes in drug use pose major new problems for law enforcement. Interdiction and crop eradication are also made vastly more difficult by the growing internationalization of the drug trade. Supplies now come into New York from many more parts of the globe than in earlier decades. Because of the millions of dollars to be made, it seems that drug traffickers will always find a way to meet the demand for drugs. They might seek to market new drugs; find different routes to smuggle drugs; seek new partners among various organized crime groups in different countries; exploit new manufacturing and communication technologies; and they might recruit more educated, skilled, or vulnerable individuals into the work of trafficking.

A detailed understanding of the tasks involved at each link in the trafficking chain will help in developing measures to control the drugs reaching the street. To date, there are just a handful of ethnographic research studies that provide a detailed understanding of street level selling strategies (Johnson and Natarajan, 1995). In some cases, this kind of research has helped to develop law enforcement strategies for controlling retail sales (Zimmer, 1987; Vera Institute of Justice, 1992). However, very few scientific analyses of higher level trafficking have been made (Adler, 1985; Mieczkowski, 1986 and 1989; Williams, 1989), and more are needed to improve the effectiveness of anti-smuggling activities.

Acknowledgments

This review was primarily supported by a National Institute on Drug Abuse grant (1K21DA00242-04). Viewpoints in this paper do not necessarily represent the official positions of the U.S. Government, the National Institute on Drug Abuse, or John Jay College of Criminal Justice.

References

Abadinsky, H. (1997). Drug Abuse: An Introduction. Chicago: Nelson Hall Publishers.

Adler, Patricia, A. (1985). Wheeling and Dealing. New York: Colombia University Press.

Alexander, Shana. (1988). The Pizza Connection: Lawyers, Money, Drugs, Mafia. New York: Weidenfeld.

Belenko, S. (1990). Demographic Characteristics of Felony Arrestees in Manhattan in 1989 New York City Criminal Justice Agency (unpublished tables).

Belenko, S., J. Fagan, & Chin, K. (1990). Changing Patterns of Drug Abuse and Criminality among Crack Cocaine Users: Final Report to National Institute of Justice. New York: New York City Criminal Justice Agency.

Blumenthal, R. (1988). Last Days of the Sicilians: At War with the Mafia. New York: Times Book.

Drug Use Forecasting. (1990). Drug Use Trends 1986-89. Washington, D.C.: National Institute of Justice.

Executive Office of the President. (1997). The National Drug Control Strategy 1997.
Washington, D.C.: Office of National Drug Control Policy.

Farah, D., & Coll., S. 1998. The Cocaine Money Market. In Annual Editions Criminology 98/99.
Connecticut: Dushkin/ McGraw-Hill.

General Accounting Office. (1984). Investigations of Major Drug Trafficking Organizations.
Washington, D.C.: United States General Accounting Office.

Goldstein, P., Lipton, D. S., Preble, E., Sobel, I. , Miller, T., Abbott, W., Paige, W., and Soto, F.
(1984). "The Marketing of Street Heroin in New York City." Journal of Drug Issues, 14 (3): 553-
566.

Johnson, B. D., Hamid, A., Sanabria, H. (1991). "Emerging Models of Crack Distribution." In T.
Mieczkowksi (ed.) Drugs and Crime: A Reader: 56-78. Boston: Allyn-Bacon.

Johnson, B. D., Kaplan, M.A., Schmeidler, J. (1990). "Days with Drug Distribution: Which Drugs?
How Many Transactions? With What Returns?" In R. A.   Weischeit (ed.), Drugs, Crime, and the
Criminal Justice System. Cincinnati, Ohio: Anderson Publishing Company.

Johnson, B. D., Williams, T., Dei, K., Sanabria, H. (1990).   "Drug abuse and the inner city: Impact
on hard drug users and the community." In M. Tonry and J. Q. Wilson (Eds.): 9-67, Drugs and
Crime. Chicago: University of Chicago Press. Crime and Justice Series, V. 13.

Johnson, B.D. & Natarajan, M.   (1995). "Strategies to Avoid Arrest: Crack Seller's Response to
Intensified Policing." American Journal of Police 14 (3/4): 49-69.

Johnson, B.D., Natarajan, M., Dunlap, E., and Elmoghazy, E. (1994). "Crack Abusers and Noncrack
Abusers: A Comparison of Drug use, Drug sales and Non Drug Criminality." Journal of Drug Issues
24 (1): 117-141.

Liddick, D. (1997). "Race, Ethnic Succession and Organized Crime: The Ethnic Composition of the
Narcotic Gambling Industry in New York City." Criminal Organizations, 10(4): 13-17.

Moore, R. The French Connection: The World's Most Crucial Narcotics Investigation. Boston:
Little Brown and Company.

Moore, Mark H. (1977). Buy and Bust: The Effective Regulation of An Illicit Market in Heroin.
Lexington, Mass: Lexington.

Natarajan, M., Clarke, R., Johnson, B. (1995). "Telephones as Facilitators of Drug Dealing: A
Research Agenda." European Journal of Criminal Policy 3 (3): 137-154.

Natarajan, M., & Belanger, M. Understanding the Organization of Trafficking Drug Dealing in New
York City (submitted to the Journal of Drug Issues).

National Institute of Law Enforcement and Criminal Justice. (1977)."The Nation's Toughest Drug
Law: Evaluating the New York Experience." Washington, D.C. United States, Department of
Justice.

Nickerson, G. W. and P. A. Dynia (1988). From Arrest to Jail: Arraignment Processing and the
Detention Population. New York: New York City Criminal Justice Agency. June.

Pileggi, N. (1982)."There's No Business Like Drug Business." New York Post (December 13:38-
44).

Reuter, P., & Kleiman, M.A.R. (1986). "Risks and Prices: An Economic Analysis of Drug
Enforcement." In M.Tonry and N. Morris (Eds.) Crime and Justice: A Review of Research. Chicago:
University of Chicago Press.

Reuter, P. (1998). "The Decline of the American Mafia." In Annual Editions, Criminology 98/99.
Connecticut: Dushkin/ McGraw-Hill.

Ross, R. A., & Cohen, M. (1988). " New York State Trends in Felony Drug Processing 1983-87."
Albany: New York State Division of Criminal Justice Services.

Schurr, C. (1989). "Godfather knows best." ABA Journal: 107-108.

Silbering, R. (1994). Office of Special Narcotics Annual Report 1994. New York City: Special
Narcotics Prosecutor's Office.

Uchida, C. D., & Forst, B. (1994). "Controlling Street-level Drug Trafficking: Professional and
Community Policing Approaches." In D.L. Mackenzie and C.D. Uchida (Eds.) Drugs and Crime:
Evaluating Public Policy Initiatives. Thousand Oaks: Sage.

U.S. Department of Justice. (1994). Worldwide Heroin Situation Report-1992. Washington, D.C.:
Drug Intelligence Division.

U.S. Department of Justice. (1992). A National Report: Drugs , Crime and the Justice System.
Washington, D.C.: Bureau of Justice Statistics.

Vera Institute of Justice. (1992) Evaluation of Tactical Narcotic Teams. New York: Vera Institute
of Justice. (Unpublished)

Williams, P. 1995. "The New Threat: Transitional Criminal Organizations and International
Security." Criminal Organizations, 9(3): 3-19.

Zimmer, L. 1987. Operation Pressure Point: The Disruption of Street-level Drug Trade on New
York's Lower East Side. Occasional Papers from the Center for Research in Crime and   Justice,
New York University School of Law.

Chapter 7

THE CHANGING DRUG SCENE IN BROOKLYN NEIGHBORHOODS

by

Prof. Richard Curtis

Department of Anthropology

Excerpted with permission from the
Journal of Criminal Law and Criminology

At the peak of the crack epidemic, when people seemed ready to write off inner cities as hopelessly lost -- a remarkable transformation began to take place. In a global economy where the gap between the haves and the have-nots continues to increase at an alarming rate, the residents of poor neighborhoods in New York City defied nearly all expectations and with minimal outside intervention, mounted an improbable comeback. The most striking manifestation of this rebirth was a plummeting crime rate which, in the latter half of the 1990's, fell to lows not seen in more than 30 years. Incumbent politicians and law enforcement officials scrambled to take credit, while the media and social scientists tried to explain how this seemingly unlikely turn of events could have happened in communities whose vitality was undermined by drug selling and using, violence, unemployment, failing schools, and other social problems.

Very little research has been done on the impact of growing up in a violent environment and how it may contribute to greater or lesser violent behavior during adolescence and later in life. Clearly, social and/or environmental factors shape the developmental trajectories of large segments of the population. But anthropological researchers are interested in what people actually do and the choices they make within the parameters that bound their everyday lives. Ethnographic research has shown that even drug abusers have agency and possess the capacity to intervene meaningfully in their own lives, though not always in ways that they intend (see Maher, 1997). Young people, in particular, are known for their malleability and capacity to adapt in novel ways to their environments;

but they have also been recognized as possessing the ability to alter the status-quo (see Farber, 1987). While the inner cities of many large metropolitan areas in the United States have experienced severe social and economic problems since at least the 1960's, case studies and comparative analyses — cornerstones of anthropological inquiry - have shown remarkable variation between cities and neighborhoods that are divided by race/ethnicity, class, immigrant status, housing patterns, crime, violence, employment opportunities, and many other factors, including the prevalence and tolerance of drug use and distribution (see Sullivan, 1989). Neighborhoods and communities are important to examine because they are, in addition to family contexts, the locations where people learn to be human. They form the crucible where orientations, outlooks, behaviors, and lifestyles are forged (Arensberg and Kimball, 1965).

To understand how and why inner city life has changed in the 1990's, especially the relationship between drugs, crime, violence and youth development, it is necessary to study specific communities. This paper focuses on two Brooklyn, New York, neighborhoods, Williamsburg and Bushwick. The data is drawn from 10 years (1987-1997) of ethnographic fieldwork spanning nine different research projects examining the lives of different groups of young people, including students, gang members, and drug dealers. The one enduring feature of the ethnographic effort in each project was an attempt to situate the observed behavior of research subjects in the context of a wider community. Research participants were observed in public and private domains, allowing for descriptions of the intimate, mundane or extraordinary details of their everyday lives, the social contexts which framed them, and manner by which they comported themselves and constructed their identities. The analysis will show that the urge to invest explanatory power in structural factors (such as demographic changes and economic conditions) or institutional operations (by the police or the courts) to explain the turnaround witnessed in inner city neighborhoods, especially the plummeting crime rates, should be tempered by an appreciation of the importance of the agency of the very people who must ultimately decide whether or not to use a drug, pick a fight, or commit a crime.

Northeast Brooklyn in Transition

In the early 1960's, many New York City neighborhoods experienced a radical transformation which originated in the period's restructuring of global, national and regional socio- economic arrangements (see, e.g., Ross and Trachte, 1990). Neighborhoods which had once been populated by European-Americans were rapidly evacuated and repopulated by immigrants from Latin America and the Caribbean, where U.S.-directed modernization and development programs had transformed indigenous economies, causing mal-integration between economic sectors, widespread unemployment and uprooted rural populations (see Sassen-Koob, 1989). But as European-Americans deserted these neighborhoods, more than 500,000 manufacturing jobs also fled the city. As the city's tax base shrank, expenditure on public services was sharply reduced (Kasarda, 1992; Mollenkopf and Castell, 1991). Although a few large manufacturers remained, the typical poor-neighborhood company in the 1980's and 1990's intermittently employed workers in non-union, low-skill, low- wage, and high-risk jobs. The economy had stopped guaranteeing economic prosperity and security and offered high unemployment and underemployment instead. Thus, upon arrival, a significant proportion of new immigrants were trapped in steadily deteriorating neighborhoods by unemployment and the lack of low- income housing.

The changes which took place in Northeast Brooklyn were, in many ways, typical of what happened elsewhere. In Williamsburg, reform, conservative and orthodox Jews fled to the suburbs beginning in the late 1950's, abandoning apartment buildings on the South side of the neighborhood, while Italians on the North side entrenched themselves, fiercely clinging to neighborhood traditions (see Curtis and Maher, 1992). Bushwick, an adjacent neighborhood to the southeast, was emptied out by a rash of arson-related house fires set by building-owners who could not sell their properties and attempted to collect insurance monies instead. Where there were once bustling, viable thoroughfares which thrived on stable manufacturing jobs nearby, there were now shuttered factories and block after block of abandoned buildings and empty lots (see Oser, 1994). The section had become an urban wasteland whose charred, derelict landscape was matched by a frontier mentality where confrontation and violence were commonly used to impose order and resolve disputes (Tabor, 1992).

The high turnover of tenants and homeowners weakened voluntary associations, if they were not completely discontinued, and disinvestment in schools and community depleted PTA's, clubs, church groups, and grassroots political groupings. The informal controls which defined and protect neighborhoods were thus slackened, opening the door for organized drug distribution and a steadily increasing crime rate (Curtis and Maher, 1992).

Drug selling organizations acted as springboards to political and/or economic power within the neighborhood, and for newly arriving minority youths, aside from family connections, there were few enduring community ties to which they pledged loyalty. Lacking significant economic opportunity and entering an urban terrain where neighborhood conditions and controls were crumbling, many newcomers found themselves pulled into the orbit of drugs, either as distributors and/or users (Curtis and Maher, 1992; see also Preble and Casey, 1969). Drugs and the "fast" money circulating in drug markets proved more attractive to them than the old-fashioned ideas of previous generations that believed it possible to climb the ladder to economic success and achieve the American dream through hard work.

Drug Markets in Northeast Brooklyn

An enduring theme of illegal drugs in New York City is that although distribution has been vertically organized since the prohibition of alcohol, control over it has shifted from one ethnic population to another. In Northeast Brooklyn, Puerto Rican freelance distributors and family businesses filled the vacuum left by the withdrawal of Italian retailers in the early 1960's. As the popularity of heroin skyrocketed in the mid 1960's, they quickly cornered street-level sales in many neighborhoods and their incipient organizations grew in size and complexity (Curtis and Maher, 1992; Preble and Casey, 1969). When the heroin epidemic ended in the 1970's, just a few Puerto Rican "owners" had consolidated the market and formed monolithic enterprises, which tightly integrated wholesale, mid-level and street-level markets. Located in selected Latino neighborhoods, these businesses remained an exclusively Puerto Rican enterprise. In Williamsburg, four Puerto Rican "owners" employed a street-level staff of Puerto Ricans exclusively (Curtis and Maher, 1992).

When the popularity of crack skyrocketed in New York City in the mid-1980's, the owners of heroin and cocaine businesses in Williamsburg resisted adding crack to their menus despite increasing numbers of customers who were asking for it, and only grudgingly allowed fledgling (Dominican) crack distributors to operate on the edge of their turfs (Curtis and Maher, 1992). Even though crack eventually made inroads into Williamsburg in the late 1980's, the antipathy which heroin and cocaine distributors, shooting gallery operators and drug injectors held toward crack users initially kept the crack scene on the neighborhood fringe. But in passing on the opportunity to diversify their tightly controlled market, the owners of drug businesses in Williamsburg emboldened competitors who eventually usurped Puerto Rican dominance over the market.

Throughout the 1970's and most of the 1980's, Bushwick was a second-tier drug market in comparison with Williamsburg. Located immediately southeast of the latter and further into Brooklyn, Bushwick is more isolated and inconvenient for drug users from outside the neighborhood to reach via car or public transportation. In Bushwick, territory was much less rigidly controlled than in Williamsburg and crack, cocaine and heroin distributors, many of them newly arrived Dominicans, were able to make significant inroads into the neighborhood in the late 1980's. By 1988, fueled by aggressive crack sales and offering an entire range of street-level drugs to consumers, drug markets in Bushwick began to rival those in Williamsburg. Still, their location was bad and many drug users continued to utilize Bushwick as a secondary market, a place they would go only when no drugs could be found elsewhere. But if Bushwick's location was inconvenient, Williamsburg's was good, too good. In the mid- 1980's, gentrification in lower Manhattan began to drive many young artists and professionals to the outer boroughs and Williamsburg became an increasingly attractive option to many of them. A housing shortage in Williamsburg, which was already bad given rapidly expanding Latino and Hasidic communities (Goldman 1990), was thus exacerbated by an influx of Manhattanites. Suddenly, buildings which had been abandoned since the early 1970's and were the sites of shooting galleries and hideouts for drug dealers were valuable property. They were sealed up, cleaned up, and completely transformed within the space of a few years. Many factory buildings near the waterfront, especially those with a view of Manhattan, were turned into lofts and sold for handsome profits. Apartment buildings were rehabilitated and rented out to local low- and middle-income families who waged spirited battles to gain entry.

For Bushwick, the citywide blackout of August 1977, when many businesses and homes were burned, represented a low point. Throughout the 1980's, like Williamsburg, Bushwick too began to experience renewal, though much more modest in scope (Oser, 1994). Small industries reclaimed many vacant factories, and New York City, in partnership with landlords, slowly began to rehabilitate some of the apartment buildings which had gone untended for many years. But when Williamsburg began to gentrify, drug markets were displaced to Bushwick, aided by a crackdown on street-level drug markets in Williamsburg by the Tactical Narcotics Team in 1989 (Curtis and Sviridoff, 1994).

The modest recovery mounted by Bushwick was promptly stalled by a steady increase in the amount of street-level crack, heroin and cocaine trafficking which drew participants from throughout the New York metropolitan area (Curtis et al, 1995). By 1990, a street-level drug "supermarket" had formed in the northern tier of Bushwick and within a four-block area, more than two dozen different "stamps" of heroin were aggressively hawked by street-level sellers who called out the name of their product like Coney Island carnival barkers. Between February 1991 and May 1992, the number of distributors and users at the largest street- level market in Bushwick doubled (Curtis et al, 1995).

The NYPD, and its Tactical Narcotics Teams (TNT) in particular, enjoyed a great benefit from the contraction and concentration of street-level cocaine (crack) markets throughout New York City. They were able to focus their efforts on fewer precincts and still maintain the same high number of arrests (about 400 per month per unit) previously achieved within a much larger geographical area. For example, more than 8,200 persons were arrested between 1988 and 1992 in Bushwick alone. A common joke was that Riker's Island, the city jail, had turned into "a Bushwick block party" (Curtis and Hamid, 1997), where young women and children sat in the waiting room exchanging gossip about recent arrests, sentences received, and mounting family pressures, while young men gathered on the other side of the bars in anticipation of visits by family and friends.

The citywide conversion of more decentralized drug markets to a few supermarkets in Bushwick, East Harlem and a few other neighborhoods also precipitated greater tumult. Drug distributors have long commanded attention (Fagan, 1989; Goldstein, 1984) for their unprecedented levels of and novel approaches to violence, including the infamous "Colombian necktie," the use of box-cutters to slash faces, and their promotion of the 9mm pistol to the status of cultural icon. "Systemic" violence (Goldstein, 1984) accounts for the lion's share of incidents related to illegal drugs, and nowhere was that more apparent than in Bushwick. While some markets earned reputations for controlling violence (e.g., Hamid's, 1991) marijuana distributors), distributors in Bushwick employed it regularly and systematically (Curtis and Maher, 1992; Maher and Curtis, 1994; Maher, 1997). There, large corporate-like organizations effected street-level drug sales, and since institutional and neighborhood-level restraints had already vanished, they completely disregarded the sensibilities of residents in doing so. They also undermined the prosperity of the community which hosted them, just as their counterparts in the formal economy had done. While their sole benefit consisted of low-level, dead-end jobs for youths, the damages included plummeting property values, a greater incidence of drug misuse, high rates of incarceration, and AIDS. But their most crippling legacy was violence.

Corporate Distributors and the Legacy of Violence

By 1992, one Puerto Rican and three Dominican "owners" ruled over crack distribution at the northern end of the Bushwick. Each had a trademark, or the color of the "tops" of the crack vials they sold: white, blue, brown and pink. Dominican families monitored the day to day operations of the largest three. Younger family members and close non-kin "associates" directed street sales, while older family members, entirely removed from the street scene, were the "executives." When there were not enough family members, owners employed persons who shared a similar background. The practice earned them the resentment of street- level workers, particularly among the Puerto Ricans who had controlled distribution throughout the 1970's and early 1980's (and had similar policies), only to be toppled by the Dominicans in the late 1980's. The rivalry which had long existed between Puerto Ricans and Dominicans in New York City was thus sharpened in the drug business.

As arrests depleted the supply of eligible Latino street- level dealers, they were replaced by African Americans and European Americans (Maher and Curtis, 1992). The gulf separating management from labor widened and their already contentious and adversarial relationships turned even more distrustful and violence-prone. Resenting their harsh and dangerous conditions of labor, and the disrespect their managers showed, many street-level sellers took every opportunity to abscond with the drugs. They fully expected physical punishment for their transgressions, and often received it.

While brute force or the threat of it is the ultimate means distributors have to enforce rules, a business is ruined when it invites police attention too frequently. Accordingly, sensible or successful distributors avoided or minimized its use. But Bushwick's corporate "owners" were reckless. Violent acts were more common in their markets because of the divisions and animosities that rigidly separated different levels of the organizations, because the owners did not live in the neighborhood and did not have to witness or confront the aftermath of their deeds, and because they could easily relocate supplies to outlets they maintained in other neighborhoods. Indeed, owners encouraged their managers to regularly use public displays of force as a way of intimidating customers, untrustworthy employees, and to send the message that they should not be crossed. For example, one owner hired an "enforcer" who strolled around the neighborhood with a baseball bat on which he wrote the names of his targets. After punishing them, he rubbed off their names.

In Bushwick in the early 1990's, "face to face" or "man to man" confrontations between individuals were replaced by humiliating group beatings, or "beatdowns." Their unrestrained brutality affected local adolescents, who were its daily witnesses. Sometimes they too participated gratuitously in beatdowns and other bloody episodes in which they had no stake: they simply saw someone being chased and, wit h malicious smiles on their faces, picked up their baseball bats or bicycle chains and joined the chase. For them, "fun" was no longer spraying graffiti, playing ball, or dancing: it was the number and severity of beatdowns they administered daily, and they became so frequent that the sight of blood stopped being a cause for alarm to researchers and local residents alike.

Drug supermarkets made these atrocities an unremarkable commonplace feature of everyday life. While police operations which target street-level drug markets may anticipate the use of force, perhaps as people resist being arrested or during their attempts to flee, some members of the New York City Police Department were innovative, and conceived many unusual applications which deeply alienated neighborhood residents. For example, when "sweeping" the main drug selling areas, they would cordon off both ends of a street and require everyone in between to lie down, regardless of whom they were. While this tactic sometimes yielded a handsome body count of arrests, it also obliged elderly grandmothers and young children to grovel on the asphalt while being roughly searched -- and it enraged many residents.   When the police could not find drug distributors to arrest, they went to well-known shooting galleries. But officers loathed going into them. They believed that too many hiding places lurked in their dark and sometimes labyrinthine constructions and that they were an obstacle course of discarded HIV-infected syringes. To flush the drug users out instead, some officers used to throw large rocks through the windows. They were caught in the act by a prizewinning reporter for the Los Angeles Times, who had been interviewing heroin injectors when the projectiles whizzed by his head (Bearak, 1992). Drug users also showed the research team large welts across their torsos which officers had inflicted with whips of thick television cable as they fled the galleries.

In the summer, local police officers mercilessly and systematically harassed drug users who loitered near the major drug selling locales. Early in the morning when they had fallen asleep on the sidewalk, foot patrol officers would routinely rouse them with kicks and order them to move. Sometimes the kick simply nudged the unfortunate awake, at other times it was meant to cause pain. So habituated were they to the pastime that the police officers continued it even when video cameras were brought to photograph them. They also responded with an overwhelming show of force at almost any infraction, be it a drug user's, dealer's or passerby's. By late summer 1992, the populace was close to insurrection and television and newspaper crews came to interview unruly crowds who were protesting the mounting number of police shootings and beatings of youths. Police had responded in full riot gear, and other residents had pelted them from the rooftops with bottles, debris and hateful epithets. Apparently thinking that beleaguered drug distributors were fomenting the neighborhood's growing hostility toward them, and immediately following a sensational article in the New York Times (Tabor, 1992), the police mounted yet another major offensive against street-level drug markets in September 1992. They stationed a mobile trailer in a nearby park to serve as the base of operations for more than 300 additional uniformed officers. These were positioned around the park and on each corner of drug "hot spots." Mounted police trotted by to discourage trafficking or "loitering." Officers stopped and questioned all pedestrians and asked for their identification and destination. Nonresident were told to stay out. The heaviest drug trafficking streets were sealed with wooden barricades and police vans, and traffic was diverted to other streets. When evening came, they drove in large flatbed trucks with gas-powered generators and klieg lights which, parked at strategic corners, illuminated entire blocks. Police painted the street numbers of buildings on rooftops to enable helicopters to give additional support to officers pursuing suspects on foot. For the next 18 months, Bushwick was virtually occupied by a small army of police.

Growing Up in the 1990's: Violence, Crime and Drugs

For Bushwick youth, it would not have been unreasonable to expect that rates of crime and violence would continue to increase throughout the 1990's, and that it was only a matter of time before a new breed of super-predators made their ominous presence felt. Much evidence seemed to suggest that the dominant models of urban decay and worsening youth violence were correct. Many youth had grown up in dysfunctional multi-problem families, without positive role models, and left unchecked by the informal controls which had defined and protected previous generations. The lack of order and structure worsened as youth turned into adolescents. Where there was typically a diffusion of responsibility for social control shifting away from parents and onto societal institutions, especially schools, in Bushwick, these societal checks had been largely missing and young adults had to forge their own solutions to problems.

The daily occurrences of violence and crime etched deep furrows on the bodies and psyches of Bushwick youth. A representative household sample of Bushwick youth 18-21 conducted in 1994-95 (Friedman et al 1997b: 120) noted the pervasiveness of violence: Violence has been an important part of their lives: approximately 10% report having been physically abused by a police officer, 30% have been threatened or stabbed with a knife, 27% have been caught in a random shootout, 22% have been threatened or shot at with a gun, 33% have been mugged or robbed with a threat of violence, and 14% of the women and 5% of the men report having been sexually abused. Over half (51%) report having carried a weapon such as a knife, club or gun. But far from becoming "super-predators" as an outcome of this exposure, many youth withdrew from social life, afraid of lingering in public spaces for fear of violence. Violence had become so commonplace that they often listened in near disbelief to stories about when fighting was fair, and done for reasons that were righteous or virtuous.

Many young people who were interviewed between 1993 and 1995 said that they were so fearful of random and/or police violence that they no longer spent much time in parks, playgrounds, stoops or the other places where youths had traditionally "hung out." Indeed, the question, "where do you hang out?" seemed to offend them. Violence and crime did not disappear overnight or entirely from the lives of this generation of youth, but in moving away from exposure to high-risk settings and the performance of violent acts in public spheres, the intimate contexts of private, and especially family, life became the arena where violent episodes found their expression. Many youth had intimate experience with the variety of problems that afflicted their elders as an outcome of involvement with cocaine, crack or heroin, and they made a conscious attempt to avoid similar fates.

Given the AIDS epidemic, a growing body count in the war on drugs, and the many adverse psycho-social outcomes that follow drug misuse, many Latino and African American youth throughout New York City began to avoid heroin and crack in the 1990's (Hamid et al, 1997). In Manhattan, for example, "the rate [of cocaine/crack use] among youthful arrestees dropped from 70 percent in 1988 down to 31 percent in 1991, where it remained through 1995. It declined further to 22 percent in 1996" (Golub and Johnson, 1997:6). In place of hard drugs, they consumed only marijuana, and viewed with disfavor even cigarettes and malt liquor, which had been aggressively marketed in their neighborhoods (Marriott, 1993). This generation of youth put tremendous pressure on their age mates to eschew stigmatized substances. Bushwick youth were nearly unanimous in their opinion that their peers would not be proud of using heroin or crack.

In a neighborhood which had become nearly resigned to the presence of brazen street-level drug markets, successive generations of youth who participated in them, and high rates of HIV/AIDS (Jose et al, 1993), it initially came as a surprise when Friedman et al (1997a) discovered that less than 3% of their sample of youth said that they had used heroin, only 9% said that they had ever used cocaine, and none were infected with HIV, syphilis, or HTLV-2. After all, most models of adolescent development had suggested that inner city youth were at progressively greater risk of drug abuse and contracting pathogens like HIV (see Kandel and Yamaguchi, 1993). Even worse, models of the likely progression of the AIDS epidemic had predicted that the virus would increasingly spread via heterosexual contact - the province of sexually active youngsters (Alexander, 1996). But clearly, this generation was not using hard drugs at rates characteristic of earlier generations. Given the low rates of HIV and other markers of risk that were discovered, apparently their drug use and sexual networks overlapped little with those already infected (Friedman et al, 1997b). Even the handful of young people interviewed in Bushwick who admitted that they had used heroin confessed that they were terrified to try it. The widely reported drop in crack and other hard drug use among inner city youth in the 1990's (Golub and Johnson, 1997) was, on one hand, an outcome of the natural progression of drug eras (Hamid, 1992), but changes in drug preferences coincided with and were deepened by more fundamental changes in youth culture. Where crack in the 1980's had emptied out the inner city and left neighborhoods and their residents looking like skeletons, the anti-crack/heroin generation of the 1990's sought to fill out their bodies. They visually displayed this attitude in the too-large designer clothing they wore, and through the language of "living large" where everything good was "phat" (fat) and "butter." Compared to the 1980's, their style was very much muted, devoid of the garish clothing and gaudy accessories that characterized the crack-era "gangsta" persona.

The reconfiguration of drug markets in the mid-1990's appreciably reduced the level of neighborhood violence. As distribution retired indoors, turf battles were eliminated, and since organizers of drug businesses hired a few trusted friends rather than easily replaceable workers, there was less conflict between them. Distributors were robbed by users less frequently because they were more protected selling indoors to known customers. Like other neighborhood residents, drug distributors and users had also adapted and contributed to dramatic changes in neighborhood conditions.

Toward the Future

The future of inner cities in the global economy of the approaching millennium does not appear particularly bright. The residents of inner city neighborhoods did not share equally in the fruits of the economic revitalization of the 1990's which created new (though less secure and rewarding) jobs and low unemployment, and led to an optimism not seen since the post-WWII economy of the 1950's. For inner city residents, the economy did not promise prosperity, security or upward mobility, but rather, more unemployment, underemployment and substantially less help from local, state and federal agencies to combat poverty and its effects. But in spite of their marginalized status and bleak prospects, many inner city residents not only forestalled their expected slide into economic ruin and social disintegration, they confounded the schools of economic, cultural and genetic determinism that had predicted a steady march toward oblivion and showed a new vitality, graphically illustrated by precipitous drops in crime and violence. Yet many scholars, journalists and policy makers continue to believe that poor people are incapable of helping themselves much less their communities, and the urge to explain their turnaround on external factors is great. The most popular of these unidimensional explanations is that innovations in policing (especially in the area of technology) are driving the extraordinary transformation of inner city neighborhoods (see Anderson, 1997). With great fanfare Mayor Giuliani and the New York City Police Department introduced their "quality of life" crackdown as the keystone ingredient in turning the city around, and they hammered this message home to the public and the media, but most urgently, to rank and file police officers who were instructed to aggressively pursue even the most petty offenders, like those engaging in jaywalking, riding bicycles on sidewalks, loitering, trespassing, or drinking beer in public. The advocates of the "fixing broken windows" approach contended that by concentrating on the "little things, the big things will take care of themselves," but with fewer serious crimes occurring and drug distributors more difficult to catch, police were able to concentrate on the lesser offenses. While aggressive policing certainly resulted in a reluctance by many people to linger in public spaces, including the reviled "obstreperous youth" who were said to spoil neighborhood civility (Kelling and Coles, 1996), police repression can hardly account for the profound changes which occurred in the daily lives of inner city residents.

The combination of factors which precipitated inner city change varies from city to city and neighborhood to neighborhood. In New York City, for example, rapidly declining rates of crime and violence, the hallmarks of this urban renaissance, have been observed in every neighborhood, not simply those where conditions had become intolerable. To disentangle and account for the multiple influences which frame behavior and the choices people make, it is useful to examine the intimate contexts where people learn to become human and construct their lives - families, social networks, workplaces and communities. But regardless of the constellation of variables which precipitated the startling turnaround observed in inner city neighborhoods, the capacity of people to alter their everyday lives and confound the "experts" has been highlighted in the current period. After being socially, culturally, economically, politically and physically stripped, demolished and deconstructed for more than 30 years, Northeast Brooklyn was ripe for rebuilding in the 1990's. In Bushwick, where neighborhood conditions had become intolerable, young people were at the forefront of this effort, and they responded to the multiple threats against their daily lives and futures by repudiating those elements which endangered them: unchecked street-level drug markets, out-of-control violence, and hard drugs. The palpable change which washed over the neighborhood beginning in 1993 was initiated and carried through by young residents who, though far from uniform in their responses to those dangers, shared a conviction that they would not succumb to the same fate that nearly erased the preceding generation. In altering their own lives, they shattered the myth that they were powerless against a "criminogenic" environment which was said to mass-produce "super-predators," and threw into question the assumption that violence must beget violence. Life in the postmodern global economy is one in which identity formation is less dependent upon the influence of family, neighborhood, race/ethnicity, nationality and history (Giddens, 1991), and more than anywhere else, the inner city is an empty canvas, an urban frontier where new structures, institutions and conventions are waiting to be built. Where the unprecedented changes that the current generation has begun are going, and whether they can be sustained is uncertain, but the outcome is by no means predetermined. In the face of the many obstacles which inner city residents must still overcome, the failure of those in power to recognize and reward the struggle of inner city youth to build a better world may yet prove the naysayers right.

References

Alexander, NJ. 1996. Sexual Spread of HIV Infection. Human Reproduction. Vol. 11:111-120, National Supplement.

Arensberg, C., & Kimball, S.T. 1965. Culture and Community. Glouchester, MA: Peter Smith. Bearak, B. 1992. A Room for Heroin and HIV. Los Angeles Times, September, 27: A1.

Curtis, R., & Maher, L. 1992. Highly Structured Crack Markets in the Southside of Williamsburg, Brooklyn. Paper prepared for publication under contract with the Social Science Research Council and the Guggenheim Foundation Working Group on the Ecology of Crime and Drugs.

Curtis, R., Friedman, S.R., Neaigus, A., Jose, B., Goldstein, M., Ildefonso, G. 1995. Street-Level Drug Markets: Network Structure and HIV Risk. Social Networks 17:229-249.

Curtis, R., and Hamid, A. State-sponsored Violence in New York City and Indigenous Attempts to Contain It: The Mediating Role of the Third Crown (Sgt. at Arms) of the Latin Kings. NIDA monograph.

Curtis, R., & Sviridoff, V. 1994. The Social Organization of Street-Level Drug Markets and its Impact on the Displacement Effect. In RP McNamara (ed.), Crime Displacement: The Other Side of Prevention. East Rockaway, NY: Cummings and Hathaway.

Fagan, J. 1989. The Social Organization of Drug Use and Drug Dealing Among Urban Gangs. Criminology. 27:633-670.

Friedman, SR, Curtis, R., Jose, B., Neaigus, A., Zenilman, J., Culpepper-Morgan, J.,Borg, L., Kreek, MJ., Paone, D., Des Jarlais, DC. 1997a. Sex, Drugs, and Infections Among Youth: Parenterally- and Sexually-Transmitted Diseases in a High-Risk Neighborhood. Sexually Transmitted Diseases, vol 24, no 6:322-326.

Friedman, SR, Neaigus, A., Jose, B., Curtis, R,. McGrady, GE, Vera, M., Lovely, R., Zenilman, J., Johnson, V., White, HR., Paone, D., Des Jarlais, DC. 1997b. Adolescents and HIV Risk Due to Drug Injection or Sex with Drug Injectors in the United States. In L Sherr (ed.) AIDS and Adolescence. Chur, Switzerland: Harwood Academic Publishers: 107-131.

Giddens, A. 1991. Modernity and Self-Identity. Stanford, CA: Stanford University Press. Goldman, AL. 1990. Brooklyn Project Shakes Hispanic-Hasidic Peace. New York Times: B4. Goldstein, PJ. 1985. The Drugs/Violence Nexus: A Tripartite Conceptual Framework. Journal of Drug Issues. 15(4):493-506.

Golub, AL, & Johnson, BD. 1997. Crack's Decline: Some Surprises Among U.S. Cities. National Institute of Justice: Research In Brief. July.

Hamid, A. 1992. The Developmental Cycle of a Drug Epidemic: The Cocaine Smoking Epidemic of 1981-1991. Journal of Psychoactive Drugs. 24(4):337-48.

Hamid, A. 1991. From Ganja to Crack: Caribbean Participation in the Underground Economy in Brooklyn, 1976-1986, Part 2. International Journal of the Addictions, Vol 26 (7) 1:735-744.

Hamid, A, Curtis, R., McCoy, K., McGuire, J., Conde, A., Bushell, W., Lindenmayer, R., Brimberg, K., Maia, S., Abdur-Rashid S., Settembrino, J. 1997. The Heroin Epidemic in

New York City: Current Status and Prognoses. The Journal of Psychoactive Drugs. December.

Jose, B., Friedman, SR, Neaigus, A., Curtis, R., Grund, JPC, Goldstein, MF, Ward, TP, Des Jarlais, DC. 1993. Syringe-mediated drug-sharing (Backloading): A new risk factor for HIV among injecting drug-users. AIDS, 7:1653-1660.

Kandel, DB, & Yamaguchi, K. 1993. From Beer to Crack. American Journal of Public Health. 83:851-855.

Kasarda, JD. 1992. The Severely Distressed in Economically Transforming Cities. In AD Harrell and GE Peterson (eds.), Drugs, Crime and Social Isolation: Barriers to Urban Opportunity. Washington: The Urban Institute Press.

Kelling, GL, & Coles, CM. 1996. Fixing Broken Windows: Restoring Order and Reducing Crime in Our Communities. New York: Free Press.

Maher, L. 1997. Sexed Work: Gender, Race and Resistance in a Brooklyn Drug Market. New York: Oxford University Press.

Maher, L., & Curtis, R. 1992. Women on the Edge of Crime: Crack Cocaine and the Changing Contexts of Street-Level Sex Work in New York City. Crime, Law and Social Change. 18:221-258. Marriott, M. 1993. For Minority Youths, 40 Ounces of Trouble. New York Times, April 16: A1. Mollenkopf, JH, & Castells, M. 1991. Dual City: Restructuring New York. New York: Russell Sage Foundation.

Oser, AS. 1994. The Quest for Shops Below Bushwick El. New York Times. Sunday, Feb. 27. Preble, E.,Casey, JJ Jr. 1969. Taking Care of Business: The Heroin Users Life on the Street. International Journal of the Addictions. 4:1-24.

Ross, RJS, & KC Trachte. 1990. Global Capitalism: The New Leviathan. Albany, NY: Stae University of New York Press.

Sullivan, M. 1989. Getting Paid: Youth Crime and Work in the Inner City. Ithaca, NY: Cornell University Press.

Sviridoff, M., Sadd, S.,Curtis, R., Grinc, R. 1992. The Neighborhood Effects of New York City's Tactical Narcotics Team on Three Brooklyn Precincts. New York: Vera Institute of Justice. Tabor, M. 1992. The World of a Drug Bazaar, Where Hope Has Burned Out. New York Times. Oct. 1: A1.

Chapter 8

FEAR OF CRIME IN A NEW YORK CITY NEIGHBORHOOD: THE GAP BETWEEN PERCEPTION AND REALITY IN BROWNSVILLE, BROOKLYN

by

Professor Delores D. Jones-Brown

Department of Law and Police Science

THE PARADOX:

While tales of murder and mayhem continue to top the highlights of many evening news shows, by all official statistical accounts, crime rates are declining virtually nationwide. FBI figures for serious crimes (including murder, forcible rape, robbery, and burglary) in the 1990s indicate reductions are being registered in most jurisdictions, especially in the largest cities.

The estimated crime rates derived from the National Crime Victimization Survey (NCVS) confirm the trends evident from police data. The situation is really improving, and is not a false impression created by changes in rates of reported victimization. Regardless of the source of information or the measurement used, there are verified indications that crime actually is subsiding. And, most notably, in New York, crime rates have plummeted more dramatically than in any other major U.S. city (see Lattimore et al, 1997).

However, when it comes to crime's counterpart, **fear**, there appears to be little cause for celebration. At the national level, a U.S. Department of Justice report indicated that in 1995, the percentage of U.S. households which identified crime as a neighborhood problem had declined by only 0.4 percent since 1991. The authors of the report noted specifically that " . . .similar to the Nation's general pattern of violent victimization rates, household perceptions of crime as a problem rose during the late 1980's and early 1990's and then leveled off" (DeFrances and Smith, 1998:1). In contrast to this pattern, however, the researchers observed that the sharp decline in crime from 1994 to 1995 was accompanied by perceptions of crime that remained "relatively stable."

Similarly, at the local level, the results of polls targeting New York City residents also reveal perceptions of crime and feelings of safety that are not commensurate with the dramatic decrease in criminal occurrences reflected by police records.

It appears, therefore, that while official statistics indicate remarkable reductions in rates of crime commission, survey data suggests that there has **not** been a comparable reduction in the high levels of fear that burden the general public. This paradox is especially true for racial and ethnic minorities living in urban neighborhoods hardest hit by the violence "epidemic" of the late 1980's and early 1990's (Snyder, et al, 1996:14; Lattimore et al, 1997). Evidence from these locales suggests that reports of falling rates of crime have been met with skepticism, and are far less effective at reducing fear of crime than might be anticipated.

Why reports of dropping crime rates, especially reductions in crimes of a serious nature, have not led to increased feelings of safety for residents of one New York City neighborhood - Brownsville in Brooklyn - is the focus of this chapter.

PERCEPTIONS OF CRIME AND VICTIMIZATION EXPERIENCE:

It has been suggested that the gap between the reality of reduced crime and people's perception of crime as a continuing problem within certain neighborhoods is linked to the residents' likelihood of becoming a crime victim, which in turn is influenced by gender, race/ethnicity and economic status.[1]

In the Justice Department report cited previously, the researchers found that, "as a general matter, the gap between perceptions of crime and the actual experience of crime varied among different subpopulations." Included within the subpopulations which continued to perceive crime as a significant neighborhood problem in 1995 were Blacks, central city residents, renters of non-public housing and both Black and White residents of public housing.

The cumulative effect of these characteristics was also evident. Among central city residents, a higher percentage of Black than White households cited crime as a problem. And, among the residents of public housing projects, 25% of Black respondents, as compared to only 13% of White ones, considered crime to be a problem. This more widespread perception of crime as a neighborhood problem among Black residents of public housing projects might be due to the higher likelihood of criminal victimization that African-Americans face, in terms of both lethal and non-lethal violent crime (DeFrances and Smith, 1998).

However, this explanation alone is not satisfactory, given the fact that during the same time period (1995), the percentage of all Black households, reporting crime as a "problem" was almost 2.5 times greater than the percentage of White households expressing this view; even though the two groups of households experienced only a 4% difference in actual victimization. Twenty-seven percent of Black households compared to 23% of White households were victimized by one or more crimes during the course of a year. Narrowing the focus to urban households and violent crime victimization, the difference across race was even smaller. A difference of only 2% was found between the violent crime victimization of Black urban households and White urban households (DeFrances and Smith, 1998:2).

In New York City, where 70 percent of poor Blacks live in poverty-stricken neighborhoods while 70 percent of poor Whites live in nonpoverty neighborhoods (Sampson and Wilson, 1995)[2], perceptions of crime and vulnerability to victimization show clear patterns of difference. In a poll of New York City residents conducted by The New York Times in March of 1997, responses reflected that views of the "crime problem" varied by race, ethnicity and economic class. Of the roughly 1,400 respondents answering the question: "In the last four years, do you think that life in New York City has generally got better, or got worse or stayed the same?": 43% of Blacks and 40% of Hispanics felt that life had gotten worse, while only 25% of Whites shared that sentiment (Nagourney, 1997:A1). Comparable results were obtained in polls reported in the Daily News (Saltonstall, 1996) and Newsday (Willen, 1997).

In the 1997 Quinnipiac College poll featured by Newsday, 49% of New York City residents surveyed said they did not feel safer and 81% still considered crime a big problem.

Two-thirds of all respondents feared becoming a crime victim. Blacks and Hispanics were described as being "somewhat" less inclined to say that their communities were safer than in previous years.

In response to the question "Compared to 1990, do you now feel safer in your neighborhood?," the Daily News survey revealed that only 30% of all respondents reported feeling safer while 24% reported feeling **less** safe. The Daily News survey results are noted to have "exposed some compelling differences among ethnic groups" (Saltonstall, 1996:2). In addition, poor people generally were, "far more likely to say that the city feels 'less safe.'" A full 32% of residents earning less than $25,000 a year said that they felt **less** safe. Only 20% of those in upper income brackets shared this sense of greater vulnerability.

Given the poll results, it is little wonder that residents of Brownsville report not feeling safer despite significant drops in the community's level of crime. Brownsville Brooklyn is one of the City's poorest neighborhoods and has one of the highest murder rates of any community. According to the 1990 U.S. Census, 81% of the nearly 85,000 residents in the 73rd precinct were Black, and 17% were Hispanic. The median household income was only about $15,000. More than one third of all families received public assistance. An even greater proportion, 37% of all families, were living below the poverty line. Officially, in the recession year of 1990, the unemployment rate for males more than 16 years old stood at nearly 13%, the worst in any precinct. And in 1990, less than 6% of all residents were enrolled in college (NYPD Crime Analysis Unit, 1993).

OFFICIAL REPORTS OF SERIOUS CRIME IN THE 73RD PRECINCT

One of the complaints lodged against those who use official crime statistics to support the argument that minorities, especially African Americans, are primarily responsible for crime, and the consequent high levels of fear in urban neighborhoods, is that such statistics mix together both serious and non-serious offenses. The result of this mixing, it is argued, is an inflation of the number of minorities involved in crime, which in turn feeds feelings of fear within the communities (Mann, 1993). In an effort to circumvent this argument, the focus here is on official statistics for serious crimes.

Homicides

For purposes of this discussion, the term "serious" will be limited to felony offenses which if resulting in a conviction, exposes the offender to a sentence of imprisonment for one year or more; and/or acts which involve the actual, threatened, or potential use of physical harm to another human being. With regards to the offense of homicide, Table 1 presents the statistics for Brownsville for the years 1993 to 1995. As noted by Lattimore et al (1997:1), one advantage of examining homicide statistics is that the offense of homicide "represents the most serious level of violence and is the most precisely measured offense in the Nation's crime-reporting systems."

Table 8-1:
Homicides* and Clearances 1993 to 1995 for the 73rd Precinct in Brooklyn

1993	1994	1995	
78	50	29	Total Homicides
74	48	28	Less Justifiables
32	20	18	Current Year Clearances**
8	16	16	Prior Year Clearances

Source: Records of the 73rd Precinct Detective Squad

*Homicide is the broad legal term referring to the killing of a human being. Consistent with the classification of crimes under the FBI's Uniform Crime Reports, Table 2 uses the narrower term, "murder" to account for murders and non-negligent homicides, excluding those deaths ruled justifiable. These distinctions may account for any numerical differences in "homicides" versus "murders" shown on the Table 8-1 and Table 8-2 for the years 1993, 1994, and 1995.
**The term "clearance" refers to those homicide incidents that resulted in the arrest of a suspect.

The Brownsville section of Brooklyn is located within the 73rd police precinct. An examination of Table 1 reveals significant decline in the number of homicides known to the police from 1993 to 1994 and from 1994 to 1995. Once the total number of homicides for each year is adjusted to omit those there were determined to be justifiable (i.e. committed under legally defensible circumstances), precinct records indicate that in 1994 and 1995 the total number of homicides dropped by 26 and then an additional 20 deaths. Thus, the two-year span represents a decrease in the number of homicides by more than 50%.

If homicides in Brownsville are typical of the national patterns, it can also be assumed that a significant number of the slayings were intra-racial, involved acquaintances, and were committed by a firearm (Witkin, 1998; NCVS, 1997; Lattimore et al, 1997; Snyder et al, 1996). Consequently, when interviewing individuals about their perceptions of crime, interviewers were keyed into listening for information in these areas.

However, among those interviewed, residents of the community lacked awareness of the significant drop in the murder rate. Most found it hard to believe; and, several reported hearing as much gunfire as ever. One young mother expressed fear for the safety of her children and noted that she plans to move. Thus, despite official evidence that within a three-year period, killings in Brownsville had decreased by more than half, residents did not feel more safe.

Other Serious Offenses
In addition to the falling rates of homicide, the figures in Table 2 indicate that the Brownsville section of Brooklyn is a community that statistically seems to have benefited a great deal from the general, citywide decline in violence and theft since 1990.

Table 8-2:

SERIOUS CRIME IN BROWNSVILLE, BROOKLYN
73rd Precinct, 1990-1996

Type of Crime	Number Of Cases Known To The Police							
	Year							Change
	1990	*1991*	*1992*	*1993*	*1994*	*1995*	*1996*	*1990-1996*
Murder	60	78	63	74	47	27	34	43%
Rape	113	82	93	80	82	66	75	-34%
Robbery	2,914	2,900	2,368	2,316	1,839	1,465	1,024	-65%
Fel. Assault	1,519	1,368	1,219	1,205	1,066	981	857	-44%
Burglary	1,313	1,214	903	776	882	619	555	-58%
Grand Larceny	1,293	1,019	1,018	966	815	647	436	-66%
Vehicle Theft	1,031	866	939	733	545	418	337	-67%

Source: NYPD Complaints and Arrests Annual Reports, 1990 - 1996, for the 73rd Precinct

These figures, drawn from records kept by the police in the 73rd precinct, indicate that compared to the grave dangers that prevailed at the start of the decade, by 1996, the residents of Brownsville faced greatly reduced risks of being killed, wounded, robbed, or raped. As shown in Table 2, the chances that burglars and car thieves would steal their personal possessions also dropped sharply.

In fact, the last column in Table 2 confirms that by 1996, incidents of serious crime in Brownsville were down dramatically across the board. Robberies, grand larcenies and motor vehicle thefts were only one-third the problem they had been in 1990. And, burglaries, murders and rapes were down by between 34% and 58%.

Yet, when interviewed in 1996 and 1998, local residents (and persons who provide services to the local residents), questioned whether their security had really improved. There were even allegations that the official statistics had been manipulated in order to further some unknown political purpose.

There are any number of factors which may have led to this mistrust of statistical reports issued by government agencies. Included among them could be the fact that when the community asked for its own high school (so its students would not have to travel to the adjoining community of East New York), city officials gave them a juvenile correctional facility instead. Surely this sent conflicting messages to residents who were supposed to believe that crime was subsiding as a serious problem. If the community was getting safer, why would it need to lock up more of its youth? And secondly, the residents of Brownsville may have gotten the impression that key decision-makers view their community as composed of people who need or deserve punishment more than education.

Indeed, these are both loaded questions to which there can probably be no agreed upon honest answers. It is important to note, however, that given the results of the various polls,

Brownsville is not atypical. Evidence that other neighborhoods have continued to regard crime as a serious problem despite police statistics that document declines in crime, suggests that there is a real problem that warrants addressing.

COMMUNITY PERCEPTIONS OF CRIME IN BROWNSVILLE: 1996-1998

As noted previously, recognition of the gap between the perception of crime and safety, versus official reports of crime in Brownsville, grew out of an analysis of results from qualitative interviews conducted with community residents, service providers, and political figures. While, to date, the sample is relatively small, encompassing approximately 30 individuals and 20 organizations, there is little to suggest that the sentiments expressed below are not representative of a meaningful portion of the population.

Findings From Interviews With Community Residents

During 1996 two sets of group interviews were held with John Jay College students who lived or worked in Brownsville. The interviews were designed to gather information regarding the students' perceptions and impressions of life in Brownsville with the advent of declining crime. The students were asked how their neighborhood had changed over the two-year period beginning approximately February, 1994. Interview questions were drawn around five major areas: the homicide rate; policing in the precinct; the local drug scene; handgun carrying; and positive developments within the community. Six students participated in the interviews. There were an equal number of men and women respondents.

Responses regarding the homicide rate have been reported earlier in this chapter. However, it warrants reiterating that all of the students were unaware of the decline.

When asked about the police in the precinct, three respondents stated that they did not have the impression that officers were present in greater numbers. They noted that the police only seemed to appear in response to emergency calls to 911. The other respondents did feel that police presence had increased, particularly in the form of plainclothes and undercover officers. The majority of the respondents had the impression that the precinct's officers, including the truant patrol, were more aggressive in stopping, frisking and questioning people. However, they also noted that a downside to the increased police activity was that innocent people got caught up in the drug sweeps.

Regarding the drug scene, most of the respondents confirmed that drug activity has moved indoors to hallways, apartments, or corner grocery stores. Only one student was aware of heroin being sold in the neighborhood; most thought that the main drugs for sale were marijuana and crack cocaine. At the time of these interviews, by all accounts, plenty of crack vials still littered the ground in parks and other public areas. The respondents reported that numerous crack houses were still operating at full potential. It was also reported by one respondent that some school security guards purposely ignored drug activity at schools and others even took part in it. All respondents noted that juveniles were still heavily involved in the drug trade, acting as steerers or couriers.

On a related note, none of the respondents felt safe regarding the issue of handgun carrying. They had no confidence in the possibility that youth were unarmed or less likely to be carrying handguns. They were not convinced by data that suggested that youths were leaving their guns at home.

While the respondents did not perceive any improvement in the availability of jobs, they did report perceptions of some positive developments. Some of them had the impression that a substantial number of housing units were being rehabilitated. They were also aware of a number of existing programs to benefit young people, but, they did not detect any evidence of expansion or greater outreach by those programs.

Perceptions Among Service Providers and Political Figures

Two sets of interviews were conducted with service providers and political figures. The first interviews were conducted during 1996 and the second set took place in March of 1998. The responses from individuals in this group were more mixed, with a leaning towards being more positive than those of the community residents; however, in several subject areas, the responses of service providers and political figures mirrored those of the community residents. For example, among the service providers and political figures interviewed in 1996, there was no perception that firearms were less available to youth. However, there was a belief that the increased police presence made young people reluctant to use their handguns. There was no belief in the notion that there were fewer guns on the street.

While the aggressive, problem-oriented approach of the police was somewhat welcomed by this group of respondents, there was a clear perception that police brutality occasionally occurred against innocent residents. This caused the respondents to be rather guarded in their praise for the police. They did, however, feel that the increased police presence reflected greater interest in the community and had the potential for improved police-community relations. The crackdown by the local precinct on minor quality of life offenses was perceived as having had some role in the reduction of more serious crimes.

In 1996, there was general agreement that neighborhood improvements were taking place, particularly the rehabilitation of vacant lots and buildings, along with enhanced investment in both private and government subsidized housing. Besides these important positive developments on the housing front, the respondents believed new businesses were being attracted to commercial avenues in the area.

Responses during the March 1998 interviews were less positive. One respondent stated plainly that s/he (phrased this way to protect the anonymity of the person interviewed) questions whether there is a real decrease in crime. S/he believes that the statistics are being manipulated by the police--that the Department is intentionally fostering the illusion of declining crime rates to suit their own purposes. S/he also has a sense that gang activity and prostitution involving juvenile and young adult males and females is on the rise in Brownsville. On the other hand, the respondent acknowledges that there has been a decrease in the juvenile delinquency caseload within the agency where s/he provided services.

In contrast to residents, one service provider believes that there are less young people involved in the local drug trade; although s/he also believes that the community's youth were attracted towards drug trade involvement because of the lack of legitimate economic opportunities within the neighborhood. S/he also believes that police presence had increased, but that this fact has been a mixed blessing. S/he noted that, overall, community policing and the targeting of drug locations for enforcement efforts has had positive effects on reducing crime over the past year and has helped to establish a better relationship between the police and the community.

However, s/he complained that Black males in particular are indiscriminately subjected to harassment by aggressive police tactics and that some police officers are very verbally abusive towards community residents. In the respondent's experience, community policing has not achieved its full positive potential because some police officers treat members of the community disrespectfully.

TOWARDS COMBATTING FEAR

In sum, the good news is that crime is down in New York City. The bad news is that not everyone believes it. Some New Yorkers don't trust the official count. Others are simply unaware of these dramatic trends, despite all the publicity surrounding the City's "comeback." One serious negative consequence of this situation is that residents lacking either trust or awareness continue to be fearful of crime. Fear of crime paralyzes neighborhoods, breeds mistrust, and drives criminal justice policy decisions that have unintended counter-productive consequences. (The current controversy surrounding the extremely severe penalties for possessing or selling crack as opposed to powdered cocaine, growing out of legislation enacted during the height of the crack epidemic, is but one example).

Those most vulnerable to crime--minorities, urban dwellers, occupants of rental property, and the poor--are also those most fearful; although, it appears that their fear is disproportionate to their actual victimization. Given the apparent disconnection between actual rates of crime and fear of victimization, it may be argued that for some New Yorkers, perhaps it is as important to measure and combat their level of fear, as it is to actually reduce the risks they face. The results of interviews reported above, clearly indicate that it is not enough for officials to proclaim that crime rates are down. They must also devise ways to make members of high-crime communities feel safer. This is the challenge.

Despite efforts to implement community policing and to create a more racially and ethnically diverse police force, members of minority communities in considerable numbers do not trust the police or the statistics that police departments compile. Ironically, some of the very tactics designed to help communities feel safer, particularly drug sweeps and other aggressive police investigations, have occasionally had the effect of exacerbating feelings of mistrust, in both directions -- community towards police and police towards community. This lack of trust retards the development of cooperative alliances that might help foster feelings of safety and further reduce crime.

What then is the solution to building trust and helping community members feel safer? Some suggest that a stronger bond between police and community can be achieved by requiring that officers live within the city. Poll results indicate that this approach is particularly appealing to Blacks and Hispanics. Seventy-eight percent of Black respondents and 73% of Hispanic interviewees favored residency requirements for officers in a recent survey (Willen, 1997). Other suggestions for reform include requiring "hands-on" training within the community, as a supplement to academy training for new recruits; and the inclusion of comments from members of the community as a component in annual evaluations of active precinct officers (Alpert and Dunham, 1997).

Whatever the approach or combination of approaches taken, efforts at trust-building must be continuous, with special precautions taken to modify police strategies and tactics that have been shown to have the potential for recreating mistrust. The preliminary findings from the Brownsville field study demonstrate that what is necessary is an ongoing give-and-take process open to community feedback and subject to adjustment over time.

Acknowledgements:

The author appreciates the significant field research contributions made by Dr. Benjamin Bowling of Cambridge University and Dr. Rosalea Hamilton, formerly of John Jay College and now in Jamaica, West Indies.

References

Alpert, G. and R. Dunham (1997). Policing Urban America, 3rd ed., Prospect Heights, IL: Waveland Press, Inc.

City of New York, Department of City Planning, (1993). Socioeconomic Profiles: A Portrait of New York City Community Districts, 1980 and 1990, Censuses of Population and Housing. New York City.

DeFrances, C. and S. Smith (1998). "Perceptions of Neighborhood Crime, 1995." Bureau of Justice Statistics Special Report, U.S. Department of Justice. Washington, DC: Office of Justice Programs.

Lattimore, P. et al (1997). Homicide in Eight U.S. Cities: Trends, Contexts, and Policy Implications, National Institute of Justice Research Report. Washington, DC: Office of Justice Programs.

Mann, C. (1993). Unequal Justice, Bloomington, IN: Indiana University Press.

Nagourney, A. (1997). "Poll finds optimism in New York, but race and class affect views." The New York Times, March 12, p. A1, B4.

National Crime Victimization Survey Report (NCVS) (1997). Criminal victimization in the U.S., 1994, U.S. Department of Justice. Washington, DC: Bureau of Justice Statistics.

New York City Police Department (1993). Selected 1990 Census Socio-economic Indicators By Precinct. New York: Crime Analysis Unit.

New York City Police Department (1990-1996). Complaints and arrests statistical report. New York: NYPD Crime Analysis Unit.

Saltonstall, D. (1996). "City coming back, New Yorkers roar." Daily News, Sept. 29, p. 2.

Sampson, R. and W. J. Wilson, Jr. (1995). "Toward a theory of race, crime and urban inequality." In J. Hagan and R. Peterson, (Eds.), Crime and Inequality, Stanford, CA: Stanford University Press.

Snyder, H., Sickmund, M., and E. Poe-Yamagata (1996). Juvenile Offenders and Victims: 1996 Update on Violence. Office of Juvenile Justice and Delinquency Prevention, Washington, DC: U.S. Department of Justice, Office of Justice Programs.

Willen, L. (1997). "Poll: New Yorkers want cops to live in City." Newsday, February 13, p. A32.

Witkin, G. (1998). "The crime bust," U.S. News and World Report. May 25, 1998, p. 28-37.

Chapter 9

THE CHANGING ECONOMY, DISENTITLEMENT AND THE GROWING INVOLVEMENT OF WOMEN IN STREET CRIME

by

Professor Joan Hoffman

Economics Division, Department of Public Management

THE IMPORTANCE OF TAKING ECONOMIC CONDITIONS INTO ACCOUNT WHEN STUDYING CRIME

Macroeconomic conditions can have an impact on crime in several ways. One way is by shaping the structure of legal opportunities available to people, depending in part on their gender, race, class and age. Another way is through cyclical variations in factors such as unemployment and inflation that affect economic standing and opportunities. A third way that the economy can influence criminal activity is by changing the characteristics of work itself, such as bringing about a shift from a manufacturing-based to a service-based job market.

The structural analysis carried out in this chapter will examine the impact of macroeconomic conditions in New York City in recent decades on women's arrest rates for the street crimes of robbery, burglary, possession of stolen property, motor vehicle theft, gambling, and possession or sale of illegal drugs. The economic conditions that affect poor women who largely lack marketable skills will be closely examined. These women who have the fewest options in the legal economy are the most likely to be drawn into illegal moneymaking activities and become exposed to arrest. In this chapter, economic opportunity is conceptualized in terms of entitlements, which extend beyond the normal market measures such as income from employment and can include government programs and family and community rights (Sen, 1977; Osmani, 1995). Unemployment and welfare benefits and access to community soup kitchens would be examples of entitlements in a city like New York. Disentitlement can be defined as the deterioration of legal economic opportunities; disentitlement enhances the attractions of the illegal economy (Hoffman, 1997a).

Besides economic conditions, women's arrest rates for street crimes are also affected by demographic factors and by police policies.

Changes in New York City's Economy That Could Affect Crime Rates

Since the 1960's, the entire U.S. economy has undergone a structural transformation due the globalization of production and the computerization of work. These changes have had a marked impact on the economy of New York City. Industrial jobs that are open to persons with limited marketable skills have been disappearing from the City's economy. There has been a steady drop in the number of manufacturing jobs since the start of the 1960's; as a result, fewer New Yorkers are employed in the low skill occupational categories termed "operators and laborers." The occupational category which contains clerical work has also shrunk in size since 1970. In contrast, highly skilled managerial and professional work has grown steadily over this time period (See Table 9-1).

In addition to the decline in low skill positions, there has been a marked change in the conditions of work. The economic climate has made it politically possible to hold back increases in the minimum wage; the purchasing power of minimum wage workers has fallen over much of the past three decades and was actually lower in 1996 than in 1960. Furthermore, the reliance by employers on part-time and temporary labor across the U.S. and in New York City has grown dramatically. The number of people involuntarily working only part-time or temporarily, increased during the 1970's, 1980's, and again during the recession of the early 1990's (Carre' and Tilly, 1998). This transformation of the job market has exacerbated existing inequalities of class, race, and gender because these positions pay less and lack fringe benefits like health insurance. As a result of these economic transformations, the proportion of New Yorkers in the lowest economic class (those receiving less than 80% of the median income for all city employees) has grown, and their absolute and relative poverty has increased, according to a variety of measures. From 1960 to 1990, analysis of U.S. Census data shows that the percent of families receiving less than 80% of the City's median income more than doubled. Almost half of all New Yorkers lived in low income families in 1996, and despite a period of relative improvement in the 1980's, this proportion was higher in 1996 than at the end of the 1970's (see Table 2). The real purchasing power of the incomes of these poor households fell steadily over this period and averaged only $7,770 in 1996. Meanwhile, the relative incomes of the New Yorkers in the richest class climbed. The ratio of upper to lower class income widened from about 12 to one in 1977 to 17 to one in 1996. In other words, within New York City, the rich became richer and the poor became poorer.

Educational credentials have grown in importance. There has been a steady rise in the proportion of persons without a high school degree in the lowest economic class. Due to the cumulative disadvantages of racism and sexism, minorities and women were especially unlikely to be prepared for the structural transformations of the late 20th century. By 1996, about two-thirds of female headed households in New York were in this lowest economic class (see Table 9-2). The lower educational attainment of minorities as well as the informal barriers of racism they encounter in school and at work both contribute to the lower earnings of black and Hispanic New Yorkers. The proportion of the labor force without high school degrees is significantly higher for minorities than for whites; but even minorities with similar levels of education earn less than whites. In fact, in both 1980 and 1990, white workers without high school degrees made more money on average than minorities who were high school graduates, and even most minorities who have taken some college courses (Department of City Planning, 1995: 40-45). Furthermore, minority unemployment rates are consistently higher than those of whites, as are minority rates of involuntary part-time employment, according to figures released by the U.S. Bureau of Labor Statistics.

During the economic transformation, many female-headed households slid down into the lowest income class as a shift in family structure occurred. The proportion of families that fit the two parent norm has been declining steadily since the 1960's. By 1990, about 30% of all households were headed by women who were raising children, and nearly half of the children growing up in New York City were not living in a married couple family (see Table 3). Increasingly, low income women had to balance the day-to-day responsibilities of raising children with their need to earn money, limiting them to part-time jobs and making it more difficult for them to attain an education.

A housing crisis has exacerbated the above problems. There has been a growing gap between the need for and the supply of decent low cost housing, both in the City and across the country. Furthermore, during this time of need, the Federal government has ceased to add to the supply of public housing, although government housing benefits for the middle and upper classes (in the form of tax write-offs for mortgage payments) continue (Barry 1998). Homelessness has been one result of this crisis. Increasingly, the homeless population consists of women and children. And, of course, homelessness creates many barriers to obtaining employment and earning a living wage that could support a family. The net effect of these changes from the 1960's to the 1990's has been a structural shift that has resulted in a disentitlement of women with limited marketable skills. They have lost purchasing power as the number of unskilled jobs and real wages have declined. If these women live with partners who also have limited job skills, these partners have also lost occupational opportunities and experienced a decline in real earnings. If these women are raising children alone, they have lost the expected family entitlement of the other parent's earnings. Furthermore, access to low income housing has declined, and government housing entitlements for low income people have shrunk. Finally, for reasons similar to those that held down the real value of the minimum wage, the purchasing power of welfare payments, the major nonmarket entitlement to income for poor women, has declined steadily since the mid-seventies and has been lower than the 1960 level since the early 1980s , according to Department of Social Services statistics. In sum, poor women with low skills have been struggling to survive in a city with rising rents, fragmenting families, shrinking job opportunities, declining remuneration for work, and a diminishing real value of public assistance support payments.

The Growth of Illegal Opportunities

At the same time that the ongoing economic transformation was shrinking legal opportunities for poor and low skilled women, the illegal drug economy was expanding. Illegal drugs are used by many groups, from prosperous people to poverty-stricken persons (Inciardi, Lockwood, and Pottieger, 1993; Hill and Crawford, 1990: 614, 621). But, ever since the turn of the century, illegal drug selling markets have been concentrated in inner cities (Inciardi, Lockwood, and Pottieger, 1993). Thus, poor and minority women are more likely than others to be exposed to the opportunities that abound within the drug business. Research shows that poor women are drawn to work in the illegal economy for primary employment, or for supplemental income, and/or to support their own drug habits (Inciardi, Lockwood, and Pottieger, 1993: 33-35).

The advent of crack cocaine in the mid 1980's attracted even more poor women into the illegal drug economy. While women had largely resisted snorting cocaine and injecting heroin, crack was readily smokable. Poor women who smoke crack are more likely to be arrested than more affluent users because the latter can buy discretely from an intermediary (at work, for instance) (Hoffman, 1997a). Furthermore, abusers of addictive substances like crack are unlikely to make bulk purchases for future use, as marijuana users do. Thus, there is a greater risk of arrest per transaction or "per hit" of crack than of marijuana.

Thus, an increase in arrests of poor women for street crimes would be expected over the period of this study, 1960 to 1996. Given the nature of the prevailing socioeconomic institutions and the City's demographics, it would be expected that these arrests would be disproportionately of minority women.

THE ECONOMY'S IMPACT ON THE CRIME PROBLEM

Women's Arrest Rates for Street Crimes: 1960-1996

The above analysis of the economic problems burdening poor women in New York City leads to the prediction that as their legal opportunities decline, their involvement in illegal activities should correspondingly increase. Therefore, women's arrest rates should be significantly linked to the intensifying economic disentitlement of women. The expectation is that poor, low skilled women would be increasingly drawn into the illegal economy both for economic gain and because of dependence on drugs. To test this hypothesis, women's arrest rates for seven street crimes were examined for the years 1960-1996. The crimes are drug sale or possession, robbery, burglary, larceny, motor vehicle theft, stolen property possession, and gambling. Both per capita arrest rates and female arrests as a percent of total arrests were tracked. The general patterns of and trends in arrests appear in Graphs 1, 2, 3, and 4. These patterns and trends will be discussed and then analyzed in terms of the explanatory power of demographics, deployment of police resources, business cycles and economic transformation.

Demographics

When the proportion of the population that is between 15 and 29 years old grows, criminologists anticipate a rise in crime. In New York City, this age group grew during the 1960's and 1970's and could thus be a part of the reason for a rise in women's arrest rates for some crimes during these decades. However, the role of demographics (see Table 4) as a dominant explanation for changing crime rates is undermined by several factors. Although this age group was expanding, there was a sharp drop in arrests for drugs and gambling in the early 1970's (see Graph 2). Furthermore, women's arrest rates rose sharply for drugs and robbery in the 1980's even though the size of this crime-prone age group was declining. So there must be other factors, besides sheer demographics, that influence involvement in criminal activity and arrest rates.

Police Resources and Policies

More police officers can make more arrests. Changes in the number of police officers available to make arrests (data not shown on the graphs) appear to be correlated to some degree with women's arrest patterns for some crimes during some periods. However, during other time periods, arrest rates unexpectedly move in the opposite direction from personnel availability. During the 1960's, both the size of the police force and the number of women arrested grew (but so did the crime-prone age group, as previously discussed). A sharp drop in NYPD personnel took place during the 1970's, but women's arrest rates leveled off rather than dropped, except for drugs and gambling. The drug arrest drop was due in part to a specific policy decision to de-emphasize arrests of users and street level dealers (Hoffman, 1997a). The gambling decline resulted from the withdrawal of personnel available to make discretionary arrests as the contracted police force concentrated its resources on more serious crimes. The increased hiring of police officers since the 1980's is most clearly reflected in drug arrests, but the drug arrest pattern shows greater variability than the personnel pattern. For the other crimes, arrest rates rise and fall in a manner that differs from the slow but steady rise in police personnel from 1980 to the present.

Since 1994, the NYPD has intensified "quality of life" arrests in high crime areas, based on the theory that perpetrators of more serious crimes also engage in minor crimes and might thus be at least temporarily deterred or perhaps apprehended. In the mid-1990's, drug arrests hit all time highs while apprehensions for robberies, motor vehicle thefts, and possession of stolen property declined (review Graphs 1 and 2). A cause and effect relationship is possible. However, these crimes were falling before 1994; meanwhile, burglary arrests increased. Also, it is important to note that even with the drops in arrests, and the fact that the number of police in uniform in the nineties is lower than in the 1960's, women's arrests were running at a higher rate in the 1990's than in the 1960's. Apparently, the availability and deployment of police personnel do have an effect on arrest rates during some periods; but again, it is not the only or dominant explanation for the overall arrest patterns and trends between 1960 and 1996.

Business Cycles

Periods of business contraction, when the City's economy was gripped by a national recession and jobs become harder to find, are indicated by the dashed vertical lines in Graphs 1 and 2. Since there have been four recessions since 1960 and arrest rates for seven crimes are being tracked, it is not easy to summarize the relationships. In general, the two graphs reveal that for some crimes the business cycles are compatible with arrest patterns: during recessions when unemployment rises, arrest rates also go up (reflecting greater involvement in illegal activities by women desperate for cash). But for other time periods and different crimes, the cycles do not correspond to the arrest patterns and often move in counterintuitive directions. For example, arrests for robbery and possession of stolen property did rise during the 1969-70 contraction, as did burglary and stolen property arrests in mid-1970's downturn. However, arrests for robberies and burglaries rose during the economic expansion of the late 1980's, when unemployment rates dropped. Furthermore, arrest rates for all of the street crimes except gambling dropped during the 1990's contraction (review Graphs 1 and 2). Therefore, arrests do not necessarily rise during hard times and fall during periods of relative prosperity.

There are several reasons why the impact of business cycles may not be reflected in arrest rates. For one thing, their effects can be swamped by police resource allocation, such as the decrease in hiring during the mid-seventies contraction, when New York City suffered through a fiscal crisis (Hoffman, 1983). Also, these periods of contraction are relatively short and may largely affect the exit from the labor force of more skilled rather than less skilled workers (Kohfield and Sprague, 1988; Hoffman, 1997a). The net effect of boom and bust economic cycles on low skilled women who commit street crimes may be to increase their long term unemployment. The rehiring rate for this group of women during periods of economic recovery may be low. A study of time lagged effects of the business cycle on arrest rates for specific crimes might show more discernible connections.

Structural Change

When the entire period from the 1960's to 1996 is considered, the overall pattern of women'sarrests strongly suggests that the transformation of the City's economy that reduced the legal entitlements of poor women had an impact on their participation in street crime. Arrest rates for six of the seven street crimes (all except gambling) were higher in 1996 than in 1960 (review Graphs 1 and 2). The structural change theory helps to explain patterns that seem to contradict expectations based on demographic trends and police personnel availability. Arrest rates have increased even though the size of the police force has not yet returned to its level in 1960. As for demographics, the decline in the proportion of the city's population that is between 15 and 29 years old leads to the expectation of lower arrests rates these days than several decades ago, but they are higher in the 1990's (except for gambling).

Women's Involvement, As Compared to Men's, In Street Crime

To examine the possibility of women's growing participation in what was formerly the overwhelmingly male-dominated field of street crime, breakdowns of arrestees by sex were calculated. The percentages of all females arrested for robbery, burglary, motor vehicle theft, and possession of stolen property, appear in Graph 3. The proportions of females arrested for drug sale/possession, larceny and gambling appear in Graph 4.

These two graphs indicate that most of the people arrested for street crimes in New York City continue to be mostly boys and men, not girls and women. However, these graphs also show that the percent of arrestees who were female has risen, and for all seven street crimes are significantly higher in the 1990's than in the 1960's. Since male involvement in street crime generally has gone up over the years, female involvement has soared even faster. In recent years, certain crime categories - larceny, possession of stolen property, robbery, and motor vehicle theft- have manifested particularly steep rises in the percent of arrestees who were female. Even when arrest rates declined in the mid-1990's, women's proportions did not drop back to the level of the 1960's.

Even though women's arrests rates are still much lower than men's, there is evidence that women have, over the long run, become more involved in illegal economic activities. An important driving force behind women's participation in crimes such as robbery, motor vehicle theft, and burglary is drug abuse. As has been discussed, the increased participation of poor women with few marketable skills in the drug economy can be significantly related to their limited opportunities in the legal economy.

Crime-Fighting Strategies

The economic analysis presented above has indicated that the structural changes in New York City's economy have hurt the chances of women with limited marketable skills to pull themselves out of poverty. Unfortunately, as a result, a growing number of poor women have become caught up in the illegal drug economy and have been arrested for committing street crimes. However, it is critical to note, that although women have experienced significant economic disentitlement, their arrest rates for street crimes are still much lower than those of men. This suggests that the role of gender in explaining reactions to impoverishment and

Table 1   Shift in Occupational Structure

Percent of employed persons (16+) in Occupations

	Operators & Laborers	Admlinistrative Support including Clerical	Managerial & Professonal
1960	22.4*	21.0* **	20.7*
1970	18	26.2	22.5
1980	14.5	24.9	25.8
1990	11.6	20.6	30.6

NYC Dept of City Planning. 1995   *age 14 plus   ** clerical & kindred

Table 2   Percent of New Yorkers with Low Class Income
(less than 80% of famliy adjusted median income)

	1977	1989	1991	1996
% persons living in families	45.7	41.1	41.9	48.6
% Black persons living in famlies	59	50	52	60
% female headed households	71.6	56.5	67.9	67.2
% with less than highschool degree	68.3	68.2	72.5	79.6

Rise of absolute and relative poverty in Lowest Class

	1977	1989	1991	1996
Real($1996) low class hshold income	8014	7792	7159	7770
Ratio:Upper/low class income	11.894	12.067	13.703	17.006

Source:McMahon, Thomas, Larian Angelo and John Mollenkopf. 1997.
    "Hollow in the Middle". Finance Divison, New York City Council .

Table 3 Shift in Family structure

	1960	1970	1980	1990
married couples as % of famlies	0.846	0.7939	0.6845	0.6331
% children under 18 living with both married couple parents	83.4*	72.6*	58.0**	52.2**

* living with both parents   ** in married couple famliy

 Bureau of the Census, Census of the Population (1960,1970,1980,1990); GPO,
      1980-90 source:NYC Department of City Planning. 1992. " Demographi

Table 4   Young Women (15-29) as % of NYC Population

Year	1960	1970	1980	1990*
Percent	19.1	22.4	24.7	22.9

US Census of the Population (1960,1970,1980,1990); GPO, Washington, D.C.
NYC Department of City Planning. 1995. "Population Projections.."
* Estimates for the year 2000 also indicate a shrinkagein this age goup.

arrests per 100.000 women

Graph 1 : Women's Arrest Rates: NYC, 1960-96

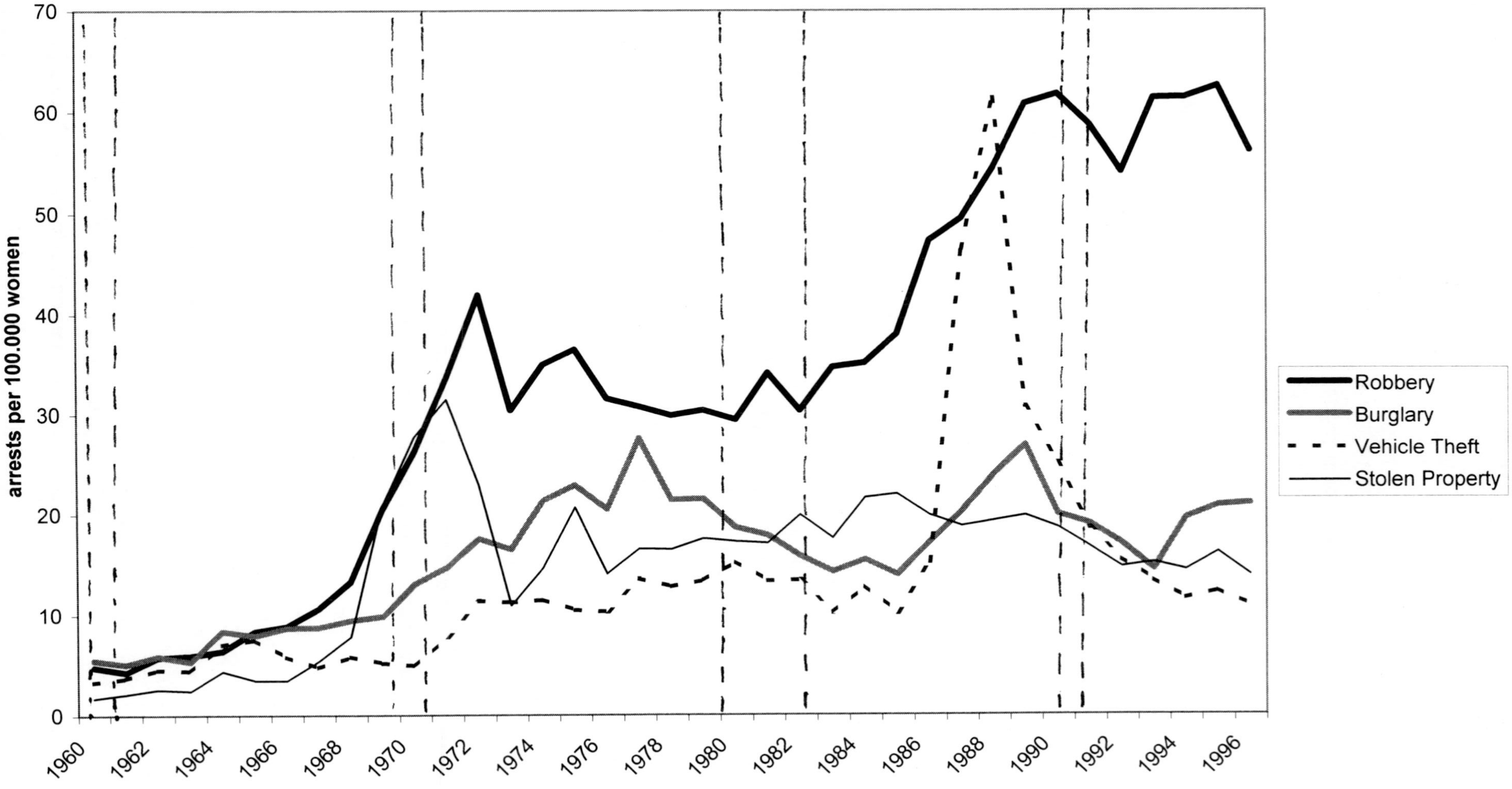

Robbery
Burglary
Vehicle Theft
Stolen Property

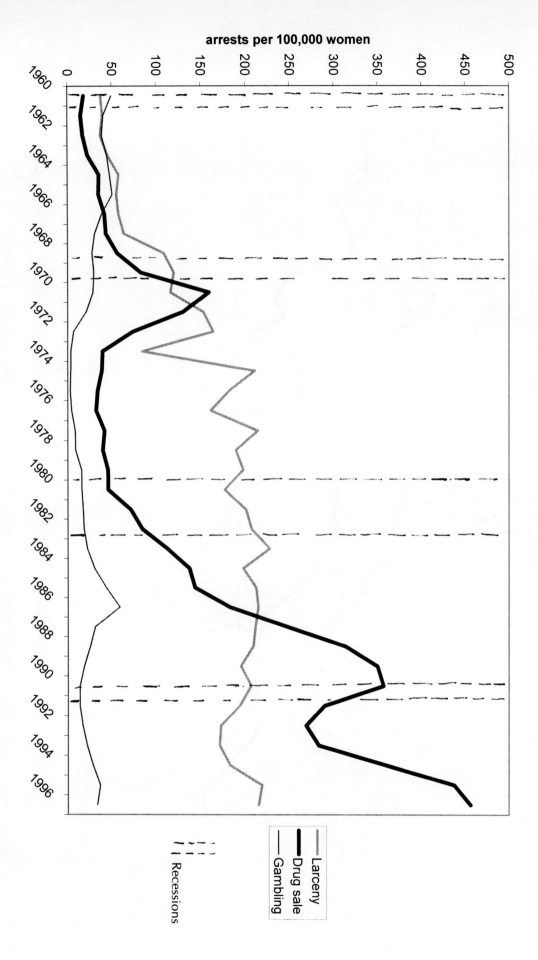

Graph 2 : Women's Arrest Rates: NYC, 1960-96

arrests per 100,000 women

Larceny
Drug sale
Gambling

Recessions

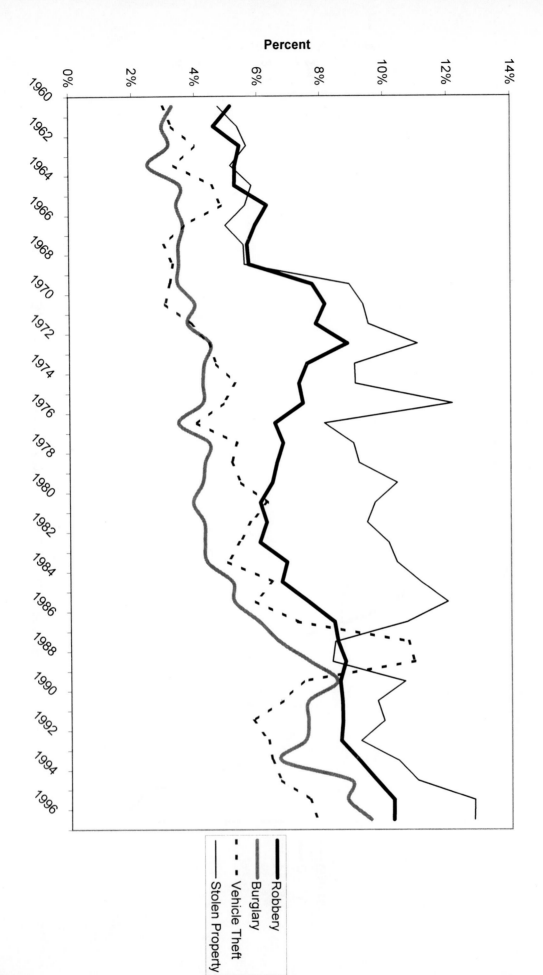

Graph 3 : NYC Female Arrests As A Percent Of Total Arrests: 1960-96

Percent

0%
2%
4%
6%
8%
10%
12%
14%

1960
1962
1964
1966
1968
1970
1972
1974
1976
1978
1980
1982
1984
1986
1988
1990
1992
1994
1996

Robbery
Burglary
Vehicle Theft
Stolen Property

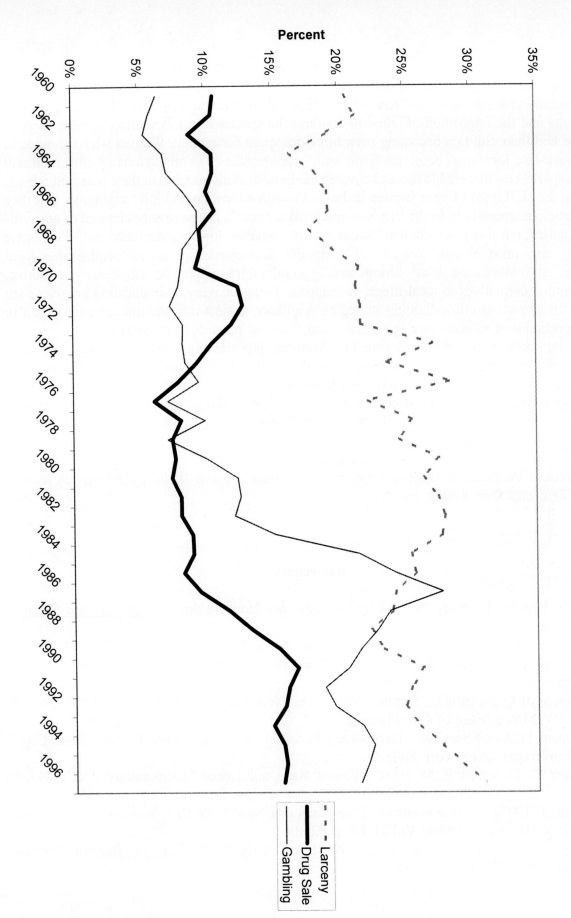

Graph 4: NYC Female Arrests As A Percent Of Total Arrests: 1960-96

Percent

35%
30%
25%
20%
15%
10%
5%
0%

1960
1962
1964
1966
1968
1970
1972
1974
1976
1978
1980
1982
1984
1986
1988
1990
1992
1994
1996

Larceny
Drug Sale
Gambling

involvement in illegal activities remains an important topic of research.

Several policy recommendations flow from the above findings about the importance of the economy as a motivation for committing crimes. Recent reductions in the amount of welfare payments and the imposition of time limits raise the specter of an increasing number of poor women and their children becoming even more desperate for money. Women who are made to take work-fare jobs must be given "grow skill" opportunities - combinations of education and work experience - that enable them to develop marketable skills suitable to their potential talents. Raising the skill level of poor women and men through education and job training, so that they can participate more fully in the City's restructured economy, is a necessary element of any anti-crime policy, but it is not sufficient. Access to safe, reliable, low cost day-care and low income housing also must become available. Community development programs emphasizing local services and mandating local hiring and apprenticeships might be particularly effective, augmenting alternatives to local illegal economies. Drug recovery and education programs are called for as well as crime-fighting strategies. Vigilance against informal racism and sexism in the apportionment of economic opportunity and financial rewards must continue.

Research shows that investing in education, job training, child nurturing, and anti-discrimination efforts pay off in the long run in the form of higher growth rates for the economy as a whole (Hoffman, 1997b). While such investments cost taxpayers money, so too does spending for police protection, arrest processing, court proceedings, jails, prison, probation, drug treatment, parole and other criminal justice expenditures.

Acknowledgments:
I appreciate the excellent work of my research assistant Antonia Walker, the research help of David Erps and Sara Russel.

References

Barry, S. January/ February 1998. "City Families Face Housing Squeeze."Dollars and Sense. #215:32-36.
Carre', F., & Tilly, C. "Part-Time and Temporary Work." Dollars and Sense. #215:22-25.
Department of City Planning. August 1992. "Demographic Profiles."NYC Department of City Planning.
Department of City Planning. Summer 1995. "The New York City Labor Force 1970, 1980 & 1990." NYC Department of City Planning.
Department of Social Services. "Dependency Economic and Social Data for New York City." Annual (averages). New York State.
Hill, Gary C., Crawford, E. M. 1990. "Women, Race, and Crime." Criminology Vol. 28 No. 4: 601-25.
Hoffman, J. 1997a. " Macroeconomic Conditions and New York City Women's Drug Arrest Rates: 1960-88."Social Justice Vol.24. No.1:.82-106.
Hoffman, Joan. 1983. "New York City Fiscal Crisis." Review of Radical Political Economy.15(3): 29-58.

Hoffman, Joan. 1997b. "Maintaining the Roots of Economic Development in an Era of Globalized Production Futures." Vol. 29. No. 9:811-25.

Inciardi, James A., Lockwood, D., Pottieger, A. E.1993. <u>Women and Crack-Cocaine.</u> New York: Macmillan .

Kohfeld, C. W., & Sprague, J. 1988. <u>Urban Unemployment Drives Urban Crime.</u> Urban Affairs Quarterly, 24 (2): 215-41. Sage Publications, Inc.

McMahon, T., Angelo, Larian, Mollenkopf, J. 1997. "Hollow in The Middle." New York City Council Finance Division.

New York City Police Department. Internal Data on Personnel.

Osmani, S.1995. "The Entitlement Approach to Famine…." in Bane, K, Pattanaik, B. and Suzumura, K. (eds.) <u>Choice, Welfare and Development.</u> New York: Clarendon Press: Oxford.

Sen, A.K. 1977. "Starvation and Exchange Entitlements…." Cambridge Journal of Economics, 1: 33-53

U.S. Bureau of Labor Statistics. "Geographic Profiles of Employment and Unemployment." Annual.

U.S. Bureau of the Census. U.S. Census of the Population. New York. Social and Demographic Characteristics.1960, 1970, 1980, 1990.

Chapter 10

MURDERS OF POLICE OFFICERS

AND

JUSTIFIABLE HOMICIDES BY OFFICERS OF THE NYPD

By

Professor Andrew Karmen

Department of Sociology

On television and in the movies, heavily armed criminals and law enforcement officers engage in wild chases and bloody shootouts, with each side taking heavy casualties. Fortunately, real life is not as violent as Hollywood pictures it to be. Several hundred thousand arrests of potentially violent individuals are carried out each year without shootings of or by police officers. But the loss of lives arising from police-civilian confrontations in New York City in the 1990s remains a real problem: each year several officers are murdered and between 20 to 30 suspects are justifiably slain by the police. This 1998 case illustrates both types of killings:

Two police officers enter an apartment in Brooklyn to serve an arrest warrant on a parolee who had failed to show up in court. With the help of a female accomplice, the parolee shoots one of the officers four times. The injured officer returns the fire and slays the attacker, a justifiable homicide. But the officer succumbs to his wounds on the operating table, a line of duty death due to a felonious assault (see Cooper, 1998).

CAPITAL OFFENSES: OFFICERS SLAIN IN THE LINE OF DUTY

When recruits take an oath to uphold the Constitution, they are pledging to risk their lives to protect complete strangers from harm. Police officers have the courage to run towards trouble while everyone else flees in the opposite direction; as a result, some officers make the ultimate sacrifice and lose their lives in the line of duty. Killing a police officer is an aggravating factor that can sway a jury to vote for execution under the death penalty law passed by the New York State legislature in 1995. As far back as 1894, the problem was serious enough in New York that a patrolman's benevolent association was set up, in part to look after the needs of the widows and orphans left behind when officers were slain in felonious assaults. Today an organization known as "Survivors of the Shield" carries on this function.

Due to its sheer size, and because it patrols some of the nation's toughest neighborhoods and meanest streets, the NYPD has suffered more line of duty deaths than any other single department or law enforcement agency. During the 26 years between 1970 and 1997, a total of 88 police officers were murdered while on the job (accidental deaths, from incidents such as patrol car crashes, are not counted) (see the NYPD Firearms Discharge Annual Report, 1994). Most of the members of the service who lost their lives in felonious assaults were killed by gunfire (93%). The worst year of all was 1971, when 11 officers became homicide victims. During the early 1970s, a small revolutionary group, the Black Liberation Army, was implicated in the murder of several patrolmen. No officers were slain during four years: 1976, 1985, 1995, or most surprisingly, 1990 (when a record 2,262 murders were committed in New York). The death toll from felonious assaults against on-duty NYPD officers over the years since 1970 is indicated by the lower line in Graph 10-1 (Suspects Killed, Officers Killed).

Although the city's worst year occurred in 1971, the country's worst year was 1979, when the collective death toll of felonious slayings in the line of duty rose to over 100 law enforcement agents. On-the-job killings generally have dropped throughout the 1980s and 1990s, according to data published in the FBI's annual Uniform Crime Reports (but 64 officers were slain across the country in 1997, up from 56 the year before). Most officers were murdered while responding to a crime-in-progress (like a hold-up or burglary), or to a report of a fight (for example, among family members or bar patrons), or while investigating a suspicious occurrence (like a prowler), or when stopping a vehicle for a traffic infraction. Besides when serving arrest warrants, taking suspects into custody, and handling prisoners, grave dangers could materialize unpredictably and instantaneously if adversaries suddenly ambushed officers, FBI analysts discovered (UCR Section, 1993; 1998). In New York City up to the late 1970s, more officers lost their lives chasing after robbers than trying to break-up domestic disturbances (Margarita, 1980). Undercover officers (especially if they are black or Hispanic) are much more likely than their uniformed colleagues to be shot (or to fire their weapons). Transit officers are at greater risk than their above-ground counterparts to become murder victims (Geller, 1992).

To safeguard the lives of police officers, police departments need to provide bulletproof vests, reliable weapons, dependable communications equipment, constant training, clear guidelines about when to use firearms, and policies that win public support for law enforcement activities (Malcolm, 1990).

A great irony surrounds the dangers of police work. Nationwide, many more officers are killed each year by their own hands (through suicides, usually involving their service-issued handguns), by their colleagues (from accidental discharges and by "friendly fire" during gunfights), and by their acquaintances (family members and lovers, when off-duty) than by their criminal adversaries (see Geller, 1992).

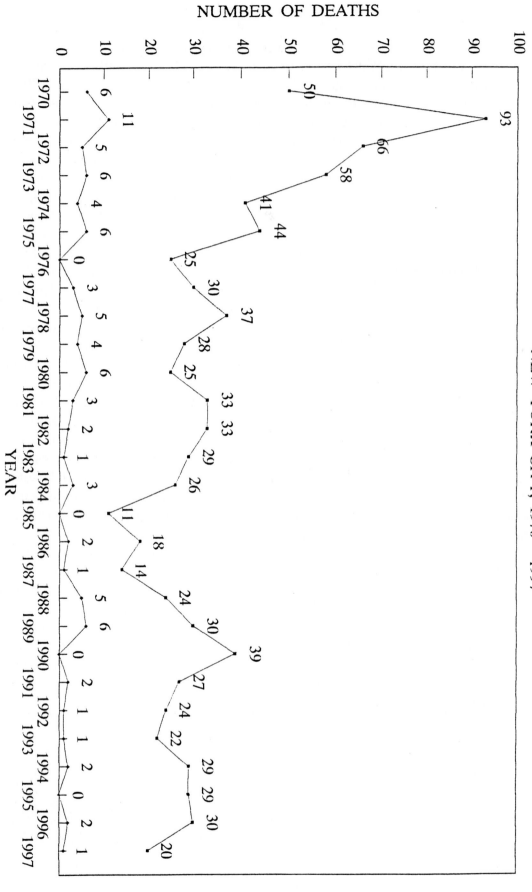

SUSPECTS KILLED, OFFICERS KILLED
NEW YORK CITY, 1970 – 1997

NUMBER OF DEATHS

YEAR

—■— Suspects Killed By NYPD   —◆— Officers Killed By Criminals

Sources: NYPD's Firearms Discharge Assault Report, 1994; 1995–1997: NYPD press releases

JUSTIFIABLE HOMICIDES: SUSPECTS KILLED BY THE POLICE

A man who once broke his girlfriend's jaw and recently slashed her throat disregards an order of protection and barges into her apartment. He grabs a kitchen knife and threatens to cut her heart out and to stab her 8 year-old daughter in the neck. For the sixth time in their stormy four-year relationship, she calls the police. When two officers arrive, the enraged man threatens them with the knife. When he refuses to drop his weapon, one officer draws his service pistol and kills him with a single bullet to the chest (Roane, 1998b).

When the legal system designates some incidents resulting in a loss of life as "justifiable homicides," that decision underscores the important criminological insight that certain killings are not murders, and that all crimes are socially defined. The circumstances surrounding each case in which one person causes the death of another must be evaluated by authorities who determine whether or not laws have been broken and punishments are merited. Put more bluntly, "what happened" is entirely a question of the audience's interpretation of the killing and its reaction to it. Accidental deaths are not brought about intentionally and are not punishable. Killing is not murder during wartime; soldiers who inflict the most casualties upon enemy troops win medals. Causing someone to expire is not murder if an executioner puts to death a person ordered to die by a judge and jury in a state that has restored capital punishment. Taking the life of an assailant is not murder if the survivor had to use deadly force in self-defense against an aggressor armed with a lethal weapon who is threatening serious bodily harm. (Statistics about the number of slayings that are ultimately ruled to be acts of justifiable homicide in self-defense, as when a store owner shoots an armed robber, are not readily available for New York City). Similarly, if a police officer uses duly authorized deadly force in accord with state law and departmental guidelines to subdue an assailant, the slaying is not a murder. In the eyes of the law, some homicide victims are actually dead offenders. Their final act on Earth was an attempt to commit a violent crime, or their behavior was viewed as dangerous or reckless, in wanton disregard of other people's well-being and specific lawful commands (like "Stop or I'll shoot"). These dead suspects are victims to the extent that they were executed on the spot - short-circuiting the entire criminal justice process - by officers provoked to fire their guns by what was perceived to be threatening behavior.

Although the particular circumstances surrounding any given incident must be reconstructed and evaluated, socio-cultural forces may be at work as well, having to do with landmark decisions by the Supreme Court (especially Tennessee v. Garner, 1985), state laws, official departmental policies, informal understandings between officers and their superiors, police-community relations, and the willingness of suspects to resist arrest, brandish weapons, and fire at officers. Consequently, the rate at which officers slay suspects varies from place to place and from time to time. Some police departments and some periods in history have much higher rates of killings deemed to be justifiable homicides than others (for example, see Robin, 1967). The NYPD ranks as relatively "restrained" compared to other big-city police departments, if the appropriate denominator is the number of officers (as opposed to the number of arrests, or the city's violent crime rate, or the frequency of gun carrying on its streets). In the late 1980s, about one suspect was killed for every 1,000 officers per year in New York, as compared with about 4 per 1,000 officers annually in San Diego, and roughly 3 per 1,000 per year in Los Angeles, Dallas, Atlanta, Memphis, and St. Louis (Kocieniewski, 1998b).

Most reasonable people agree that police shootings should be minimized as much as possible, as long as the safety of the officers and the public is not sacrificed. Officers should try to issue warnings (like, "Police, freeze!; Hands up!; Drop it!;"); and show restraint until the last possible moment, if conditions permit; and then employ deadly force only as a last resort, when all other measures to subdue a suspect and make an arrest have failed. Officers are trained to minimize their reliance on guns through lessons in "verbal judo" (to disarm opponents through persuasion) and via role playing and shoot/don't shoot exercises in simulated confrontations.

The number of New Yorkers killed by the NYPD over nearly three decades is depicted by the upper line in Graph 10-1 above. Since 1970, more than 900 people have lost their lives for acting in ways that officers considered to be threatening. Police gunfire claimed many more lives before the department placed restrictions on the use of service revolvers. In the aftermath of the corruption scandal investigated by the Knapp Commission, strict new "defense of life" guidelines regarding deadly force were adopted, under Commissioner Patrick Murphy. The number of suspects killed (as well as the number of officers killed) dropped sharply as soon as shooting at most fleeing felons (and the firing of warning shots) became impermissible in 1972. However, an entire page in the Patrol Guide still details the complicated instructions that are supposed to influence the "tough calls" that officers are forced to make in highly charged, real-life situations (McKinley, 1990). However, department records indicated that the overwhelming majority (94%) of NYPD officers in 1997 had never fired their guns even once during their entire careers, except at the Rodman's Neck firing range in the Bronx (Kocieniewski, 1998a).

"Police involved shootings" in which suspects are mortally wounded are investigated by each borough's District Attorney's Office, and the facts are presented to a grand jury for their review, to see if there was any criminal wrongdoing on the part of the officer involved. The officer can be indicted for what the police call a "bad shooting" only if the grand jury concludes he had no legitimate reason to believe he or anyone else was in imminent danger. The vast majority of slayings are deemed to be justifiable homicides. During the decade of the 1980s up to 1991, fourteen officers were indicted for killing suspects in ten different incidents. Only one was convicted of any criminal charges, and that case was not about deadly force; a sergeant was found guilty of vehicular manslaughter for driving drunk and running over a pedestrian ("Previous cases...," 1991).

One of the very rare occasions in which an officer was found guilty of misusing the privilege of resorting to deadly force, and in which the person who was killed can be considered to be a murder victim, took place in 1997. After a bench trial, the officer's actions seemed so indefensible that the judge found him guilty of manslaughter and sentenced him to prison:

An off-duty cop tells a uniformed transit policeman that a man is stalking a woman on a subway train. The policeman stops the train, locates the man and frisks him, but finds no weapon. The officer takes the man (who is considerably larger than he is) off the train and they wrestle with each other on the platform. Twice, the officer frantically radios for help on his radio. He then fires two shots at close range, striking the edges of the man's clothing. The man tries to flee but only gets a few feet before he is struck in the back by a third, fatal bullet (Levitt, 1997).

Controversial Issues Surrounding The Use Of Deadly Force

Does The Use of Deadly Force By Police Correspond To The Level Of Violence In The City?

Over the twenty year period from 1978 to 1997, the number of suspects killed by the police mirrored fairly closely the number of "civilians" killing each other. As civilian vs. civilian murders rose in the late 1970s, so did police killings; as murders among members of the general public fell in the early 1980s, police killings declined as well; when civilian murders rose in the late 1980s, suspects died more often at the hands of the police; after peaking in 1990, both civilian and suspect deaths declined until 1994. But when the NYPD drastically shifted its policies towards aggressively cracking down on minor quality of life offenses, the body counts of suspects killed by the NYPD crept up and then remained constant (at 29 or 30 a year), until 1997 (when 20 died at the hands of the police). Meanwhile, the number of murders between New Yorkers dropped steadily and sharply (by 51%, from 1572 in 1994 to 767 in 1997).

How Should Killings Under Questionable Circumstances Be Handled?

Even though most of the suspects who die from police gunfire were violent felons posing an imminent threat to the officers who confronted them, or to hostages or innocent bystanders, several cases each year become the focus of heated controversies. New Yorkers engage in heated arguments over whether these deaths are "justifiable homicides" or "on-the-spot executions by uniformed agents of the state." For example, these cases provoked strong emotions in 1997:

Responding to a report of shots fired late one night, officers encounter a sixteen-year-old running away from a brawl that erupted after a party. One officer orders the fleeing youth, who is holding something two feet long, to halt and drop his weapon. But the drunken youngster turns, looks over his shoulder and then keeps going. Fearing that the youth is armed with a shotgun, the officer fires his service revolver. As the young man lies dying on the pavement, the officer discovers that what looked like a shotgun is actually a machete painted black, with a hilt resembling a pistol grip. Original accounts from police sources contend that the youth, who had a record of arrests for robbery, was advancing and was brandishing the machete. But the autopsy performed by the Medical Examiner's Office determines that he was shot in the back. Nonetheless, a grand jury decides that the policeman fired his weapon in accordance with the law and departmental policy (Editors, New York Times, 1997).

A man leaves an apartment with no telephone in a housing project to call his mother to tell her he will be bringing his family over to visit for Christmas. Downstairs, he sees dozens of police officers who are searching for a person who fired a gun from a nearby rooftop. He becomes panicky and runs and hides in a grocery store, ignoring a cop's orders to halt. Two officers enter the store with guns drawn, order the customers and workers to get out or lie down, and yell to the suspect to drop his weapon and come out with his hands up. After eluding the officers for awhile, the suspect rises up suddenly with something in his hand. Mistaking the object for a lethal weapon (from a distance of about six feet), the officer shoots him. But it turns out the dead man was only holding a knit cap and a ring of keys on a leather strap. Police sources reveal that he had a record of arrests for assault, robbery, resisting arrest, and marihuana possession, and theorize that he ran because he knew he could be jailed because of several outstanding arrest warrants for minor charges. But they also concede that the officer who shot him, in addition to 13 commendations for exceptional, meritorious and excellent police work for making nearly 250 arrests, had been the subject of 12 civilian complaints (all determined to be "unsubstantiated") and had been involved in 8 shootings (wounding at least two suspects) in 14 years, more than any other officer on the force (Kocieniewski, 1998a).

Incidents like these two, in which police officers, particularly white officers, use deadly force under questionable circumstances, especially against black or Hispanic suspects, trigger angry marches, intense media coverage, and bitter shouting matches in which partisans for one side or the other trade insults, challenges, and counter-charges. As these political conflicts unfold, different groups weigh in and take predictable positions, reflecting their perceived interests (see Karmen, 1982).

The Patrolmen's Benevolent Association (PBA), which portrays itself as the voice of the rank-and-file cop-on-the-beat, almost always defends the officer's action as justifiable within departmental guidelines. PBA spokesmen usually argue that the officer found himself in a kill-or-be-killed situation, and did nothing wrong. Furthermore, the public should not "second-guess" those who are "on the front lines" where they are compelled to make "split-second decisions" that are "matters of life-and-death." PBA representatives argue that the public should be more concerned about the violence and firepower unleashed by hardened criminals against the police, and less apprehensive about the defensive shots fired by officers facing imminent danger and possible death while trying to do their jobs, to maintain order, enforce the law, and protect the innocent.

The top leadership of the police department (referred to as the "brass" or "suits" by their subordinates) generally adopts a different stance. Spokesmen for the Commissioner assert that the department is handling the problem in a professional manner. All incidents involving the discharge of firearms are thoroughly investigated. Serious breaches of departmental policy are examined at hearings, which can result in disciplinary actions like demotions, suspensions, and even expulsions. All candidates are subjected to psychological testing to weed-out violence-prone individuals, and recruits are carefully trained at the academy to observe all the legal restraints on the use of deadly force. Patrolmen and detectives are closely monitored and tightly controlled by their supervisors in the field.

In some highly charged incidents, in which a white officer shoots a minority suspect, black and Hispanic officers might feel compelled to take an independent stance. Through their organizations, the Guardians, 100 Blacks in Law Enforcement, and the Latino Officers Association, they express doubts about the ability of the department to "police" itself, and tend to call for outside investigations by other law enforcement agencies, such as the state police, the FBI, or a special prosecutor.

Civil liberties groups, warning the public about the menace of an evolving "police state" and the immediate danger posed by "trigger-happy" cops, insist that civilian review boards are necessary to oversee departmental operations, and that other restraints on the use of deadly force must be imposed.

Civil rights organizations and activists fear that "cover-ups" will "whitewash" the department's complicity in what they perceive to be race-based double standards. Civil rights groups believe that the overt discrimination of the past stubbornly persists: that white officers in general show appropriate restraint when dealing with white suspects, but that a small percentage are much too quick to shoot if given the slightest pretext when the suspect lined up in their sights is black or Hispanic. As a result, civil rights activists demand criminal prosecutions of "racist killer cops" and urge the families of people slain by the police under questionable circumstances to file multi-million dollar wrongful death civil lawsuits against the city, as a way of compelling the authorities to implement reforms.

Are The Police Quicker To Shoot Black And Hispanic Suspects?

Obviously, the problem of the misuse of deadly force by officers is the most disturbing part of a much larger historical and nationwide problem called "police brutality," defined as the unnecessary and excessive application of physical force to subdue a suspect or make an arrest. Across the country, including New York City, shootings and killings under questionable circumstances have touched off urban "riots" (which can also be seen, in a political sense, as uprisings or rebellions) since the 1960s. The risk of becoming a victim of police brutality falls unevenly, of course. Those who face the greatest chances of being verbally humiliated, physically beaten, and even killed under questionable circumstances are the city's negatively stereotyped poor black and Hispanic teenage boys and young men. NYPD training materials warn officers to avoid the "symbolic opponent syndrome," recognized as a mind-set that assumes that an individual is a "bad guy" merely because of his race, nationality, grooming, or mode of dress. Officers are urged not to reach any premature conclusions that may lead to irreversible actions because of a suspect's appearance, and are reminded that looks can be deceiving (Noel, 1998).

After a series of controversial killings during the early 1980s, New York Governor Mario Cuomo appointed "The State Commission On Criminal Justice And The Use Of Force" chaired by former U.S. Attorney Paul Curran, to see if there was evidence of discrimination. Although the commission had trouble compiling the necessary data, it's report stated that it found no evidence of "...systemic nor pervasive misuse of deadly or physical force..." and "...does not find that race is a significant factor in police decisions..." (Moses, 1987). Seventy-five recommendations for reform were included in the three volume report.

A study of NYPD shootings in the 1980s turned up what at first glance seems to be a surprising finding: that black and Hispanic officers were more likely than their white counterparts to fire their guns and wound or kill suspects. However, this apparent anomaly was easily explained: minority officers were more likely to be stationed in high crime precincts, and given dangerous undercover or front-line assignments which brought them into direct contact with violent offenders; and they tended to live in high crime city neighborhoods, where they were drawn into life-and-death confrontations when off-duty (Fyfe, 1988).

In the late 1990s, the controversy flared up again. Defenders of the NYPD argued that the infrequent events in which the police kill suspects under questionable circumstances receive such extensive media coverage that some New Yorkers might misjudge the threat posed by officers who may harbor racial prejudice as compared to the threat posed by criminally inclined members of their own communities (see for example, see Crouch, 1997; and Mayor Giuliani, quoted in Marzulli, 1998).

The relative magnitude of the two sets of dangers can be put into some context or perspective by comparing the number of people killed by the police to the number killed by fellow New Yorkers. A statistical breakdown of the racial and ethnic background of the 161 suspects killed by on-duty cops for the years 1991 through 1996 was released by the NYPD to a newspaper columnist (Crouch, 1997) and appears in Table 10-1.

Table 10-1:

SUSPECTS KILLED BY THE NYPD
1991 - 1996

Race/Ethnicity Of Deceased	Number Killed 1991-1996	Percent Of All Suspects Killed by Officers 1991-1996
Black	82	51%
Hispanic	57	35
White	20	12
Asian	2	1
Total Deaths	161	99%

Source: NYPD statistics, cited in Crouch, 1997.

The third column of Table 10-1 shows that about half of all justifiable homicides claimed the lives of black people. The question arises, Is this 51% portion suspiciously and disturbingly high? The answer is that it all depends on the choice of an appropriate standard for comparison purposes. Compared to the proportion of New Yorkers who are black (about 25% in the 1990s), 51% seems out of line by a factor of 2. But other standards for comparison might be the percent of all suspects that attacked police officers who were black, or the percent of all offenders who were black, or the percent of all arrestees for violent offenses who were black, or even the percent of all victims of violence who were black. A proportion of 51% corresponds closely to the 1991-1996 percent of murder arrestees - as well as murder victims - who were black..

Similarly, the percent of suspects killed by the police who were Hispanic is disproportionally high (35%), if the standard for comparison is the proportion of the city's population that is Hispanic in the 1990s (about 25%). However, this 35% figure is in line with the proportion of Hispanic murder defendants and murder victims during the 1990s (roughly one-third) . The percentages of whites and Asians killed by police actions were both disproportionally low, but this probably reflects the lower level of involvement in criminal violence of these two population groups.

Calculating ratios from the data shown in Table 1 above, for each black suspect killed by a member of the NYPD during the period 1991 to 1996, 59 black New Yorkers were murdered by fellow "civilians." Similarly, for every Hispanic suspect slain by a police officer, 62 Hispanic residents were killed by other New Yorkers (Crouch, 1997).

However, critics make several counter-arguments. They point out that law abiding black and Hispanic New Yorkers, who are victimized by violent criminals at a high rate, should not have to live in fear of police officers who are supposed to serve and protect them. Criminal violence is difficult to control; the unnecessary use of deadly force by agents of the government should be much easier to curb. And in some of these controversial cases, the punishment (death) did not fit the crime (making a "suspicious move" that was misinterpreted by the officer as life-threatening).

Controversies Spur Demands For Reform

Tragedies and crises always provide opportunities for improvement. The sustained public outcry surrounding certain killings under questionable circumstances has prodded the NYPD to re-examine some of its departmental policies and training practices.

The 1984 death of a 67 year old grandmother, who was slain by a shotgun blast after she lunged with a knife at officers who had come to evict her from her apartment in a housing project, inspired new training programs about dealing with emotionally disturbed persons and caused departmental guidelines to be revised concerning the use of non-lethal weapons like shields and mace (McKinley, 1991).

In 1987, after a 27 year old Harlem street vendor who had beaten a policeman with a steel pipe was killed by a hail of bullets fired by three of the six officers who had surrounded him, Commissioner Benjamin Ward approved a search for better non-lethal weapons, somewhere in-between nightsticks and service revolvers, such as stun guns and dart guns, that could effectively and humanely restrain suspects (Purdum, 1987).

In 1993, after a young man whose football hit a police car in the Bronx was asphyxiated by the arresting officer, Commissioner Ray Kelly banned the use of the arm choke hold and the nightstick choke hold (Smith, 1994). The department also initiated a program to monitor officers with repeated civilian complaints about brutality (Kocieniewski and Weiser, 1998).

In 1994, after a young man on Staten Island died while being taken into custody, Commissioner William Bratton ordered a review of the part of the curriculum at the Police Academy that dealt with how to subdue unarmed suspects who resist arrest (Smith, 1994).

In 1997, after an unarmed man was slain by an officer who had previously been involved in 8 shootings, Commissioner Howard Safir ordered the department to create a new unit to keep track of the number of shootings per officer and to monitor the actions of all officers who fire their guns on three or more occasions, to see if they require retraining or new assignments (Weiss, 1998).

In 1998, a Brooklyn grand jury took the unusual step of publicly criticizing the NYPD for providing insufficient firearms training and supervision for the plainclothes officers in the elite Street Crime Unit that seeks out suspects believed to be armed and dangerous. Months earlier, the same grand jury failed to indict two officers for criminal wrongdoing, even though one pumped sixteen rounds and his partner eight bullets into a suspected car thief after he reached under his seat for a steering wheel lock that was mistaken for a gun (Roane, 1998a).

To minimize the use of deadly force by officers against suspects, police departments need to adopt well thought-out written policies, to teach officers to internalize these procedures, to incorporate new tactics and equipment into training programs, to maintain close supervision in the field, to carefully monitor the performance of individual officers, and to hold officers and their supervisors accountable for violations of departmental rules (see Van Blaricom, 1998).

References

Cooper, M. (1998). "Officer is killed in Brooklyn; suspect, a parolee, also dies." New York Times, May 27, pp. A1, B6.

Crouch, S. (1997). "Cop-bashers ignore real enemy." New York Daily News, September 21, p. 28.

Editors, New York Times (1997). "A police shooting." New York Times, April 10, p. A28.

Federal Bureau of Investigation (FBI). (1993). Law enforcement officers killed and assaulted. Washington, D.C.: U.S. Department of Justice.

--------------------------------------- (1998). Officers killed and injured, 1997. FBI Press release, May 11. Internet website.

Geller, W., (1992). "Put friendly-fire shooting in perspective." Law Enforcement News, December 31, p. 9.

Karmen, A. (1982). "The controversy over the use of deadly force by police: Competing interests and clashing ideologies." American Journal of Policing, 2, 1: 19-47.

Kocieniewski, D. (1998a). "Officers facing added scrutiny over shootings." New York Times, January 1, 1998.

--------------------- (1998b). "Police's use of deadly force in New York is low for nation." New York Times, January 2, p. B1, B6.

-------------------- and Weiser, B. (1998). "U.S. trial evidence shows how police protect their own." New York Times, June 26, pp. A1, B6.

Levitt, L. (1997). "Family in blue abandons cop." Queens Newsday, May 27, p. A16. "

Malcolm, A. (1990). "Change in enforcement said to cut violence between police and public." New York Times, September 2, p. B32.

Marzulli, J. (1998). "Rudy lauds his Finest for drop in fatal force." New York Daily News, January 3, p8.

Margarita, M. (1980). Criminal violence against police. Ann Arbor: University Microfilms.

McKinley, J. (1990). "'Tough call' for police on when to fire." New York Times, February 2, p. B3.

------------ (1991). "Toll is rising in shootings by the police in New York." New York Times, January 5, p. B1, B23.

Moses, P. (1987). "Cops not trigger-happy in racial deaths: probers." New York Post, May 18, p. 4.

New York Police Department (1994). Firearms Discharge Annual Report.

"Previous cases and their outcomes." (1991). New York Times, March 21, p. B6.

Noel, P. (1998). "I thought he had a gun." Village Voice, January 13, pp. 41-43.

Purdham, T. (1987). "Options sought to deadly force." New York Times, June 9, p. B1.

Roane, K. (1998a). "Training of some officers is criticized by grand jury." New York Times, February 14, p. B3.

--------- (1998b). "Police fatally shoot Bronx man after he threatens two with knife." New York Times, May 31, p. A26.

Robin, G. (1967). "Justifiable homicide by police officers." Pp. 88-102 in M. Wolfgang (ed.),

Studies in homicide. New York: Harper and Row.

Smith, C. (1994). "Good cop, bad cop: The (unauthorized) NYPD. handbook." New York Magazine, July 11, pp. 27-28.

Van Blaricom, D. (1998). "Doing something about excessive force." Law Enforcement News, January 15, pp. 9-10.

Weiss, M. (1998). "NYPD launches unit to track trigger-happy officers." New York Post, January 1, p.8.

Chapter 12

THE NEW YORK CITY POLICE DEPARTMENT'S NEW STRATEGIES

By

Prof. Eli B. Silverman

Department of Law and Police Science

and

Paul E. O'Connell, Ph. D Program

John Jay College of Criminal Justice

INTRODUCTION AND BACKGROUND

Since 1994, when Mayor Rudolph Giuliani and Commissioner William Bratton presided over a thorough overhaul of the New York City Police Department, crime rates have continued to fall sharply within the City of New York. The numbers of reported murders, robberies, automobile thefts, and other 'street' crimes continue to decline rapidly under Commissioner Howard Safir, who took over the helm of the NYPD in 1996. It seems logical and reasonable to attribute the sudden improvement in public safety during the mid- and late 1990's to the new, smarter policing strategies that the department is currently implementing.

And yet, criminologists are reluctant to give the NYPD credit for driving down the city's crime rate. Perhaps they still adhere to one or more of three basic themes that have been derived from earlier research in the field of police management and administration.

The first theme is that traditional police practices can have only a limited impact on crime. The academic community's focus on a host of external factors, called "social roots," has contributed to a diminished view of the role of the police in crime reduction. As recently as 1990, two criminologists observed: *"no evidence exists that augmentation of police forces or equipment, differential patrol strategies, or differential intensities of surveillance have an effect on crime rates"*. (Gottfredson & Hirschi, 1990: 270) Moreover, police officials were warned that if they took credit for declining crime rates, they would later be blamed when crime rates went back up as part of an inevitable cyclical rise and fall in illegal activities.

During periods of increasing crime rates, criminological research has repeatedly stressed the importance of economic, demographic and political conditions. One scholar has recently noted that crime rates in large cities can be predicted accurately 80 percent to 90 percent of the time when one takes into account such economic and social factors as income, unemployment, education, prevalence of minorities households headed by single women, household size and home ownership (Bayley 1996: 40-41).

The second theme is that police have to change their ways and do things very differently if they are to have any substantial impact on crime rates. This requires major reforms: from reactive, incident-driven responses to more coherent and coordinated operations that work in concert, not at cross-purposes; where generalist police officers and specialist units, such as detectives, do not work in isolation from one another and the community; where organizational decisions are made at the level where they will be most effective; where accurate and timely information is systematically gathered and combined with forethought, insight and collective wisdom to diagnose problems rather than react to discrete, random isolated incidents.

The third principal theme is that these types of much-needed police reforms have been historically blocked and will always be frustrated by inherent bureaucratic resistance and a wide range of barriers. Scholars of organizations have long commented on the insularity of big city police departments which have been especially resistant to change due to their organizational rigidity and inflexible role assignments, as well as the distinctive nature of their work. These obstacles, it has been maintained, have prevented police forces from refocusing and reorganizing themselves, their values and their missions and hence have hindered redeployment and proper matching of resources with crime patterns (See Goldstein, 1990; Sparrow, 1990; Carter, 1990; Hoover, 1992).

It is important to acknowledge the place of situational crime prevention in bringing down New York's crime rate. This approach, reflected in more recent research, clearly demonstrates that improved policing can have a great impact.

This chapter explores the new managerial philosophy that is now guiding NYPD operations; reviews how this large and complex bureaucracy was reengineered; describes how areas of authority and responsibility were reassigned; summarizes the major crime-fighting strategies that were adopted; and explains how the discussions at Compstat meetings enable top administrators to coordinate the department's attack on criminal operations within city limits.

A NEW MIND SET

The New York City Police Department, since 1994, has demonstrated its capacity to recast its strategic, managerial and organizational approaches. These changes constitute a virtual revolution of significant and monumental proportions. Those who hold that "policing is policing" (and hence can have only a limited impact on crime) are not aware of important new developments. The plummeting crime rates in New York provide a dramatic demonstration that more is at work than can be explained by comparatively slow, even glacial changes in the social fabric. A virtual avalanche of changes in law enforcement strategies must be accorded a prominent role.

An entirely new mind set has developed within the NYPD. This revolution is a product of: revised thinking of police ends and means; a willingness to draw upon and expand previous departmental approaches such as problem solving, decentralization, and quality of life concerns;

an eagerness to raise questions about existing obstacles; and a genuine commitment and willingness to try innovative strategies, decision making processes and organizational arrangements.

Prior to 1994, crime prevention was not the primary focus of the entire New York City Police Department (NYPD). Part of the explanation for this shortcoming lies in the long held scholarly as well as practitioner views noted above that the police can have only a limited impact on crime due to the alleged greater influence of a host of social, economic and demographic factors. The police role, therefore, was centered on efficiently and effectively responding to crime, maintaining stable relationships with the community and combating police corruption.

In regard to the role and mission of the police, the 1993 Mayoral campaign set the groundwork. The successful candidate, Rudolph Giuliani, featured law enforcement issues. There was a clear desire to focus more specifically not only on major crimes but also on so-called quality of life crimes, such as graffiti, aggressive panhandling, street peddling, unwanted car window washing, noise making, prostitution, maintaining disorderly premises, low level drug dealing, and the operation of illegal social clubs. The belief was that these activities not only contribute to fear of crime and disorder, but they provide the conditions which breed further community decline and more serious crime. The notion that there is a connection between disorder and crime is no longer just a hypothesis. The studies and examples are legion. One 60-day pilot study of illegal window washers revealed that 50% had previous arrests for serious felonies and 50% had previously committed drug related offenses. What's more, it is the quality of life crimes which consistently cause citizens' greatest concerns and demands for police services.

REVAMPING THE ORGANIZATION

The new mind set not only championed the police doing different things, but also doing traditional tasks differently. This focus is evident in the simultaneous generation of policy and personnel changes as well as critical organizational self-examination. The commitment to significant change was coupled with an awareness that large scale public bureaucracies, like the NYPD, possessed an enormous capacity to resist change.

Top Level Changes

Several early occurrences and actions stand out as watershed events in revamping police approaches and strategies. One of the new commissioner's first orders was to direct top level bureau chief personnel to submit crime reduction plans for their areas of responsibilities. These were not accepted. By the end of Commissioner Bratton's first month in office (January 1994), the First Deputy Commissioner, the Chief of Patrol, the Chief of the Organized Crime Control Bureau (OCCB), the Chief of Detectives, the Deputy Commissioner for Community Affairs and others in high ranks all retired and were replaced by younger commanders with reputations for being aggressive risk takers. This represents an early and swift replacement of personnel (compared with previous changes in administration) by a commissioner who prided himself on change. In addition, over two-thirds of the city's 76 precinct commanders were replaced during Commissioner Bratton's first year in office.

Supporting these high-ranking changes was a large infusion of resources. The increase in personnel began in 1990, when the police force grew from 26,000 to its current level of approximately 38,000 uniformed officers. About half of this 12,000 person increase resulted from general and special city funding, and the other half came from the 1995 merger of the previously independent Transit and Housing Police Departments with the New York City Police Department.

Introducing Organizational Changes

By the end of the first month of the new commissioner's tenure, significant policy changes were also announced. For example, some of the responsibilities of the Organized Crime Control Bureau, which is charged with handling drug enforcement, auto theft, and public morals, were transferred to lower levels: borough and precinct commanders. In addition, progress was made to integrate traditionally independent detective squads into closer coordination with precinct commanders.

The overhaul of the department could not, of course, solely proceed with the enlistment of new leaders and new goals. To use the lexicon of organizational change (as the department often did), it was important to engage a "critical mass" of the organization. Two major vehicles were crucial to this process. They were the use of focus groups and reengineering committees. Their impact as agents for change can best be appreciated in the context of the difficulty encountered by previous reform efforts. Earlier attempts at innovation were frequently short lived or limited to isolated units in the department. Restrictive top down department rules and regulations are difficult to modernize. They provide numerous obstacles to change.

Changing the Rules

If the Department's recent history was burdened by centralized rigidities and insular decision making, then the very basis of decision making had to be changed. The extensive use of focus groups and the reengineering groups by the department allowed officers to meet and express their grievances with the department. The term *"reengineering"* is used in modern management writings to convey a willingness to start anew and question all organizational goals and strategies. Reengineering groups were key to the involvement of the rank and file officers. Their meetings highlighted a sense of crisis and problems and pointed the way toward solving longstanding problems.

The themes of 12 reengineering committee reports centered on: (1) the need for devolution of decision making authority from headquarters to the precincts; (2) the matching of resources with problems; and (3) the benefits of shifting from decision making based on functional specialization rather than one based on geographic authority. Two key documents were issued, the "precinct organization" document and the "geographic vs. functional" document.

The precinct organization document presented plans to streamline the lines of communication and authority within each precinct by: 1) changing the structure of the precinct to geographically-based teams that operated in defined areas and were supported by precinct-wide special resources; 2) replacing incident-based strategies with problem solving strategies to attack crime and quality of life concerns; and 3) changing the methods of accountability for all personnel in the precinct by measuring results as well as efforts.

Similar themes emerged in the "geographic vs. functional" report which stressed streamlining the lines of authority and placing "resources closer to the point of impact at the delivery level." It called for a concurrent increase in the levels of accountability, this time on a department-wide basis. The ultimate goals were to significantly reduce crime, fear of crime and disorder. The report recommended that precinct commanders should be allocated the resources and latitude of deployment necessary to address local conditions. It recommended revising department guidelines which limited the total number of precinct personnel assigned to anti-crime units, street narcotics duty, special posts, and community beats.

DEVISING BOLD, NEW, ANTI-CRIME STRATEGIES

Perhaps the most significant initial changes introduced by the new police administration were the six specific crime fighting strategies directed at violence, disorder and fear. Issued as pamphlets, they were entitled: 1) "Getting Guns off the Streets of New York"; 2) "Curbing Youth Violence in the Schools and on the Streets"; 3) "Driving Drug Dealers out of New York"; 4) "Breaking the Cycle of Domestic Violence"; 5) "Reclaiming the Open Spaces of New York"; 6) "Reducing Auto-Related Crime in New York." These strategies were widely disseminated throughout the NYPD and implemented during 1994 and 1995.

Each strategy contained certain techniques and methodologies in common. They relied upon a coordination of effort and resources; the institution of problem-solving techniques; and additional specialized training. In each instance, the Department clearly articulated the exact criminal condition(s) to be addressed as well as a precise "game plan" for correcting them. Such systematic efforts were unprecedented in NYPD history and represented a dramatic new way of coordinating crime fighting.

Getting Guns Off the Streets:

The primary goal of this strategy was to dramatically reduce the number of people carrying illegal handguns, which were involved in a majority of the violent crimes perpetrated in the city. "Gun-toting" represented the most visible and immediate threat to the lives and general welfare of the people of New York. For that reason, the department's new strategic assault on violent crime began with an all-out campaign against illegal weapons.

Prior to the implementation of this strategy, emphasis was placed simply on the seizure of guns, with only a scattered follow-up investigation, or an occasional coordination of efforts into other gun-related offenses, such as illegal gun trafficking. The strategy states that:

> *Rarely have gun confiscations been used to attack a series of related crimes: the trafficking and purchase of the gun in the first instance, other crimes committed with the same weapon, or the crimes of accomplices who have not been systematically pursued once the arrest of one defendant is made.*

It also noted that gun arrests made at the patrol level were weak and that the conviction rate for felony weapons charges in the city had dropped significantly between 1981 and 1992, due to an overall lack of experience and training.

To combat this, the strategy directed officers to aggressively pursue both accomplices and suppliers (gun traffickers) and called for the active participation of detective squads in debriefing *all* prisoners and in "strengthening" each gun arrest. The goal was to "encourage results-oriented police and investigative work." It called for greater cooperation between the precinct commands and the Department's various specialized units, such as the Career Criminal Investigation Unit (CCIU) and the Robbery Identification Program (RIP) units, and augmented the resources of these pre-existing units.

The strategy also called for a revised and expanded training program to "teach detectives case development of gun investigations," as well as the effective use of confidential informants and search warrants.

Curbing Youth Violence:

Strategy Number Two targeted the apparent breakdown in the department's internal lines of communication with regard to the criminal activities of youthful offenders. It noted that information concerning such behavior had been accumulated in the past, but was stored primarily for "record-keeping purposes." It was not comprehensively used for crime analysis purposes and, in fact, could not even be retrieved by most precinct personnel. The strategy also noted that a majority of field officers (both supervisory and rank and file) were extremely confused about proper juvenile arrest procedures, and were reluctant to carry out arrests in these situations.

Strategy Two called for the purchase of new computer equipment and the acquisition of additional programming support for the purpose of cross-referencing all police reports relating to truancy, unlawful behavior, and intelligence about gang activities. A new data base would then be accessible to precinct personnel and, ultimately, officials in family court. The strategy sought greater coordination of effort and a systematic approach to youth crime by tripling the number of youth officers in each precinct (from one to three) and by assigning one entire detective squad (consisting of one supervisor and six detectives) to the Office of the Corporation Counsel's Family Court Division. This squad's mission was to backstop the work performed by precinct detective squads, including strengthening of cases, pursuit of accomplices, apprehension of those selling guns to minors, locating witnesses and complainants, and execution of warrants.

While these tactics might, at first blush, appear to be mere redundancies of the tactical suggestions contained in strategy one, closer inspection reveals that these initiatives build upon, complement, and indeed require many of the fundamental changes put forth in the gun strategy. The efforts to crack down on juvenile gun violence, for example, would be fruitless, were it not for the changes contained in the first strategy that call for a more coordinated approach to the investigation of gun crimes. Strategy two would have had little real impact on such crime if the department had been content to simply make arrests for gun possession with little effort to follow-up and determine who is supplying such weapons in the first place. Once the department redirected its efforts into a more coordinated and "results-oriented" approach, it could build upon these changes in additional specific strategies.

Driving Drug Dealers Away:

This strategy called for an aggressive campaign against open air drug markets, by emphasizing the detection, arrest and prosecution of illegal narcotics dealers. It cited earlier enforcement efforts that employed the tactical use of police resources in specific geographical areas for the purpose of "severely disrupt[ing] narcotics traffic" and reducing the overall level of crime (such as "Operation Pressure Point" in 1984 and "Operation Take Back" in 1990). In a candid self-appraisal of its previous efforts, the Department found that it had indeed "reclaimed" certain areas of the City from drug dealers but that *it had inadequate resources, insufficiently coordinated efforts, and too-limited participation by Patrol Services personnel to be able to hold these areas long enough for neighborhoods to help reestablish themselves as drug-free.*" In response, the Department declared a "No Tolerance" policy for drug dealers and purchasers.

Strategy Three called for a "refocusing" of police personnel and resources. Previously, uniformed patrol officers (who were in a position to directly observe such illegal drug operations) were discouraged from making street-level drug arrests. As the strategy indicates, *"While there was no written policy [at the time] forbidding uniformed officers from making such arrests, the intent of commanders was made clear in a number of ways."* This policy was adopted by previous administrations due to "concern among police administrators that the temptations of the lure of narcotics trafficking would be too great . . . "

The strategy proposed a straightforward solution - allow patrol personnel to act against narcotics activity that they witnessed. Once again, however, this directive would be virtually meaningless without adequate organizational support, such as additional manpower and more timely and accurate information. Policies were revised, efforts were coordinated, information was shared and resources were placed closer to the ultimate point of delivery, at the precinct command level. Specific locations were targeted by precinct commanders who were given enhanced levels of authority as well as corresponding degrees of responsibility.

Breaking the Cycle of Domestic Violence:

Strategy Four attempted to "instill proactive, problem-solving practices in the Department's day-to-day domestic violence work." An attempt was made to simplify department guidelines concerning arrests in domestic violence incidents and thoroughly document instances of police intervention. The strategy called for: 1) the creation of a new reporting form to record all such calls; 2) the development of a computer database of Orders of Protection, which would become available to precinct personnel; and 3) the creation of two new positions within precinct commands, that of Domestic Violence Prevention Officer and Domestic Violence Investigator.

Resources were redeployed and the informational processes of the department were streamlined in order to enable officers to access the most current and accurate information possible. Armed with these new tools, they could now engage in a comprehensive and effective campaign to drive down the overall rate of domestic violence.

Reclaiming Open Spaces:

Strategy Five criticized the amount of "overspecialization" within the Department and attempted to establish a more comprehensive approach to crime fighting. Previously, the Department's Public Morals Division had been called upon to address all street prostitution complaints in all precincts at the same time. The strategy noted with frustration that precinct commanders were forced to "wait their turn" before specialized units could be dispatched to address such conditions. Perhaps most important, the strategy noted that uniformed police officers were discouraged from making prostitution or narcotics arrests, primarily due to a fear of corruption. Such arrests were delegated to Citywide "specialty units," such as the Public Morals Division and the Narcotics Division. The new strategy altered this policy in a dramatic fashion.

Precinct commanders were provided with the authority and resources necessary to increase street-level enforcement of a wider variety of offenses (such as "panhandling" and drinking in public) and to direct their personnel to make arrests for prostitution and possession/sale of narcotics while in uniform. Precinct Commanders now had the freedom to design and institute their own "buy and bust" or "sting" operations within the command. Specialty units were still, however, responsible for 'inside' locations, where drug, prostitution or gambling operations were being conducted behind closed doors, as opposed to being conducted on street corners.

Commanding officers could now innovate and design specific enforcement programs for their precincts. In an effort to increase the overall "quality of life" within the city, the police engaged in a crackdown that enabled them to arrest and interview more suspects, thus providing them with more intelligence concerning criminal activity and more background information that could be stored and drawn upon for future investigations.

Reducing Auto Crime:

The sixth strategy was used to convey the department's renewed commitment to combating auto theft. No longer would stealing automobiles be viewed as a low-priority crime. The Department's previous policy of leaving the bulk of such enforcement efforts to its citywide auto crime unit, was abandoned. The Department again refocused its efforts into a more comprehensive problem solving approach on the precinct level. This strategy authorized precinct commanders to institute their own "sting" operations to close suspected "chop shops" and enabled them to develop tactical strategies that would increase the number of arrests and dramatically reduce the overall amount of auto crime. In sum, the department's efforts were refocused, transferred to the precinct level, and coordinated by the open access and transfer of necessary information.

THE COMPSTAT PROCESS - PUTTING IT All TOGETHER: COMMANDING OFFICERS UNDER FIRE

Information is key to a police department's ability to manage crime. Early in 1994, the Department made a concerted effort to overcome the lag of three to six months in its reporting methods which generated crime statistics. New updated data appeared in a document known as the "Compstat" (comparative statistics) book, which included current weekly, monthly, and year-to-date statistics for criminal complaints and arrests for major felony categories and gun violations. Statistics were compiled on a citywide, patrol borough, and precinct basis.

The need to know about the extent of and events related to crime had to precede the Department's ability to reduce crime. Crime mapping is not new, but the Compstat data supplanted previous pin mapping efforts. The use of sophisticated computer technologies and software mapping capabilities were integrated with statistical analyses and deployment data. These twice-weekly crime strategy meetings represent the first time that multiple sources of crime information were assembled for display before all the key members of the Department at a meeting devoted solely to fighting crime.

At the crime strategy meetings, precinct commanders are held accountable for the levels of crime in their areas. Since they were familiar with community needs, commanders were provided with greater authority and latitude to deploy their personnel to address community-specific conditions. However, they were held accountable if crime rates did not go down. Compstat has been a central tool to clinch the devolution of crime management responsibilities to the local level. It assesses the effectiveness of commanders' crime-fighting strategies and results. Compstat enables Commisioner Safir and the Department to evaluate the rigor and effectiveness of its anti-crime strategies (such as the debriefing of arrestees by detectives and the search for all accomplices). It also provides a unique opportunity for administrators to observe and evaluate their subordinates.

CONCLUSION

This chapter has highlighted some of the most significant innovations in the police department's strategies to combat crime. Since 1994, the key principles have been informed decision making, decentralization, a closer match between problems and resources, greater commanding officer accountability, and an emphasis on performance as well as effort. The results of these changes are a huge reduction in crime rates.

References

Bayley, D. (1996). "Measuring Overall Effectiveness," in L. T. Hoover (ed.). Quantifying Quality in Policing, Washington, D.C., Police Executive Research Forum.

Brown, L.P. (1991). Policing New York in the 1990's New York City Police Department.

Carter, D. H. (1990). "Methods and Measures" in Trojanowicz, R.& Buqueroux, B.Community Policing, A Contemporary Perspective, Cincinnati, Anderson.

Citizens Crime Commission of New York City. (1996). Reducing Gun Crime in New York City: A Research and Policy Report, New York.

Erez, E. (1995), "From the Editor," Justice Quarterly 12(4) December: 619.

Gladwell, M. (1996). "The Tipping Point." New Yorker, June 10: 32-38.

Goldstein, H. (1990). Problem Oriented Policing. New York: McGraw Hill.

Gottfredson, M. and Hirschi, (1990). A General Theory of Crime, Stanford: Stanford University Press: 270.

Hammer M. and Champy J. (1993). Reengineering the Corporation New York: Harper Business.

Hoover, L.T. (1992). "Police Mission: An Era of Debate" in Hoover, L.T. (ed) Police Management, Perspectives and Issues. Washington, D.C. Police Executive Research Forum.

Koper, C. (1995). "Just Enough Police Presence: Reducing Crime and Disorderly Behavior by Optimizing Patrol Time in Crime Hot Spots," Justice Quarterly, Vol. 12, No. 4

McElroy, J.E. et al. (1993). Community Policing, The CPOP in New York. Newbury Park, CA: Sage.

Reppetto, T. (1978). The Blue Parade, New York: Macmillan

Sherman, L.W. (1986). "Policing Communities: What Works" in Reiss, A.J. Jr. and Tonry, M. (eds.) Communities and Crime, Chicago, IL. The University of Chicago Press.

Sherman, L. and Rogan, D. (1995.) "Effects of Gun Seizures on Gun Violence: Hot Spots Patrol in Kansas City," Justice Quarterly, Vol. 12, No. 4.

Silverman, E. (1995.) "Community Policing: The Implementation Gap," (in Kratcoski P. and Dukes D.(eds.)) Issues in Community Policing. Cincinnati: Anderson

Silverman, E (forthcoming) The Next Police Revolution, Boston: Northeastern University Press Sparrow, M.K., Moore, M.H. and Kennedy, D.H. (1990.) Beyond 911. New York: Basic Books.

Wilson, J. Q. and Boland, B.(1978). "The Effects of the Police on Crime," Law and Society Review, Vol 12: 367-390.

Wilson, J.Q. and Kelling, G. L., (1982). "Broken Windows: The Police and Neighborhood Safety," The Atlantic Monthly: 29-38.

NYPD Documents:

*Strategy No 1 "Getting Guns off the Streets of New York," March 7, 1994.

*Strategy No. 2 "Curbing Youth Violence in the Schools and On the Street," April 6, 1994.

*Strategy No 3 "Driving Drug Dealers out of New York," April 6, 1994.

*Strategy No 4 "Breaking the Cycle of Domestic Violence,"April 26, 1994.

*Strategy No 5" Reclaiming the Public Spaces of New York," July 18, 1994.

*Strategy No 6 "Reducing Auto Related Crime in New York," 1995.

*Strategy No 7 "Rooting Out Corruption, Building Organizational Integrity in the New York Police Department," June 14, 1995.

Report of the Re-engineering Committee on Precinct Reorganization, NYPD, 1994.

Report of the Re-Engineering Committee on Geographic V. Functional Specialization, NYPD, 1994.

Chapter 12

POLICING NEW YORK CITY'S SUBWAY SYSTEM

By Professor Vincent Del Castillo

Department of Law and Police Science

Say the word "subways" and people think of crime. For decades the New York City subways have been portrayed as dangerous places by the news media and in television and motion pictures stories. Scenes of heavily grafittied trains with marauding bands of adolescent criminals preying on helpless travelers have provided grist for the entertainment industry's image mill. The crazed person who pushes an unsuspecting passenger into an oncoming train shows how vulnerable all commuters can be.

Police and City officials offer another perspective, however, that of a subway system that is both efficient and safe. But are the subways safe? Is it realistic to expect any public place in a large urban area to be totally free from crime? Actually, when compared to the total crime problem in New York City, the rate of crime underground is relatively low. Nevertheless, crime and fear of crime in the subway continue to be a subject of concern and seemingly never-ending debate.

This chapter will attempt to shed some light on the issue of crime in the subways and will review some of the techniques used by the police to respond to and prevent subway crime.

FEAR OF CRIME

Public places generally earn their reputations for danger in three ways; personal observations, word of mouth and media reports. Personal observations include not only the actual commission of crime but also certain kinds of behavior by disruptive people. Drunks, drug addicts, panhandlers, prostitutes, and rowdy youths are all symbolic of dangerous places (Wilson & Kelling, 1982). Evidence of their behavior is often found in the form of graffiti, litter and vandalism. People also learn of criminal activities from accounts given by friends, families and acquaintances.

News media reports provide the most comprehensive, frequent, and graphic accounts of criminal victimization. Each day, news reports detail the more serious crimes that occur in neighborhoods, the city, the region of the country, and indeed from the whole world. Crimes that occur closer to home are more likely to raise concerns about personal safety than similar crimes in other areas.

The New York City subway system is a public place, but it differs from other public places in a number of ways. First, the subway functions as a social equalizer; everyone who travels by subway shares the same facilities. Middle class or poor; well educated or not; black, white,Hispanic, Asian, foreign born or native; home owner or homeless: all share the same seats in the same subway cars, walk the same platforms, and rely upon the same passageways and stairways. There are no first class accommodations in the subway. Money cannot increase protection from crime in the subway as it can elsewhere. There are no alarm systems, extra security devices or security personnel available to improve any one individual's safety or sense of safety in the subway.

Another way that the subway differs from other public places is in people's reaction to reports of crimes that occur in the subway as compared to crimes committed in neighborhoods other than their own. In this regard the subway might be considered everyone's second neighborhood.

If the subway is a neighborhood, at least in the context of its common interest for people, it is a neighborhood inhabited by strangers. Virtually all passengers in the subway are strangers to each other. People entering subway stations and especially trains, frequently make quick assessments of the other passengers based on their appearance, dress and demeanor. This is particularly true during the hours when there are fewer passengers than might be found in the peak rush hour periods.

Strangers in the subway are not perceived as unique individuals. Instead, visible characteristics, such as age, sex, dress, demeanor, race or ethnicity and mode of speaking, are used to place a stranger in a social category associated with certain expected behaviors. For some, displaying "symbols of deviance" such as the wearing of dark sunglasses, maintaining a "stony silence" or an intimidating body posture function as a strategy for communicating a "tough" appearance of one who is to be feared (Katz, 1988). Personal experiences and shared cultural expectations are used as a basis for category assignment. Social categories provide a foundation for social interaction in otherwise uncertain, unstructured situations (Merry, 1981).

THE NEW YORK CITY TRANSIT SYSTEM

The New York City subway system is the nation's largest and most complex. With more than 230 route miles of track, more than 465 stations and more than 6,400 subway cars, it moves an average of more than 3.7 million passengers a day. The system is old, with the earlier tunnels and stations dating back to 1904. It is also a diverse system, a combination of tunnels, some nearly 200 feet below ground, and elevated rails and stations, some of which are almost 100 feet above ground. The subway's population varies by time of day and day of week. The system typically carries as many as 700,000 passengers during the traditional rush hour periods and as few as about 4,000 passengers in the early morning hours. The Transit Authority estimates that on average, passengers travel about seven miles per trip, requiring about 30 minutes.

The subway is a closed system that provides rapid mobility to those within it and at the same time limits and structures their movement. Rapid mobility, which is the primary function of a public transit system is a benefit to riders and, ironically, is often used as an advantage by criminals.

Criminals take advantage of the mobility of the system in a number of ways. First, because many stations reflect the community they serve, strangers exiting and entering stations in high crime neighborhoods become opportunistic targets for the criminals in those areas. Second, criminals commit crimes on trains while they are in motion, then make their escape at the next station. Criminals also take the trains to specific stations in order to commit their crimes. Stations with high passenger density provide a large number of potential crime victims. Criminals can mingle with the crowds, and then after striking, can take a train out to another part of the city.

Subway Crime Compared to Crime in The Rest of New York City

Felony crime figures are presented in order to demonstrate the historical consistency in the proportion of New York City crime committed in the subways. New York City Police Department felony crime reports have been used to provide a basis for comparison. Those reports are categorized in terms of: murder and non-negligent manslaughter, forcible rape, robbery, felonious assault, burglary, and grand larceny.

Table 12-1 compares felony crimes committed throughout the entire city to felonies carried out within the subway system for the years 1981, 1988 and 1995. It shows that crimes committed in the subway rise and fall largely in step with crimes carried out in the rest of the city, and are probably influenced by the same social forces. Table 12-1 also reveals that the volume of crime committed in the subway is relatively low. For example, during 1995 on an average day, about 18 felonies were reportedly committed in the subway as compared to an average of about 1,000 felonies per day reported in the rest of the city. The last column shows that historically, the proportion of city crime that occurs in the subway remains fairly constant at about two percent. In terms of the risk of becoming the victim of a felony, the daily probability for subway riders is about one out of every 205,000 trips.

Table 12-1:

Comparison of Crimes Committed in the Subway to the Entire City

Selected Years: 1981, 1988, and 1995

Year	Total Felonies in Entire City	Above Ground	%	Subways	%
1981	637,451	622,156	97.6%	15,295	2.4%
1988	540,165	525,859	97.4%	14,306	2.6%
1995	375,424	368,699	98.2%	6,725	1.8%

Source: N.Y.C. Police Department and N.Y.C. Transit Authority

Table 12-2 reveals that incidents of the most serious crimes against persons, murder and rape are relatively rare in the subway. Robberies and grand larcenies are not so unusual. The most common serious crimes committed in the subways involves the stealing of property from passengers. This is accomplished either by stealth (pick pocketing and opening handbags for example), or by the use of force (such as robberies). In fact, many of the small number of murders committed in the subway result from robberies in which the force used ended the victim's life. Additionally, unlike typical confrontational crimes where the offender is known to the victim, most subway crimes involve victims and offenders who are strangers to each other. This tends to make it more difficult to successfully investigate those crimes, particularly murders.

Table 12-2:

Comparison of Different Categories of Crimes Committed in the Subway to the Entire City 1995

Crime Category	Total Felonies Entire City	Above Ground	%	In Subways	%
Murder	1,180	1,174	99.5%	6	0.5%
Forcible Rape	2,374	2,362	99.5%	12	0.5%
Robbery	59,280	56,754	95.7%	2,526	4.3%
Felony Assault	34,302	33,764	98.4%	538	1.6%
Burglary	75,058	75,026	99.9%	32	0.1%
Grand Larceny	66,061	63,001	95.4%	3,060	4.6%

Source: N.Y.C. Police Department.

The bulk of the crimes committed in the subways are relatively predictable and follow readily discernible patterns. Those who steal by picking pockets or opening hand bags prefer a crowded environment, such as trains or station platforms filled with rush hour passengers. Even crimes of violence, especially robberies tend to follow predictable patterns. For example, certain stations and parts of stations (such as stairways and station entrances) have a higher probability of robbery than others. Also, robberies involving students often occur around school dismissal times. Gangs of students prey on other students from either the same school or from neighboring schools. Robberies occur most frequently during certain times of the day and on certain days of the week. Evening hours and weekend nights are preferred by opportunistic criminals, those who will take advantage of someone who might have had too much to drink after work or others who appear to be particularly vulnerable. Robbers often congregate around stairways leading to the street. They will usually position themselves in one of two general locations. Some lurk on a subway stairway landing. From that position they can observe passengers entering or leaving the station, as well as police officers or others on the street or in the station who might interfere with their plans. Some robbers prefer to wait where the subway stairs meet the street. There, they can quickly grab property from an unsuspecting target and the escape on foot. This particular plan of attack is preferred by teenagers who are usually fast enough to outrun most pursuers. Street stairway robberies are usually

142

committed by criminals who live in or are familiar with the surrounding area. Also, this type of criminal will often return to the same location in search of additional victims, sometimes on the same day if their profits from the first robbery were not substantial enough.

Policing Subways

Police responses to these crimes take a number of operational forms that are adapted to the circumstances, and frequently involve the use of officers in plain clothes.

Larcenies

There are a number of criminals who specialize in larcenies of stealth. They are particularly skilled at picking a person's trouser or jacket pocket or opening a woman's handbag without the victim realizing that their property was taken until they have occasion to look for their wallet. For the most part, they ply their trade in crowded places such as subway trains and platforms during the morning and evening rush hours, after sporting events and in shopping districts, especially during holiday seasons. The crowds allow them to make close contact with their "mark" without drawing attention to their activities.

Express trains such as the Lexington Avenue line from Grand Central Station to Union Square provide the larcenists with enough time between stations to complete their crime. They will usually try to wait until others have entered a crowded train and then squeeze in behind their intended mark. They sometimes carry a newspaper for the dual purpose of hiding hand movements and distracting the victim. As a moving train lurches forward, stops abruptly, or makes any movement that tends to cause people to shift positions, the larcenists will "accidentally" bump into their mark, temporarily distracting the victim while they relieve them of their wallet.

Being positioned next to the door allows the larcenist to quickly leave the train after the crime has been committed. Although they will sometimes take the next train in the same direction, they prefer returning to their station of origin to repeat the process.

Because of the inability of officers to effectively move through heavy crowds or observe waist level activities in crowded trains, this type of crime is almost impossible to control with uniformed police patrols. On the other hand, specialized plain clothes patrols have been successful in observing the larcenists in action and arresting them. Plain clothes officers typically patrol the areas favored by these criminals and watch for suspicious persons following the behavior outlined above. The officers are alert to persons getting off one train only to enter the next train or persons repeatedly appearing at the same station. When the officers believe they have a suspect either one or two officers will enter the train with him in an effort to observe the attempt to commit the larceny.

There is a somewhat complicating aspect to the operation, however. Sometimes men who commit sex crimes follow the same pattern of behavior as the larcenists. They will position themselves next to a woman in a crowded train and as the train is in motion they will unnecessarily crowd her and rub against her pretending that the motion of the train is controlling their movements. In fact, the pattern of behavior of both criminal acts is so close that it is not unusual to pick up suspects whose criminal records show both sexual abuse and attempted grand larceny arrests.

Robberies

The circumstances and conditions of robberies in the subway are nearly opposite to those of larcenies by stealth. Robbers prefer isolation so that they can be free of interference from police and others and also so that they can observe any police activity in the area. Station stairways are preferred, especially where there is a landing at a 90-degree turn of the stairway. Plain clothes officers are generally assigned to stake out a station where a street stairway has recently experienced robberies. If they can blend in with the area, they might take up a position on foot or in a van or other suitable vehicle. Armed with information about the previous crimes, including the profile of past victims and descriptions of the wanted persons, they patiently wait for the robbers to strike again. Being creatures of habit, criminals tend to return to places where they have been successful.

Responses to robberies by opportunistic criminals present a more difficult challenge as many of these crimes occur in trains. The usual target is an apparently easy victim with a gold chain or bracelet, expensive watch, handbag, or other easily taken item of value. Once the potential victim has been chosen, the robbers usually position themselves next to or in the general area of the target and wait until the train is approaching their desired station before committing their crime. Once the property has been taken, the robbers exit the train and continue on their way. By the time the victim has an opportunity to report the crime, the culprits are long gone.

In addition to deploying highly visible uniform patrols to deter such robbers, there are generally two responses to this problem. Firstly, plain clothes officers with sufficient experience and skill, if they are alert enough, can spot potential victims as well as others in the train whose behavior follows the criminals' method of operation. When the culprits make their move, the officers can arrest them as they commit the crime.

Secondly, the Transit Police have had considerable success using decoy operations to catch this type of criminal. Armed with victimization data that describes the type of person most likely to fall prey to such crimes of opportunity, decoy teams set out to replicate the circumstances that those criminals find attractive. Decoy teams are generally composed of the decoy officer and approximately eight backup officers. Decoy operations can be particularly dangerous for the decoy officer, and it takes a high degree of team work and cooperation to use this technique effectively and safely.

In a typical operation, the decoy poses as a vulnerable or likely target of a robbery or larceny. The decoy might appear to be sleeping or drunk, or an elderly or infirm passenger. Such operations can take place on a station platform bench or in a train. The backup team must blend in with their surroundings, and yet position themselves so that they can either observe the decoy or listen to the decoy by way of a radio. The trick is to be close enough to respond quickly in the event that the decoy is in trouble, and yet far enough away so as not to alert the would be robber to the trap.

Decoy operations have a number of advantages over other strategies for catching criminals in the act, or subsequently apprehending them. First, because there are a number of police officers involved in the operation and because they are alert to the impending event, they can usually provide a more comprehensive description of the crime and a more reliable identification of the suspect than the victim and other citizens who may have witnessed a crime. Second, victims and witnesses are sometimes reluctant to cooperate for a number of reasons, particularly fear of retaliation and concern over losing time from work. Many also want to avoid the stress of pursuing the criminal justice process, especially having to testify at trial. Third, the decoy operation provides a better opportunity of catching the criminal in the act. Finally, and perhaps most important, the decoy officer serves as a surrogate for the potential victim thereby sparing a citizen that kind of trauma.

Graffiti

The desire to leave one's mark or name on a tree or rock, or to pen a humorous or political message, or to simply deface property is a phenomenon experienced by nearly all societies. The problem is particularly prevalent in urban areas where identities are easily lost in the crowd. Subways have historically been the target of graffiti, especially by the young. The opportunities are readily available to nearly 200,000 youths who use the subways for travel to and from school. During the 1970's and into the 1980's, with the introduction and popularity of felt tip markers and spray paint the subways became a popular medium for a plethora of the subway graffiti.

Graffiti crews began to spring up throughout the city. Gang members and those who wanted to emulate them used the subways to scrawl their nicknames (street names) and street numbers. "Tags," as they are known, were even the subject of the 1985 Hollywood movie, "Turk 182". Although there were those who defended the mural painters as artists, by 1983 virtually every one of the more than 6,400 train cars in the system was covered with graffiti, inside and out. Station signs could not be seen through the train windows; passengers could not read the subway maps and the sheer volume of graffiti gave the appearance of an environment that could not be controlled. The connection between graffiti and fear of crime and the appearance of urban decay is well documented (see Del Castillo, 1992; Glazer, 1979; Wilson & Kelling, 1981).

The Transit Police employed traditional law enforcement tactics to deal with the graffiti problem: intelligence gathering; increased surveillance of train yards and areas between stations where trains are stored during off peak hours; and arresting and summonsing offenders. The identities of hundreds of the youths responsible for graffiti became known for their "tags" and by their repeated apprehensions. More than 150,000 such apprehensions were effected annually; yet the problem persisted. Because most of the vandals were either adolescents or younger, the overburdened juvenile and criminal justice systems failed to impose any meaningful penalties, which simply emboldened the graffiti-ists to continue their activities.

In 1984, the Transit Authority embarked on a comprehensive "Clean Car Program" to take control of the graffiti problem. Noteworthy is the fact that this program was not exclusively the responsibility of the police but rather a coordination of all Transit Authority departments. Central to the program's success was the strategy of taking small bites out of a big problem rather than trying to solve the entire problem at one time. The idea was to take control of graffiti one train line at a time.

The Number "7" line, which extends from Main Street in Flushing Queens to Times Square on the West side of Manhattan, was the first in the Clean Car Program. A security survey of the train storage areas for this line was conducted and any broken fences or other potential breaches of security were repaired. Also, every train car was thoroughly cleaned inside and out before it was put into service. Part of the success of the program was the commitment to the principle that no train would be allowed in service if it contained any graffiti at all.

About twenty-five police officers were assigned to this line for uniform train patrol and for plain clothes assignments in and around the Number "7" line train storage areas. This contingent of officers supplemented the normal patrols in the area. The plain clothes officers often dressed in work clothes wearing orange reflective vests like those worn by Transit Authority workers. After several arrests, the graffiti-ists were conditioned into thinking that anyone dressed in that way could be a police officer. With the large number of workers in the train terminal areas the police had the added benefit of seeming to represent larger numbers than was actually the case. This also provided residual apparent police presence after the police had been redeployed.

The increased patrols, as well as the fact that no graffiti would be allowed to remain on the trains, removed much of the incentive for graffiti, especially the large murals. After all, if no one can see the finished product why expend the effort? The graffiti problem on the Number "7" line began to decline steadily over the first several weeks of the program. Because the train cars were not filled with graffiti as in the past, the small amount that persisted was easier to spot and enabled the police to concentrate on the time periods and general locations where the graffiti was likely to occur. This insight helped the patrols to be more efficient in preventing incidents of graffiti and in making arrests.

Detailed records on the incidents of graffiti were kept. When it appeared that the Number "7" line was under control, the decision was made to move onto the next train line in the Clean Car Program. The original contingent of officers was gradually redeployed to the next assignment and eventually normal police patrols were able to maintain control over graffiti on the Number "7" line. This basic pattern of gradually taking control of one train line at a time continued for about five years until, in 1988, every one of the more than 6,000 trains cars in the subway was graffiti free.

Fare Evasion

Fare evasion is a major concern for officials of the New York City subway system. Although the true extent of the problem is undeterminable, the Transit Authority estimates that between 60 million and 80 million dollars a year is lost through fare evasion, and although those fiscal losses have remained relatively constant over the years, the problem is likely to become more pronounced if fares increase.

In addition to the loss of revenue, there are a number of secondary, but serious concerns about fare evasion. Especially important is the copycat syndrome, in which it is feared that if fare evasion becomes commonplace, it will be emulated by others. This is especially likely to occur if it is perceived that there is an absence of any deterrent force. In practice, individuals who would normally pay their fare are encouraged not to do so through the realization that others are evading payment without sanctions. Although this will not impact on all riders, because some will pay under all circumstances, there are many situational offenders who will take advantage of the opportunity of the moment. For example, if rush hour passengers are waiting on a long line to purchase tokens while a train is entering the station and one person leaves the line and successfully enters the station illegally, many of the others will leave the line and follow the fare evader.

Equally important is the concern that if fare evasion becomes commonplace, the quality of life of the system will deteriorate. Free and open access to the system will encourage more of the homeless to reside in the subway, increase the numbers of undesirables frequenting the system, and invite petty criminals to switch their illegal activities from the streets to the subway. The latter poses the greatest threat to the system, for as the ambiance deteriorates and perception of fear increases, rider-ship will diminish as passengers seek other modes of transportation. When this becomes pronounced, the viability of the subway system is threatened (Brantingham et al., 1991; Felson et al., 1990).

A number of police strategies are available to deter fare evasion. As a general rule, uniformed police officers prevent crimes from occurring, particularly when those officers are highly visible. Plain clothes officers are more effective in making arrests after the fact. Combinations of these patrol strategies tend to be an effective enforcement tool for a variety of crime problems including fare evasion.

The mere presence of a uniformed officer at a subway entrance is generally sufficient to prevent fare evasion. However, if more than one entrance is accessible, the officer's ability to completely prevent fare evasion at that station will be limited, as some fare evaders will simply move the locus of their actions to an unguarded entrance. Additionally, when uniformed officers leave the entrance areas to patrol other parts of the station, those who are intent on entering the station illegally have the opportunity to do so. Plainclothes officers are usually assigned to those stations that experience increases in fare evasion, particularly by those who are not easily deterred. Because plain clothes officers blend in with their environment they can be quite effective in summonsing and sometimes arresting fare evaders. After concentrating on a particular station for a few days, or in some cases more than a week, the incidents of fare evasion diminish, allowing the plain clothes officers to move to other stations experiencing high numbers of fare evaders. Depending on the station's clientele the residual effects of these operations can be long lasting, for weeks and sometimes months. Some are dissuaded from future fare evasion because of the high cost and inconvenience of having to appear at a hearing and pay a summons while others are simply displaced to other stations where they can successfully enter without payment.

The use of sweeps and mini-sweeps are also effective in combating fare evasion. Mini-sweeps, as the term implies, are small scale operations usually conducted simultaneously at three or four stations that are adjacent to each other. Compared to single station operations, this approach has the added advantage of catching displaced fare evaders, those who would move from station to station looking for an unprotected entrance.

Sweeps are large scale anti-fare evasion efforts involving scores of police officers assigned to a large number of stations in either a train line or in a geographic area that encompass a large number of stations, for example, business districts in downtown Brooklyn or midtown Manhattan. These sweeps are highly coordinated and involve not only police but other components of the justice system. Typically, a sweep will result in well more than one hundred apprehensions and virtually all will result in an arrest. Because these operations are well-publicized, they produce a deterrent effect not only on those who are apprehended but many of those who hear about the operation through the news media.

Although the obvious purpose of these sweeps and mini sweeps relates to the control of fare evasion, a secondary or less obvious goal may be equally important in terms of effective policing and crime prevention. Sweeps often result in the apprehension of the more serious and violent criminals, many of whom either use the subway as their locus of criminal activity or simply as a means of travel. For example, unlike routine fare evasion stops, where the offender is simply issued a summons, sweep apprehensions result in an arrest which includes a search, fingerprinting and a criminal record check. Fare evaders are often found to be carrying concealed guns and other contraband and many are also wanted for other crimes and have outstanding arrest warrants. An example of the effectiveness of this type of operation is illustrated in the 1992 Transit Police records of sweep activity resulted in the arrest of 3,651 persons with outstanding arrest warrants and the confiscation of more than 100 illegal firearms (NYCTA, 1993:6).

The Transit Police and Passengers' Fears

Fear of crime operates on an emotional level and is influenced more by what a person perceives and feels rather than what a person knows. In a study of fear of crime on the New York City subways, three factors relating to environmental control were associated with fear of crime. The perceived effectiveness of transit police in order maintenance was related to fear of crime in that those who rated the transit police high on maintaining order were less likely to report being fearful than those who believe the transit police were doing poorly in that regard. Those who felt that passengers were routinely being hassled by disorderly youths were also more likely to report being fearful. Finally, the perception of graffiti as a serious problem was also strongly related to fear of subway crime victimization (Del Castillo, 1992).

References

Brantingham, P.L., Brantingham, P.J., & Wong, P.S. (1991). How public transit feeds private crime: Notes on the Vancouver "Skytrain" experience. Security Journal, 2:91-95.

Del Castillo, V. (1992), Fear of Crime in the New York City Subway. Unpublished doctoral dissertation, Fordham University, New York.

Felson, M. et al. (1990). Preventing crime at Newark subway stations. Security Journal, 1: 137-142.

New York City Transit Authority (NYCTA), (1993). Fare evasion status report.

Katz, J. (1988). Seductions of Crime. New York: Basic Books.

Merry, S. E. (1981). Urban Danger. Philadelphia: Temple University.

Wilson, J. Q. & Kelling, G. L. (1982). Broken Windows. The Atlantic Monthly, 249: 29-38.

Chapter 13

**THE DEVELOPMENT OF HOSTAGE NEGOTIATION
BY THE NYPD**

by Robert Louden

Director, Criminal Justice Center
John Jay College

The sub-headline of a story in the New York Times read, "gunshots, officers and a tank for the backdrop for a manhunt." The article referred to a four-hour siege in Queens, N.Y. during which New York City detectives negotiated with an armed burglary suspect who had fired upon officers responding to a 911 call. Although many units of the police department participate in such events, the focus is often on the role of hostage/crisis negotiation. The negotiation function in the NYCPD is housed in the Detective Bureau. William H. Allee, the Chief of Detectives commenting on the dramatic and dangerous event, noted, "Our commitment, our resources that you see here tonight, had one purpose, and that purpose was to prevent any further violence and have this end peacefully. That's what we did, and that's what we're most proud of" (Chen, 1998: p. B3).

On May 19, 1998, the New York City Police Department Detective Bureau Hostage Negotiation Team marked the 25th anniversary of its founding at a daylong series of retrospective presentations at John Jay College of Criminal Justice/CUNY. New York City was the first police jurisdiction in the United States to institute and formalize the practice of negotiation as a tactic to solve hostage holding problems.

The fact that the event was held at John Jay College is significant in that three of the five individuals who have commanded the team during the past quarter century earned degrees from John Jay, and the other two have taken courses there. John Jay College also provides advanced training for police negotiators and tactical officers, *Managing Situations Involving Mentally Disturbed Persons.*

A DEFINITION OF HOSTAGE/CRISIS NEGOTIATION

Negotiation is a transaction between two parties, representing themselves or others, which is designed to arrive at a mutually agreeable resolution. A dictionary definition of negotiation (American Heritage, 1983) includes, "to confer with another in order to come to terms." Negotiation does not automatically presuppose an equality between parties but does recognize the relative strength or power of each side. Implied in the negotiation process is that each side has something that the other wants, that there is no better mutually acceptable solution immediately available, and that there is a willingness to communicate and to compromise.

Police officers engage in the practice of negotiation throughout their daily assignments, especially in these times of community policing and collaborative approaches to problem solving. They negotiate events such as noise complaints, neighborhood disputes, situations with disorderly youth, and parking conditions. Hostage negotiations are somewhat more complex because issues of safety, matters of life and death, are always present. These situations typically involve the response of a large number of law enforcement personnel, a potentially confusing command structure, and an adherence to special procedures. Media attention is a given at virtually every hostage/crisis negotiation scene.

"Hostage-taking is a very ancient form of criminal activity. In fact, it was even an accepted tool of diplomacy when used by legitimate authority"(Crelinsten and Szabo, 1979: ix). Hostage-taking is defined by the United Nations as *"the seizing or detaining and threatening to kill, injure, or continue to detain another person to compel a third party to do or abstain from doing any act as a condition for the release of the hostage"*(Levitt, 1988:14). *"Hostage takers act in order to create an extortionate transaction with the police."* (Rogan, et al, 1997: 3).

Hostage/crisis negotiation is a police strategy which consists of responding to a situation that involves imminent danger to the life or limb of a person(s) being held against their will. There is not necessarily an immediately apparent connection between captor and victim. Individuals are often *"taken hostage only because they are available and vulnerable."*(Buhite, 1995: xv).

A law enforcement organization designates an individual as the negotiator to engage the hostage holder in a dialogue in an effort to find a peaceful resolution to the instant problem. The hostage holding may originally be motivated by criminal intent, emotional crisis, or political considerations. The negotiator will attempt to persuade the holder to release the hostage(s) unharmed in return for a pledge that the captor will not be harmed and may be assisted in resolving problems in a legitimate way. *"Negotiation is thought of as the process of discussion engaged in by two or more parties, each of which wants to achieve a desired aim"* (Edleman and Crain, 1993: xii). For situations where negotiation does not seem to be effective, the police will attempt to facilitate the rescue of the victim and the apprehension of the perpetrator by distracting the hostage- holder. A common element in hostage and barricaded subject incidents is defiance by the subject of orders from the authorities to come out peacefully. *"A standoff develops between the overwhelming power -- manpower, firepower and legal authority -- of the police, military or other authorities and the defiant, trapped offender."* (Bahn, 1987: 1)

Police negotiators are law enforcement officers who are selected and trained for the task and who are acting on behalf of their employing agency (Volpe & Louden, 1990:308). For many years the commonly used term was "hostage negotiation" and in many jurisdictions it still is. Since approximately 1989 (Kaiser, 1990), the FBI has switched to "crisis negotiation" and many agencies have followed suit. The International Association of Chiefs of Police (1991) utilizes the term "hostage communicator."

Police hostage/crisis negotiators and communicators view *"the negotiation of substantive and non-substantive wants or demands in similar terms: agreement making through bargaining or problem solving, typically via quid pro quo"* (Rogan, et al, 1997:11). Police hostage/crisis negotiation involves bargaining for the life of an innocent person, or may involve dealing with a non-hostage holding barricaded criminal, or dealing with individuals who may be emotionally disturbed or mentally ill. Police generally engage in hostage/crisis negotiation in order to save the hostage's lives, without unnecessarily endangering the lives of the helpers.

Development of Hostage/Crisis Negotiation as a Strategy in U.S. Police Organizations

In the late 1960's and early 1970's, Morton Bard (1974) conducted pioneering research which contributed to major shifts in the way police reacted to domestic violence, sexual assault and hostage holding. Each of these areas involves a wide range of dispute, conflict and crisis intervention issues. Bard acknowledged that "considerable gaps" still existed between police and academics but stressed their "commonality of interest." His work sought to establish the "development of a mechanism for coupling the practitioner and the researcher " (Bard, 1974:20). His applied research during the period 1967 to 1969 employed crisis intervention techniques for police officers in dealing with domestic violence. He was also a significant contributor to the original application of similar practices for investigators responding to reported rapes and other sexual assaults. His work in domestic violence and sex crime was well received by many in the New York City Police Department. His research findings were integrated into the Police Academy curriculum. Bard's work with sex crime victims was contemporaneous with the development of the new hostage negotiation program. Since both activities were functions of the Detective Bureau, a serendipitous expansion of Bard's interest and techniques was realized. He became an early advocate and adviser of the innovative specialty of hostage/crisis negotiation (Bard, 1975; 1976; 1978; Donovan & Sullivan, 1974).

Two hostage events which occurred in New York State, one in 1971 and the other in 1972, are often referred to in the literature of hostage situations but did not at the time prompt any changes in law enforcement policy. The September 1971 Attica prison riot and hostage holding in northwest New York State resulted in death for ten correction officers and twenty-eight inmates during a rescue attempt. This tragedy prompted controversy in criminal justice and social science circles over using force versus restraint in approaching hostage incidents (Garson, 1972; Wicker, 1975; Useem and Kimball, 1989: Shelton, 1994; Strollo and Wills-Raftery, 1994). It did not, however, prompt interest by the New York City Police Department, perhaps because it involved prisoners and was contained within the walls of a correctional facility located hundreds of miles away. Similarly, a 1972 bank robbery hostage situation in Brooklyn,(a fictionalized account appears in the popular 1975 movie Dog Day Afternoon), did not immediately result in new responses to situations involving hostages. However both Attica and Dog-Day, as well as additional incidents, eventually led to the acceptance of negotiation as a viable strategy for dealing with hostage situations (Bolz & Hershey, 1979; Moorehead, 1980).

A shift in official responses to hostage situations took place following the 1972 Munich Olympics incident. Two members of the Israeli Olympic team were killed in the original takeover. Additionally, one West German police officer, five PLO terrorists and eight Israeli hostages died during an attempt to free the hostages by force (Schreiber, 1973; Moorehead, 1980; Cooper, 1985; Soskis & Van Zandt, 1986).The Munich event alerted the New York City Police Department that their jurisdiction could provide a similar opportunity for some group to engage in terroristic diplomacy. The fact that the hostage holding occurred during the International Olympics, involved

American allies, (Israel and West Germany), and was broadcast live by the media was enough to prompt an immediate study of the issues (Gelb, 1977; Bolz and Hershey, 1979; Gettinger, 1983).

A literature search consisting of four social science data bases, NCJRS, Criminal Justice Abstracts, Sociofile, and PsychLit, revealed that the first two published articles about police hostage negotiation in the U.S. were separately authored by two New York City Police Department commanders who had a role in the early formulation of the policy. Donald F. Cawley (1974) was the Chief of Patrol during the post-Munich policy study period and the first field-test, albeit spontaneous, of the new Recommended Guidelines: Incidents Involving Hostages (1973). These contingency plans stressed that *"The primary consideration in such circumstances is to secure the lives and safety of the threatened hostages, the police officers, innocent bystanders, and the criminals themselves"* (Culley, 1974:1). A Detective Bureau lieutenant, referring to the same document, noted that Chief Inspector Michael J. Codd had recently *"reviewed and approved plans for hostage situations, plans which [Codd] had been working on with various units of the police department since September 1972."* This original plan did not specifically mention using hostage negotiators.

Shortly after the Munich incident in 1972, Patrick Murphy, then New York City Police Commissioner gave the order that New York should prepare itself for terrorist hostage-taking (Gettinger, 1983:14). His Chief of Special Operations, Simon Eisendorfer, formed a committee consisting of patrol, detective, training and psychological services representatives. The FBI followed suit in 1973 when it initiated research and training in hostage negotiation. One of the original FBI negotiators, Conrad Hassel, noted that this speciality was not even conceived until 1972, but that it soon spread across the country (see Gettinger, 1983). Now the majority of police departments in the US which employ at least one hundred sworn officers utilize the hostage negotiation concept. Some started soon after New York City and others as recently as 1997.

Evolution of the Detective Bureau Hostage Negotiating Team and its Relationship to Other New York City Police Department Units

In January 1973 a significant event in the evolution of hostage negotiation took place over a two-day period in Brooklyn, New York at a location known as John & Al's Sporting Goods Store. The local precinct police had responded to a silent alarm call of a possible robbery in progress and were met with gunfire from within the store. Reenforcements arrived, including Emergency Service Unit tactical officers, which is the equivalent of SWAT Team personnel in some other jurisdictions. One ESU officer was killed and two other officers were wounded in the quickly unfolding event. One of four suspects was also wounded and eight hostages were held in the store. The new operational plan for incidents involving hostages, which Chief Eisendorfer had organized a few months earlier at Commissioner Murphy's direction, was implemented for the first time. Its primary concerns were with containment of the scene, control of personnel and resources and communication with the captors (Cawley, 1974). Prior to this, police procedures basically called for a location to be surrounded; a demand for immediate surrender was to be announced, followed by a forced entry, often supported by gunfire. But experimenting with the newly evolving system, forty-seven hours after the incident began, all of the hostages were safe, the four perpetrators were in custody and there was no further injury to police officers or other responders. Although the police were fired upon hundreds of times during the event, the police did not return fire after the initial confrontation.

A comprehensive critique of the incident at John & Al's was undertaken. Although the plan had not been eagerly received throughout the Department, its basic principles were validated by the activities surrounding the forty-seven-hour siege. Even though the original plan had stressed the importance of communicating with hostage holders, there had been no prior indication as to whom the negotiator would be. The critique made commanders aware of "negotiation deficits." A wide variety of police and non-police persons had 'negotiated' during the forty-seven hours, largely without measurable success. As a result of the incident, the idea of having specific individuals designated as hostage negotiators was introduced into the New York City Police Department for the first time. By April 1973 a team of negotiators had been selected from the ranks of the Detective Bureau and put through a four week training program (Welch, 1984:66).

Police Commissioner Michael J. Codd (1977:3) in a report on police preparedness for terrorist events indicated that the hostage situation guide had been designed to "focus on functional team work, effective communications, and skilled coordination of tactics, under the management of a high ranking police commander." A major change to the original draft of the plan, following John & Al's, was the establishment of "a group of specially trained negotiators responsible for communicating with barricaded suspects" in place of "the more traditional response of unconditional assault" (Taylor, 1983:64).

The first formal practice of police hostage negotiation was established in New York City during the period between September 1972 and April 1973 (Bell, 1978; Moorehead, 1980; Bolz and Hershey, 1979; Schlossberg and Freeman, 1974; Douglas & Olshaker, 1995). In 1974, the New York City Police Department received a grant from the New York State Division of Criminal Justice Services to support the efforts which had been initiated post-Munich and revised as a result of John & Al's. A hostage confrontation response system, utilizing Detective Bureau investigators and Emergency Service Unit tactical specialists, was formalized. The investigators and the tactical officers were trained to "meet the problem of hostage negotiating and rescue" under the direction of an incident commander, according to a Police Department document Terrorism Control in New York City (1979). The recommended guidelines had evolved into a Tactical Manual for Hostage Situations (1974).

The Emergency Service Unit of the New York City Police Department was a highly diverse mobile force of uniformed officers with full-time citywide responsibilities. The members of this all volunteer group had to have extensive uniformed patrol experience before applying for a transfer into the Emergency Service Unit. The members were rescue oriented and performed a wide range of specialized tasks. According to their Operational Policies and Tactics (1977:1,20), among other tasks, they are certified Emergency Medical Technicians who take potential jumpers off bridges and buildings, handle radiation accidents, search for and transport improvised explosive devices and operate the Emergency Rescue Vehicle (a tank). *"They are the [New York City Police] Department's Firearms Battalion. They are the only members qualified to use tear gas. They are also skilled in the use of anti-sniper rifles, carbines, machine guns, and the shotgun, their most basic weapon."* One chapter of their Operational Policies and Tactics manual was devoted to confrontations, which included *"sniper, barricaded criminal/hostage, disorderly group/mob, civilian clothed member [and] dangerous psychotic."* The Emergency Service Unit was selected to be the tactical [SWAT] component of the new hostage confrontation program because of its involvement in closely related activities for many years.

It was an Emergency Service Police Officer, Steve Gilroy, who was killed in the early stages of the siege at John & Al's. It was not surprising that officers assigned to Emergency Service might resent, if not resist, creation of a new team of officers to perform part of their [ESU] jobs (Welch, 1984).

The decision to house the negotiator component of the new program in the Detective Bureau rather than Patrol or Special Operations was based on a variety of personnel factors to locate appropriate candidates to become successful hostage/crisis negotiators (Schlossberg & Freeman, 1974 ; Bard, 1978; Symonds, 1980). Since assignment to the Detective Bureau had been preceded by a range of other policing experiences, the investigators would be chronologically and experientially mature. Investigators worked in civilian clothes which fit with the crisis intervention notion of non-hostile representation of authority. Detective assignments are normally case-driven as compared to those of uniformed patrol officers who are often radio-run-incident driven, so investigators do not have to be readily available for the next routine radio-run. Investigators are also expected to be competent in gathering and analyzing intelligence as well as in conducting interviews and interrogations. These skills were deemed necessary for success in hostage/crisis negotiation.

To be accepted as a negotiator, the volunteer investigator needed a positive recommendation from his commander; to pass a paper and pencil psychological examination and a follow-up interview with a police department psychologist; and to be favorably interviewed by the Hostage Team Coordinator. Those chosen were then assigned to a four week training program, designed specifically for the purpose, that covered psychology, physical fitness, firearms, electronic equipment, and liaison (Culley, 1974:3). They were assigned full time in civilian clothes to various Detective Squads, and were called for an incident based on geographic area of assignment, scheduled work time, and special qualifications. After the incident, the negotiators returned to their regular investigative duties. These individuals performed the additional duties of hostage/crisis negotiator without additional pay, although their base investigator's salary was higher than the base pay of the uniformed Emergency Service Officers.

During approximately the first ten years of existence, the New York City Police Department Detective Bureau Hostage Negotiating Team was a function without a permanent home. When the hostage confrontation program was formally launched, as a result of the critique of the John & Al's siege, the newly designated Hostage Coordinator, a Lieutenant assigned to the Brooklyn Detective command, was placed in charge and transferred into the Major Crimes Section of the citywide Special Investigation Division. In 1983, the hostage/crisis negotiation function was transferred to a staff unit in the Detective Bureau, the Central Investigation and Resource Division. In addition to coordinating a hostage team, the Lieutenant was responsible for supervising kidnaping and extortion investigations, and was also accountable for various other activities including the unit which provided technical support and surveillance at hostage situations. The changes which occurred during 1973 to 1983 were due to resistance or a lack of acceptance on the part of some senior police commanders during a period of adjustment. The personality of the hostage team coordinator and positive media attention to early successes of the team also created resentment. The original team coordinator was an extremely outgoing individual who was also active in many social organizations within the Department. The New York media provided extensive coverage to the highly successful operational activities of the hostage negotiators and the coordinator made himself available to a variety of interviewers. This was with the approval of the press office of the Police Department, but it engendered negative reaction by other commanders. This is consistent with Welch's observation about organizational resistance to innovations (Welch, 1984).

Another change which took place during this same time period was in the types of incidents to which hostage/crisis negotiators were dispatched. Originally they responded only to confirmed hostage-holdings, and the request for hostage/crisis negotiators was initiated by the Emergency Service Unit supervisor at the scene. Gradually, based on hostage/crisis negotiation success, and accompanying positive media attention, they were dispatched to some non-hostage crisis situation such as barricaded criminals and people threatening suicide. Both of these functions previously had been the exclusive purview of the Emergency Service Unit. Contemporaneous with these expanded duties, hostage/crisis negotiation personnel were also being utilized in kidnap and extortion cases, and in operational planning for high risk raid and warrant execution. A significant change took place with the publication of the Police Department's Interim Order # 51 (1984) when for the first time it was mandated that negotiators be dispatched to certain situations involving non-hostage holding emotionally disturbed persons. These situations were previously handled by the Emergency Service Unit. Likewise, prior to this, calls for the immediate services of hostage/crisis negotiators had been initiated by the Emergency Service Unit Supervisor. However, the new Interim Order specified that the requesting authority was to be the Incident Commander, normally the on-scene Duty Captain, who was usually the highest ranking uniformed officer at the incident. Graph 13-1 shows the workload - that is, the number of incidents in which they were called upon to intervene. Graph 13-1 also shows the number of incidents in which a person barricaded-in or holding a hostage was armed with a gun.

The practice of hostage/crisis negotiation is a good example of the interdisciplinary nature of police work and the importance of merging academic knowledge with real world problems to arrive at responsible solutions to life-threatening situations. Hundreds of lives - those of hostages, police officers, and even the perpetrators of these crimes - have been saved as a result of the adoption and refinement of this approach to resolving stand-offs.

References

American Heritage Dictionary. (1983). Second College Edition. New York: Dell Publishing.

Bolz, F., & Hershey, E. (1979). Hostage Cop. New York: Rawson Wade.

Bahn, C. (1987). Sieges and their Aftermaths. New York: John Jay College of Criminal Justice. Unpublished Manuscript.

Bard, M. (1974, July). Implications of Collaboration Between Law Enforcement and the Social Sciences FBI Law Enforcement Bulletin.v. 43, n. 7.

Bard, M. (1975). The Functions of the Police in Crisis Intervention and Conflict Management. Washington: U.S. Department of Justice.

Bard, M. (1976). Role of Law Enforcement in the Helping Systems in Monahan, J., Ed., Community Mental Health and the Criminal Justice System. New York: Pergamon Press.

Bard, M. (1978). Hostage Negotiations; Part I, Tactical Procedures, & Part II, Negotiating Techniques. New York: Harper & Row Films.

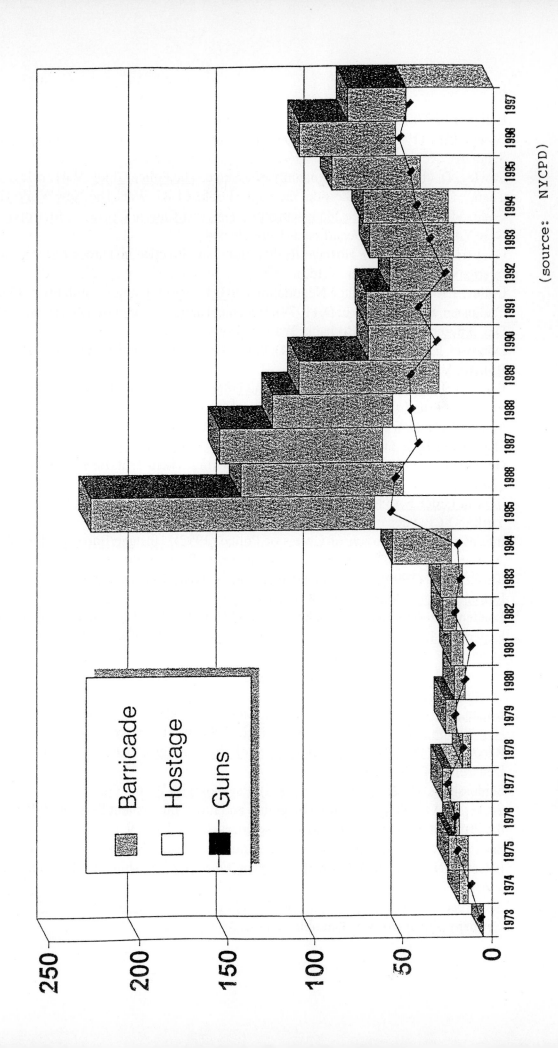

NEW YORK CITY POLICE DEPARTMENT - HOSTAGE NEGOTIATIONS UNIT
HOSTAGE/BARRICADE SITUATIONS
1973-1997

Barricade
Hostage
Guns

(source: NYCPD)

156

Bell, J.B. (1978). A Time of Terror. New York: Basic Books.

Buhite, R.D. (1995). Lives at risk: hostages and victims in American foreign policy. Wilmington: Scholarly Resources Inc.

Cawley, D. (1974, January). Anatomy of a Seige. The Police Chief. V.41, n.1.

Chen, D.W. (1998) In Bayside, the Night Looked Like War. The New York Times, March 19.

Codd, M.J. (1977). Police Management of Terrorist Caused Crises; A Metropolitan Perspective. New York City Police Department: Unpublished

Cooper, H.H.A. (1985). Hostage Rights - Law and Practice in Throes of Evolution Journal of International Law. Winter. V.15, n.1.

Culley, J.A. (1974). Hostage Negotiations FBI Law Enforcement Bulletin.v. 43 n.10.

Crelinsten, R.D. and Szabo, D. (1979). Hostage-Taking. Lexington: D.C. Heath and Company Dog Day Afternoon. (1975). Burbank: Warner Brothers.

Donovan, E.J., & Sullivan, J.F. (1974). Police Response to Family Disputes FBI Law Enforcement Bulletin.V.43, n.9.

Douglas, J., & Olshaker, M. (1995). Mind Hunter. New York: Simon & Schuster.

Edelman, J. and Crain, M.B. (1993). The Tao of Negotiation.New York: Harper Business.

Garson, G.D. (1972). Force versus Restraint in Prison Riots Crime and Delinquency . V.18, n.4.

Gelb, B. (1977). The Cop Who Saves Lives New York Times Magazine, April 17.

Gettinger, S. (1983). Hostage Negotiators Bring Them Out Alive Police Magazine.V.6, n.1 (January).

Interim Order No.51 Aided Cases, Mentally Ill or Emotionally Disturbed Persons. (1984). New York: NYCPD departmental order.

International Association of Chiefs of Police (1992). Hostage/Barricaded Subject Incidents. Arlington, VA: IACP National Law Enforcement Policy Center.

Kaiser, N.F. (1990). The Tactical Incident; A Total Police Response FBI Law Enforcement Bulletin. V.59, n.8 (August).

Louden, R.J. (1993). How Much is Enough? How Much is Too Much? . Recommendations of Experts for Improvemnets in Federal Law Enforcement After Waco. Washington: U.S. Department of Justice.

Moorehead, C. (1980). Hostages to Fortune.New York: Atheneum.

Operational policies and Tactics (1977). New York City Police Department. Unpublished.

Rogan, R.G., Hammer, M.R., and Van Zandt, C.R. (1997). Dynamic Processes of Crisis Negotiation; Theory, Research and Practice. Westport: Praeger.

Recommended Guidelines: Incidents Involving Hostages. (1973). New York City Police Department.Unpublished.

Schlossberg, H., & Freeman, L. (1974). Psychologist With a Gun. New York: Coward McCann

Soskis, D.A. (1983). Behavioral Scientists and Law Enforcement Personnel: Working Together on the Problem of Terrorism Behavioral Sciences & The Law. V.1, n.2.

Soskis, D.A., & Van Zandt, C.R. (1986, Autumn). Hostage Negotiation: Law Enforcement's Most Effective Non-Lethal Weapon Management Quarterly. Washington: U.S. Department of Justice. V.6, n.4.

Schreiber, M. (1973). After-Action Report of Terrorist Activity; 20th Olympic Games Munich, West Germany .Quantico, VA: Unpublished FBI Manuscript

Shelton, P.T. (1994). Attica -1971- LeBastille Extraordinaire <u>History of the New York State Police 1917 - 1987</u>. New York: Trooper Foundation of the State of New York.

Strollo, A.R., & Wills-Raftery, D. (1994). <u>Four Long Days: Return to Attica</u>.Hurley, NY: American Life Associates.

Symonds, M. (1980). Victim Responses to Terror <u>Annals of the New York Academy of Sciences</u>. V.347 (June):129-136.

<u>Tactical Manual for Hostage Situations</u> (1974). New York City Police Department: Unpublished.

Taylor, R.W. (1983, March). Hostage and Crisis Negotiation Procedures: Assessing Police Liability <u>Trial</u>. V.19, n.3.

<u>Terrorism Control in New York City</u> (1979). New York City Police Department: Unpublished.

Useem, B., & Kimball, P. (1989). <u>States of Siege - U.S. Prison Riots 1971 - 1986</u>. New York: Oxford University Press.

Volpe, M.R. & Louden, R.J. (1990). Hostage Negotiations: Skills and Strategies for Third Party Intervention in High Stress Situations. <u>Dispute Resolution and Democracy in the 1990's: Shaping the Agenda</u>. Washington: Society of Professionals in Dispute Resolution.

Welch, M.F. (1984). The Applied Typology and Victimology in The Hostage Negotiation Process <u>Crime and Justice</u>. V.7:63-86.

Wicker, T. (1975). <u>A Time To Die</u>. New York: Quandrangle.

Chapter 14

PROSECUTION IN NEW YORK CITY

By

Professor Martin Wallenstein

Department of Speech and Theater

Orientation -

"Be tough but fair." The words rang out clearly from the front of the room. There stood Charles J. Hynes, the District Attorney for Kings County in the Borough of Brooklyn New York, addressing a room full of new law school graduates hired to be prosecutors, the Borough's famous name. We were promised hard work and a chance to do an important job. We were sitting in a large but crowded room in the office of the District Attorney where much of our early training would take place. Outside the window, one could see the golden statute of justice, with her scales raised on the Supreme Court building across the street, but, no one was looking out the window now.

Like all of the other new hires, I felt lucky and honored to be there. I was going to be an Assistant District Attorney, a prosecutor. I had just taken the oath to uphold my role as a "Brooklyn A.D.A." I had not yet found out whether I'd passed the bar, but, I would be prosecuting cases in Criminal Court provisionally along with most of the rest of the "Class of 1990." In the year that followed as an Assistant District Attorney and the year after that, as a Special Assistant District Attorney, I discovered a lot about why being "tough but fair" in that office is so crucial for justice in our criminal justice system. This paper examines the role of the prosecutor in New York City.

THE PROSECUTOR'S ROLE

At the time we took the oath of office, many of my fellow "freshman" Assistant District Attorneys probably were not aware of how uniquely American the office of the District Attorney really was. The prosecutor's office is not under the auspices of the Courts; nor is it a loosely organized group of private attorneys. In Europe, prosecutions are conducted by civil service persons who fall under the organization of the judiciary. In England, prosecutions are conducted by private barristers (courtroom attorneys) who may prosecute in one trial and defend the accused in the next (Sullivan, 1986). When at the end of his speech, the Brooklyn District Attorney, grinned, and said, "And, remember, I hired you; you work for me," he was pointing out an important aspect of prosecution in New York and throughout the country. Unlike civil service positions, we were employed at the will of the District Attorney, and, we could be fired at his displeasure.

Prosecutors investigate organized crime, domestic violence, fraud, official corruption, and police misconduct. Prosecutors serve as legal advisors to the police as they investigate crimes. After a suspect is arrested, and, sometimes before that arrest ever takes place, the job of seeing the case through to trial and if necessary, to defend the state's action on appeal belongs to the prosecutor. Since a police officer needs only "probable cause" to arrest a suspect while a conviction requires "proof beyond a reasonable doubt," often there is much work to be done after a suspect has been arrested. The responsibility for justifying the case for the government and the actions of the police falls upon the prosecutor. At the same time, the prosecutor must serve as the first check on unjustified police actions. The prosecutor makes the first determination about whether to pursue the charges made by the police or to drop these charges and let the suspect go. If the defendant's actions warrant more serious charges than those brought by the police, it is the prosecutor's responsibility to upgrade those charges. The prosecutor recommends whether bail should be set, what amount bail should be, or whether to recommend remanding a defendant without bail. Then, it is the prosecutor who has to present the case before the grand jury to obtain an indictment, and to the jury at trial. If the government wins a conviction, the prosecutor has to defend the actions that led to the conviction in Court as fair, just, and lawful if the defendant appeals his conviction. Prosecutors have a responsibility to make recommendations to the state legislature to improve of the criminal justice system as well.

THE STRUCTURE OF DISTRICT ATTORNEY'S OFFICES IN NEW YORK CITY

In some rural localities, the prosecutor may be an individual attorney holding the office on a part-time basis, handling the few cases that come his way on his own. (Bjorkman, 1981). In New York City, the prosecutors who are in charge of handling cases involving state violations, misdemeanors and crimes from the time a defendant is arrested to the time a convict has exhausted his appeals, are the five elected District Attorneys (See, N.Y. Constitution, Article XIII § 13). These District Attorneys are elected in borough-wide elections and serve for four year terms in office. However, these District Attorneys rarely if ever try cases themselves. They are busy running some of the largest law offices in the Country. Occasionally, the New York State Attorney General's Office will conduct prosecutions in New York City as well. In very rare instances, the Governor of the State of New York will appoint a special prosecutor to handle a case that is particularly sensitive and controversial. District attorneys are assisted by hundreds of Assistant District Attorneys as well as large staffs of investigators, secretaries, clerks, and paralegal workers. Federal prosecutions are handled by one of two federal prosecutors who also have fairly large staffs. While the District Attorney has no direct superior, the Federal Prosecutor is an employee of the United States Justice Department and works under the supervision of the Attorney General of the United States. There is also a special citywide office to conduct drug prosecutions in New York, The Office of Special Narcotics. This office is staffed by Assistant District Attorneys from the offices of the five District Attorneys and by attorneys from the federal prosecutor, and has jurisdiction throughout the city.

Prosecutors' offices at the county ("borough") level are run as a bureaucracy with an elected official at the top and experienced appointees just below. However, the front lines are staffed by relatively inexperienced and young attorneys who are paid far less than they would make working for large prestigious law firms or in other jobs in the private sector. Because of the low pay, heavy work load, and the value placed upon the litigation experience an Assistant District Attorney receives, the District Attorney's offices generally require a minimum commitment of between three and four years from prospective job applicants.

The five borough prosecutors' offices structure the way cases are handled differently. One basic difference is the degree to which the office uses "vertical" or "horizontal" structure. Some of the offices, such as that in Manhattan, use a *horizontal* structure for handling most cases. Unless the case is earmarked for a specialized bureau when it first comes into the office, the attorney, who first "catches" the case will handle the case in early case assessment, at arraignment, in preparation for trial, in plea negotiations, and at a trial, if necessary. Richmond County and Bronx County use a modified horizontal structure where attorneys are assigned to the case before or at arraignment, but a different attorney may be assigned if the case is upgraded from misdemeanor to felony. That attorney will then follow the case through to its conclusion. The Kings County and Queens County District Attorney's offices use a *vertical* structure. Where the vertical structure is used, the case will be handled by one attorney during early case assessment, by another during arraignment and bail, by another for trial preparation, by still another before a grand jury, and yet another at trial.

Both vertical and horizontal structures have their advantages and disadvantages. The horizontal structure allows the attorney to persevere with a case from beginning to end. This allows the police officers and witnesses involved in the case to have a feeling of continuity because they deal with the same representative at each stage of the proceedings. But, the vertical structure has advantages as well. It allows the attorney to devote full attention to that one specific function. There are admittedly different skills required for early case assessment, initial case preparation, presentation before a grand jury, in plea negotiation and at trial. The horizontal structure allows the prosecutor's office to let less experienced attorneys handle cases at earlier less crucial stages and lets the more experienced A.D.A.'s handle the more difficult tasks of advocacy at trial.

CONFLICTS BETWEEN OFFICES

Generally, the various offices handling prosecutions in New York City have clearly defined jurisdictions which discourage conflicts between them. Federal prosecutors concern themselves with federal crimes. State prosecutors concern themselves with violations of state laws. The District Attorneys concern themselves with State crimes committed within the County that they serve. Usually, the Governor and the Attorney General of the State leave the District Attorneys free to handle these cases as they see fit. However, there are cases where conflicts arise.

When there is a conflict between the U.S. Attorney's Office and the county District Attorney, the doctrine of 'preemption' determines jurisdiction. Federal prosecutors have the power to preempt state charges with federal charges for the same or similar offenses. For example, the U.S. Attorney for the Eastern District of New York took over a case involving securities fraud from the New York County (Manhattan) District Attorney over the protestations of that office in 1998. The federal prosecutor could do this because federal law in this area preempted, or took precedence over the State law in the area of securities fraud.

In some areas, however, the county District Attorney's office and the U.S. Attorney's office can work in conjunction. For example, the Kings County District Attorney's office was not able to obtain a conviction against Lemrick Nelson for the murder of Yankel Rosenbaum, a Jewish man stabbed to death in 1991 during an anti-Semitic riot in the Crown Heights section of Brooklyn. The stabbing followed an automobile accident in which a black child was killed by a Jewish driver in a rabbi's motorcade. However, after the State prosecution failed, the United States Attorney for the Eastern District (partly at the urging of the Kings County District Attorney's Office) prosecuted Nelson for the violation of Rosenbaum's civil rights, although the accused had been found "not guilty" of the state charge of murder. The Federal Prosecutors were able to try Mr. Nelson in this case because, while the state murder prosecution and the Federal prosecution for violation of civil rights stemmed from the same factual incident, the crimes charged were different enough that for the purposes of these charges, State and Federal authorities were deemed to be two separate sovereigns. Thus, Mr. Nelson's constitutional protection against "double jeopardy" did not apply. In other less publicized cases, A.D.A.'s have been cross designated and worked together with the U.S. Attorney's office.

Whenever the Governor believes that a case may be too sensitive to be handled fairly by the county prosecutor, the Governor may appoint a "Special Prosecutor" to handle that case. For example, in 1986, when in a racially charged attack, a young Black man was killed by young white men in Howard Beach, Queens County, Governor Cuomo appointed a special prosecutor to handle this racially charged case. More recently, in 1996, after The Bronx District Attorney made public statements to the effect that he would never seek capital punishment under New York's death penalty statute, Governor Pataki removed him from a case involving the killing of a police officer and put State Attorney General Vacco in charge of the case (see Matter of Johnson v. Pataki, 229 A.D.2d 242, 1st Dept. 1997; affirmed by sharply divided Court of Appeals, New York Law Journal 12/5/97: 25 Col.1, Ct. App.). However, this authorization to appoint a special district attorney is sparingly invoked and narrowly interpreted (People v. Leahy, 72 N.Y.2d 510, 1988).

TRAINING OF ROOKIE PROSECUTORS

Classes of newly hired prosecutors receive several weeks of intensive training from more experienced attorneys in the office. The training includes an orientation to the various bureaus in the office, advanced training in criminal law and procedure, an orientation to the kinds of paperwork that the prosecutor will receive from the police, and practice in interviewing victims and suspects. The rookie prosecutors then begin their work under supervision in one of the various bureaus.

Within weeks, new Assistant District Attorneys find themselves interviewing police officers, writing up accusatory instruments, arguing in court about bail and sufficiency of cause to arrest and search, preparing cases for trial, asking for orders of protection for victims, and negotiating plea bargains with defense counsel, or in the midst of writing appellate briefs in felony cases. As responsibilities increase, A.D.A.s receive continued training for the new roles.

THE IMPORTANCE OF PROSECUTORIAL DISCRETION

In Brooklyn's early Case Assessment Bureau, an unhappy police officer is informed that the suspect he has just arrested for possessing marijuana will not be prosecuted. The officer threatens to take the case elsewhere to be prosecuted. "Oh yeah," responds the A.D.A., "and who will you get to prosecute this case?"

Prosecutors have wide latitude to exercise their discretion in deciding what crimes to prosecute and how vigorously to go after defendants. Indeed, the power to prosecute a crime and to control the prosecution after the accusation has been made rests with the District Attorney (see People v. DiFalco, 44 N.Y.2d 482, 1978). Moreover, just because a crime has been committed does not mean that the prosecutor must prosecute the person who committed it. The office of the District Attorney can decide not to prosecute as a matter of public policy (In Matter of Hassan v. Magistrates Court, 20 Misc. 2d 509, 514; Leave Denied, 8 N.Y.2d 750, 1960). In fact, even the Court cannot force a prosecutor to let a defendant plead to a lesser offense than the one with which the prosecutor has charged him unless the prosecutor gives consent (McDonald v. Sobel, 272 A.D. 455, 2d Dept. 1947). Prosecutorial discretion extends to starting investigations, initiating prosecutions,

determining what charges to submit to the grand jury, whether to bring a case to trial, and, whether to prosecute an appeal against an Appellant fighting a guilty verdict (see Sullivan, 1986). When New York reenacted the death penalty in 1995, the District Attorney became the only elected official in New York with discretion to seek an offender's death. This power of discretion implies a heavy weight of responsibility.

THE PROSECUTOR'S EXTRA ETHICAL RESPONSIBILITIES

In Brooklyn, we were reminded that we had taken two oaths. We had taken an oath when we became members of the New York State Bar, but, we had also taken an oath when we signed the book as members of the District Attorney's office. Prosecutors in New York are aware that they must answer to a tougher ethical standard than do other attorneys. The prosecuting attorney must follow the general ethical rules governing all attorneys. As must any attorney, the prosecutor must represent her client "zealously," but "within the bounds of the law" (DR 7-102). She must not make any misleading or inaccurate statements to the accused ("Rule" 3.5). She should be truthful in Court ("Rule" 3.5). The prosecutor should follow the rules about contact and candor with persons who do not have legal representation ("Rule" 4.3). The Prosecutor should adhere to the limitations on trial publicity and avoid trying a case in the media ("Rule" 3.6). Indeed, the prosecutor is prohibited from making extrajudicial statements and must exercise "reasonable care" that members of the staff don't make them either ("Rule" 3.6 and 3.8(e)). Finally, prosecutors must adhere to rules of courtroom decorum ("Rule" 3.5).

The prosecutor's role calls for additional stricter standards of ethical conduct, because while the A.D.A. must be a vigorous advocate, she represents the People of the State of New York (in the case of county prosecutors) or the People of the United States of America (in the case of Federal prosecutors). This means that the prosecutor must protect the rights of all citizens, including the accused. Thus, the prosecutor has an ethical duty not to prosecute unless probable cause exists (Rule 3.8(A); DR 7-103(A)). A defense counsel, by contrast, should defend with vigor even if she thinks her client is guilty. Moreover, the defense counsel should not turn down the chance to represent a potential client simply because she thinks the defendant is guilty.

Indeed, the American Bar Association Model Rules of Professional Conduct exempt the defense attorney from the prohibition against making frivolous claims or defenses for a criminal case in which the defendant faces incarceration (*see Rule 3.1*). The defense counsel can and should put the People to its proof. The prosecutor must make sure that the accused has been informed of his right to counsel and has been given a reasonable chance to obtain counsel (Rule 3.8(B)). The prosecutor is not supposed to tell witnesses not to talk to a defense attorney. Defense attorneys routinely tell defendants to exercise their fifth amendment rights not to speak to anyone in law enforcement, and, the defense attorney may advise the defendant's friends or relatives that they might not be helping the defendant by speaking to the prosecutor.

Because, the prosecutor should not lie or misrepresent either the law or the facts to anyone, an A.D.A. cannot use some of the techniques employing deception that police favor in investigations. For example, a police officer trying to get a confession might tell a suspect that a co-defendant has confessed when this is not true; the prosecutor could not do so. The police officer might tell a suspect that the copy machine in the corner was really a new kind of remote lie detector, and that the suspect has failed the polygraph test; the prosecutor could not do so. A police officer can pay an informant for information; the prosecutor is barred from paying any witness except for reimbursing ordinary expenses unless the witness is an expert (see, A.B.A. Standard 3.1.).

Moreover, the prosecutor has both a legal and a moral obligation to disclose all evidence that would negate the guilt of the accused or that would lead to a reduction in the crime charged or to a reduction in the sentence that the accused might receive (see Brady v. Maryland, 373 U.S. 83 (1963); (Rule 3.8(d); DR 7-103 (B)).This obligation to turn over exculpatory information dramatically distinguishes the prosecuting attorney from the attorney for the defense for whom that obligation is very much limited by lawyer-client privilege and the doctrine of confidentiality. In order to encourage clients to rely on their attorneys and be truthful to them, much of the conversation between a lawyer and a client and much of the attorney's work product are cloaked in the same kind of confidentiality that a doctor and a patient or a priest in the confessional would have. Both Federal and State Constitutions require the disclosure of much of this kind of information by prosecutors (see Kyles v. Whitely, 514 U.S. 419, 1995). Indeed, an accused is deprived of due process if a prosecutor fails to disclose evidence, including impeachment matter, when there is a reasonable probability that the evidence would have led to a different result (People v. Bagley, 473 U.S. 667, 1985). Moreover, the prosecutor must turn over any police reports to defense counsel as well if defense counsel requests them (see People v. Rosario, 9 N.Y.2d 286, 1961; People v. Scott, 88 N.Y.2d 888, 644 N.Y.S.2d 913, 1996).

Even in the heat of battle while trying a case, the prosecutor must keep in mind that with the power and the oath of the office come a special responsibility. When presenting an argument to a jury, the prosecutor must avoid referring to inadmissible evidence as must any attorney (Rule 3.4). However, the prosecutor, unlike the defense attorney, has an ethical responsibility to pursue evidence that might hurt her own case or be helpful to the defense counsel (DR 7-103(B); "Rule" 3.8(d)). The defense has no such parallel duty. In fact, should undue emotionalism or other conduct by the prosecutor result in a guilty verdict, the defendant may appeal and might have his conviction reversed as a result. Should a prosecutor lose a case in part due to undue emotionalism or other unsavory tactics by the defense, the prohibition against double jeopardy would prohibit the prosecutor from seeking a new trial, and even if there are sanctions taken against the defense counsel, the acquittal would stand.

The Prosecutor's Responsibility to Victims

While prosecutors represent all the "People," they owe a special responsibility to one class of individuals. "Until recently, the criminal justice system in general has viewed the crime victim as nothing more than a witness to a crime," and some prosecutors might treat the victim as just a person whose testimony was necessary to obtain a conviction (Brindle, 1990). Prosecutors now must receive training in victim assistance, especially for cases involving domestic violence, sex offenses, elderly victims, child victims, and the families of homeless victims (N.Y.S. Executive Law § 642 (5)). Prosecutors must seek to ensure that victims are protected from intimidation, notified of all proceedings involving their case, given back their stolen property promptly, informed that crime compensation might be available to them, and made aware of counseling through both public and private programs. For violent crimes, or where there was a threat of serious physical injury, or in the case of crimes involving loss of significant amounts of money or destruction of property, the prosecutor must consult with the crime victim about the options of dismissal, plea bargaining, and going to trial with the case (Executive Law § 642(1)). During sentencing, the prosecutor must bring the opinion of the violent crime victim to the attention of the Court (Brindle, 1990).

The Prosecutor's Role Before the Grand Jury

One legal proceeding that is highly secret and very powerful is controlled by the prosecutor. Indeed, the prosecutor is the only attorney allowed to speak in this closed door presentation of evidence. That proceeding is the grand jury. Even where a case begins as a misdemeanor, the prosecutor can insist that the Criminal Court adjourn the case while the Prosecutor presents it to the Grand Jury to consider felony charges against the defendant (N.Y. CPL § 170.20).

Grand Juries are made up of citizens impaneled for the purpose of determining whether criminal activity should be prosecuted. New York requires that the Grand Jury have between 16 and 23 people sitting in order to indict a suspect. However, while sixteen grand jurors are necessary to constitute a quorum, only twelve need be present to have heard essential evidence in order to return an indictment provided that all twelve vote for that indictment (People v. Collier, 72 N.Y.2d 298, 1988). Grand Juries were originally intended to be a check against unwarranted prosecutions. The U.S. Constitution guaranteed that *"[n]o person shall be held to answer for a capital or otherwise infamous crime, unless on presentment or indictment of a grand jury"* (except in the case of military personnel in time of war) (U.S. Constitution Amendment V). Indeed, even today, unless a defendant waives indictment by a grand jury, he may not be prosecuted in New York State Court without an indictment (N.Y. CPL § 200.10). However, a grand jury need not be passive. It has the right on its own initiative to investigate any offenses regardless of whether there was a preliminary hearing to determine probable cause (People v. Edwards, 19 Misc. 2d 412, 414, Ct. of Gen. Sess. N.Y. Co. 1959; People v. Hobbs, 50 Misc. 2d. 561, 565, Monroe Co. Ct. 1966; Rudich, Grand Jury Procedure, 1990; Murphy & Rudich, 1998).

The prosecutor wears two hats before the grand jury. She is both the attorney presenting the evidence for the state, and, she is also the surrogate for the judge, ruling on admissibility, relevance, and giving instructions as to the law. This dual role gives the prosecutor tremendous influence over the Grand Jury Proceedings (Murphy, 1990; Rudich & Murphy, 1998).

The Prosecutor's Role at Trial and on Appeal

At trial, the prosecutor bears the burden of proving a defendant's guilt. Thus, while a defense counsel, in theory, can remain silent throughout a proceeding, the prosecutor must make the case for the People from the very beginning. She must battle for the admissibility of evidence in motion papers and at hearings, she is responsible for coordinating the appearance of witnesses and securing the evidence. To a large extent, the prosecutor is the director and producer of the show. Indeed, the prosecutor must give an opening statement that previews a *prima facie* case for each charge in an indictment in a felony case, and must then prove her case beyond a reasonable doubt. The one big advantage of the prosecutor is that of having the last word at trial. In New York State courts, the prosecutor gets to give the closing argument last. In federal court, the prosecutor gets to give a rebuttal after the defense's closing argument.

On appeal, the burdens dramatically shift. For, while the prosecutor bore the burden of proof at trial, the responsibility for raising and proving most issues on appeal shifts to the defendant/appellant. However, New York is unusual in one respect. The Appellate Divisions where the Courts receive their first appeal from the rulings of the trial judge can review both matters of fact and law (CPL § 470.05). This means that at the first level of appeal, the prosecutor may have to argue not only that the Court was right as to the law, but that the proof at trial was beyond a reasonable doubt and that the People provided the preponderance of the evidence. The New York Court of Appeals will only review questions of law, except in the case of capital cases which go directly to the Court of Appeals for review (CPL § 450.70; 450.80).

Normally, the appeals process is started by the defense, because, once a verdict is rendered, the prosecutor is barred by considerations of double jeopardy from raising the issue of the defendant's guilt at another trial. However, there are some issues where the appeal will be initiated by the prosecutor. The prosecutor may appeal an order dismissing an accusatory instrument before trial, an order setting aside the verdict, a sentence other than a death sentence, an order to vacate a judgment other than a death sentence, an order suppressing evidence or an order setting aside or modifying an order of forfeiture (see Freidlander, 1990; Collins, Bressler, Levine, & Shiffrin, 1991).

Being Tough But Fair

The prosecutor's role is a unique one. She is an investigator, the arbiter of the facts, a check on illegal police action, a check on official corruption, the instructor on the law to the grand jury and also the advocate presenting the case for the People. Because in addition to bringing cases to prosecution, the prosecutor also must protect the accused from abuses by the police, police officers may have an uneasy relationship with prosecutors. Indeed, the prosecutor has as much of a duty to prosecute police officers for criminal behavior as she does to prosecute any citizen for wrongdoing. For this reason, police often see the prosecutor as an adversary instead of an ally. In bringing charges, recommending bail, preparing and trying cases and handling appeals, the prosecutor must indeed be "tough but fair." If the prosecutor is not tough, the law will not be enforced; if a prosecutor is not fair, justice will not be served.

166

References

Table of Statutes

U.S. Constitution Amendment IV, V, IV, & XIV.
N.Y. Constitution Article XIII § 13.
N.Y. Criminal Procedure Law § 170.20, § 190, §200.10, § 450.70, §450.80 §470.05.
N.Y. Executive Law § 642(1), § 642(5)

Table of Ethical Rules and Standards

A.B.A. Model Code of Professional responsibility (1980) DR 7-102, 7-103 (B).
A.B.A. Model Rules of Professional Conduct (1983) Rule 3.1, 3.5, 3.6, 3.8(A), 3.8(B), 3.8 (D), 3.8 (E) 4.3.

Table of Cases

Brady v. Maryland, 373 U.S. 83 (1963).
McDonald v. Sobel, 272 A.D. 455 (1947).
Matter of Hassan v. Magistrates Court, 20 Misc.2d. 509; Leave Denied, 8 N.Y.2d 750 (1960).
Matter of Johnson v. Pataki, 229 A.D.2d 242 (1997), *affirmed* 90 N.Y.2d 900 (1997).
Kyles v. Whitely, 515 U.S. 419 (1995).
People v. Collier, 72 N.Y.2d 298 (1988).
People v. DiFalco, 44 N.Y.2d 482 (1978).
People v. Edwards, 19 Misc.2d 412 (Ct. of Gen. Sess. N.Y. Co. 1959).
People v. Hobbs, 50 Misc.2d 561 (Monroe Co. Ct. 1966).
People v. Leahy, 72 N.Y.2d 510 (1988).
People v. Rosario, 9N.Y.2d 286 (1961).
People v. Scott, 88 N.Y.2d 888 (1996).
United States v. Bagley, 473 U.S. 667 (1985).

Secondary Sources

Bjorkman, (1981) The part-time State's Attorney in South Dakota: the conflict between fealty to private client and service to the public. 27 S.D.L.Rev. 1.
Brindle, & Currier (1990) Victims' rights and the role of the prosecutor. Basic Course for Prosecutors. New York: Division of Criminal Justice Services.
Collins, Bressler, Levine, & Shiffrin (1991) Appeals in criminal cases. New York Criminal Practice Handbook, edited by R.W. Vinal. New York State Bar Association.
Freidlander (1990) Appellate Practice. Basic Course for Prosecutors. New York: Division of Criminal Justice Services.
Morgan & Rotunda (1987) Professional Responsibility: Problems and Materials. University Casebook Series, Foundation Press, Mineola, New York.
Murphy & Rudich (1998) Grand Jury Proceedings. New York Criminal Practice Handbook, edited

by L.N.Gray, New York State Bar Association.

Murphy, (1990) Grand Jury procedure. <u>Basic Course for Prosecutors</u>. New York: Division of Criminal Justice Services.

Sullivan, (1986) The prosecution function. <u>Basic Course for Prosecutors</u>. New York: Division of Criminal Justice Services.

Chapter 15

NEW YORK CITY'S COURT SYSTEM

By

Prof.essor Daniel R. Pinello

Department of Government

HOW THE COURT SYSTEM IS ORGANIZED

New York State has one of the most complex court systems in the country (Flango & Rottman, 1992). To understand why it's complicated, first consider what a simple **court-organization system** looks like. Take neighboring Connecticut, with just three levels of courts handling criminal cases. The highest is named the Supreme Court; the lowest, the Superior Court; and the middle, the Appellate Court — as in Figure 15- 1. The Superior Court is also known as the **trial court** since criminal cases begin there and proceed to trial or other disposition (like plea bargains). The remaining court levels are **appellate**, reviewing proceedings in the trial court. Appeals from the trial court go first to the middle level (called the **intermediate appellate court**), and under special circumstances, from there to the highest level (termed the **court of last resort**).

By comparison, New York State has *eleven* kinds of trial courts and *two* intermediate appellate courts. This complexity appears in New York City courts dealing with criminal cases (Figure 14- 2). Three trial courts handle criminal cases in the City, depending on the kind of **criminal offense** charged and the age of the accused. New York law defines two major categories of crimes: (A) **misdemeanors** are offenses punishable (1) by one year in prison or less or (2) by fine of $1,000 or less; (B) **felonies** are offenses punishable by more than those amounts. The **New York City Criminal Court**, with branches in each of the five boroughs, has **jurisdiction** (or power) (A) over all misdemeanor prosecutions through the trial stage and (B) over felony cases until time of **indictment**, when **grand juries** determine whether sufficient credible evidence exists to believe individuals charged with felonies should stand trial. Once grand juries indict **defendants** in New York City, jurisdiction shifts to the **Criminal Term** (or part) of the **Supreme Court of the State of New York**, with branches in each borough. Despite its misleading name, the New York Supreme Court is not the highest one in the State. Rather, it's the trial court with the broadest power over the most kinds of cases, including civil lawsuits (people suing each other for money). The New York Supreme Court, therefore, is called the trial court of general jurisdiction, and indictments in New York City proceed to trial or other disposition in the Supreme Court.

Figure 1

Connecticut's Criminal Court System

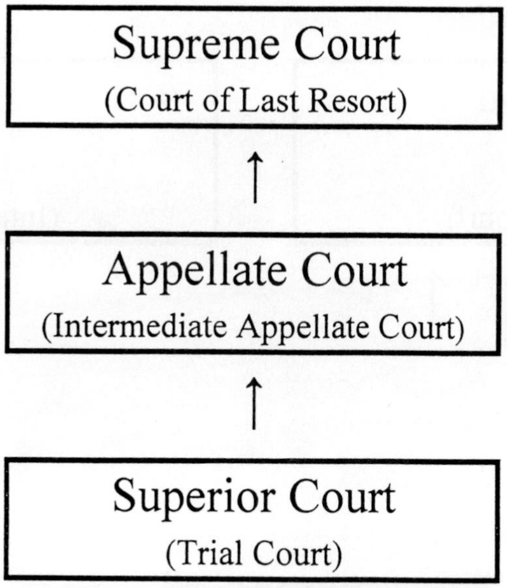

```
┌─────────────────────────────────┐
│        Supreme Court            │
│     (Court of Last Resort)      │
└─────────────────────────────────┘
                ↑
┌─────────────────────────────────┐
│        Appellate Court          │
│  (Intermediate Appellate Court) │
└─────────────────────────────────┘
                ↑
┌─────────────────────────────────┐
│         Superior Court          │
│         (Trial Court)           │
└─────────────────────────────────┘
```

Figure 2

New York City's Criminal Court System

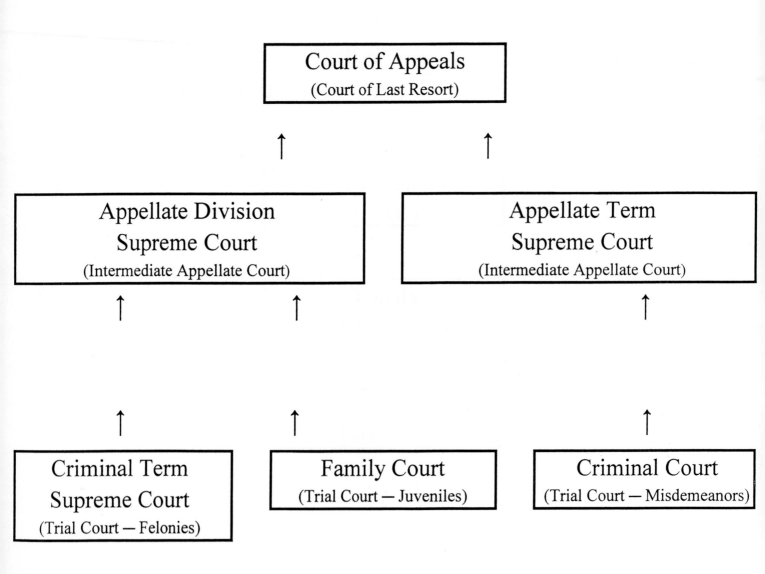

The **Family Court of the State of New York**, with branches in each borough, handles **juvenile delinquents** (people under age 16 charged with criminal offenses), although individuals as young as 13 may be prosecuted as **juvenile offenders** in the criminal courts when accused of the most serious felonies. As a result of recent reform, a specialized division of the Court will handle the 5% of its total cases involving delinquency (Lewis, 1998).

When criminal prosecutions end in trial courts with findings of guilt, defendants have a right under state law to an appeal. Intermediate appellate courts thus have no choice but to hear these appeals, resulting in the **mandatory appellate jurisdiction** of those courts. People guilty of misdemeanors in the New York City Criminal Court appeal to the **Appellate Term** of the New York Supreme Court. Those guilty of felonies in the Supreme Court, as well as delinquents in the Family Court, appeal to the **Appellate Division** of the Supreme Court. Another complexity of the New York judicial system, then, is that the state's Supreme Court is both the intermediate appellate tribunal and the trial court of general jurisdiction. The Appellate Division is separated into four **judicial departments**. The First Department consists of the Bronx and Manhattan. The Second Department covers Brooklyn, Queens, and Staten Island, as well as Dutchess, Nassau, Orange, Putnam, Rockland, Suffolk, and Westchester Counties.

The losing side in the intermediate appellate court may want to appeal further, to the state court of last resort — called the **New York Court of Appeals**. But since there is no absolute right to a second appeal, litigants seeking review by the Court of Appeals must petition for leave (or permission) to appeal, and the Court grants only about 2% of requests. In addition, defendants convicted of state crimes sometimes claim violations of their federal constitutional rights and petition the **United States Supreme Court** to examine their cases. Again, such extra judicial scrutiny is **discretionary** not mandatory, and fewer than 1% of applications to the U.S. Supreme Court are granted. Hence, the resolution reached in the state intermediate appellate court is the final one in most appealed cases.

Adding to the confusion of the state court system in New York City is the existence of separate federal courts also handling criminal cases. **Federalism** — the political concept of dividing power between the centralized authority of the national government and the more local control of the states — requires the federal (or national) government to prosecute people accused of criminal violations prohibited by federal law in federal courts. Fortunately for students of crime and justice, the federal court system is the simple variety, as in Connecticut, although the names are slightly different: the federal trial court is the **United States District Court**; and the intermediate appellate court is the **United States Court of Appeals**. Further, New York City covers two federal judicial districts. The Bronx and Manhattan make up the **Southern District of New York**, while Brooklyn, Queens, and Staten Island are in the **Eastern District of New York**. Thus, federal criminal prosecutions in the Bronx and Manhattan begin in the United States District Court for the Southern District of New York, while federal cases from the rest of the City start in the United States District Court for the Eastern District of New York. Appeals from those two courts go to the United States Court of Appeals for the Second Circuit, located in Manhattan.

Proposals to simplify New York State's court system have been suggested for a long time (Barbanel 1983; Glass 1987). Most recently, New York's Chief Judge, Judith S. Kaye, recommended the consolidation of state trial courts into just two categories from the current eleven: a District Court to handle low-level cases and the Supreme Court for the rest. New York Governor George

Pataki has endorsed Judge Kaye's plan, which influential media like the *New York Times* support as well ("Pushing for Court Reform" 1998). Yet, although Judge Kaye's idea does simplify trial courts statewide, it would have little impact on criminal cases in New York City. The only reform affecting the City would be the consolidation of all trial courts into one, so every criminal case would be processed in the same tribunal.

Such comprehensive consolidation, however, is very unlikely. Consider what happened in 1987, the last time the state legislature seriously considered it. On the merits of court unification, opponents argued that trial-court specialization is desirable and pointed to how the Family Court, in recognition of the special needs of minors and personal family matters, was established to be less adversarial than other courts (Glass, 1987). An even greater obstacle to court simplification was political partisanship. Republicans, who dominate judicial elections in suburban Nassau, Suffolk, and Westchester Counties, were frustrated that the Democratic strongholds of Brooklyn and Queens in the Second Judicial Department allow the elevation of more Democratic judges to the Appellate Division when the Governor is a Democrat. Accordingly, state Republican leaders refused to support court consolidation without the creation of a Fifth Judicial Department separating Nassau, Suffolk, and Westchester from Brooklyn and Queens — a move Democrats opposed (Glass, 1987; Lynn, 1987; Schmalz, 1987). At the same time, the Supreme Court Justices Association fought court unification because its members resisted sharing power and prestige with lower-court judges (Lynn 1987; "Court Reform at Risk" 1987). State unions representing court personnel also raised questions about their members' pay and working conditions in the event of consolidation (Lynn, 1987). In the face of such combined opposition, trial-court reform failed.

How Judges Are Selected

Reflecting its complex court system, New York's method of selecting judges is complicated, too. A neighboring state again offers a simple system for comparison. New Jersey's Governor appoints state judges and the New Jersey State Senate confirms them, just as the President of the United States appoints federal judges and the U.S. Senate confirms them. In contrast, New York uses *three* different methods of judicial selection: **executive appointment**; **popular election**; and the so-called **Missouri Plan**. (Regardless of method, candidates for all trial and appellate judgeships in New York City must be members of the state bar for at least ten years to be eligible.)

Appointment

Judges of the New York City Criminal Court and of the Family Court in New York City are appointed by the Mayor of New York City for ten-year terms. Annual salaries in the Criminal Court are $103,800; the Family Court, $113,000. Justices of the Appellate Term of the Supreme Court, earning $115,500 annually, are selected from sitting Supreme Court justices by the Chief Administrative Judge of the Supreme Court with the approval of the Presiding Justice of the Appellate Division in which the Appellate Term is located. Appellate Division justices are appointed by the Governor for five-year terms from sitting members of the Supreme Court. Associate justices earn $119,000; presiding justices, $122,000.

Election

Justices of the New York Supreme Court, earning $113,000 annually, are elected for fourteen-year terms after being nominated to the November ballot by political parties.

Missouri Plan

Named after the first state to use it, this judicial-selection method seeks to equalize the influence of political parties and to insure participation of nonlawyers in the process. The **Commission on Judicial Nomination** (CJN) consists of 12 members, four appointed by the Governor, four by the Chief Judge of the Court of Appeals, and one each by the Speaker of the Assembly, the Temporary President of the Senate, the Minority Leader of the Senate, and the Minority Leader of the Assembly. Regarding each group of commissioners appointed by the Governor and by the Chief Judge, no more than two can be from the same political party, and no more than two can be lawyers. The CJN evaluates candidates for the Court of Appeals and, acting on at least eight concurring votes of the 12, recommends to the Governor from three to seven candidates for positions on the Court. The Governor must choose from these recommendations, and the State Senate confirms the Governor's choice. The term of office is 14 years. Associate judges earn $125,000; the chief judge, $129,000.

New York law limits the number of judges officially sitting on particular courts, further complicating judicial selection. For example, only one Supreme Court justice is authorized for every 50,000 people. Manhattan's population thus warrants approximately 30 Supreme Court justices. Yet, Manhattan's criminal caseload alone necessitates more than 40 justices staffing its Criminal Term — not to mention those required for the Civil Term, Appellate Term, and Appellate Division.

As a result, the Chief Administrator of the Courts often designates judges from other state courts to serve as "acting" members of the criminal courts. Accordingly, popularly elected judges of the **New York City Civil Court** sit on the Criminal and Supreme Courts, and judges of the **New York Court of Claims** (appointed by the Governor and confirmed by the State Senate), as well as judges of the Criminal Court, serve on the Supreme Court.

The phrase "**politics** of judicial selection" refers to the informal forces surrounding the choice of judges. Each selection system involves political dynamics that go on behind the scenes. Executives like governors and mayors, for example, often are concerned about the political **ideology** or philosophy of the people they appoint to the bench. For criminal-court appointments, questions of whether judges favor the prosecution or defense arise. For instance, Governor Pataki denied reappointment to a justice of the Appellate Division in Manhattan who had a pattern over 20 years on the bench of generally ruling in favor of defendants (Hoffman, 1997). Critics of chief executives who act upon ideological criteria to select judges claim such conduct undermines judicial independence and politicizes the judiciary (Hoffman 1997; "Governor Pataki's Message to Judges" 1997). Popular election of judges likewise evokes criticism. For example, some charge that political party bosses stage bogus elections that fail to reflect genuine popular will (James, 1986; Vance, 1988). Even though a plan designed to minimize political influence in judicial selection was adopted, New York's experience in choosing Court of Appeals judges indicates partisanship and ideology do play important roles. In 1983, for instance, Governor Mario Cuomo, a Democrat, successfully persuaded the legislature to increase the number of candidates the Commission on Judicial Nomination recommends, thereby expanding gubernatorial choice (Margolick, 1983; "Cuomo Signs Measure on Court Nominations" 1983). In 12 years as governor, Cuomo was able to name moderate and liberal judges to the Court of Appeals, while Republican Governor Pataki's first appointment was more conservative (Pérez-Peña, 1998).

Partisan politics also affects judicial expansion. When the legislature considers adding more judges to understaffed courts, political **patronage** is always a concern. How many of the new judges will be Democrats versus Republicans is important to the success of proposed judicial additions (Greenfield, 1988; Kolbert, 1988; Vance, 1988). For instance, when the mushrooming use of crack cocaine in the 1980s required augmenting the number of criminal-court judges to handle new drug arrests, Democrats and Republicans in Albany had to work out a deal dividing the 23 new judges between the parties before the judgeships would be authorized (Schmalz, 1986).

The Handling of Criminal Cases in New York City

An **arrest** usually initiates most prosecutions for "street crimes" like robbery, burglary, drug possession and sale, prostitution, rape, and auto theft. When the police make arrests in New York City, they have the **discretion** or power to release accused people from custody when charged only with misdemeanors. Those suspected of committing felonies have to await **arraignment**, the defendant's first formal appearance in court, before given the opportunity of release.

At arraignment, formal notice of charges is given, either by reading them aloud in open court, or more frequently, by giving the defense attorney a copy of the **accusatory instrument** (complaint, indictment, or information). In addition, the accused is informed of his or her right to be represented by an attorney, and if the accused is indigent, counsel is assigned by the court. In response to the charges against him or her, the defendant enters a **plea** or response of "guilty" or "not guilty" to the charge(s).

As a practical matter, the most important event occurring at arraignment is the judge's determination of **bail**. In theory, bail guarantees the presence of an accused in court at all stages of the prosecution against him or her. Historically, this has meant posting a bail **bond** or written promise to pay a specified amount of money to the court upon defendants' failure to appear when scheduled, such failure resulting in forfeiture of the money. Bail **bondsmen** act like insurance companies issuing bail bonds for defendants paying premiums of 10% of the total amount of bail and providing collateral (like homes or other substantial property) to secure the bonds in the event of forfeiture.

If bail is set and the defendant cannot pay it, he or she must wait in jail until a trial or other disposition of the case — which often takes as long as three to six months, even more.

An alternative to bail is releasing defendants on their **own recognizance** — their promise voluntarily to return to court when necessary. Courts use simple predictors to determine whether an accused is a good risk to be released without bail: Does the defendant have a residence in the area? How long has he or she lived there? Does he or she have a job? Does he or she have family ties? What is his or her prior criminal record? How serious is the crime charged?

Criminal cases do not have to start with arrests. Often, with so-called white-collar crimes (like embezzlement or stock manipulation), the prosecution begins with the filing of charges by means of an indictment.

A grand jury is a group of 16 to 23 citizens who listen to evidence against individuals charged with felonies and who, with the concurrence of 12 or more grand jurors, serve several functions. First, they act in a judicial capacity to determine whether sufficient credible facts or evidence exist to believe a felony has been committed by the person charged. In other words, grand juries eliminate frivolous accusations, screening out charges of serious criminal conduct which are not well supported by the prosecution's evidence.

Second, grand juries serve an investigative function. If prosecutors believe serious crimes have been committed, grand juries have **subpoena power** to compel witnesses to appear before them to testify about the alleged criminal conduct.

Grand jury proceedings are secretive and not open to the public like other criminal proceedings. Prosecutors are the only participating attorneys. Defense attorneys may be present when their clients testify, but cannot take part in any way (such as raising objections or asking questions).

If someone is arrested, charged with a felony, and kept in custody, and a grand jury has not heard the charge within 120 hours, the defendant has the right to be released or to have a **preliminary hearing**, where a judge hears the evidence against him or her to see whether there are sufficient credible facts to believe the defendant has committed a felony, which would allow the case to proceed. In short, the judge serves the same judicial function as the grand jury in sorting out credible serious charges from insupportable ones.

During **discovery**, the defense requests the prosecution reveal certain factual details of its case to the defendant so he or she can be aware of what the prosecution will allege happened when the case proceeds to trial. Examples of such details are the time and date when the alleged crime occurred and its location and whether the defendant made statements to authorities which will be offered in evidence. The prosecuting attorney has a right to receive advance notice of the defendant's use of an alibi or of psychiatric evidence for a defense of mental disease or defect.

Pre-trial hearings allow the court to determine whether any of the defendant's constitutional rights were violated when the evidence was collected.

Defendants charged with Class A misdemeanors or with any felony have a constitutional right to **trial by jury**, the first phase of which involves the **voir dire** — the jury-selection process. The trial judge and the attorneys for both prosecution and defense question members of the **venire** — the pool of prospective jurors at trial — to select a **petit jury** of six people (in misdemeanor trials) or 12 (in felony cases) who will decide the defendant's fate. The judge has the discretion to select from one to six alternate jurors (or more in death-penalty cases).

After questioning, each side may request **challenges** against certain venirepeople. That is, the attorneys will want people removed from the jury box in a process of elimination. The first kind of challenge is **for cause**. Here, an attorney objects to a specific person's sitting on the jury because he or she is clearly unable to act in an unbiased or unprejudiced way, or is unable to follow the law as applied to the case by the judge. Jurors are excused only if the judge agrees with counsels' objections. After challenges for cause, the attorneys for each side may exercise **peremptory** challenges. These are objections to specific people sitting on a jury for which generally no reasons need be given. If the prosecution or defense simply doesn't like the way a person "looks" (except when disapproval is motivated by race or gender), then the judge must excuse him or her from service. However, the number of peremptory challenges each side has is limited, ranging from as few as three in misdemeanor trials to as many as 20 in the most serious felony prosecutions.

After all challenges have been exercised in the case, the venire members remaining in the jury box become the jury. Note that jury selection is a process of elimination, not of affirmative choice.

After the voir dire is completed, and the jury is sworn in, each side has the opportunity to make an **opening statement** to the jury. This is nothing more than a preview of what each side intends to prove later in the trial by means of calling **witnesses** to testify or by other kinds of proof.

The prosecution gives its opening statement first, followed by the defense. However, the defense has no affirmative obligation to do anything other than be responsive during the trial. Thus the defense may **waive**, or give up, its opening remarks, while the prosecution is obliged to make them.

Next comes the **People's case**. The **district attorney** offers evidence of the defendant's guilt. This usually consists of calling individuals to testify, but also may include the introduction of **physical evidence** such as weapons or drugs found in a defendant's possession. In addition, **expert witnesses** may be called — people with training in special fields of knowledge important to the prosecution (or the defense), such as ballistics experts in weapons cases or forensic pathologists in homicide prosecutions.

After the prosecution "rests" — that is, after its evidence is completed — the **defendant's case** may proceed. If the defense chooses to offer evidence in its behalf, it too may call eyewitnesses and expert witnesses and introduce exhibits.

After the Defendant's case is presented, the prosecution has an opportunity for **rebuttal**. In other words, it may try to repair any damage made to its version of events during the defendant's presentation.

Summations or **closing statements** follow the conclusion of evidence. These are comments by the attorneys, summarizing and organizing evidence and trying to persuade the jury of the truth of their cause.

Next, the judge **charges** or instructs the jury on how the law should be applied to the facts in the case. Among other things, the judge gives the jury "recipes" of ingredients or **elements** of the crimes charged for the jury to search for in the evidence.

After the judge's charge, the jury retires to **deliberate** in order to reach a **verdict**. In most circumstances, the verdict is one of two kinds: "not guilty" or "guilty." Note that a verdict of "not guilty" does not necessarily mean the defendant is "innocent."

If the jury's verdict is "not guilty" on all charges, the case is finished. If the verdict is "guilty" on any charge, the judge must **sentence** the defendant for his or her misconduct.

Nonjury trials occur when either defendants are charged with only the least serious kinds of crimes (Class B misdemeanors), bringing no legal right to trial by jury, or when defendants waive their right to trial by jury and agree to have a judge act as the trier of fact. Such "bench trials" are more common in the Criminal Court (representing roughly two-thirds of misdemeanor trials commenced) than the Supreme Court (no more than one in ten felony trials commenced).

Although all trial-court proceedings take place before single judges, appeals are decided by multimember panels. Either two or three Appellate Term justices together review Criminal Court decisions, with two justices' concurrence necessary to decide an appeal. Panels of four or five Appellate Division justices hear appeals from the Criminal Term of the Supreme Court and from Family Court, with three justices' votes necessary to resolve a case. If it agrees to hear an appeal, the Court of Appeals acts *en banc*, that is, with all seven judges hearing the case and a simple majority of four (or more) needed to decide it.

Caseload

New York City state-court criminal caseload statistics for 1997 are summarized in Table 14-1. Note that caseloads among the boroughs vary dramatically, even taking population differences into account. For example, the number of new cases in the Criminal Court varies from 3,030 per

100,000 residents in Queens to almost 9,300 per 100,000 residents in Manhattan. Likewise, the number of new (felony) cases in the Supreme Court is as little as 200 per 100,000 residents in Staten Island to as much as 820 in Manhattan — a fourfold difference. Of course, Manhattan's higher rates reflect its commercial nature; the other four boroughs are primarily residential.

Table 14-1:
State-Court Criminal Caseloads, 1997

New York City Criminal Court
New cases

	Bronx	Brooklyn	Manhattan	Queens	Staten Island	Total NYC
Felonies	23,040	19,812	27,563	13,209	3,104	86,728
Misdemeanors	47,381	71,871	95,120	39,789	7,414	261,575
Violations	1,002	4,092	5,844	3,490	1,673	16,101
Other	3,590	5,155	9,818	2,564	416	21,543
Total	75,013	100,930	138,345	59,052	12,607	385,947
Dispositions						
Pleas	45,756	42,788	75,337	29,096	6,513	199,490
Verdicts	208	102	151	98	22	581
Dismissals	18,869	44,997	41,730	21,146	4,859	131,601
To Grand Jury	6,484	5,887	10,130	3,665	553	26,719
SCI*	2,540	1,386	1,355	2,299	243	7,823
Other	3,695	5,890	10,141	2,542	405	22,673
Total	77,552	101,050	138,844	58,846	12,595	388,887
Cases Disposed At Arraignment	37,908	45,822	79,832	24,725	3,590	191,877

Criminal Term, Supreme Court (Felony Cases)

	Bronx	Brooklyn	Manhattan	Queens	Staten Island	Total NYC
New Cases	8,573	9,048	12,236	6,055	767	36,679
Dispositions						
Guilty Pleas	8,286	8,543	11,515	5,281	733	34,358
Verdicts	646	580	860	600	63	2,749
Dismissals	803	1,038	1,475	683	47	4,046
Other Outcomes	132	145	270	6	7	617
Total	9,867	10,306	14,120	6,627	850	41,770
% Pleas	84.0	82.9	81.6	79.7	86.2	82.3
% Verdicts	6.5	5.6	6.1	9.1	7.4	6.6
% Dismissals	8.1	10.1	10.4	10.3	5.5	9.7
% Other	1.3	1.4	1.9	1.0	0.8	1.5

*Superior Court Information

Second, the New York City Criminal Court is clearly a workhorse, processing approximately eight times more cases than the Supreme Court's Criminal Term. Moreover, the Criminal Court disposes of almost 50% of cases at arraignment by means of pleas and dismissals. Indeed, trials reaching verdicts for misdemeanors are virtually nonexistent in the Criminal Court, representing less than two-tenths of one percent (.2%) of dispositions — around one in every 669. By comparison, trial verdicts in the Supreme Court are almost 7% of dispositions there. However, the Criminal Term's having about 45 times more verdicts than the lower court isn't surprising when one recalls the Supreme Court handles only the most serious offenses, carrying high stakes for everyone. Citywide jury-trial conviction rates in the Supreme Court ranged from 67 to 75 percent between 1992 and 1996, with a high of 86% in Staten Island during 1993 and a low of 59% in the Bronx during 1992.

Third, New York City's criminal justice system depends heavily upon defendants' voluntary guilty pleas, representing more than 80% of all dispositions and more than 90% of all findings of guilt in the Supreme Court and more than 99% of all findings of guilt in the Criminal Court. In short, the City's criminal-court system couldn't exist without plea bargaining.

By comparison, the federal-court criminal caseload in New York City is minuscule. The combined number of felony cases filed annually in the Eastern and Southern Districts of New York is fewer than 4,000, less than 10% of state-court felony filings.

CONCLUSION

New York City and State have one of the most complex judicial systems in the country. Proposals to simplify New York's courts have been suggested for a long time. But in the face of powerful political opposition, significant court reform is difficult to achieve. New York's method of selecting judges is complicated, too. Partisan politics directly affects judicial selection and expansion. The handling of criminal cases is an elaborate process. Court caseloads vary significantly among the five boroughs, with findings of guilt overwhelmingly the result of plea bargains, not trials.

References

Barbanel, Josh. 1983. "Task Force Proposes Merging New York's Major Trial Courts." *New York Times*, June 9, sec. II :B1.

"Court Reform at Risk." 1987. *New York Times*, May 18, sec. I: A18.

"Cuomo Signs Measure On Court Nominations." *New York Times*, April 7, sec. II: B4.

Flango, Victor E., and David B. Rottman. 1992. "Research Note: Measuring Trial Court

Consolidation." *Justice System Journal* 16:68-69.

Glass, Judy. 1987. "Bar Group Opposes Court Amendment." *New York Times*, May 17, sec. XXI: 18.

"Governor Pataki's Message to Judges." 1997. *New York Times*, December 16, sec. I, p. A30.

Greenfield, Edward R. 1988. "Governors, Too, Have Political Interests." *New York Times*, May 22, sec. 4: 30.

Hoffman, Jan. 1997. "A Prominent Judge Retires, Objecting to the Governor's Litmus Test." *New York Times*, December 14: 49.

Kolbert, Elizabeth. 1988. "Budget Slows A Bid to Add 17 Judgeships." *New York Times*, June 5: 35.

Lewis, David L. 1998. "Family Court Overhaul." *New York Daily News*, February 25:23.

Lynn, Frank. 1987. "Court Merger Seen as Dead in Legislature." *New York Times*, June 8: B1.

Margolick, David. 1983. "Picking of Judges Assailed by Cuomo." *New York Times*, August 15, sec. I: A1.

Pérez-Peña, Richard. 1998. "A Liberal on Top Court is Resigning." *New York Times*, February 21, sec. II: B1.

"Pushing for Court Reform." 1998. *New York Times*, January 19, sec. I : A16.

Schmalz, Jeffrey. 1986. "Cuomo and Top Legislators Agree to Add 23 Criminal Court Judges." *New York Times*, October 29, sec. I : A1.

Schmalz, Jeffrey. 1987. "Judges Add Confusion to Merger." *New York Times*, June 20 : 29.

Vance, Cyrus R. 1988. "Now, Party Bosses Decide the 'Elections.'" *New York Times*, May 22, sec. 4 : 30.

Chapter 16

JURIES IN NEW YORK CITY
By

Professor. James Levine

Dean of Graduate Studies

Bernhard Goetz, a white mass transit commuter, became a nationally known figure in 1984 when he shot four black youths on a crowded New York City subway train and then fled from the scene of the shooting. Although he ultimately contended that the youths were trying to rob him, when he turned himself into a New Hampshire police station only nine days later, he made a videotaped confession. Said Goetz: *"[I am] a cold-blooded murderer, . . . a vicious rat, a monster."* The media dubbed Goetz "the subway vigilante."

Goetz subsequently pleaded self-defense, claiming at his trial for attempted murder that the youths surrounding him appeared menacing-even though they had brandished no weapons when they "asked" him for five dollars. He testified that he was "acting out of goddamn fear," stating that one of the teenagers had a "funny" smile and a "shine" in his eyes. A Manhattan jury, comprising ten whites and two blacks, acquitted him of all charges except illegal possession of a deadly weapon, his unlicenced handgun.

One of the four youths who suffered brain damage and permanent paralysis from the shooting subsequently sued Goetz, and the case came to trial almost a decade later. The six-person Bronx civil jury, made up of four blacks and two Hispanics, rejected Goetz's claim of self-defense and ordered him to pay $43 million in damages. They apparently focused on the repeat shootings, placing emphasis on the second bullet fired into the plaintiff's back as he was cowering in fear and, at that moment at least, not posing a threat. In the face of these two seemingly contradictory verdicts, the question occurs: are Bronx juries different?

The answer is yes. Some of the Manhattan jurors may well have had empathy for Goetz as an understandably fearful potential victim of unchecked urban crime, and they may well have stereotyped young black males as aggressive and dangerous (Fletcher, 1988). The Bronx jurors, on the other hand, were perhaps struck by the evidence demonstrating Goetz's paranoid fear of racial minorities. From *their* vantage point, Goetz was a trigger-happy perpetrator of crime rather than a victim. Two juries; two boroughs; two points of view; two diametrically opposed verdicts.[1] This chapter will show that the two Goetz verdicts are *not* anomalies. Jury behavior in New York varies significantly as one travels through the city's five boroughs and it varies even more as one ventures beyond the city limits. The jury tries very hard to do justice, but what constitutes justice depends to some degree on who is meting it out. Jury behavior in New York is a tale of five cities.

The Jury and the Criminal Justice System

In American jurisprudence, defendants have a constitutional right to have a jury of peers decide whether they are guilty of criminal charges brought against them.[2] After a trial in which the prosecution attempts to prove culpability and the defense has an opportunity to rebut the charges, it is the province of the jury to determine whether guilt has been proved beyond a reasonable doubt. The judge, relying on statutory law and previous judicial opinions, determines the applicable law which is presented to the jury in the form of instructions. Once the judge has defined and explained the law, the jury alone weighs the evidence, determines the facts, and applies the law to the case at hand. The truly awesome responsibility of determining whether a defendant goes free or is subject to punishments such as imprisonment is thus vested in a group of ordinary citizens drawn from all walks of life. For better or for worse, the jury is a democratizing element in the criminal justice system.

The Impact of Local Opinion on the Jury

Although jurors generally try very hard to base their decision-making on the evidence produced at the trial and make good faith efforts to understand the sometimes incomprehensible instructions given to them by the judge, their own predispositions have some bearing on the judgements they make (Levine, 1992b). The trial record amassed through an adversary system in which both the prosecution and the defense are trying to win rather than ascertain the truth is often fraught with uncertainty and contradiction. Finding out *what really happened* entails some degree of guesswork, and jurors cannot help but rely on their own backgrounds, circumstances and perspectives to sort things out. One psychologist, who is an expert on juries (Ellsworth, 1989: 206), has observed *"that much of what is perceived is a function of the perceiver; it is a particular construct of the events perceived, rather than a true reflection."* Which scenario of events among a number of plausible ones is most believable to jurors will in some measure reflect their understanding of the world.

The jury selection process includes a probing of jurors' biases (called the *voir dire)*. Normally it results in the exclusion of outright bigots and those who have made up their minds in advance of the trial, but those who do get chosen as jurors inevitably harbor points of view which color their thinking. Personal sentiments of jurors almost never play a role when the facts are crystal

---

[1]It must be noted that other factors besides the locus of the trial may have been responsible for the divergent results, including the lesser burden of proof needed to win a lawsuit than is needed to convict of criminal charges and the lower quality of Goetz's legal representation in the second case.

[2]Duncan v. Louisiana, 393 U.S. 145 (1968). The Supreme Court has ruled that the right to trial by jury extends to any case where a defendant faces at least six months of imprisonment.

clear; it is rare that jurors will consciously convict those thought to be innocent or exculpate defendants when they are absolutely convinced of their guilt. But when the law is vague or the facts are confused, subjective views and opinions can tilt the jury one way or the other.

These verdict-affecting viewpoints are not random; they reflect the political culture from which jurors are drawn. The now commonplace use of multiple sources from which names of jurors are selected has made jury selection more inclusive, a state of affairs which produces juries that are more representative of the body politic than used to be the case when middle-aged, middle-class white males dominated the pool. Consequently, the "mainstream" political views that characterize the venue in which a defendant is tried are likely to be reflected in the outlooks of jurors drawn from that venue. The idiosyncracies of jury selection, especially the use of peremptory challenges which allow lawyers on both sides to excuse potential jurors without providing a reason, may on occasion produce a peculiarly composed jury at odds with prevailing opinion, but over the long haul jury verdicts echo the views of the local majority.

The Vagaries of Jury Decision-Making in New York

No where is the influence of community sentiments and norms demonstrated more clearly than in New York City. A study of 35,595 verdicts rendered by juries in criminal cases in New York State between 1986 and 1995 revealed substantial variation in jury behavior within the New York City metropolitan area (Levine, 1997). The same research also indicated that New York juries function differently from their counterparts in the rest of New York (known as "upstate"). In fact, these aggregate data strikingly show that the varying political and social contexts from which juries emerge affect the decisions that they make.

Table 16-1 below compares the outcomes of jury trials in the five counties or boroughs comprising New York City and the adjacent two suburban counties. It is seen that the jury acquittal rate ranges from a low of 20.1 per cent in Long Island's Nassau County just east of the city to 38.4 per cent in Bronx County. Even within the city proper, there is substantial variation: Bronx juries acquit almost twice as many defendants as juries in Staten Island (Richmond County) and they exonerate nearly 50 per cent more defendants than do juries in Queens.

Table 16-1: Jury Acquittal Rates in the Metropolitan Area, 1986-1995, by County

	Jury Acquittal Rate	Number of Jury Trials
Bronx	38 %	4,893
Kings (Brooklyn)	31	7,595
Queens	28	4,186
New York (Manhattan)	24	8,817
Richmond (Staten Island)	21	202
Westchester	21	918
Nassau (Long Island)	20	1,324

One reason for this variation in the propensity to convict is suggested in Table 16-2, which compares the acquittal rates of counties with their racial and ethnic demography. There is a close correspondence between the percentage of citizens who are either African-American or Hispanic-American and the tendency to acquit.[3] By and large, the "whiter" the population of a county, the fewer the acquittals generated by its juries. Bronx County has the highest percentage of minority residents and the highest jury acquittal rate, while Nassau County on Long Island is lowest on both counts.

Table 16-2:

**The Relationship between Racial Demography and Jury Verdicts
New York City Metropolitan Area, 1985-1996**

	Percent Black and Hispanic	Jury Acquittal Rate
Bronx	74%	38%
Kings (Brooklyn)	55	31
New York (Manhattan)	44	24
Queens	40	28
Westchester	23	21
Richmond (Staten Island)	15	21
Nassau (Long Island)	14	20

What these data strongly suggest is that the discrepant Goetz verdicts mentioned at the outset of this chapter exemplify a recurring pattern. The Bronx is quintessentially an "inner city" milieu and its juries reflecting this environment truly are more lenient, confirming the aptness of the headline of a <u>New York Times</u> article on jury behavior (Kifner, 1988): "Bronx Juries: A Defense Dream, a Prosecution Nightmare." Staten Island, on the other hand, while part of New York City, is closer demographically to the suburbs in Westchester and Nassau counties in that blacks and Hispanics are a relatively small proportion of residents. Their juries act accordingly, convicting to a much greater degree.

Why does the racial composition of venues matter? No doubt there is a bit of sheer prejudice-white jurors quick to pronounce black and Hispanic defendants guilty out of racial malice and minority jurors siding with defendants of color out of racial favoritism. But such blatant race-based

---

[3]The statistical correlation (Pearson's r) between percentage minority population and acquittal rates across these seven counties is .95, significant at the .005 level.

judgements are probably rare in that almost all jurors are genuinely committed to basing their verdicts on the law and the evidence (Hans and Vidmar, 1986).

A more compelling explanation of the tendency of nonwhite jurors to acquit more often than white jurors is that they honestly see the evidence differently. They are more likely to be skeptical of the truthfulness of police testimony, having had more firsthand and secondhand knowledge of fabrications made by law enforcement officers than is true of white jurors. This is confirmed by a nationwide study of 800 ex-jurors which shows that blacks are much less likely than whites to believe police officers when their testimony conflicts with that given by defendants ("Racial Divide," 1993). This point was bluntly expressed in the novel Bonfire of the Vanities (Wolfe, 1987: 133):

> Bronx juries were difficult enough for a prosecutor .
> . . [having been] drawn from the ranks of those who
> know that in fact police are capable of lying. Bronx
> juries entertained a lot of doubts, both reasonable and
> unreasonable, and black and Puerto Rican defendants
> who were guilty, guilty as sin, did walk out of the
> fortress free as birds.

The incredulity of Bronx jurors about police testimony was illustrated in a 1998 civil case brought by one Darryl Barnes against a New York City police officer who had shot and paralyzed him during a chase on the streets that occurred in 1988. Shortly after the incident, the police department, accepting the officer's claim that Barnes had himself fired a gun during the encounter, not only cleared the officer of any wrongdoing but gave him a commendation for meritorious service and promoted him to the rank of detective as a reward for his conduct. But the jury that decided the case a decade later thought otherwise, awarding Barnes $76.4 million in damages. The plaintiff's lawyer (quoted in Rohde, 1998) offered a cogent explanation of the verdict: *"I think that the jury was sending a message that if you're going to do a misdeed you're going to be punished . . . I think people [in the Bronx] believe the police act with a great deal of excessiveness in minority areas."*

Another factor, besides attitudes toward the police, that accounts for the difference between white and nonwhite jurors' conclusions is stereotyping, the use of generalizations about a group to characterize particular members of the group. A good number of white jurors surely harbor negative racial stereotypes, indiscriminately attributing crime proneness to an entire race; in their eyes black defendants are ipso facto guilty as charged. Black jurors, on the other hand, having dealt with a full gamut of people within their own race, can make more discerning judgements. Mock-jury research substantiates the idea that race-stereotypic thinking affects the juror judgement process (Gordon, 1990; King, 1993).

Race and ethnicity are not the only source of juror predispositions that may account for variance in jury behavior. In this regard, political ideology of a more general nature has been said to be a "permanent hidden agenda" throughout the criminal justice system (Miller, 1973). The clash between the liberal perspective with its concerns about protecting the rights of the accused and the conservative outlook which emphasizes crime control and punishment affects lawmakers who regularly make criminal justice policy. This ideological schism also affects those who carry out policy: police, prosecutors, judges and jurors. Local communities vary enormously in their ideological composition, from highly liberal to very conservative; juries' decisions over the long haul reflect these political differences.

This is suggested in Table 16-3, which compares the propensity of juries to acquit across seven counties with the political behavior of county electorates. The data show a significant correspondence between a county's support for two relatively liberal candidates and the rate at which it acquits defendants.

Table 16- 3

The Relationship Between Voting Behavior and the Jury Verdict in the New York Metropolitan Area, 1986-1995

	Percent voting for Clinton in 1996	Percent Voting for Cuomo in 1994	Jury Acquittal Rate
Bronx	82 %	72 %	38 %
N. Y. (Manhattan)	78	78	23
Kings (Brooklyn)	77	68	31
Queens	71	60	28
Westchester	56	46	21
Nassau	55	44	20
Richmond (Staten Is.)	50	46	21

The higher the support for Democratic Governor Mario Cuomo in his losing race for reelection in 1994 against Republican George Pataki, the higher the acquittal rate.[4] Likewise, greater support for President Clinton in his successful race for reelection against conservative Robert Dole in 1996 was also commensurate with higher acquittal rates.[5] Ballot box decisions and jury box decisions have something in common, as political ideology to some degree wends its way into both domains.

The effect of local sentiments is demonstrated even more clearly by contrasting jury behavior in some ultraconservative, racially-homogenous counties far removed from New York City with the prevailing New York City patterns. For example, Ontario County, upstate, which is 3 per cent black and Hispanic, gave Clinton only 46 percent of its vote in 1996 and gave Cuomo only 24 percent of its vote; its juries acquit only 12.3 percent of all defendants! It is thus considerably tougher than even Staten Island in New York City, which convicts at a much higher rate than any other of the

---

[4]The correlation (r) between county support for Cuomo and the acquittal rate of counties is .81, significant at the .01 level.

[5]The correlation (r) between county support for Clinton and the acquittal rate of counties is .67, significant at the .05 level.

city's five boroughs. Indeed, the 57 counties outside New York acquit at the rate of 23.7 per cent in contrast to the 29.5 percent rate in the city.

It should be noted that these intrastate variations are not peculiar to New York State. Another study has identified a similar phenomenon in two other populous states, California and Florida (Levine, 1992a). Comparison of three Southern California counties showed that juries in somewhat liberal Los Angeles acquit most often, juries in conservative San Diego County acquit less frequently, and juries in ultraconservative Orange County acquit least of all. Likewise in Florida, the ideological bent of counties as measured by voting statistics matches the behavior of juries. The variations witnessed in New York are thus a manifestation of realities in jury behavior generally, and are not a geographical oddity.

In assessing the above data, a couple of qualifying points must be mentioned. One is methodological: it is possible (though doubtful) that the inter-county disparities discussed above result from either different mixes of cases facing jurors in different areas, or from divergences in prosecutorial policy such that juries in one locale may generally be presented with more solid evidence than juries hearing cases in other jurisdictions. Suffice it to say here that scrutiny of such possibly confounding factors has not revealed all that much difference from county to county.

It should also be noted that jury behavior in different parts of the New York metropolitan area actually shows more similarities than differences. The acquittal rate in the toughest county is only 18 percentage points lower than the rate in the most lenient, and it is noteworthy that the allegedly "softhearted" Bronx juries actually convict nearly two-thirds of the time. What this suggests is that in cases with overwhelmingly incriminating proof, virtually all juries convict- whether they are predominantly black, white, or Hispanic and whether liberal or conservative. Contrariwise, shaky prosecutions that are fraught with evidentiary shortcomings are typically doomed to failure no matter what the racial or political complexion of the venues in which they are tried.

In general, New York juries stick to the evidence when the evidence seems incontrovertible; the political inclinations of jurors surface only when the law or the facts are murky. Jurors strain to be fair, but their commitment to rationality and evenhandedness falters when trials end in confusion. Popular sentiment holds sway when objective analysis fails to give answers.

Reforming the Jury

In recent years, New York has put into place a number of reforms inspired and prompted by the report of a broad-based panel created by New York Court of Appeals Chief Judge Judith Kaye, that was charged with the task of a "top-to-bottom" review of the state's jury system (McMahon, 1994). The ostensible goals of the reformers were to make juries more representative, to make the jury system more efficient, and to make jury service less burdensome. However, taken together, the changes implemented as a result of the panel's recommendations (New York State Unified Court System, 1996), may well serve an even more profound purpose - enhancing the jury's capability for objectivity and thereby reducing some of the disparities in decision-making discussed above.

A number of initiatives were aimed at diversifying jury pools and thus increasing the likelihood that any given jury would accurately reflect the underlying population from which it is drawn. Sources of jurors were expanded to add public assistance and unemployment rosters to the previously used voter registration, driver's license and state income tax lists. All of the many automatic exemptions from jury service that excused attorneys, police officers, members of the clergy and even embalmers and podiatrists were eliminated, thus making most citizens eligible to serve as jurors. A number of enforcement mechanisms were created to insure that prospective jurors contacted by the courts actually fulfill their duty to serve rather than ignoring initial inquiries and summonses from jury officials as so many had previously done. By vastly augmenting the numbers of potential jurors arriving at the courthouse and by bringing in a much greater cross-section of the community, these measures provide for a broadening of perspectives that inform deliberations. Diverse juries are better suited to finding the truth than homogenous ones.

A second set of initiatives dealt with improving the amenities and reducing the burdens of jury service. The average time of service has been cut almost in half; compensation for jurors was increased from $15 per day plus carfare to $40 per day; facilities for jurors are being upgraded; and greater information about trial proceedings is now being furnished through an orientation video and a jurors' handbook. By lessening the stress which jury service often elicits, these changes ought to increase the rationality and decrease the emotionality of juror decision-making. A more relaxed juror is a more sensible juror.

Thirdly, courthouses are being redesigned and re-outfitted to enable jurors to better receive the evidence. Relatively simple modifications can significantly help jurors: perfecting amplification systems can make testimony more audible and correcting poor lighting can enable jurors to see physical exhibits more accurately. Beyond this, there has been some experimentation with "high-tech" trials courts such as "Courtroom 2000," recently set up in a State Supreme Court in Manhattan that allows jurors to see physical evidence close-up by use of video-imaging tools and flat-screen monitors in the jury box. Trials which do a better job of educating jurors about the facts are more apt to produce reasonable verdicts.

Finally, the unique rule in New York State requiring mandatory sequestration of jurors during deliberations of all criminal cases has been eased. Having to spend time in a hotel rooming with a total stranger if a verdict cannot be reached in one day is an unnerving experience detested by jurors which can undermine the pursuit of justice by prompting premature judgements, by engendering the scapegoating of defendants, or by fostering closed mindedness (Levine, 1996). The state legislature has experimentally taken a step toward remedying this dubious practice by allowing judges in all but the most serious cases to do what judges in all of the other 49 states have long been able to do: order sequestration only when heavy media coverage threatens to have a biasing impact on the jury. By eliminating routine sequestration, a particularly insidious disruption in jurors' personal lives, and by allowing them the opportunity to return home at night, the new regulations should facilitate sound judgement and reduce the impact of extralegal factors on verdicts.

CONCLUSION

New York juries indisputably "beat to their own drummer," but so too do *all* juries. United States Supreme Court Chief Justice Oliver Wendell Holmes (1920: 237-238), after many years of experience as a judge in the Massachusetts courts, conjectured long ago that juries *"will introduce into their verdict a certain amount--a very large amount, so far as I have observed-of popular prejudice."* Holmes' speculation was validated by a nationwide study (Kalvin and Zeisel, 1966: 495) of 3,576 criminal trials taking place in all 50 states that revealed the significant influence of public opinion on verdicts.

Even though the adjudication process of New York City juries is nothing special, New York City *is* special and a couple of its boroughs are *very* special. The Bronx and Brooklyn are counties with uncommon concentrations of persons of color and they tend to have a decidedly liberal ethos, qualities which incline their juries to produce more acquittals. But areas as remote from New York City as Washington, D.C., and Detroit that have a similar racial and political demography reveal the same proclivity to give defendants the greater benefit of the doubt (McCoy, 1994; Holden, Cohen and deLisser, 1995).

Juries in New York City try with considerable success to avoid bias in deciding verdicts, and recent reforms in New York should enable them to do an even better job of performing their mission dispassionately. But the ambiguities of the law and the uncertainties of the evidence confronting jurors at the end of many trials inescapably impel them to resort to subjectivity in exercising discretion; there is really no way out. Juries are the most democratic institution of the judicial process, so it should come as no surprise that their decision-making is influenced by the political climate of the venues in which trials are held.

New York City juries thus to a considerable degree act politically. This is hardly news: Alexis de Tocqueville (1835/1946: 282), writing 165 years ago in his classic work Democracy in America, recognized that *"the jury is, above all, a political institution."* Inner city juries of today reflect inner city politics, just as suburban juries reflect suburban politics. In New York City and elsewhere, the jury and the community are inextricably linked.

References

Ellsworth, P.(1989). Are twelve heads better than one? Law and Contemporary Problems, 52: 205-224.

Fletcher, G.(1988). A Crime of Self-Defense: Bernhard Goetz and the Law on Trial. New York: Free Press.

DeTocqueville, A.(1833/1946). Democracy in America. New York: A. A. Knopf.

Gordon, R. (1990). Attributions for Blue-collar and White-collar Crime: The Effects of Subject and Defendant Race on Simulated Juror Decisions. Journal of Applied Social Psychology, 20: 971-983.

Hans, V. & Vidmar, N.(1986). Judging the Jury. New York: Plenum.

Holden, B., Cohen, L. & de Lisser, E. (1995). Race seems to be playing an increasing role in many jury verdicts. The Wall Street Journal: October 4, p.A1, A5.

Holmes, O.(1920), Collected Legal Papers. New York: Harcourt, Brace.

Kalven, H. & Zeisel, H. (1966). The American Jury. Boston: Little Brown.

Kifner, J.(1988). Bronx juries: A defense dream, a prosecutor's nightmare. The New York Times, December 5, p. B1.

King, N.(1993). Postconviction Review of Jury Discrimination: Measuring the effects of race on jury decisions. Michigan Law Review, 92:63-130.

Levine, J.(1992a). The impact of local political cultures on jury verdicts. Criminal Justice Journal,

14(2):163-180.

Levine, J.(1992b). Juries and Politics. Pacific Grove, CA: Brooks/Cole.

Levine, J.(1996). The Impact of Sequestration on Juries. Judicature, 79(5):266-272.

Levine, J.(1997). The Impact of Racial Demography on Jury Verdicts in Routine Adjudication. Criminal Law Bulletin, 33(6): 523-542.

McCoy, C.(1994). If Hard Cases Make Bad Law, Easy Juries Make Bad Facts: A response to Professor Levine. Legal Studies Forum, 18(4: 497-508.

McMahon, C.(1994). The Jury Project: Report to the Chief Judge of the State of New York. New York: The Jury Project.

Miller, W.(1973). Ideology and criminal justice policy: Some current issues. Journal of Criminal Law and Criminology, 64:141-162.

New York State Unified Court System (1996). Jury Reform in New York State: A Progress Report on a Continuing Initiative. New York: New York State Unified Court System.

"Racial Divide Affects Black, White Panelists" (1993). National Law Journal (February 22) :S8-S9.

Rohde, D.(1998). "$76 Million for Man Shot by the Police." The New York Times, April 9: B6.

Wolfe, T.(1987). Bonfire of the Vanities. New York: Farrar.

Chapter 17

THE HISTORY OF PROBATION IN NEW YORK CITY

By

Professor Charles Lindner

Department of Law and Police Science

At 54th Street and 9th Avenue in New York City, a short distance from the John Jay College of Criminal Justice, is a narrow, three story building constructed in the late 1800s. It now houses a "community court," a return to its original function after serving the city in a number of different ways. Passersby are unlikely to notice the words "Eleventh District Municipal Court," engraved high on the front of the building. Fewer still know that the first major scandal in the history of probation occurred at this site.

Complaints were made in the early 1900s that the full complement of 16 male police/probation officers would congregate in the courthouse on Friday evenings to watch as female probationers, many of whom were prostitutes, reported to their female probation officers. When questioned at an investigatory hearing (New York State Commission: Proceedings, 1909), the male officers testified that they gathered in full force to protect the eleven female probation officers. When that explanation was rejected, since no female officer had ever been assaulted, these men claimed that it was essential to good police work to be able to identify which women were prostitutes. This testimony was a part of a 1908 Commission hearing in New York State which was primarily devoted to emerging issues in the newly evolving field of probation, including the appropriateness of staffing probation agencies with individuals who were also police officers.

THE EMERGENCE OF PROBATION IN THE UNITED STATES

The first probation departments were created in various states around the turn of the century. Although probation type activities were performed some years earlier, in 1878 probation was regulated by statute for the first time when Massachusetts enacted a law authorizing the appointment of a paid probation officer to accept cases in Boston's criminal courts (Dressler, 1969:27). Massachusetts expanded the role of probation in 1890 and again in 1898, and a number of states created probation systems around the turn of the century. As early as 1901, the probation system was in actual operation or was provided by statute in fifteen of the twenty-five largest cities of the United States (Folks, 1902: 234).

The creation of the first juvenile court in Chicago, Illinois in 1899 proved to be a major impetus for the growth of probation. At first, the public was more willing to accept probation as a sentence for juveniles rather than for adults.

THE EVOLUTION OF PROBATION IN NEW YORK CITY

In 1901 the New York State Legislature created a probation system which was limited to justices of courts having original criminal jurisdiction in all cities of the state (Prison Association, 1902: 48-49). Unfortunately, concerns that probation was not adequately punitive, coupled with the reluctance of many jurisdictions to fund probation services, and widespread misunderstandings about probation's role in the justice system, retarded its growth and limited its use in many parts of the State..

The lack of a clear understanding of probation's function, even among judges, court officials and probation officers themselves, led to frequent abuses, an absence of standards, and great inconsistencies in terms of policies and practices. One divisive issue was whether probation work should be rooted in a social service orientation or based on a police/law enforcement model. Other important and controversial issues of the times concerned whether probation officers should be paid, what appropriate qualifications for the job should be, and what size caseloads were manageable.

The first probation officers in New York City were an extremely heterogeneous lot, reflecting a broad range of vocational experiences. Some were social workers whose services were often contributed on a part-time basis by their agency, some were members of the clergy, some were retired civil servants, and others were police officers or court personnel temporarily reassigned to probation work. A large number were volunteers from varied backgrounds, some of whom hoped to move into full-time, paid positions. Such a diverse group suffered from little or no professional contacts, an absence of training, and great variations in work standards, styles, and performance. Although in many states, probation services were originally limited to juveniles, the opposite was true in New York. Because of conflicts with the New York Society for the Prevention of Cruelty to Children, which perceived probation as a threat to their work, eligibility for supervision and services was originally limited to persons 16 years-of-age or older. However, following a series of compromises with the Society, the probation law was revised to permit supervision of juveniles less than 16 years old (Folks, 1910).

Although the original probation law prohibited payment of salaries to probation officers, it was soon realized that this would not only discourage many qualified applicants, but would impede the professionalization of probation. A 1905 modification of the law authorized local authorities to pay salaries to probation officers for their work (N.Y.S. Probation Commission, 1906: 10), thereby contributing to job security and staff stability, enhanced professionalism, and the eventual demise of volunteer help.

EARLY CRITICISMS

Virtually from its beginning years, the New York State probation system was the target of extensive criticism. The opprobrium was widespread and voiced by the judiciary, public officials, and even the very leaders of the probation movement. The major criticisms, some of which are not unlike the complaints voiced today, included the following:

1. There was a widespread belief that probation was too lenient a sanction for many offenses, and was an inappropriate alternative to incarceration for many offenders, and thus contributed to increases in crime. Although probation at its outset was generally limited to non-violent minor crimes, many people in those days felt that virtually all crimes should be punished through incarceration. The early literature is replete with attacks on sentences of probation in particular cases by public officials and other influential figures, many of whom were ideologically opposed to it in principle. In 1921, for example, the New York State Probation Commission (1922: 3) responded to allegations "that hardened and habitual offenders convicted of serious crimes have had their sentences suspended or were released on probation or parole" by acknowledging that although a serious problem did exist, it was "attributable mainly to the failure on the part of public officials in many states to provide either adequate salaries for or a sufficient number of probation officers" .Virulent denunciations of the alleged leniency of probation caused the Law Enforcement Committee of the American Bar Association to consider recommending the withdrawal of the power of trial judges to place offenders on probation (N.Y.S. Probation Association, 1922: 3).

2. The work of probation officers was generally viewed in a negative light. The criticisms extended to their excessive caseloads, lack of standards, inadequate supervision of probationers, infrequent home visits, and alleged incompetence. While the shoddy quality of probation work is well documented in the literature and was substantiated by the investigatory committees of the day, it may have been a function of the questionable work of volunteers, police-probation officers, and political appointees; inadequate funding; and confusion about the purposes of probation. Early probation services have been characterized as generally superficial, careless, a more or less hit-or-miss affair, and a blundering ahead approach; one researcher (Rothman, 1980:83) pointedly asked how probation could have continued to grow in the face of such failures.

3. Many observers were critical of the services provided by volunteers, asserting that they lacked formal training and often were unsupervised, and that some individuals were unsuitable for probation work. To paid officers they represented a bar to professionalism, respectable status, and good salaries. A report of the Prison Association of New York (1902:11) alleged that "the labor of unpaid volunteers "... cannot take the place of the unremitting service of an officer" who devotes full time to probation work. Similarly, the New York State Probation Commission (1906: 75-77) argued that in the larger centers of population "the amount of probation work to be done is so great that volunteer service alone is inadequate."

As the number of paid officers increased, criticism of volunteers intensified. Typical was the contention that volunteers who could not be properly supervised or held accountable for their work "without the authority which pay gives" only should be involved in less difficult cases (Eliot, 1914:58). The use of volunteers declined with the appointment of paid officers, and it was reported by the New York State Probation Commission (1917:112) that although used in many courts, they were no longer relied upon as in the early years . By the 1930s, their use in New York City had been phased out and was generally restricted to rural areas of the State.

4. Professionally oriented staffers, especially those with a social work orientation, were critical of the work of police officers assigned to serve as probation officers. Known as police/probation officers, they continued to serve into the 1920s. As in several other cities, police officers in New York City were employed as a temporary expedient during the earliest years. Some believed that police officers were ideally suited for probation work because they would command the respect of

the public and would not be afraid to carry out home visits in dangerous parts of the city. Nevertheless, like volunteers, they were perceived as a threat to professionalism and the antithesis to the social work counseling model which the founders of probation considered ideal. Social workers believed police officers to be unsuited for probation work either by training or temperament, and stereotyped them as punitive, controlling and law enforcement oriented (Lindner: 1994).

In practice, the police probation officer experiment in New York City was a disaster. The position was often viewed as a "political plum" for older officers who were past their prime. Usually assigned to a specific magistrate rather than a court, loyalty was often to a judge rather than to a probation agency. Few did any significant probation work, often supervising only a handful of cases in a year, and instead functioned more like a court officer. Testimony at a 1908 hearing revealed that many of these former police officers had few actual contacts with probationers, knew little about their cases, and often failed to maintain records and written case histories. The overall quality of their work was superficial.   They received little training and often lacked any basic concept of their job responsibilities. Some officers spent most of their time as court officers, and viewed as their prime responsibility to "keep the hall clear and keep the peace inside the court" (N.Y.S. Commission: Proceedings, 1909: 436-469). A member of the State Probation Commission (Wade, 1923) asserted that "their judgements have been harsh and their patience short in dealing with human weaknesses and they are being gradually eliminated from
the service."

GROWTH OF PROBATION

With the passage of time, probation gained acceptance as an alternative to incarceration both in New York State and throughout the nation. As a general rule, caseload growth was usually more rapid in the cities than in rural areas. The number of adults under probation supervision grew from about 1,100 in 1907 to about 15,500 in 1921, with the number of full-time officers climbing from 200 to 400 Wade (1923: 3). Nevertheless, growth in rural areas continued to be lethargic because of limited caseloads and budgetary concerns. For example, in 1933 it was reported that approximately 63 percent of the probation officers in the State were serving in the City (New York State Commission to Investigate Prison Administration and Construction, 1933: 14).

The New York State Probation Commission, organized in 1907, was the first state probation commission and it proved to be a significant force for professionalization. It advocated expanded probation services, encouraged the appointment of paid probation officers, moved to extend services to rural parts of the State, helped draft probation legislation, held and published the proceedings of annual conferences, and investigated and reported on the quality of probation services throughout the State.

A number of early legislative enactments helped shape the character of probation. Originally viewed as a source of patronage, the "State Civil Service Commission in 1913 classified all positions of salaried probation officers as competitive" (Wade, 1923:5). The success of adult probation work in New York State served as a model for the creation of a Domestic Relation Court in the City of Buffalo in 1910 and shortly after in Brooklyn and Manhattan. All of these courts collected money for the support of families "from lazy and self-indulgent husbands and fathers," and succeeded in restoring family ties and rebuilding homes. The "Court promises to be one of the most useful ... in its economic and constructive influence, on demoralized, disunited and deteriorated families..." one official noted (Wade, 1923: 7).

Probation's jurisdiction and caseload grew when a statutory amendment in 1918 gave the court the power of unrestricted discretion in placing offenders on probation, except in cases punishable by death, life imprisonment or for a fourth or more felony convictions. Significant also was a 1930 amendment to the Penal Law which required a presentence investigation for all convicts placed on probation or given a suspended sentence on a felony conviction (New York State Commission to Investigate Prison Administration and Construction, 1933: 19).

SUPERVISION OF THE OFFENDER

Then, as now, supervision of the offender was seen as at the heart of probation work . The Chairman of the New York State Probation Commission expressed the views of many early probation advocates when he stated "that supervision is the crux of probation (Wade, 1933: 6). Its importance was recognized at the outset, practiced from the very beginning of probation, and was a carry-over from the concept of "friendly visitation" (Lindner, 1992: 45). In the earliest years supervision was informal, often unstructured, and tended to follow a "big brother" model. This was a role particularly envisioned for the volunteers who were seen as providing guidance and support for one or two juvenile probationers at a time. In the absence of the constraints of social work professionalism which developed later on, the probationer/officer relationship was often close and personal. For example, in some instances, the probationer would report to the officer's home (New York State Probation Commission, 1918: 76). To accommodate employed probationers, some reporting offices were open both evenings and Saturdays. In addition, some officers took juveniles on trips for cultural or entertainment purposes and held group meetings with the boys. Services provided to the probationers were more varied than they are today, including referrals to libraries, night schools, Y.M.C.A.s, and to open bank accounts. Some officers even acted as buffers between the probationer and his debtors. Emphasis was placed on
the importance of employment, so some officers canvassed businesses, social service agencies, and their own acquaintances to find jobs for the probationers in their caseload.

Consistent with the moral standards of the day, some probation agencies excused women from reporting for fear of contamination through co-mingling; or these agencies had the women report to the officers' homes or meet them in a library or park (New York State Probation Commission, 1906: 16; 1918: 76, 251). In virtually all agencies, male and female probationers reported to the office on different days. Furthermore, a female could not be placed under the direct supervision of a male officer (New York State Probation Commission, 1930: 16).

A federal probation system, which today supervises cases in New York City and throughout the nation, was not created until 1925, and until 1930 did not handle a substantial number of cases (Bates, 1936: 284). There was intense opposition to a federal system based on the idea that probation would undermine the Volstead Act (Prohibition Amendment) by providing a substitute to incarceration for criminals involved in the illegal alcohol trade; many judges believed that lenient probation sentences would undermine law enforcement in general. The intensity of that debate was reflected by the approximately 34 bills introduced between 1909 and 1925 to establish a federal probation agency until one was finally passed (Evjen, 1975).

Over the years, the number of probationers under supervision has consistently increased. By the end of 1996, it reached a new high of 3,180,000 adult offenders nationwide (U.S. Department of Justice, 1997). Even more significant than the overall increase in population is the dramatic growth over the last few decades, especially in New York City, but in other parts of the nation as well, of felons under probation supervision. Strategies developed to deal with "felony probation" include a philosophical shift from the "rehabilitative" focus to the "crime control" model, which emphasizes closer supervision to protect the public. Felony caseloads require an increased reliance on classification systems to identify which probationers must be watched more carefully than others, the adoption of intensive supervision for a smaller number of cases, and the use of intermediate sanctions like house arrest and electronic monitoring.

One last debate that continues to rage today as passionately as in the past relates to the question of probation's effectiveness. Probation has grown bigger, but is it any better? Moreover, how can "better" be measured? Critics have always pointed to the high recidivism rates of probationers who don't seem to have benefitted from the experience of being watched and counseled. In response, some skeptics would ask whether the quality of the service delivered by probation departments is really relevant. They would contend that probation's actual functions are alleviating the overcrowding pressures facing institutional corrections (the shortage of cells in jails and prisons), and allowing courts to quickly and efficiently dispose of case backlogs through negotiated pleas of guilt in return for leniency. The existence of probation as a potential sentence provides the judiciary with an option that carries a degree of insurance from condemnation; when a convict is placed on probation, there is a perception of community protection and of punishment through supervision. There is even a perception of rehabilitation and treatment for the "more deserving" probationers, such as juveniles and first time offenders, to ease the societal conscience. If these perceptions are important, then the statistical effectiveness of probation as a means of reducing criminality remains an illusory concern, since these other functions are more significant. The continued growth of probation is assured, even if the delivery of services to offenders often turns out to be largely a failure.

References

Bates, S. (1936; Reprinted 1971). Prisons and Beyond. Freeport, N.Y.: Books for Libraries Press.

Dressler, D. (1969). Practice and Theory of Probation and Parole, 2nd ed. New York: Columbia Univ. Press.

Eliot, T.D. (1914). Juvenile Court and Community. N.Y.: The Macmillan Co.

Evjen, V.H. (1975). "The federal probation system: The struggle to achieve it and its first 25 years." Federal Probation, Vol. 39, #2: 3-15.

Folks, H. (1902). The care of destitute, neglected, and delinquent children. New York: Johnson Reprint Co.

Folks, H. (1910). Juvenile probation in New York. The Survey; pp. 667-673.

Lindner, C. (1992). The Probation Field Visit and office report in New York State: Yesterday, Today, and Tomorrow. Criminal Justice Review. Vol. 17, No. 1: 44-60.

------------- (1994). The police contribution to the development of probation: An historical account. Journal of Offender Rehabilitation, Vol. 20, 3 & 4, 61-84.

New York State Commission to Inquire into the Courts of Inferior Criminal Jurisdiction in Cities of the First Class (1910). Proceedings. Albany, NY.

New York State Commission to Investigate Prison Administration and Construction (1933). Probation in New York State: Special Report.

New York State Probation Commission (1906). Report of the Probation Commission of the State of New York Appointed Pursuant to the Provisions of Chapter 714 of the Laws of 1905. Albany, N.Y.: Brandow Printing Co.

New York State Probation Commission (1918). Eleventh Annual Report. Albany, N.Y.: J.B. Lyon Co., Printers.

New York State Probation Commission (1922). Probation in New York State. Albany, N.Y.: J.B. Lyon Co., Printers.

New York State Probation Commission (1930). Twenty-Third Annual Report. Albany, N.Y.: J.B. Lyon Co., Printers.

Prison Association of New York (1902). Fifty-Seventh Annual Report for the Year of 1901. Albany, N.Y.: J.B. Lyon Co., Printers.

Rothman, D.J. (1980). Conscience and convenience: The asylum and its alternatives in Progressive America. Boston, MA: Little, Brown & Co.

U.S. Department of Justice, Bureau of Justice Statistics. (1997). Probation and Parole, 1996. Washington, DC: U.S. Government Printing Office.

Wade, F.E. (1923). Adult Probation in New York State. N.Y.S. Probation Commission. Albany, N.Y..

Chapter 18

THE NEW YORK CITY DEPARTMENT OF PROBATION TODAY

By
Professor Charles Lindner

Department of Law And Police Science

Across the country, probation is the Cinderella of the criminal justice system: overworked, inadequately funded, low in status, and subjected to frequent criticism by the media, the judiciary, and the public.

National studies have pinpointed some of the specific problems faced by probation departments: limited resources, staff shortages, an increasingly difficult clientele to supervise, an absence of meaningful supervision for large numbers of cases, an abandonment of routine home visits, and widespread public misconceptions about the nature and purpose of conditional liberty (see Guynes, 1988; and Lindner and Bonn, 1996). Not surprisingly, most of the problems faced by large probation agencies in other jurisdictions are similarly experienced by the New York City Department of Probation. This chapter will identify and critique the major strategies used by the Department to cope with budgetary setbacks, increased caseloads, and clients that are more difficult to supervise and assist. It will also explore the increased reliance on new technologies to enhance the supervision process. Finally, it will examine some indicators of operational success and failure.

HEAVILY USED BUT INADEQUATELY FUNDED

Probation agencies have never been given enough money to meet their responsibilities, since the time they were first established at the turn of the century. Perhaps the problem of chronic shortfalls can be traced back to one of the few errors made by John Augustus, appropriately credited with being the "Father of Probation," because he attempted to sell the idea of probation to a skeptical public as an inexpensive alternative to incarceration. Indeed, during the early years, probation costs were artificially kept low through the use of strategies that would be unacceptable today: a reliance on volunteers, and the practice in certain jurisdictions of not paying full time staff. If probation is still seen as a cost-savings way to deal with offenders, that is because in the competition for the criminal justice dollar, it is low on the totem pole. Community corrections (as opposed to institutional corrections) has expanded to relieve the corrections budget crisis. It costs taxpayers between $22,000 and $25,000 to incarcerate a prisoner for one year. A nonviolent offender sentenced to a supervised probation caseload will cost the government between $3,000 and $7,000 (Boone, 1997).

Although held in low esteem by many, probation is the most commonly used sentence in the United States. In fact, its use as the disposition of choice continues to increase. Nationally, the number of offenders on probation (and parole) supervision has been increasing by more than three percent annually since 1990. Approximately 3.2 million adult offenders were on probation as of the end of 1996 (Bureau of Justice Statistics. August 14, 1997). The unending budgetary crisis is particularly painful for probation agencies. Lacking a positive public image and a core constituency to support its interests, and often criticized by liberals and conservatives alike, community-based corrections agencies have been assigned growing caseloads unmatched by commensurate funding increases. In the absence of the kind of population constraints imposed by the brick, mortar and steel bars of a corrections facility, probation caseloads appear to lawmakers and judges to be infinitely expandable.

The inadequate funding of probation agencies arises because they are unable to compete effectively for scarce public funds. As a result, they receive less than ten percent of the dollars set aside by state and local governments for corrections expenses (Petersilia, 1997). The decline in spending for community corrections, coupled with drastic increases in the number of offenders sentenced to community corrections not only brings about a problem of caseloads that are too large but also limit the ability of the agency to secure the services needed to rehabilitate offenders (Lindgren, 1997).

The historical under funding of probation agencies has been a serious problem in New York City as well. For example, in 1976 when the City faced a fiscal crisis, the Commissioner of Probation noted that the Department, hidden deep in the system and lacking the visibility to rally public support, suffered greater staff layoffs than other components of the criminal justice system.

Today, the New York City Department of Probation is one of the largest probation agencies in the nation. As of the end of fiscal year 1997, the Department employed a staff of 810, of whom 498 served as probation officers (N.Y.C. Department of Probation, 1998). During fiscal year 1997, the Department completed more than 47,000 adult pre-sentence investigations and reports, of which 38,000 were felonies and almost 10,000 were misdemeanors. They also completed more than 7,000 juvenile court investigations.

These investigations, known as pre-sentence investigations and reports, primarily serve to assist the judge in reaching sentence. They are prepared by the probations service after conviction, but prior to sentence. They focus on the lifestyle of the defendant, the nature of the crime, the prior legal history, and a sentencing recommendation which is advisory. In New York State the pre-sentence investigation, unless waived, is mandatory in all felony cases, and the court may not pronounce a sentence of probation, a sentence of imprisonment for a term in excess of ninety days, or consecutive sentences of imprisonment with times aggregating more than ninety days in the absence of a pre-sentence report. In its discretion, the court may order a pre-sentence report in any case (NYS Criminal Procedure Law Supplement, 1997/98, Section 390.20).

During fiscal year 1997, the Department supervised more than 78,000 adult probationers and a juvenile court caseload of more than 2,000 cases. The average adult caseload per case-bearing probation officer was more than 200 supervisees per month, while the average juvenile caseload per case-bearing probation officer was 84 cases per month (NYC Department of Probation, 1998).

FELONS ON PROBATION: THE AGENCY'S LITTLE WHITE LIE

Most people assume that probation is used as an alternative to incarceration mostly for youths, and for adults who are first-time offenders who have committed only minor crimes. That may have been true in the past, but no longer reflects reality. One of the sweeping changes that took place in New York, as well as in most large city probation departments, has been the transition from a population predominantly of misdemeanants to one made up overwhelmingly of felons. In New York City, the percentage of persons under supervision who were convicted of a felony stands at about 75% (Russi, n.d.). Nationwide, almost 60% percent of all adults on probation had been convicted of a felony (BJS, August, 1997).

Probation serves as an escape vent to relieve institutional overcrowding; whenever there is an acute shortage of prison space, convicted felons are placed on probation instead of being locked up. The changeover to a felony caseload has had serious consequences for probation officers, the agency, and the public. For the officers, the presence of so many felons in their caseloads increases the likelihood that some persons under supervision will violate the conditions of probation, often by committing another serious crime. Although, many felons under probation supervision have not been convicted of violent acts, others have both a history of violence and extensive arrest records. Moreover, felons are a more dangerous population to deal with, and could pose a threat to the officers supervising them, especially during the course of home visits. Finally, violent felons or those with extensive criminal records are often viewed by probation officers as chronic recidivists with little motivation for change. Except for pro forma referrals for services, the agency and the officers will stress control over treatment when handling them.

For the agency, a population composed mostly of serious offenders requires increased supervision costs because caseloads must be smaller; often felons are placed on intensive supervision. Although felons usually need closer surveillance, their serious personal problems also require enhanced services.

Finally, an agency's supervision of a predominantly felony population poses a threat to the very existence of probation departments. Many members of the public would be shocked to learn that most probationers have committed felonies and are not first offenders. The public's faith in the criminal justice system's ability to mete out harsh punishment as retribution and for the purpose of deterrence might be severely undermined should they learn how frequently violent persons and repeat offenders escape incarceration. Furthermore, the administrators of probation agencies live in fear of the threat of negative exposure: the media and political opponents are quick to pounce on stories of felony probationers committing horrendous new crimes.

A MORE DIFFICULT PROBATIONER POPULATION

Evidence from various sources confirms the suspicion that probation supervision is more difficult now than in the past for several reasons: caseloads have increased; a greater proportion of the clientele is made up of felons; and more probationers suffer from emotional illnesses, substance abuse, and AIDS. The large number of probationers in need of substance abuse treatment is documented by a recent study, which reports that, *"More than 2 of every 5 probationers were required to enroll in some form of substance abuse treatment. An estimated 29% of probationers were required to get treatment for alcohol abuse or dependency, and 23% for drug abuse."* (Bonczar, Dec., 1997) In a nationwide survey of probation and parole personnel, at least three-fourths of the respondents said they believed that the supervision needs of offenders are greater now than in the past (Guynes, 1988: 8). Similarly, a nationwide study about probation officer victimization reported trends toward assigning teams rather than individuals to conduct home visits, offering street safety training, and permitting officers to carry defensive weapons (Lindner & Bonn, 1996). Even caseloads assigned by family court are increasingly populated with more violence-oriented youthful offenders (See U.S. Dept. of Justice, 1997).

RESTRUCTURING IN THE 1990'S: RISK LEVELS

In the early 1990's the Department of Probation, together with a number of other New York City agencies, were ordered to downsize so as to reduce operating costs. Although public relations statements would refer to the new mandate as "doing more with less," the restructuring was mostly an attempt to save monies through the prioritization of services. Essentially this was accomplished by focusing supervision efforts on the higher risk potentially violent probationers at the expense of decreasing services to offenders classified as low risk. The Agency reports that the current re-arrest rate for their 63,000 adult probationers, while under supervision, is approximately 25% (Ryan, 1998).

At the heart of the restructuring process was the development of a sophisticated "risk assessment" instrument to classify probationers according to their probability of committing future violent criminal acts. Accordingly, all probationers are now classified at the outset to determine whether they should be placed in violent or nonviolent supervision tracks, based on such factors as their potential for violent behavior, treatment considerations, the existence of special conditions of probation, and the existence of allegations that they have violated the conditions of their probation. Consistent with a behavioral modification model, probationers may move to a more or less intrusive level of supervision based on their behavior and the time remaining before they are released from supervision.

Higher risk offenders receive more intensive oversight. In addition, all offenders with a history of violence are assessed to determine what treatments would be appropriate. In this way, scarce resources are reserved for those who are most likely to benefit from services or to cause trouble.

The concept of classification is not new to probation. Even in the earliest years, individual officers informally and unofficially prioritized the degree of supervision they would devote to each offender in their caseload. In later years, formal classification systems were developed, often based on an individualized assessment of needs and risks. Although the Department of Probation's current classification system is more methodical, statistically-based, and differentiated, like all systems it is intended to serve the goal of conserving scarce resources through a triage strategy which provides higher risk cases with the lions' share of the agency's time and money.

Upon placement on probation by the court, all offenders are assigned to an Intake and Assessment Unit for classification into a violent or nonviolent category. Those classified as nonviolent will be placed in a track with minimal degrees of supervision. Those found to be of high risk for violence undergo a secondary assessment which includes a structured interview, a mental health screening, and a determination as to suitability for group counseling. Based on the secondary assessment, higher risk probationers are placed in one of four specialized units of an "Enforcement Track " (Russi, n. d.).

The Blue Unit:

Probationers remain in this unit for between 7 and 8 months. During the major part of this time they will meet twice a week for 2 hour group therapy sessions based on the technique called "cognitive skills development." This unit is characterized by small caseloads allowing for close interaction between officer and probationer. Successful completion of the program results in a transfer to the less intensively supervised Green Unit. Those failing are sent to the Blue Unit (Russi, n.d.).

The Amber Unit:

Probationers remain in this unit for an average of one year. While no group work services are provided, caseloads are small to allow for frequent contact and close supervision. When appropriate, referrals are made to outside treatment providers. Upon completion, they enter the Green Unit.

The Green Unit:

Probationers remain in this unit for an average of one year. Caseloads are larger than in the units cited above. Supervision - including face-to-face meetings, and telephone or collateral contacts, as well as treatment referrals - takes place, but is less intense. Basically this is a relapse prevention unit. Probationers graduate to either the Special Conditions Track or to the Reporting Track.

The Red Unit:

The primary function of this unit is to supervise all probationers who have violated their conditions of probation, either by committing a new crime or by breaking the rules (technical violations). Supervision is close, with protection of the public from further harm as the overriding goal. Probationers remain in this unit until their violation of probation charges are resolved.

These four supervision tracks - blue, green, amber, red - for high risk, violence-prone offenders appropriately serve the goal of maximizing public safety, but they are costly in terms of the expenditure of Agency resources. To compensate for this, lower risk nonviolent probationers receive minimal degrees of supervision or services.

Those probationers with court ordered special conditions, such as attendance in a drug treatment program, must maintain regular contact with their probation officer for the first 2 months, and comply with their special requirements. They are then placed in a "passive management phase," which calls for one face-to-face contact meeting every six months, and monthly reporting through a questionnaire or by checking in via an Automated Reporting Machine System (ARMS).

An even larger group of nonviolent probationers meet only once with their assigned officers, and thereafter report monthly by ARMS, unless there is an allegation of misconduct or some other problem. Obviously, caseloads are exceptionally high for officers supervising these lowest risk probationers, who are largely left alone (Russi, n. d.).

The Use of Intermediate Punishments

The use of "intermediate punishments" is a popular practice among probation agencies throughout the nation, including New York City. Intermediate punishments include a range of court ordered sanctions more punitive than ordinary probation supervision, but less severe than incarceration. It can be thought of as "probation plus." The stated aim is to match the sanction to the offense, but the real goal is reduce reliance upon incarceration (Abadinsky, 1997: 411). In addition, intermediate sanctions provide the court with a greater range of sentencing options, and enable the criminal justice system to exercise greater control over offenders by punishing them in ways just short of locking them up. The availability of these options means, "it is no longer necessary to equate criminal punishment solely with prison. The balance of sanctions between probation and prison can be shifted, and at some level of intensity and length, intermediate punishments can be made the more dreaded penalty" (Petersillia, 1997: 6). Intermediate punishments that can be added to the sentence of probation include fines, restitution, community service, house arrest with or without electronic monitoring, and intensive probation supervision.

Like other agencies, the New York City Department of Probation applies a range of disciplinary interventions and intermediate sanctions, when needed. Together with drug testing and intensive supervision, the Agency runs a day treatment center for violent and nonviolent offenders who do not successfully complete treatment, enforcement and reporting programs" (Russi, n. d.).

Intensive Probation

Intensive probation supervision is an intermediate sanction which is reserved for high risk and special need offenders. It's designed to protect the community by keeping more careful watch over potentially troublesome probationers and, if needed, by providing them with additional rehabilitative services. Probation officers conducting intensive supervision have caseloads of 25 or less. Intensive probation supervision can be used for both juvenile and adult cases; because low caseloads consume scarce resources, as of fiscal 1998, only approximately 1,800 probationers were being monitored this closely.

The Department also runs a Juvenile Intensive Supervision Program for delinquents who would otherwise be placed in a detention facility, or a community-based group home. The average daily enrollment in this program was about 350 at the start of Fiscal 1998. The program's violation rate, including both technical misconduct and re-arrest, was almost 17 percent during 1998.

Unlike other probation costs, which are shared by the city and state governments, the state provides 100 percent reimbursement for intensive probation caseloads. The apparent generosity of the state government is understandable since New York State saves money by placing youths on intensive probation supervision while they live at home rather than incarcerating them in state facilities for delinquent youths.

It is not clear whether intensive probation supervision reduces recidivism rates. As with many new correctional treatment programs, including Scared Straight, Intensive Probation Supervision was heralded as a panacea, a magic bullet that would work wonders. The earliest experiments in Georgia claimed to achieve a great degree of success, and provided probation with new hope. Unfortunately, these claims have not withstood the test of empirical research; subsequent evaluations of other programs operating in different states have not yielded such impressive results. Although the professional literature suggests that intensive supervision falls short of fulfilling its intended goals of enhancing public safety, providing a cost-effective alternative to incarceration, and resolving the prison crowding problem, these programs have been a public relations success.

THE MISCONDUCT REVIEW BOARD

During restructuring, the Agency undertook several especially creative steps. One was the establishment of a Misconduct Review Board, which is based on the "Parole Board Model." Allegations by officers of probationer misconduct, including all technical violations (with the exception of absconding), are heard by an administrative board. The board can impose intermediate sanctions, such as a curfew, community service, placement in a day treatment center, or assignment to an intensive probation supervision unit. Serious misconduct may result in the filing of a violation of probation charge with the court. The advantages of running a Misconduct Review Board include a reduction of court caseloads for violation of probation charges, a shortening of the time it takes to resolve allegations of misconduct, and greater consistency in the Agency's handling of misbehavior by probationers.

CENTRAL RESOURCE UNIT

The Department will also benefit from the creation of a Central Resource Unit which handles telephone inquiries from field officers on both a regular and emergency basis. Staffed by officers with expert knowledge of social service resources, the purpose of the unit is to provide current information on dependable treatment providers. This is an advance over systems which depend on printed human resource directories, which tend to become quickly out-of-date; or on the field officers' own knowledge, which is often limited. As a result, referrals for service are now more likely to be current, appropriate, and based on the needs of individual probationers.

THE DAY TREATMENT CENTER

The Smith-Bell Day Treatment Center is an alternative to incarceration programs for probationers who are in violation of their conditions of probation. It serves male probationers over 16 years of age from Manhattan and the Bronx. It is also used by probationers in a violation status under the citywide Intensive Supervision program and in the Kings Juvenile Offender Program. They recently began servicing juvenile offenders sentenced in the Supreme Court Youth Parts.

As an alternative to incarceration, probationers attend the program from 8-10 hours a day, and otherwise reside in their homes. To enter the program the probationer must be in violation status, must pass a screening interview, and receive approval for entry into the program from the District Attorney, and the sentencing Judge. On the calendar date of the violation of probation, the probationer must waive his right to a hearing and plead guilty to the violation. The conditions of probation are then enhanced to allow for participation in the program, and dates for court review of a progress review are established. Participation in the Day Treatment Center is a form of intermediate punishment which serves as an alternative to incarceration, and offers a myriad of treatment services.

Educational services within the program include literacy training, GED preparation and computer assisted instruction. Drug treatment and drug abuse prevention education are provided and enhanced by frequent testing to monitor the use of drugs. Cognitive skills, as well as life skills, are taught in a group setting. All probationers must perform up to 24 hours of community service while in the program.

Probationers in the program are closely monitored by a special Field Services unit, which is responsible for verifying residence, checking on curfews, and responding to probationers who have failed to attend. Probationers participate in the Day Treatment Center for 6 to 9 months, and upon graduation, are placed in an Intensive Supervision Program for an additional 6 to 9 months of supervision (N.Y.C. Department of Probation, 1998).

Nova Ancora

One of the unique programs run by the Department is Nova Ancora (new anchor). Essentially a job-training and employment program, it was first initiated in the 1980's with a $100,000 grant from the Ford Foundation. It was suspended in 1990 because of budgetary cutbacks; it was reactivated in 1994. The mission of the program is to reduce recidivism by providing life skills preparation, vocational training and employment for probationers (Gelormino and Weiss, 1997). Nova Ancora seeks to recruit small and large businesses, and trade unions, to provide on-the-job training and subsequent employment for probationers. Contracts have been developed with government and not-for-profit organizations to offer training and, in some cases, subsidized employment. In the past few years, probationers have been placed in a number of positions ranging from entry-level jobs to relatively skilled labor, including employment as computer technicians, construction work, clerical work, messenger service and catering. The program is especially successful in that these businesses are willing to take the risk of hiring persons with criminal records.

In fiscal year 1996, the program served more than 500 probationers. In 1996 a preliminary evaluation of the program compared the re-arrest rates of "successful" participants (those who remained in the program for 3 months or more) with a control group of probationers who did not participate in the program. It was found that the "successful" participants had a 50 percent lower re-arrest rate. Since employability is a key factor in preventing recidivism, this preliminary evaluation is especially encouraging (Gelormino, L. & Weiss, E.J., 1997).

Alternative To Court (ATC)

The Alternative to Court program is a diversion program designed to divert juvenile first offenders accused of misdemeanor or low-level felony cases out of the court system. The diversion occurs during the probation intake service (or preliminary procedure) and before the drawing of a petition to initiate court action. The program provides short-term individual and family counseling, referrals to outside social service agencies, mandatory educational classes, and services of a Computerized Learning Lab. Parental involvement is stressed and parent education groups meet monthly. The prosecutor and the victim must agree to the diversion, and the child's parents must be willing to cooperate fully in the program. While in the program, the juveniles are under the supervision of a probation officer with whom they meet twice weekly.

In fiscal year 1996, while in the intake process, 1407 children were screened for the Alternative to Court program. Approximately 450 or about 32% of these children were diverted into the program, thereby removing them from court jurisdiction (Russi, 1996).

The advantages of diversion programs include freeing the child from the stigma of being labeled a "juvenile delinquent," reducing the workload in family court, conserving scarce resources, and intervening early so as to deter further delinquency.

ALTERNATIVE TO DETENTION (ATD)

The Alternative to Detention program, which has been in operation for many years, is designed to allow children facing charges in Family Court to remain under the supervision of their parents in their homes pending court disposition, rather than be detained at a youth detention facility. Selection for participation in the program is based on risk considerations as to whether the child will keep his court appointment and/or might commit another criminal act. Children in the program are closely supervised by probation officers and report to an Alternative to Detention Center every school day. Activities at the Center include counseling, education, recreation, and cultural programs.

The Alternative to Detention program spares many children from the trauma of detention, allows their attorneys to have greater access to them, and saves the City the very expensive costs of juvenile detention (Lindner,1981).

DOMESTIC VIOLENCE

As is true of many agencies, special attention is now being paid to the handling of domestic violence cases. All probation officers currently receive specialized training in domestic violence issues, "so as to enhance services both to domestic violence victims and to probationers under supervision for domestic violence offenses." (N.Y.C. Department of Probation, 1998). In addition, specially trained probation officers have been placed in the domestic court parts of the Criminal and Supreme Court to prepare customized pre-sentence reports on domestic violence cases. These reports assist the court in imposing special conditions in domestic violence cases and requiring that abusers receive therapeutic services.

THE PRE-SENTENCE INVESTIGATION AND PST REPORT

Preparation of the pre-sentence investigation and report is a traditional role for all probation agencies. The primary purpose is to provide a report on the defendant that will assist the judge to hand down an appropriate sentence that takes into account both the defendant and the crime. Secondary purposes of the pre-sentence report include the use of the report for risk classification purposes should the defendant be incarcerated, and for risk classification purposes should he be placed on probation, and for research studies.

During fiscal year 1998, more than 50,000 investigations were completed by the Department of Probation, of which more than 42,000 concerned felonies and nearly 8,000 were about misdemeanors. The Department runs an Accelerated Pre-sentence Investigation Program that attempts to reduce the number of days between pleading guilty and sentencing for incarcerated felony defendants to as few as 10 calendar days (NYC Department of Probation 1998). However, the quality of the Department's pre-sentence investigation is of questionable value. This is especially true in misdemeanant cases, which generate reports of a little more than a two pages, the first of which is essentially a "face sheet."

Probation officers are assigned more than twenty investigations per month, which explains in part the poor quality of their work. By comparison, in the Federal Probation System's Southern District of New York, officers are assigned approximately 6 investigations a month, about one fourth of the workload.

In many investigations little effort is made to verify the information volunteered by the parties, to establish collateral contacts, and to reconcile conflicting statements. Moreover, there is little critical analysis, and the body of the report often constitutes an unsubstantiated recitation of the defendant's statements. Of course, the large workloads of investigatory officers constrain the quality of their work. It should be noted, however, that to upgrade the quality of the report, special field units of officers are assigned to make home visits to cases under investigation to verify the residence of the defendant.

Since cases are resolved by negotiated pleas in more than 95% of the time in New York, the pre-sentence investigation is more ceremonial that substantive because it is rare for a judge to revise the degree of punishment agreed upon by the assistant district attorney and the defense lawyer. In reality, the Pre-Sentence Investigation Report might easily be done away with, since it merely perpetuates the myth of "individualized justice" (Rosecrance, 1988).

THE TECHNOLOGICAL REVOLUTION

Technological advancements primarily have had an impact on the probation officers' law enforcement functions, with little benefit to the rehabilitative process, as predicted (Moran and Lindner, 1985). For example, low-risk probationers who formerly reported by mail now check in by inserting their hand into a fingerprint recognition device in a kiosk located in a lobby. In terms of surveillance, a kiosk is an improvement that saves money. Electronic monitoring systems control the movement of adult probationers. A voice-tracking system enforces the curfews of juveniles who are given beepers and must call into the probation office upon demand. These technological improvements have permitted the Department to restructure its operations along the lines of a triage model, with the high risk cases receiving great attention at the expense of the low risk cases.

SUMMARY AND RECOMMENDATIONS

As true of probation agencies throughout the nation, the New York City Department of Probation has been challenged "to do more with less." To accomplish this goal, the adult supervision service was restructured to provide the greatest "bang for the buck."

Unlike past years, when the medical model of corrections reigned supreme and virtually all criminals were considered sick and in need of treatment, social services are now reserved for those most likely to benefit from treatment.

Obviously a conscious policy decision has been made by the Department to work within its limited budget by expending the bulk of their resources on higher risk cases, even at the price of neglecting the needs of low risk offenders. It can be argued that the policy is sound from an administrative point of view in that it is consistent with public safety.

Probation administrators, however, should address the issue of continuing to prepare pre-sentence investigations which are wasteful, resource consuming, and essentially of symbolic value. Unlike the federal pre-sentence report, which "has become more a legal document than a diagnostic tool, citing facts statutes and guidelines" (Denzlinger and Miller, 1991), the City pre-sentence report has been rendered obsolete by plea negotiation and mandatory sentencing. In reality, the sentence has already been agreed upon prior to the officer being assigned to look into the case. Not only is the report more ceremonial than substantive, but it is also destructive to the Agency. This work assignment is demoralizing to officers who understand the worthless of their efforts; their work product is of such low quality that it undermines the creditability of the Agency. Although currently required by law, probation administrators might consider advocating legislative change in relation to the mandatory nature of the report. Possible changes include limiting the reports to felony cases, encouraging greater use of waivers, reducing the contents of the report, or leaving the preparation of the reports to para-professionals. In this way, much of the scarce resources unnecessarily expended could be used for the supervision of probationers.

Acknowledgments

The author appreciates the assistance of Commissioner Russi, Public Relations Director Ryan, Deputy Commissioner Siegel, and Manhattan Branch Chief Dobbs.

References

Abadinsky, H. (1997). Probation and Parole: Theory and Practice, 6th ed. New Jersey: Prentice Hall.

Boone, H., Jr. (1997). The Money Trial: Following the trends in correctional dollars. Perspectives, 21(4) Fall: 32-33.

Bonczar, T.P. (1997). Characteristics of Adults on Probation, 1995. Bureau of Justice Statistics, Special Report, December. Washington, DC: U.S. Department of Justice..

Bureau of Justice Statistics (1997). National Institute of Justice Journal (September): 4.

Denzlinger, J.D. & D.E. Miller (1988). The Federal Probation Officer: Life before and after guideline sentencing. Federal Probation.55(4): 49-53.

Guynes, R. (1988). Difficult clients, large caseloads plague probation, parole agencies. U.S. Department of Justice, Office of Justice Programs, National Institute of Justice (Research in Action) August: 1-8.

Gelormino, L. & E.J. Weiss (1997) Corrections Compendium, 22 (2) Feb.: 1-4.

Lindner, C. (1981). The Utilization of Day/Evening Centers as an Alternative to Secure Detention of Juveniles/ Journal of Probation and Parole: Vol. 13.

Lindner, C. & R. Bonn (1996). Probation Officer Victimization and Fieldwork Practices: Results of a National Study. Federal Probation. 60 (2) :16-23.

Moran, T. & Lindner, C., (1985). Probation and The High Technology Revolution in Criminal Justice Review, 10:25-32

New York City Department of Probation (1997). Mayor's Management Report. New York: 44.

New York State Criminal Procedure Law Supplement, 1997/8, Section 390.20, New York: Looseleaf Publications.

New York City Department of Probation (1998). Mayor's Management Report.

Petersilia, J. (1997). Probation in the United States: Practices and challenges. National Institute of Justice Journal. Sept.. U.S. Department of Justice, Washington, DC: 2-8.

Rosecrance, J. (1988). Maintaining the myth of individualized justice: Probation pre-sentence reports. Justice Quarterly, 5(2): 235-256.

Russi, R. (n.d.). Restructuring Adult Supervision Services: A Program Overview. New York: The City of New York Department of Probation.

Russi, R. (1996). Testimony of Probation Commissioner Raul Russi before the City Council Committee on Youth Services, New York, December 10: 1.

Ryan, J., (1988). Interview with Jack Ryan, Public Relations Officer of the Department of Probation

Chapter 19

NEW YORK CITY'S JAILS

By

Professor Andrew Karmen

Department of Sociology

Note:
The following information was drawn from the Department of Correction homepage linked to the Official New York City website maintained by Mayor Giuliani's administration (go to http://www.ci.nyc.ny.us/html/doc). The posted material reviews the Department's history and describes its detention facilities, inmates, training academy, and new strategies to prevent gang fights and other forms of violence. It does not address problem areas like cellblock living conditions, the smuggling in of contraband by visitors and employees, charges of brutality and corruption, the degree of effectiveness of rehabilitation efforts, or the recidivism rates of former inmates.

A BRIEF HISTORY AND OVERVIEW OF THE DEPARTMENT OF CORRECTION

In most jurisdictions, the local jails are run by the county sheriff's department. But in New York, for more than 100 years, the city's houses of detention have been operated by the Department of Correction (DOC). The DOC was set up in 1895, when the Department of Charities and Correction was divided into two separate agencies. The responsibility of running hospitals and almshouses was given to the Department of Public Charities. The Department of Correction took over administration of the penitentiary and workhouse on Blackwell's Island (now called Roosevelt Island), the Manhattan House of Detention (then called the "Tombs"), five other local facilities, and the cemetery on Hart Island (the proverbial "Potter's Field" where poor people have been buried since 1869). In the 1930's, the old Blackwell's Island facilities were phased out and the Department's focus of operations shifted to Rikers Island, connected to Astoria, Queens by a bridge. Rikers Island was enlarged from its original 90 acres to its current size of more than 400 acres by the addition of sanitary landfill. Over the decades, ten separate jails were built on Rikers Island, which together now have the capacity to house more than 16,000 prisoners. Moored at the island to house overflow crowds are two small floating detention centers, which were formerly Staten Island ferries. The island also has its own power plant, marine unit, K-9 dog unit, bakery, laundry, print shop, tailor shop, and bus transportation facility.

The massive scale of the Department of Correction's operations mirrors the size of the city's crime problem, the number of arrests made by the NYPD, and the number of cases processed by the court system. During fiscal year 1997, about 443,000 prisoners passed through the DOC's lock-up facilities and were delivered to court appearances (some prisoners were arrested and processed more than once during the year). In addition to the ten jails on Rikers Island, the Department runs six borough detention centers (two in Brooklyn, two in the Bronx, one in Manhattan, and one in Queens); fifteen court holding pens (one in every Criminal Court, Supreme Court, and Family Court building in each of the five boroughs, where inmates scheduled for that day's proceedings are kept); and four prison wards. Many of the facilities have specialized functions; there is a maximum security one person-per-cell building; a place for misdemeanants serving up to a year behind bars; a facility housing the relatively small proportion of female detainees and misdemeanants, plus a nursery for up to 25 infants; a reception center for adolescent male detainees 16 to 18 years old; two infirmaries and three prison wards in hospitals for prisoners who are physically or mentally ill; a methadone detoxification unit for detainees addicted to narcotics; a separate ward for those with contagious diseases like tuberculosis; a special dormitory for inmates afflicted with AIDS; and a hospice for terminally ill inmates. Added together, the grand total of inmates under the control of the City's Department of Correction (not counting those imprisoned by the State's Department of Correctional Services) approaches 20,000 and outnumbers the inmate populations of 40 of the 50 states. The average cost to taxpayers of keeping someone behind bars for a year was about $41,000 during FY 1997.

Another indication of the scale of the DOC's operations is the size of its transportation division. A staff of 375 uniformed and civilian employees support a fleet of more than 400 vehicles that jointly travel more than 2 million miles a year carrying more than 2.5 million riders (inmates, staff members, and visitors). Inmates are driven to and from court appearances, hospital visits, and significant family events (such as funerals), plus they take one-way rides to upstate prisons.

The Department of Correction has been running the nation's first urban boot camp since 1990 on Rikers Island. Called the High Impact Incarceration Program (HIIP), its highly disciplined military regimen is intended to foster self-discipline and lifestyle changes. Marching, drilling and exercising is coupled with vocational/educational training, substance abuse counseling, and community service (work details do painting, landscaping, graffiti removal and other maintenance tasks). HIIP is an intense "voluntary program" for willing participants that lasts for only 61 days and accepts up to 100 parolees who have committed technical violations, plus some City-sentenced inmates more than 19 years old convicted of nonviolent misdemeanors. Nearly 500 inmates entered the program during fiscal year 1997; 64% made it through to graduation and release.

CORRECTIONS OFFICERS

Almost 13,000 people worked for the DOC in 1997. About 11,340 (88%) were uniformed officers; the rest were civilian employees.

Attracting, preparing, and retaining a qualified staff has always been a challenge. From 1927 until the 1930's, the Police Department trained raw recruits to be "prison keepers." Since then, the DOC has operated a training academy (currently, it is located in the Middle Village section of Queens). The academy offers pre-service and in-service training necessary for the successful performance of officers' duties in a highly charged institutional environment. Topics in the twelve-week curriculum range from survival skills (the appropriate use of force, firearms and baton training, defensive tactics, hostage situations, control of contraband) and legal matters that can arise on the job (concerning Constitutional law, criminal procedural law, penal law, search procedures, preserving crime scenes, courtroom testimony, identifying ethical issues) to basic health training (about first aid and CPR, resuscitation techniques, recognizing infectious diseases, suicide prevention).

THE INMATES

About 19,200 inmates were incarcerated on an average day during fiscal year 1997. However, during the course of the entire 12 month period, about 133,300 people passed through the City's jail system.

There are several types of prisoners under the control of the Department of Correction. Most (67%) are "detainees" who have not been convicted (yet) of any crime. After their arrest and arraignment, they were unable to raise sufficient funds to make bail, or were remanded without bail, pending trial (if they were charged with murder, for example). Of the remaining one-third of the inmates under DOC supervision, about 17% are people convicted of misdemeanors who are serving sentences of up to a year in jail; the others (16%) are convicts who have just been sentenced to more than one year behind bars for committing felonies and are waiting to be transferred to upstate prisons run by the State Department of Correctional Services; also, a small number are probationers and parolees facing revocation hearings for violating the terms of their conditional liberty. The average length of stay for detainees (many of whom faced felony charges) was around 46 days; individuals who quickly pled guilty to committing misdemeanors were incarcerated for an average of 37 days during fiscal year 1997.

All the inmates under DOC custody were more than 15 years old (juvenile delinquents are handled by a different city agency). The average prisoner was 31 years old. About one quarter of all inmates (27%) were between the ages of 16 and 24. The overwhelming majority were teenage boys and men. Most of the New Yorkers who were incarcerated were black (56%) and Hispanic (35%); the rest were white (7%) and other (mostly Asian) (2%).

As for the charges inmates faced (the top charge at intake, right after arraignment), the largest group, about one third of all prisoners (32%), was in trouble for drug offenses (sale and possession). At the time of admission, about one quarter (24%) of all inmates had been arrested for a crime of violence, and one tenth were charged with crimes against property; the remainder (16%) faced an assortment of felony and misdemeanor charges. In terms of specific offenses, more than 21% were in custody for drug sale and another 10% for possession; more than 8% of all inmates were being held on charges of murder or attempted murder, more than 12% for robbery, nearly 5% for burglary, 1% for rape, and 2% for grand larceny plus 3% for petit larceny. About 30% of all inmates had been arrested in Manhattan but only 21% lived in Manhattan during fiscal year 1996 (the latest available statistics). About 4% of the people held in New York City jails did not live in the five boroughs.

An estimated 12% of the daily inmate population, perhaps as many as 1,600 prisoners, were believed to be affiliated with outside street gangs such as the Latin Kings, Netas, and Bloods during the late 1990's. To prevent inmate vs. inmate violence such as stabbings, the DOC implemented a number of new strategies: a gang intelligence unit was created, and gang identifiers and symbols like beaded necklaces were banned; a computerized system was devised to track incidents of violence and dangerous inmates; those known to be violent or security risks were kept separate in housing, recreation, and transportation; attacks were sternly handled as new offenses subject to arrests and prosecutions; officers were given chemical agents, special restraining devices, and metal detectors; and security searches were stepped up. As a result, the Department reported that incidents involving inmate violence, like slashings, had been cut dramatically from more than 100 monthly in 1994 to fewer than 100 during a four-month period in late 1997.

Jail overcrowding has been a chronic problem over the centuries, as authorities periodically coped with a shortage of cells and a surplus of commitments from police stations and courts. Two inmates per small cell (double-bunking) and crowded dormitories are the result. In 1970, inmates outraged by the overcrowded conditions rioted in four DOC facilities. When surging populations of arrestees led to a situation where the headcount was more than 20% above the officially designated maximum capacity in 1982, a federal court ordered the release of nearly 600 detainees who were being held because they couldn't post very low bail. Since then, more facilities have been built, and temporary space has been reserved for emergency situations. In the 1990's, capacity utilization has ranged from 90% to 99%.

Chapter 20

CAPITAL PUNISHMENT IN NEW YORK

by

Professor Barry Latzer

Department of Government

In 1995 New York became the 38th State to authorize the death penalty. Although no one (yet) has been executed under the new law, and no one has been put to death in New York since 1963, the Empire State still ranks third among all states (behind Texas and Georgia) in total number of executions.[1] This shows that New York has had considerable historical experience with capital punishment. It is likely that in the 21st century, New York will again be executing a small number of criminals each year. It is also likely that some of those who are executed will be from New York City, since the overwhelming majority of murders in New York State take place in the City.[2] Indeed, the first death sentence under the new law was handed down in Brooklyn in June 1998.[3] Although City prosecutors are responsible for prosecuting capital cases, the law governing the death penalty is made in Albany by the State Legislature and Governor.

This chapter will explore three different matters: 1) the recent history of the death penalty in New York; 2) the current-day capital punishment law, and how it operates; and 3) some of the major issues New York State's legal system faces in the implementation of the death penalty.

---

[1] See U.S. Dept of Justice, Bureau of Justice Statistics, *Capital Punishment 1996*, p. 10 (1997). From 1930 to 1996, Texas executed 404 persons, Georgia, 388, and New York, 329. Ibid.

[2] Over eighty percent of the State's murders occur in New York City. See State of New York, Division of Criminal Justice Services, *1994 Crime and Justice Annual Report*, p. 8 (1995); State of New York, Division of Criminal Justice Services, *1993 Crime and Justice Annual Report*, p. 8 (1994).

[3] Darrel K. Harris was sentenced to death for murdering three people in a social club in the Bedford-Stuyvesant section of Brooklyn. See Somini Sengupta, *Haunted Juror Tells Of a Divided Panel Deciding for Death*, N.Y. Times, June 8, 1998, at A1.

HISTORY

329 persons have been executed by the State of New York since 1930. All but two of these executions were for murder; the other two were for kidnaping. Of those executed, 234 (71%) were white; 90 were black (27%); and five were of other races.[4] Two were women.[5]

From the 1930's to the 1960's, the number of executions in New York declined fairly steadily, as they did throughout the United States (see Table 20-1).

Table 20-1:

Executions in New York State, by Five-Year Periods, 1930-1965

1930-34	1935-39	1940-44	1945-49	1950-54	1955-59	1960-64
80	73	78	36	27	25	10

Source: U.S. Dept. of Justice, Bureau of Justice Statistics Bulletin, *National Prisoner Statistics-- Capital Punishment* (Washington, D.C.: U.S. Govt. Printing Office, 1979):17.

Two years after the last New York execution, in 1963, the state legislature narrowed the capital punishment law, limiting the death penalty to those convicted of murdering a police officer or a peace officer, and to those who committed murder while serving a life term in prison. But this law (later amended to extend to the killing of jail and prison employees) was struck down in 1973 by the state's highest court, the Court of Appeals.[6] Replacement legislation enacted in 1974 also was declared unconstitutional.[7] Thereafter, in each consecutive year, for the next eighteen years, the New

---

[4] U.S. Dept of Justice, Bureau of Justice Statistics Bulletin, *National Prisoner Statistics-- Capital Punishment* (Washington, D.C.: U.S. Govt Printing Office, 1979):18.

[5] Ibid.: 19.

[6] See People v. Fitzpatrick, 32 N.Y.2d 499, 300 N.E.2d 139, 346 N.Y.S.2d 793 (1973). The statute was found unconstitutional based on the U.S. Supreme Court's decision in Furman v. Georgia, 408 U.S. 238 (1972). *Furman* had declared that the death penalty as administered in Georgia (and by implication, throughout the United States) was "cruel and unusual punishment" in violation of the Eighth Amendment.

[7] See People v. Davis, 43 N.Y.2d 17, 371 N.E.2d 456, 400 N.Y.S.2d 735 (1977), where the Court of Appeals held that a mandatory death sentence for someone convicted of

York State legislature approved death penalty bills, and each time the governor of the state vetoed the legislation (refused to sign the bill into law). Democratic Governor Hugh Carey successfully vetoed capital punishment legislation each year from 1977 through 1982, whereupon his Democratic successor, Governor Mario Cuomo, continued the practice from 1983 through 1994. The legislature was never able to muster enough votes to override these vetoes.

During this period, the murder rate in New York rose dramatically. In 1963, the year of the last execution in the Empire State, there were 689 murders in the state, for a rate of 3.8 murders for every 100,000 people.[8] One decade later, in 1973, there were 2,034 murders in New York, for a rate of 11.1 per 100,000.[9] By 1990, the rate reached 14.5 per 100,000, and then began to decline again.[10]

As the murder rate climbed throughout the country, public opinion polls indicated that national popular support for executions also skyrocketed. Whereas only 47% of all Americans favored the death penalty in 1966, a steady 70%-75% supported it throughout the 1980s and 1990's.[11]

In November 1994, George Pataki, a Republican, was elected governor for the first time in twenty years, defeating incumbent governor Mario Cuomo. During the campaign, Pataki promised to enact a death penalty law, and the issue may have been a significant factor in his election. In his inaugural address, the new governor spoke the following words:

---

murdering a corrections employee was unconstitutional. Just prior to the *Davis* case, the United States Supreme Court had ruled that mandatory capital punishment for murder is unconstitutional. Woodson v. North Carolina, 428 U.S. 280 (1976). Mandatory death for "lifers" who kill was struck down in People v. Smith, 63 N.Y.2d 41, 468 N.E.2d 879, 479 N.Y.S.2d 706 (1984).

[8] U.S. Dept of Justice, *Uniform Crime Reports for the United States 1963*, (Washington, D.C.: U.S. Govt Printing Office, 1963), p. 61. In the federal and New York State crime reports "murder" includes manslaughter, except negligent manslaughter.

[9] U.S. Dept of Justice, *Uniform Crime Reports for the United States 1973*, (Washington, D.C.: U.S. Govt Printing Office, 1973), p. 60.

[10] State of New York, Division of Criminal Justice Services, *1995 Crime and Justice Annual Report*, p. 8 (1996). From 1990 to 1995, the New York State murder rate was 14.5, 14.2, 13.1, 10.9, and 8.6. Ibid. The murder rate in New York City for that same period was 30.7, 29.3, 27.1, 26.5, 21.3, and 16.1.

[11] Phoebe C. Ellsworth and Samuel R. Gross, "Hardening of the Attitudes: Americans' Views on the Death Penalty," 50 Journal of Social Issues 19 (1994). A 1995 national survey showed 77% support for the death penalty. Of respondents living in the eastern part of the United States, 75% expressed such support. There was no separate indication of the views of New York residents. U.S. Dept of Justice, *Sourcebook of Criminal Justice Statistics--1995*, Table 2.71.

Our founders believed that one area where government should be strong and effective was maintaining public order and public safety. They understood society's first obligation is to those citizens who obey the law and respect the rights of others, and they expect government to protect them from those who do not. Let me also note that when a society does not express its own horror at the crime of murder by enforcing the ultimate sanction against it, innocent lives are put at risk. Not out of a sense of vindictiveness, then, but a sense of justice--indeed, a sense of compassion for those who otherwise might become victims of murder--I will ask the Legislature to pass and I will sign and enforce the death penalty. And let me say--and let me say: if one police officer's life is saved, if one less child is caught in a crossfire, if one fewer cabdriver or shopkeeper is killed in a robbery, then the death penalty will have proven itself worthwhile.[12]

A death penalty law was approved in the first few months of Pataki's administration. That legislation became effective September 1, 1995. The New York death penalty law is very complex, in part because of the need to satisfy the constitutional requirements established by the United States Supreme Court. The next section of this chapter analyzes the main features of this law.

NEW YORK'S DEATH PENALTY LAW

Murder in the First Degree

Only a person found guilty of Murder in the First Degree is eligible for the death penalty in New York. Murder in the First Degree is defined as an intentional murder committed under one (or more) of twelve "aggravating" circumstances.

Note first that the murder must be "intentional." This means that the prosecutor must prove that the killer desired the death of the victim at the time of the crime. Not included in this definition are "reckless" murders, where the murderer is aware that his conduct could cause a death, and although he is indifferent to such a possibility, he is not desirous of it. An example of a reckless murder would be shooting into a crowd, or throwing a heavy object from a tall building, without seeking to kill anyone in particular. Neither of these reckless murders are capital crimes (crimes for which one could get the death penalty) in New York.

Also not considered intentional murders are killings in which the perpetrator only intended to wound or injure the victim, and what is ordinarily called "felony-murders," which are deaths occurring during certain violent felonies.[13] Some states authorize the death penalty for

---

[12] 'The People Seek Change': Transcript of Pataki's Inaugural, N.Y. Times, Jan. 2, 1995, at A28.

[13] Ordinarily, a person may be found guilty of felony murder merely upon proof that he committed a violent felony, such as robbery, and that someone died during the commission of the crime. There is no need to prove that the defendant did the killing, or that he intended the death. Thus, an accomplice to a robbery, even a mere lookout, may

felony-murder even though the accused may not have intended or done the killing. Although such laws have been upheld by the Supreme Court,[14] unintentional murder is not a capital crime in New York.

In addition to having to prove intentional murder, a prosecutor who seeks the death penalty must prove beyond a reasonable doubt one of the aggravating circumstances enumerated in the New York statute. This is to insure that the death penalty will be applied consistently and will be limited to only the most reprehensible murders and murderers, i.e., those that are "aggravated." Box 20-1 below lists the twelve aggravating circumstances, divided into three categories: aggravators defined by the status of the victim, by the status of the defendant, and by the nature of the crime.

BOX 20-1: CIRCUMSTANCES THAT CAN LEAD TO THE DEATH PENALTY

Aggravating Circumstances in New York's Death Penalty Law

Where the VICTIM was . . .

1. an on duty police officer

2. an on duty "peace officer," including parole, probation and court officers

3. an on duty corrections employee

4. a witness or his immediate family

5. a judge

Where a DEFENDANT was . . .

6. previously convicted of Murder 1• or 2•

be found guilty of felony murder if one of his cohorts killed the victim. Indeed, it would be felony murder if the victim suffered a fatal heart attack during the crime, or if one of the other perpetrators was killed, even if he was shot by the police.

The New York death penalty statute lists "contemporaneous felony murder" as one of the aggravating factors which may be proved in order to establish first degree murder, but it is to emphasized that this applies only to *intentional* murders during the commission of a listed felony, and only to intentional murders committed or commanded by the defendant. In short, ordinary *un*intentional felony murder is not murder first degree in New York.

[14] See Tison v. Arizona, 481 U.S. 137 (1987), where the Supreme Court affirmed a death sentence for the major participant in a felony-murder who did not kill or intend to kill but had a mental state of "reckless indifference" to human life.

> 7. a serial murderer (2 or more additional killings of a similar nature within 24 months)
>
> 8. an inmate serving a life sentence
>
> Where the MURDER was . . .   9. a murder for hire
>
> 10. intentional murder during the commission of certain violent felonies
>
> 11. a multiple murder (intentional murder plus another killing at the same time)
>
> 12. a torture murder

Guilty Pleas

Even if a defendant is accused of First Degree Murder, he is not eligible for the death penalty unless the prosecutor gives notice to the accused and the court, within 120 days of indictment, of the state's intention to seek death. This notice may be withdrawn, but once withdrawn it may not be re-filed. If the prosecutor does not seek the death penalty, the defendant may still be tried for Murder First Degree, and if found guilty, may be sentenced by the judge to life without parole, or to a minimum of 20-25 years and a maximum of life in prison. Or, if the prosecutor and judge agree, the defendant may plead guilty to Murder First Degree, giving the judge the same sentencing options. A death sentence may be imposed only by a jury after a trial and verdict of guilty of First Degree Murder.

Note that if the prosecutor does not seek the death penalty, or if he accepts a guilty plea, the defendant cannot be sentenced to death. This gives prosecutors a great deal of power over potentially capital cases.

Attorneys

The new death penalty law created a statewide Capital Defender Office (CDO) to monitor and coordinate legal representation in death penalty cases. The CDO is charged with the responsibility of recruiting lawyers to defend capital cases and providing training and support services for them. It is also required to maintain a roster of attorneys certified by the courts as capable of handling a death penalty case. Two such capital-certified attorneys must be appointed by the trial court in first degree murder cases. If there is a conviction in a death penalty case, the Court of Appeals must appoint counsel to handle the appeals.

The Capital Trial

Death penalty trials are different from ordinary trials in two principal respects. First, the jury selection process is more elaborate in order to be doubly sure that jurors have no disqualifying biases and that they will be able to vote for the death penalty if such a decision becomes necessary. Second, the trial is "bifurcated," or divided into two parts: a guilt phase, and a penalty or sentencing phase. Immediately before the trial, prospective jurors summoned from the county in which the murder took place will be questioned by the prosecutor and defense attorney to determine their fitness to serve. Potential jurors may be questioned individually outside the presence of other jurors, and they may be questioned without limitation by the judge on the possibility of racial bias. Each side--the prosecution and the defense--may exclude from the jury without explanation ("peremptory challenge") up to 20 prospective jurors. Also, each side may challenge an unlimited number of prospective jurors "for cause," that is, with explanation. The explanations may include such things as kinship or friendship with one of the trial participants, or a bias for or against the accused.

As this is a capital case, jurors' views on the death penalty are especially significant, and prospective jurors will be questioned closely about their beliefs. New York law provides for "death qualification" of jurors. That is, a person being considered for the jury may be kept off the panel for cause if he "entertains such conscientious opinions either against or in favor of the death penalty" as to preclude impartiality in rendering a verdict or imposing sentence.[15] The main reason for death qualification is to ensure that the jury can be fair to the prosecution. A juror who would never under any circumstances vote for death is unfit to serve in a capital case because he is biased against one of the sentencing options. Some people have argued, however, that death qualification is unfair to defendants because the jury ultimately selected will be purged of death penalty opponents and the remaining panelists might be the kind of persons who are more likely to vote "guilty" and to support a death sentence. The Supreme Court considered these arguments and found no constitutional problem with death qualification.[16]

Once the jury is impaneled, the guilt phase of the trial begins. It is like an ordinary trial, although it may take longer than a noncapital murder trial because there may be more witnesses and their testimony may be more protracted. At the end of this part of the trial the jury decides on guilt or innocence. If the jury is not unanimous ("hung jury") a mistrial is declared and the defendant may be tried again. If there is a unanimous vote of "not guilty" the accused is set free. If all jurors vote guilty of Murder in the First Degree the same jury will sit for the second (penalty) phase of the trial.

The penalty phase is where the "aggravating factors" discussed previously come in. Unless the jury unanimously finds that one of the twelve aggravating factors was proven, it cannot impose a death sentence. During the penalty phase, the prosecutor must, through witnesses, prove beyond a reasonable doubt the existence of one of the aggravators, and the defense can try to rebut this evidence.[17]

---

[15] The quoted language is from New York Criminal Procedure Law (C.P.L.) § 270.20.

[16] See Lockhart v. McCree, 476 U.S. 162 (1986).

[17] The prosecutor may also present evidence of two "special aggravating factors": that the crime was an act of terrorism, or that the defendant had two or more serious violent felony convictions within the previous ten years. The jury may be influenced by

The defense may also present what is known as "mitigating evidence"--evidence in opposition to a sentence of death. Although the New York statute lists mitigating factors, such as mental impairment, or the domination of another person at the time of the crime, it also allows the defendant to present any other circumstance of the crime or the defendant's state of mind, character or background that is relevant to punishment. This "catchall" language allows the defense to present virtually any evidence it wishes in mitigation even though the prosecutor is limited to proving only the listed aggravators.[18]

The reason for a bifurcated trial can now be made clear. Some of the testimony at the penalty phase--evidence, for example, of defendants' prior murders (an aggravating factor), or of his background or character (mitigating factors)--would be inappropriate in an ordinary trial, as it might improperly influence the verdict. Yet the capital jury must consider such evidence before imposing sentence. By dividing the trial in two parts, evidence relevant to the sentence can be presented in the penalty phase without prejudicing the earlier guilt or innocence decision.

Once the aggravating and mitigating evidence is presented, the jury must make two determinations in order to impose a sentence. First, it must unanimously find that an aggravating factor was established and that it (along with any other aggravating evidence the jury may accept) substantially outweighs any mitigating factors. Second, and independently, it must vote unanimously for death.

The capital jury has an alternative sentencing option: life without parole. That is, the jury may unanimously agree that instead of death the sentence will be life imprisonment without parole. What if the jury is not unanimous regarding the sentence? If the jurors are unable to agree on the punishment the judge must impose a sentence of 20-25 years to a maximum of life. In short, after a guilty verdict, there are three possible sentencing outcomes: death, life without parole, or a judge-imposed sentence of 20/25 to life.

Who May Not Be Executed?

Of course, a defendant found Not Guilty by Reason of Insanity may not be punished at all, much less put to death, as he is not guilty of a crime. He may be committed to a mental institution for an indefinite period, however, on grounds of mental illness plus dangerousness. A defendant who was sane at the time of the crime but becomes insane at the time his death

---

this evidence, but the jury must still find that one of the twelve "regular" aggravating factors was established in order to vote for death.

[18] New York had no choice but to permit any relevant mitigating evidence as the Supreme Court made it a constitutional mandate. See Lockett v. Ohio, 438 U.S. 586 (1978). Partly as a way of balancing the open-ended rule on mitigating evidence, the Supreme Court has permitted the prosecution to offer in the penalty phase what are known as "victim impact statements." See Payne v. Tennessee, 501 U.S. 808 (1991). Victim impact statements consist of testimony by the family of the murder victim on the magnitude of their loss. As this chapter was being written the Pataki administration was proposing legislation to permit victim impact evidence in New York.

sentence is to be imposed may not be executed.[19]

New York law adds protection against execution of those defendants who are found in a non-jury hearing to be mentally retarded.[20] This hearing may take place before or after the guilt phase of the trial. A defendant found to have an intelligence quotient (I.Q.) below 75, accompanied by behavioral difficulties (which condition existed before the age of 18), cannot be executed in New York.[21] If found not retarded, the defendant may still offer proof of mental infirmity as mitigating evidence during the penalty phase of the trial.

The other significant death penalty exemption in New York is for age. State law bars execution unless the defendant "was more than eighteen years old at the time of the crime."[22]

Appeals

The appeals process in capital cases is lengthy and complicated. Assuming a defendant is found guilty of Murder in the First Degree and sentenced to death, it will be several years before he can be executed. First there are direct appeals, then follow what are called in New York "post-conviction motions," capped by federal habeas corpus petitions. These three types of appeals (more accurately called "post-conviction review," since direct appeal is only one type of judicial review following the trial) will be discussed in the order just presented.

Usually, the focus of post-conviction review is on procedural errors during the trial. If the reviewing court determines that there were trial errors serious enough to render the trial unfair and warrant reversal it can overturn the conviction or the sentence. Ordinarily, following reversal, a new trial or a new sentencing hearing is permitted, since the discovery of a trial error is not the same as a finding that the accused was innocent or undeserving of the death penalty.

Post-conviction review is time-consuming largely because it entails lengthy and detailed writing. After studying the trial transcript (which may be thousands of pages long for a lengthy and complex capital trial), defense lawyers must prepare a brief alleging trial errors and supporting each claim with the appropriate legal arguments. Then prosecutors must read

---

[19] This is also a federal constitutional rule. See Ford v. Wainwright, 477 U.S. 399 (1986). Such a defendant may be executed once his sanity is restored.

[20] The Supreme Court permits the execution of mildly to moderately retarded defendants. See Penry v. Lynaugh, 492 U.S. 302 (1989).

[21] There is an exception. The retardation exemption does not apply to an inmate in a correctional institution who intentionally kills an on-duty correctional employee.

[22] This is the language of New York Penal Law (P.L.) § 125.27(1)(b). It is not clear whether this means that the defendant must have been 18 at the time of the murder or 19. Clearly, however, defendants who were 17 years old or less when they killed may not be executed in New York, though such executions are permitted under the U.S. Constitution. See Stanford v. Kentucky, 492 U.S. 361 (1989).

the transcript and the defense brief and respond with their own brief seeking to refute the defense arguments. Finally, the reviewing judges have to read the briefs and relevant portions of the transcript, decide each defense claim, and prepare a written court "opinion" explaining the reasons for their decisions. Each post-conviction review could take well over one year.

As in most states, New York provides for direct appeal of capital cases to the highest court in the state (here, the Court of Appeals). (By contrast, noncapital appeals go to the intermediate appeals courts.) Such review is mandatory and may not be waived by the defendant. The Court of Appeals may reverse the conviction or death sentence because of trial errors, as in a noncapital appeal. In addition, in capital cases the court may overturn a death sentence if it was imposed under the influence of passion or prejudice, including sentences that were influenced by the race of the defendant or victim. The Court of Appeals must also determine whether the sentence was excessive or disproportionate to the penalty imposed in similar cases, considering both the nature of the crime and the relevant characteristics of the defendant. This last determination is called "comparative proportionality review" and can be very time-consuming because records of all similar cases must be studied.[23] The U.S. Supreme Court has said that it is not constitutionally required.[24]

The rulings of the Court of Appeals on federal constitutional questions may be appealed to the U.S. Supreme Court by a petition for certiorari. The Supreme Court does not have to grant such a petition, however, and the overwhelming majority are denied. Denial of certiorari means that the Supreme Court will not review the case, which leaves standing the last court ruling. If the Supreme Court grants the certiorari petition and decides the appeal, it then usually remands the case to the state court for further proceedings, including a new trial or another sentencing hearing if such is necessitated by a Supreme Court reversal. Whether it decides the case or not, the Supreme Court is the last stop in the direct appeals process.

Now the post-conviction motion phase begins. New York law provides for motions (requests to a court) to "vacate judgment" (reverse the conviction) or to "set aside sentence" on various grounds, including the discovery after trial of new evidence.[25] However, no issue may be raised on a motion if the same issue was resolved on direct appeal or if defendant unjustifiably failed to raise the issue on direct appeal. In other states the most common claim in this type of post-trial review is "ineffective assistance of counsel," the contention that the defense attorneys were incompetent. These claims are usually unsuccessful, but they also lengthen the appeals process, which, naturally, is desirable to defendants trying to stave off the imposition of a death sentence.

Post-conviction motions are initially made to the court that originally tried the case. If the motion is denied, the denial may be appealed to the Court of Appeals and then, for federal

---

[23] New York law requires the courts trying capital cases to compile data on race, sex, ethnicity, religion, geography, and other factors as will assist the Court of Appeals in comparative proportionality review.

[24] See Pulley v. Harris, 465 U.S. 37 (1984).

[25] Details may be found in C.P.L. §§ 440.10 and 440.20.

issues, to the U.S. Supreme Court (on certiorari). The motion and each appeal of its denial require additional briefing, which of course takes more time.

Once direct appeal and state post-conviction motions are complete, the defendant may petition a United States District Court for a federal writ of habeas corpus. Habeas petitions are very much like state post-conviction motions, except that only federal rights may be claimed, and a federal judge will review them. Indeed, only claims that were already reviewed and rejected by the state courts during the direct appeal or state post-conviction process may be raised on federal habeas. If the writ is granted, the conviction or sentence will probably be overturned and a new trial or a new sentencing hearing will usually be permitted. If the writ is denied, as is usually the case, the prisoner may appeal the denial to the appropriate United States Court of Appeals, and if unsuccessful there, may seek review of the denial of the writ by the United States Supreme Court. (This is likely to be a death row inmate's third Supreme Court certiorari petition, including the petitions on direct appeal and on state post-conviction motions.) Recent changes in the federal statutes governing habeas corpus limit death penalty inmates to one petition to be filed within 180 days (six months) of the completion of all direct appeals plus the time needed to complete pending state post-conviction motions.[26] This same legislation requires deference to state court decisions by the federal judges who review habeas petitions, thus disfavoring the granting of petitions.

This ends the post-conviction process. Although the New York death penalty law is too new to determine the time the process will take here, it probably will not be less than the national average for the 1990s, which is nearly ten years.[27]

Method of Execution

New York law provides for execution only by lethal injection. Use of the electric chair--developed first in New York at the end of the nineteenth century--is abolished.

ISSUES IN THE IMPLEMENTATION OF THE DEATH PENALTY

Prosecutorial Discretion

The prosecution of death penalty cases is left to the District Attorneys of each of the sixty-two counties of New York State. As already noted, these prosecutors have considerable discretion in seeking or not seeking capital charges. Several district attorneys in New York City expressed personal reservations about the death penalty when the law went into effect

---

[26] See the Antiterrorism and Effective Death Penalty Act of 1996, 110 Stat. 1214, signed into law by President Clinton in 1996.

[27] See U.S. Dept of Justice, Bureau of Justice Statistics, *Capital Punishment 1996*, p. 12 (1997). The average elapsed time (expressed in months) from sentence to execution for all death penalty states, from 1990 to 1996 was 95, 116, 114, 113, 122, 134, and 125. Ibid. The average of these figures is 117 months, or 9 years and 9 months.

in 1995, and their misgivings may be having an impact on the number of death penalty prosecutions in the City.[28]

The most forthright opposition came from Bronx District Attorney Robert T. Johnson, who at one point stated that it was his "present intention not to utilize the death penalty provisions of the statute."[29] Johnson's remarks, coupled with his failure to seek the death penalty in a few highly publicized murder cases, led to an open conflict with Governor Pataki. In December 1995, Michael Vernon was arrested and charged with the gunshot murder of five victims in a Bronx shoe store. Since this was a multiple murder, it constituted murder in the first degree, but District Attorney Johnson did not file notice of intent to seek the death penalty. In light of Johnson's public statements, the Governor asked him whether he had adopted a predetermined policy against the death penalty. Johnson responded that he intended to seek life imprisonment without possibility of parole in Vernon's case, but declined to comment on his general policy regarding the death penalty. The Governor accepted this response "with grave reservations," and indicated that he would monitor future cases in Bronx County.

A few months later, in March 1996, Police Officer Kevin Gillespie was fatally shot in the Bronx as he interrupted a crime in progress. Three suspects (Angel Diaz, Jesus Mendez and Ricardo Morales) were arrested in connection with the shooting. Governor Pataki wrote to Johnson, demanding "assurance that you do not have a policy against seeking the death penalty," and asking whether there were any "circumstances under which you will seek the death penalty in Bronx County." Criticizing the Governor's "heavy handed approach," which he called "tantamount to the disenfranchisement of the voters of the Bronx," Johnson told the Governor that he would leave "the door ajar, however slight, to exercise this option in the Bronx." Dissatisfied with that response, the Governor issued an Executive Order directing Attorney General Dennis C. Vacco to take over the prosecution of the Gillespie case. Vacco sought the death penalty against Diaz, but the case was aborted when Diaz committed suicide in his jail cell.

D.A. Johnson sued the Governor, challenging Pataki's takeover action in the Diaz case as an improper interference with the independence of district attorneys. The Court of Appeals ruled that governors had broad authority to "supersede" a district attorney and to direct the state Attorney General to prosecute a criminal case.[30] Despite the Governor's legal victory, it remains to be seen whether his threat to take over the prosecution of selected murder cases will be enough to prod New York City district attorneys into seeking the death penalty.

As of early 1998, only two of the five New York City prosecutors had sought the death penalty: Brooklyn District Attorney Charles J. Hynes (five cases), and Queens District Attorney Richard A.

---

[28] See Adam Nossiter, *In New York City, A Mixed Response to Law from Prosecutors*, N.Y. Times, Mar. 8, 1995, at B5.

[29] Quoted in Johnson v. Pataki, 229 A.D.2d 242, 655 N.Y.S.2d 463 (1st Dept. 1997). The ensuing discussion of the conflict between Governor Pataki and Bronx D.A. Johnson, including the quoted remarks of both parties, was drawn from the opinion of the intermediate appeals court in Johnson v. Pataki, ibid.

[30] Johnson v. Pataki, Nos. 227, 228, 1997 WL 749497 (N.Y. Dec. 4, 1997).

Brown (two cases).[31] Early figures also showed that, except for Brooklyn D.A. Hynes, upstate prosecutors were more aggressive in seeking the death penalty than prosecutors in the City and its surrounding suburbs.[32]

LEGAL CHALLENGES TO THE DEATH PENALTY LAW

A legal scheme as complex and controversial as the death penalty is bound to invite court challenges. These may arise from uncertainties in the meaning of the law, or from claims that the law violates the U.S. Constitution or the Constitution of New York State. It should be understood that even though New York law appears to meet or exceed federal constitutional standards, New York courts may impose higher standards based on the state constitution, or may compel revisions in the law because of the way they interpret it.[33] Three different legal challenges are described below. They are based on geographic disparities, racial discrimination, and the denial of the state constitutional right to a jury trial.

A potential basis for a challenge to the New York death penalty law could arise out of geographic disparities in the application of the penalty, such as the downstate/upstate differences in capital prosecutions alluded to earlier. "Arbitrary" infliction of the death penalty would violate the Eighth Amendment to the U.S. Constitution and probably the equivalent provision in the state

---

[31] See Davis Rohde, *Death Penalty To Be Sought For 5th Time In Brooklyn*, N.Y. Times, Feb. 20, 1998: B7.

[32] Of the first sixteen cases statewide in which the death penalty was sought, nine originated in the 55 upstate counties of New York State, while seven came from New York City, Suffolk, Nassau and Westchester. The nine upstate cases were drawn from a pool of 39 suspects indicted on first-degree murder charges, for a selection rate of 23 percent. The downstate counties, which provided seven death cases from a pool of 61 first-degree murder indictees, had an 11.5 percent selection rate. Tracey Tully, *Death Penalty Bias Upstate*, Times Union (Albany, NY), July 27, 1997, at A1 (statistics from state Capital Defender's Office and state Division of Criminal Justice Services). As of February, 1998, Brooklyn D.A. Hynes had sought the death penalty in 5 of his 21 first-degree murder more cases--more than any other prosecutor in the state. In one of these cases, People v. Harris, the jury imposed a death sentence on June 6, 1998. The Bronx and Manhattan had, respectively, 28 and 16 first-degree murder cases, and the death penalty was not sought in any of them. See Davis Rohde, *Death Penalty To Be Sought For 5th Time In Brooklyn*, N.Y. Times, Feb. 20, 1998: B7.

[33] For some possible state constitutional challenges to New York's capital punishment law see Mary R. Falk and Eve Cary, "Death-Defying Feats: State Constitutional Challenges to New York's Death Penalty," 4 Journal of Law and Policy 161 (1995).

constitution.[34] The legal meaning of "arbitrary" is not entirely clear, but opponents of capital punishment could contend that similar cases should not be treated differently depending on whether the crime occurs upstate, where prosecutors more aggressively seek the death penalty, or in the City, where the ultimate penalty is less often pursued. On the other hand, defenders of the State's death penalty law could point out that a prosecutor who is determining the appropriate charges in a case is permitted to take into account the attitudes of the citizens of his county from which juries are drawn. In other words, New York City prosecutors do not have to seek the death penalty if they conclude that City jurors will not vote for it in a given case--even if upstate jurors and upstate prosecutors would take a contrary position.

Racial disparities are another potential source of challenge. Although the U.S. Supreme Court will not permit purposeful race discrimination in sentencing, such bias is very difficult to prove, and an elaborate statistical study demonstrating different treatment of cases involving black murder victims was held insufficient proof of unconstitutional race discrimination.[35] By interpreting the New York State Constitution, however, New York courts could develop a lower standard of proof, and could accept the kind of statistical evidence rejected by the Supreme Court. The state courts of other states have so far declined to take this course, and whether New York's courts will do so is an open question.

One state constitutional challenge to New York's death penalty law was mounted even before the first death sentence was imposed.[36] This claim was based on a provision of the New York State Constitution that has no equivalent in the U.S. Constitution. In Article I, Section 2 of the state constitution it says: "A jury trial may be waived by the defendant in all criminal cases, except those in which the crime charged may be punishable by death. . . . " As we have already pointed out, New York's death penalty law permits guilty pleas to Murder in the First Degree, but prohibits a death

---

[34] See Furman v. Georgia, 408 U.S. 238 (1972). New York courts could interpret Article I, Section 5 of the New York Constitution as providing broader rights than the Eighth Amendment of the U.S. Constitution, or they could interpret the state provision as a source of the same rights, or even of narrower rights. The two provisions use virtually identical language. U.S. Const. Amdt. 8 says in part: "nor cruel and unusual punishments inflicted." N.Y. Const. Art. I, § 5 says in part: "nor shall cruel and unusual punishments be inflicted."

[35] See McCleskey v. Kemp, 481 U.S. 279 (1987), where a study by Professor David C. Baldus found that in Georgia in the 1970's, killers of whites were more often sentenced to death than killers of blacks, especially if the killer of the white victim was black. The Court held that even if the study was valid, it did not show that McCleskey's case (McCleskey was black; his victim was a white police officer) was fraught with unconstitutional race discrimination.

[36] See In re Hynes, 1997 WL 786348 (N.Y. A.D. Dec. 22, 1997), where an intermediate appeals court upheld on federal and state constitutional grounds the plea bargaining portions of the state's capital punishment law.

sentence if such a plea is accepted. The argument is that this law violates Article I, Section 2 because it authorizes waiver of a trial by jury for a crime which "may be punishable by death." If the words of the state constitution are taken literally the argument seems compelling. However, the courts may interpret those words to mean only that one cannot plead guilty and be sentenced to death.[37] Under this interpretation, the death penalty law would be upheld. This is an issue that will have to be decided by the State's highest court.

A CONTINUING CONTROVERSY

Although the murder rate in New York City and State began declining sharply in the mid-1990s, there will, unfortunately, be plenty of opportunities to invoke and to test the State's death penalty law. The first major legal test may well come from Brooklyn, when the New York Court of Appeals reviews the first death sentence under the new law, imposed on triple murderer Darrel K. Harris.[38] It is a safe bet that there will be enough homicides with the elements of "aggravated" first degree murder to put reluctant City prosecutors on the spot. In addition, there will certainly be enough capital prosecutions statewide to provide the basis for court challenges to the death penalty statute. Public debate over the death penalty issue is likely to remain vigorous, given the broad popular support for, and the fervent opposition to, capital punishment. Each highly publicized murder and each significant court decision is bound to renew the dispute. Each step closer to an actual execution--and eventually there will almost certainly be an execution in New York--will add fuel to the fire. Given these circumstances, capital punishment is destined remain a "divisive" issue in the Empire State for many years.

---

[37] If the purpose of the state constitutional provision is to protect a defendant against feeling pressured to waive his right to a jury trial then the argument against the death penalty law has some cogency. Since, under New York law, a defendant faces a possible death sentence if he goes to trial, but not if he pleads guilty, he may feel pressured to surrender his jury trial rights in order to save his life. The U.S. Supreme Court accepted a comparable argument in United States v. Jackson, 390 U.S. 570 (1968), although it subsequently repudiated its position in Brady v. United States, 397 US 742 (1970).

If, however, the purpose of the New York constitutional provision is to insure that a jury will play a role in capital cases--that a jury verdict, as opposed to a bench trial or a guilty plea, will always precede a death sentence--then the argument against the death penalty law collapses. The law protects the right to a jury trial by prohibiting the imposition of a death sentence except after a jury verdict.

[38] See Robert D. McFadden, *Test of Death Penalty Law Quickly Follows Decision,* N.Y. Times, June 8, 1998, at B4.

Chapter 21

Settling Criminal Cases in Community Dispute Resolution Programs in New York City

by

Professor Maria Volpe

Department of Sociology

Imagine the following scenario: Glen and Pierre are neighbors who have been involved in a long-standing disagreement over Glen's late night gatherings in his apartment. Glen, who lives directly above Pierre, has his friends come over to visit almost every night at about 9:00 p.m. and they stay until midnight. Each night Pierre bangs on the pipes and ceiling to let Glen know how perturbed he is with his noise. Whenever they meet face to face in the elevator, Pierre mutters that he cannot sleep at night and Glen just ignores him. On two occasions, Pierre called the police to the apartment house. They went up and told Glen to quiet down, and then left. One night, Pierre went up to Glen's apartment and pounded on the door. When Glen answered, they exchanged some words. Pierre told him that he was going to call the police if Glen's friends did not leave immediately. Glen told Pierre to do whatever he had to do. Pierre started yelling at him. Words led to a shoving match. Phillip, Glen's next door neighbor, heard the commotion in the hallway and called the police. When the police arrived, Glen and Pierre accused each other of throwing the first punch and wanted the police to arrest the other for assault, and disorderly conduct. Pierre even accused Glen of criminal trespass. After listening to their accusations against each other, the police told Glen and Pierre to go to the local mediation center to work out their differences. Simultaneously, they asked "Mediation? What's that?"

MORE THAN ONE WAY TO PROCESS CRIMINAL MATTERS

Traditionally, criminal matters like the one described above are officially disposed of in criminal courts using rules of evidence and procedure. Judges, prosecutors, and defense attorneys, with the assistance of many support staff including stenographers, bailiffs, police and court officers, gather in publicly accessible criminal courtrooms to process docketed cases. The adjudicatory approach used by these legal actors is one which pits prosecutors [on behalf of the "people" and the victims] against defendants. The focus of these proceedings is the determination of culpability based on past events and the application of the law to the facts presented. Whether or not a defendant goes to trial, the outcome will be innocence or guilt as determined by a judge or jury. Simply put, in the traditional legal setting, one either wins or loses. Moreover, this view of how criminal cases are processed is the best known and the most commonly used approach. Despite its pervasiveness, this approach is neither the only one nor necessarily the most appropriate way to resolve criminal cases.

Since the early seventies, countless innovative efforts drawing on mediation and related informal dispute resolution processes have flourished and now complement the formal processing of criminal matters throughout the country [McGillis, 1997]. Of all of the emerging developments, those using citizens who are trained in mediation and related techniques have gained the widest popularity and have been institutionalized in many jurisdictions. Central to these efforts has been the use of techniques which help individuals settle their disputes themselves at community based dispute resolution centers.

This emerging landscape, however, is quite complex. The new and ever-changing developments make it near impossible to keep track of all of the efforts blossoming around the country. There are countless program models and approaches defining how less adversarial processes can be used in the courts [McGillis, 1997]. Community-based dispute resolution programs vary in sponsorship, size, and organizational goals. For the most part, however, they handle cases where individuals have some type of relationship [landlord/tenant, relatives, acquaintances, neighbors, friends, business] and the incident is considered to be relatively minor [even though what appears to be trivial is important to the disputants involved].

All of the community-based dispute resolution programs are complemented by a wide range of other activities that further the use of less combative processes to manage criminal matters. For instance, legislatures from coast to coast have passed legislation amending criminal procedure laws, particularly for misdemeanor cases [e.g., see Rogers and McEwen, 1994], encouraging programs to bring victims and offenders together. Criminal justice professionals including prosecuting and defense attorneys, judges and police, probation, parole and correction officers, are becoming acquainted with the uses of mediation in handling criminal matters. These and other developments are contributing to a major paradigm shift in how criminal matters are perceived, processed, and disposed of. Collectively, they are beginning to have profound implications for the criminal justice system.

This chapter will focus on less combative processes, like mediation and conciliation, that are used in the processing of criminal cases in community based dispute resolution centers, including those in New York City. Each of the five boroughs houses at least one community-based dispute resolution program that processes criminal matters which could otherwise be disposed of by the courts.

Why new approaches to process criminal matters?

Historically, criminal courts have been the object of recurrent criticism. While designed to provide accused individuals with the presumption of innocence until proven guilty, the legal process can get bogged down with tactical maneuvers that impose significant costs on defendants, their support systems, the community, and the justice system. Additionally, the courts have provided very limited opportunities for victims to actively participate in the official processing of their cases. Depending on the situation, the adversarial methods used can polarize parties and even provoke further escalation. It is not surprising, then, that there has been an increasing interest in finding better, less time consuming, and less costly ways of processing matters which routinely burden overcrowded criminal courts.

In criminal matters, complainants and defendants may share a past history that includes a prior relationship, some mutual responsibility for the situation, as well as recurring scenes involving police intervention. Such cases often present criminal justice system practitioners with major challenges about how to proceed legally and what to do with the two parties. Traditional court procedures do little to help the parties to understand or deal with the underlying issues that give rise to criminal charges, or to minimize the possibility that the individuals will not experience a similar encounter in the future.

Many criminal cases are about relationships, miscommunication, misunderstandings, and lack of resourcefulness in working out differences with others. Processing such cases in the court system may only exacerbate the differences between the parties. For example, although an assault is viewed as a violation of the penal code, many assaults are the means by which individuals settle differences because they are limited in managing them in any other way. In short, for some hitting is often considered an acceptable way of responding to a conflict. In more extreme instances, a homicide can easily result from poorly managed interactions that escalate to a point where one kills the other party, sometimes over a matter that, in retrospect, can be deemed relatively insignificant by everyone, such as a dirty look, an unconfirmed rumor, or a dispute over a parking space.

All of these concerns have given rise to the questions, "Isn't there a better way than arrest, prosecution and punishment to settle differences?"

MEDIATION AND THE PROCESSING OF CRIMINAL MATTERS

When criminal cases are processed in alternative dispute resolution forums, mediation is usually the process used. Mediation is a process that uses a third party, known as a mediator, to assist disputing parties to have a conversation about their differences or perceptions. The mediator uses techniques to help collect relevant information, frame the issues, consider options, and if possible reach a mutually agreed upon understanding of where they will go from there. More often than not, nonlegal concerns are significant. Unlike the adjudicatory process, mediation does not attempt to assign blame or find guilt. Mediation empowers the parties and enables them to be creative about settling the situation that they have experienced and to consider how they would like to construct their future interactions [e.g., see Moore, 1996]

The outcomes of mediation sessions should reflect the interests and needs of all parties. Even if the parties agree to stay away from each other, the mediation session provides them with an opportunity to discuss the terms of the separation and how they will communicate with each other should it be necessary. For instance, if they live in the same apartment building and cannot avoid meeting [as when taking out the garbage], they may decide that when they must interact, they will do so only through an agreed upon intermediary.

Mediation, however, does not mean the same thing to everyone. While it is generally understood that central to the mediation process is self-determination by participants, that is, the settlement of the conflict rests with the parties involved, there is not a generally agreed upon definition of mediation including New York State. For instance, the Final Report of the Chief Judge's New York State Court Alternative Dispute Resolution Project [1996:7] notes that "Mediation ... is a term used in an extraordinary variety of ways. Some describe the role of the judge in encouraging compromise and settlement as 'mediation' of a dispute, which is very different from the more commonly accepted definition of mediation, involving exploration of the parties' underlying, and often nonlegal, interests." Additionally, a number of lively debates rage on among experts in the field about whether mediation should focus on the settlement of cases or on an evaluative, facilitative or transformative approach which can change the parties, their behavior and attitudes [see Bush and Folger, 1994; Riskin, 1996].

RESOLVING DISPUTES IN NEW YORK STATE

In 1981, New York State became a pioneer when its legislature passed Chapter 847 of the Laws of 1981 that created and funded the New York State Community Dispute Resolution Centers Program. Section 170.55 of the criminal procedure law was amended as follows, "The court may grant an adjournment in contemplation of dismissal on condition that the defendant participate in dispute resolution and comply with any award or settlement resulting therefrom."

Initial funding was appropriated for community-based programs to provide dispute resolution services in 15 counties across the state. After three years, in 1984, the pilot legislation was made permanent. At present, these programs are available in all 62 counties in New York State.

Since the inception of the NYS Community Dispute Resolution Centers Program, the community-based dispute resolution centers have been involved in the conciliation, mediation and arbitration of a wide variety of selected misdemeanor offenses including aggravated assault, aggravated harassment, assault, criminal mischief, forgery, fraud-bad check cases, harassment, menacing, noise, petit larceny, reckless endangerment, theft of services, and vandalism.

In 1986, the New York State Legislature passed Chapter 837 of the Laws of 1986 which allows selected felonies to be adjourned in contemplation of dismissal and referred to dispute resolution centers for mediation. These cases can be adjourned in a local criminal court upon arraignment or after indictment or superior court information. They must be referred to dispute resolution centers before final disposition in the courts, after an agreement is reached between the court, prosecution and defendant, and upon reasonable notice for the victim to be heard. If a case is adjourned in contemplation of dismissal, the court must release the defendant on his/her own recognizance and refer the action to a dispute resolution center. Within 45 days of this action, the dispute resolution center must inform the prosecutor whether the charges have been resolved.

If the outcome is a fine, restitution or reparation, the dispute resolution center must report on its status every 30 days to the prosecution. In those instances where the defendant has agreed to pay a fine, restitution or reparation, but has not lived up to the terms of the agreement, the prosecution may within one year have the charges restored on the court calendar. Currently, the law does not allow defendants charged as repeat felony offenders or those charged with a Class A felony, or a violent felon drug offense to be referred to dispute resolution centers.

The legislation allows for the charges to be dismissed if the defendant has lived up to the agreement for six months, or where the defendant has not paid a fine, restitution or reparation, s/he has agreed to do so within one year of the adjournment. When all charges are dismissed, all papers and records pertaining to the case will be sealed and the wrongdoer will be restored to his/her status prior to arrest and prosecution.

Since processes like mediation rely on the full and candid participation of the parties, the New York State statute provides for confidentiality to be maintained at the community dispute resolution programs. Judiciary Law, Section 849-b[6] states "All memoranda, work products, or case files of a mediator are confidential and not subject to disclosure in any judicial or administrative proceeding." Two major exceptions to this provision concern domestic violence and child abuse. The New York State Community Dispute Resolution Centers Program has developed specific guidelines to address the use of mediation in cases involving child abuse and domestic violence. Generally speaking, violence is non-negotiable. For both child abuse and domestic violence, appropriate action, including reporting incidents to the proper authorities or courts, may be warranted. In the case of domestic violence, mediation may continue if the parties voluntarily agree.

Cases brought to the community dispute resolution centers are mediated by volunteer citizens from the community who are trained in mediation and conflict resolution skills for at least 25 hours by trainers certified by the Unified Court System. Each trainee must then observe cases as well as serve an apprenticeship and undergo an assessment before being certified to mediate. Additionally, each year mediators must complete six hours of continuing education and participate in three mediations per year [CDRC Program, 1996-1997:10].

The community dispute resolution centers receive their cases from a variety of sources including courts, district attorneys, legal aid, police, public and private agencies, schools, or by walk-ins. According to the Community Dispute Resolution Centers Annual Report from April 1, 1996 to March 31, 1997, the centers conducted 23,273 conciliations, mediations, and arbitrations involving 51,659 individuals, with parties reaching agreements in 77% of those cases which were mediated. Also, in fiscal year 1996-97, 30% of the cases involved criminal matters; 81 felony cases were processed; and the average cost per conciliation, mediation and arbitration was $138 [CDRC Program, 1996-1997:1,2].

MEDIATION IN NEW YORK CITY

The processing of criminal matters by community-based dispute resolution centers has a long history in New York City, with some New York City centers in the forefront of pioneer efforts in the United States. For instance, in 1969, The Institute for Mediation and Conflict Resolution [IMCR] was established in Harlem with funding from the Ford Foundation by individuals who were interested in expanding the use of conflict resolution skills routinely used in labor relations to the management of interpersonal conflicts [IMCR, n.d.]. In addition to its work in the Harlem community, in July 1977 IMCR joined with the Victim/Witness Assistance Project of the Vera Institute of Justice to establish the Brooklyn Dispute Center to mediate felony cases [Davis, 1982:157]. This project was a result of studies...

> ...*that showed that 40 percent of the cases that became felonies involved long standing, interpersonal, prior relationships between the victim and the defendant. We interviewed the victims involved in the felony cases and found out that a very high proportion said that they were coming to court to resolve the problem, not to have the defendant incarcerated and punished. They wanted the defendant to stop doing whatever it was that brought the case to court. This suggested that mediation was a potential solution for many felony cases* [Friedman, 1983:49].

The Brooklyn Dispute Center became the site of the first experimental study of a mediation program which randomly assigned cases to either mediation or criminal court. [Davis, 1982:157].

With few exceptions, the other community-based dispute resolution centers in New

York City grew out of the funding incentive provided by the 1981 legislation referred to above. Since the outset of the statewide initiative, the Unified Court System of the State of New York has awarded partial funding to not-for-profit organizations in each borough to provide conciliation, mediation, arbitration, or related dispute resolution services at community-based dispute resolution centers. In recent years, the mediation centers in Manhattan, Brooklyn, and Queens have established additional local sites in order to provide more accessible services at more convenient locations.[1]

For the most part, the New York City community dispute resolution centers mirror all of the characteristics described in the previous section on dispute resolution in New York State. A significant difference is that in recent years complaints against other individuals in New York City have been screened by Court Dispute Referral Centers in each borough. CDRCs provide information and referral services to individuals who want to file complaints. According to the most recent Community Dispute Resolution Centers Program Annual Report, "most complaints are referred to the CDRCs by the New York City Police Department when an arrest cannot be made and the dispute is ongoing." [CDRC Program, 1996-1997:4] Of the 25,000 individuals the CDRCs screened in 1996-1997, 8,000 were referred to the community dispute resolution centers for mediation [ibid.].

Like the community dispute resolution centers throughout the country, those in New York City handle a wide range of civil and criminal disputes. The latest workload data [April 1, 1995 - March 31, 1996] available from the Community Dispute Resolution Centers Program of the New York State Unified Court System indicate that the majority of cases processed were of a criminal nature. Of the 1,889 cases, 9,749 were misdemeanors or violations and 10 were felonies.[2] Collectively, the criminal cases constituted 82 percent of the total cases in New York City.

Like the dispute resolution centers across the country, those based in New York City have been providing a wide range of services, including the introduction of innovative ways of handling criminal cases. For instance, in a recent issue of The New York Mediator, new criminal justice initiatives at two New York City dispute resolution centers were described. More specifically, in the Bronx, IMCR has been collaborating with police precincts and "police officers now carry a memo insert that provides them with information regarding alternative dispute resolution. This has increased the number of walk-ins." [1998:3] On Staten Island, the Community Dispute Resolution Program has "developed a juvenile shoplifting mediation/education program to provide an alternative to criminal prosecution and to reduce recidivism among youth arrested for petit larceny"[1998:12].

Is the Alternative Effective?

Program administrators, policy makers and researchers are increasingly faced with the need to identify meaningful and accurate measures of the effectiveness of processes like mediation within the criminal justice system. Data are sorely needed for a wide range of purposes, including a better understanding of what works best, and under what conditions, as well as how the competing goals of the criminal justice system and informal resolution can be reconciled.

Since community-based dispute resolution programs are still relatively new, evaluation research, though growing and conducted much more widely, is still in its infancy. Much of the knowledge about the effectiveness of these programs is drawn from the anecdotal data accumulated by the program personnel. At the hundreds of community-based dispute resolution programs, caseloads are low, which diminishes some of the cost effectiveness sought by these programs. Studies do show, however, that parties who attend mediation sessions are satisfied with the process, and that when they do show up, they are likely to reach an agreement.

USING CONFLICT RESOLUTION SKILLS IN OTHER PARTS OF THE CRIMINAL JUSTICE SYSTEM

Innovative uses of mediation and conciliation in the criminal justice system are increasingly encountered. Innumerable employees of criminal justice agencies have been trained and countless new programs have been introduced throughout the criminal justice system. Without all of the complementing initiatives, it is highly questionable whether the community-based dispute resolution programs could survive.

Most of these programs rely on the courts and police for a significant number of cases.

The most notable use of mediation is in what has become known as "restorative justice" programs, also referred to as victim-offender mediation programs and victim-offender reconciliation programs. These programs emphasize the need to see crime as more than a violation against the "government," which then prosecutes offenders, but as something done to victims and the larger community. The premise is that everyone gets hurt by crime. Hence, offenders are accountable to everyone who has been wronged and must take responsibility for their actions.

A key component of restorative justice is the involvement of victims, and often the larger community, in the process. As is true of other mediation programs, the overwhelming majority of victims and offenders who participate in restorative justice processes find them to be fair [Umbreit, et.al, 1994]. Additionally, victims' fear of revictimization by the offender is reduced and offenders express having an understanding of the impact of their crimes as a result of the mediation process.

CHALLENGES

Mediation and related dispute resolution processes for criminal matters have been viewed as a double edged sword. While they have been applauded for repairing relationships, empowering individuals, and enhancing the delivery of justice, they have also been challenged for a number of reasons. One of the strongest arguments against the use of mediation is that it undermines the due process safeguards of persons accused of crimes. Since mediation is an informal process that occurs behind closed doors, often with non-lawyers serving as mediators, defendants may not receive the kind of rights they are entitled to in the conventional justice system. As a result, mediation has been referred to as a second class form of justice.

Additionally, because mediation brings the parties together to work out their own terms for the future, there are to those who have been unhappy with what is perceived as an approach that is not only nonpunitive but "soft" as well. This clashes with the public's expectation that the criminal justice system should punish wrongdoers.

Since community based programs currently are underutilized and handle relatively small caseloads, there are questions about whether, to date, they are less costly than formal adjudication in court.

Finally, dispute resolution processes are largely unregulated since universally accepted standards of practice have not as yet been established for practitioners. Each jurisdiction has defined who can mediate and under what conditions. In many instances, anyone can mediate. This has raised many concerns about the qualifications of those who mediate and quality of services delivered.

The use of processes like mediation and community-based dispute resolution programs, including victim offender mediation programs, to process criminal cases challenges the very nature of the criminal justice system. Rather than relying on an adversarial system where individuals are pitted against each other in the quest of proving guilt beyond a reasonable doubt, these new approaches focus on problem solving and bringing victims, offenders and the community together in private, informal settings. Central to these processes is self determination where the victims, offenders and members of the community participate in the construction of their own future, whether together or apart.

The personalized approach common to mediation and related informal resolution processes makes it difficult to evaluate their effectiveness. Unlike official court processes that are relatively accessible, mediation and related processes occur behind closed doors. Undoubtedly, the techniques used and the outcomes reached may be markedly different. For instance, parties may agree to be respectful and ensure each other's safety in one case, and not call each other names in another. In addition, some may find that the mere opportunity to meet and negotiate with each other is sufficient to settle their differences. Comparing these kinds of practices and outcomes with those occurring in criminal courts continues to pose major challenges for researchers.

Nonetheless, there is growing evidence that processes like mediation and the many community-based dispute resolution programs, including victim-offender reconciliation programs, are a valuable complement to traditional adversarial methods of processing cases. Throughout the country, there is widespread evidence that they are being institutionalized and relied on by the criminal justice system. Over the course of the last twenty years, thousands of criminal cases have been processed by the dispute resolution centers in New York City. With their emphasis on including victims, offenders, and communities in settling problems, neighborhood-based dispute resolution centers provide a fresh, new paradigm for processing legal matters by actively involving those directly affected by the conflicts.

References

Bush, Robert A. Baruch and Folger, Joseph A. [1994] <u>The Promise of Mediation: Responding to Conflict Through Empowerment and Recognition</u> San Francisco: Jossey-Bass Publishers.

Community Dispute Resolution Centers Program [CDRC Program], Unified Court System of the State of New York, <u>Annual Report</u> April 1, 1996 to March 31, 1997.

Community Dispute Resolution Centers Program of the New York State Unified Court System, Aggregate Workload Data for the First, Second, Eleventh and Twelfth Judicial Districts for the Time Period April 1, 1995 through March 31, 1996 [unpublished data provided by CDRC].

Community Dispute Resolution Centers Program [CDRC Program], Unified Court System of the State of New York, <u>Two Year Report</u>, April 1, 1990 to March 31, 1991; April 1, 1991 to March 31, 1992: 30-31,41-2.

Davis, Robert C. [1982] "Mediation: The Brooklyn Experiment," in M. Feeley and R. Tomasic [eds], <u>Neighborhood Justice: Assessment of an Emerging Idea</u>, New York: Longman :154-170.

Friedman, Lucy [1983] "Setting Up Dispute Resolution Programs" in M. Volpe, T. Christian and J. Kowalewski[1982] [eds], <u>Mediation in the Criminal Justice System Conference Proceedings,</u> May 20-21, John Jay College of Criminal Justice, American Bar Association Special Committee on Dispute Resolution, Dispute Resolution Papers Series No. 2 - December 1983:40-54.

<u>Final Report of the Chief Judge's New York State Court Alternative Dispute Resolution Project,</u> [1996] "Court Referred ADR in New York State", May 1.

IMCR flyer, nd. "The Institute for Mediation and Conflict Resolution" [currently based in Bronx, New York]

McGillis, Daniel [1997] <u>Community Mediation Programs: Developments and Challenges</u> Washington, DC: NIJ.

Moore, Christopher W. [1996] <u>The Mediation Process: Practical Strategies for Resolving Conflict</u> San Francisco: Jossey-Bass Publishers.

<u>New York Mediator,</u> [1998]. "News From The Programs" volume 17, number 1, Winter/Spring: 4-15.

Riskin, Leonard L. [1996] "Understanding Mediators' Orientations, Strategies, and Techniques: A Grid for the Perplexed" 1 <u>Harvard Negotiation Law Review</u> : 7-24.

Rogers, Nancy H. and McEwen, Craig A.[1994] <u>Mediation: Law, Policy, Practice,</u> Deerfield, IL: Clark Boardman Callaghan

Umbreit, Mark with Robert B. Coates and Boris Kalanj, [1984] <u>Victim Meets Offender: The Impact of Restorative Justice and Mediation,</u> Monsey, New York: Criminal Justice Press.

Endnotes

1. The dispute resolution centers in New York City which receive partial funding from the Community Dispute Resolution Centers Program of the Unified Court System of the State of New York are as follows [CDRC Program 1996-1997, Appendix C]:

Bronx County:
Institute for Mediation and Conflict Resolution [IMCR]
349 East 149th Street, Suite 405
Bronx, New York 10451

Kings County:
Victim Services [VS]
Brooklyn Mediation Center [Main Office]
210 Joralemon Street, Room 618
Brooklyn, New York 11201

Brooklyn Community Offices:
Red Hook Mediation Program
East New York Mediation Program
Crown Heights Mediation Program
Flatbush Mediation Program

New York County:
Victim Services [VS]
Manhattan Mediation Center
346 Broadway, Suite 400W
New York, New York 10013

Harlem Mediation Center [VS]
1854 Amsterdam Avenue
New York, New York 10031

Midtown Community Court [VS]
Dispute Resolution Program
314 West 54th Street
New York, New York 10019

Northern Manhattan:
Washington Heights - Inwood Coalition
652 West 187th Street
New York, New York 10033

Queens County:
Community Mediation Services
Queens Mediation Network
89-64 163rd Street
Jamaica, New York 11432

Flushing:
Beacon Center at JHS 189
144-80 Barclay Avenue
          Flushing, New York 11355

Bayside:
Beacon Center at M.S. 158
46-35 Oceania Street

Bayside, New York 11361

Astoria:
Beacon Center at JHS 204
36-41 28th Street
Astoria, New York 11106

Richmond County:
Staten Island Community Resolution Center
42 Richmond Terrace
Staten Island, New York 10301

2.
Types of Disputes Processed by Community Dispute Resolution Programs in New York City

Type of Dispute	New York County # of cases %	Kings and Richmond Counties # of cases %	Bronx # of cases %	Queens # of cases %	Totals # of cases %
Misdemeanor /Violation	1,873 83.9	3,571 74.9	2,470 92.1	1,835 83.1	9,749 82.0
Felony	2 0.1	4 0.1	0 0.0	4 .2	10 0
Civil	322 14.4	594 12.5	81 3.0	357 16.2	1,354 11.4
Juvenile	24 1.1	538 11.3	127 4.7	10 .5	699 5.9
Civil - Mobile Homes	0 0.0	0 0.0	0 0.0	1 0.0	0 0
Undesignated	12 0.5	61 1.2	3 .1	0 0.0	76 .6
Total	2,233 100	4,768 100	2,681 100	2,207 100	11,889 100

Source of data: Community Dispute Resolution Centers Program of the New York State Unified Court System, Aggregate Workload Data for the First, Second, Eleventh and Twelfth Judicial Districts for the Time Period April 1, 1995 through March 31, 1996.

Chapter 22

TRENDS IN CRIMINAL JUSTICE SPENDING, EMPLOYMENT, AND WORKLOADS IN NEW YORK CITY SINCE THE LATE 1970's

By

Professor Michael Jacobson

Department of Law and Police Science

This chapter examines changes in the in City's criminal justice budget, the headcounts for these agencies, and the workloads they tackled from the late 1970's up through the late 1990's. Changes in criminal justice funding and employment will be compared to other large non-criminal justice functions of City government in order to see how elected officials and policy makers have allocated resources over this period of almost two decades. Variations in the workload handled by criminal justice agencies will also be examined with an eye toward whether they help to explain the allocation of resources. Finally, the social costs and benefits of the investments in criminal justice will be discussed, both in terms of resources which may have been diverted from other non-criminal justice functions of municipal government (such as education and social services) and the City's successes in reducing crime rates. The central thesis of this chapter is that there is no direct relationship between the amount of money spent on the operations of criminal justice agencies and the level of public safety. Increasing spending doesn't necessarily buy greater safety. In fact, as the data will show, the smallest increases in spending on and employment in criminal justice took place during the four year period from 1993 to 1997 (Mayor Giuliani's first administration), and yet crime rates dropped faster than at any other time during the past twenty years.

CHANGES IN BUDGET ALLOCATIONS

One of the best ways to gauge the priority given to certain areas of government over other publicly funded activities is to examine the financial resources which elected officials and policy makers earmark for these functions. A look at the total amount of spending and, in some ways more importantly, a monitoring of the rate of annual increases or decreases in spending gives a clear indication of governmental priorities in any particular year, as well as over time. This section will examine the trends in total spending for all the components of the criminal justice system in comparison to some other major responsibilities of the City government (education, social services) and to the entire City budget.

The increases in funding for criminal justice operations, as compared to the increases for some of the other major components of the City's budget, as well as the growth of the entire City budget from 1979 to 1997, appears in Table 22:1.

Table 22: 1
SPENDING ON CRIMINAL JUSTICE AND OTHER AREAS
New York City Budgets, 1979 - 1997
(In Millions of Dollars)

FUNCTION	YEAR				PERCENT CHANGE			
	1979	1989	1993	1997	79-89	89-93	93-97	79-97
Police (1)	$816	$1,851	$2,143	$2,457	+127%	8%	15%	201%
Corrections	118	614	760	804	421	24	6	582
Probation	19	45	60	69	135	32	16	262
Prosecution (2)	39	141	186	207	258	32	12	428
Indigent Defense (3)	26	96	130	116	275	36	-10	356
Total CRJ Costs (4)	1,018	2,747	3,278	3,666	170	19	12	258
Social Services (5)	2,850	5,114	7,168	7,533	79	40	5	164
Education (6)	2,260	5,779	7,237	8,093	156	25	12	258
Total NYC Budget	$12,949	24,664	30,365	33,981	90%	23	10	162

Notes:: All budget items are rounded off to the nearest million dollars.
   Percent changes are rounded off to the nearest integer.
   All figures are operating costs only, and exclude pension and fringe benefits costs.
   All figures are actual expenditures, not initial, planned budget allocations.
(1) Includes NYC Transit and Housing Police Departments, before their NYPD merger in 1995.
(2) Includes the Special Narcotics Prosecutor as well as the five District Attorney's offices.
(3) Includes costs of 18-B attorneys as well as the Legal Aid Society.
(4) Does not include the costs of the Department of Juvenile Justice, which was part of the
   Human Resources Administration in 1979, and didn't have a separate budget.
(5) Besides DSS, includes the Department of Homeless Services and the Administration For
   Children's Services, which became separate agencies in fiscal 1995/96.
Sources:: Data provided by the New York City Office of Management And Budget.

Simply examining the growth of criminal justice expenditures, as compared to outlays for social services, education and total spending from 1979 to 1997 reveals a few notable trends (see the last column in Table 22:1). First, the percent increase in spending from 1979 to 1997 is equal for education and criminal justice (both are up 258%). Second, they are both up far more than the increase in outlays for social services (up 164%) and total City spending (up 162%). Third, within criminal justice, spending on correction (up 582%) far exceeded any other increase in criminal or non-criminal justice spending. In fact, the spending increase for corrections was over two and a half times that for police (up 582% and 201% respectively), was more than twice education's increase (up 582% and 258% respectively) and was well over three times the rate of increase for social services (up 582% and 164% respectively). Only the money used to pay for prosecuting defendants and to otherwise run the District Attorneys' offices in the five boroughs shot up dramatically, but not as much as the Department of Correction budget (up 428% and 582% respectively). Interestingly, within criminal justice, the budget for police protection had the slowest rate of increase. In fact, the rate of growth of the police budget was less than that of probation (201% and 262% respectively); even spending to provide defense attorneys for indigent defendants (up 325%) far outpaced spending increases for the Police Department.

Every type of criminal justice expenditure, as did spending on education, significantly exceeded the overall increase in the City's budget. The increase in social services merely kept pace with the general increase in total City spending (up 164% and 162% respectively).

Another way to look at budget priorities is to compute the proportion of the entire City budget earmarked for various purposes. The percent of the total City budget spent on various governmental functions appears in Table 22:2. It shows that while education and criminal justice both took up increasing shares of the total City budget, proportionate spending on social services remained flat from 1979-1997. Education and criminal justice expenditures as a total portion of the City's budget both grew by about the same proportion (by more than one third) while social services' proportion of the budget remained absolutely constant. The proportion of the total City budget spent on correctional services more than doubled, from less than 1% to more than 2%, increasing at a rate about four and a half times greater than either education or social services.

Table 22:2 documents how a subtle shift of resources has taken place over the last two decades. Money has been diverted away from social services (as it grows at a slower rate than criminal justice and education, and lags far behind the growth in proportionate amount of total spending); and toward education and criminal justice (and specifically into correctional expenses within criminal justice). This change in proportionate spending, and the enormous increase in corrections spending in particular, merits a closer look. Since the increase in police spending over this period was much slower, and this at first seems counter-intuitive, it will be worthwhile to examine the budgets of the three mayoral administrations, and their differing political and budgetary priorities, from 1979 to 1997.

To further analyze spending patterns, refer back to Table 22:1 and the columns for the periods 1979 to 1989, 1989 to 1993, and 1993 to 1997. The reason these periods were chosen is because they coincide with the three terms of Mayor Edward Koch, the four year term of Mayor David Dinkins (1990-1993) and the first of Mayor Rudolph Giuliani's two terms (1994-1997). Because the Executive Branch in New York City has so much influence over the budget, the comparison between these three mayoral terms is revealing about some of their priorities.

Table 22:2:
PROPORTION OF THE TOTAL CITY BUDGET
DEVOTED TO CRIMINAL JUSTICE, SOCIAL SERVICES, AND EDUCATION
Fiscal Years 1979-1997

YEAR FUNCTION	1979	1997	PERCENT INCREASE in Proportionate Spending 1979-1997
Education (1)	18%	24%	+36%
Social Services (2)	22	22	0
Criminal Justice (3)	8	11	35
Corrections	0.9	2.4	167
All Other Budget Items	53%	44%	-17%

Notes: Percents are rounded off to the nearest integer,
     except for the Correction's budget.
     Spending on corrections is part of the criminal justice budget.
 (1) Costs of Board of Education
 (2) Besides DSS, includes Department of Homeless Services and the
     Administration For Children's Services.
 (3) Includes police, correction, probation, prosecution, and indigent defense costs.
Source: Data provided by the New York City Office of Management And Budget.

      Since Mayor Koch was re-elected twice from 1978 to 1989, the percent increases in the column headed "from 1979 to 1989" are a reflection of his resource allocation policies, and they stand in an interesting contrast to the next eight years when Mayor Dinkins and Mayor Giuliani were in office. Corrections spending under Ed Koch was dramatically greater than spending on any other criminal justice function or for education or social services (421% for correction, 127% for police, 156% for education and 79% for social services). The difference in the rate of spending on the City jails under Mayor Dinkins compared to Mayor Giuliani's first term may surprise some readers. Spending on corrections rose by about 24% under David Dinkins, compared to less than 6% under Rudolph Giuliani; thus Mayor Dinkins, who was widely considered to be more "progressive" or "liberal" than Mayor Giuliani, approved of an infusion of additional funds for incarceration that was roughly four times greater than his successor's budget increase (one of the reasons for that increased level of spending had to do with a greater workload, as will be explained below).

      The columns headed "Percent Change 90 to 93," and "94 to 97" reveal that the Police

Department's budget grew under Mayor Giuliani by almost 15%, compared to only around 8% under Mayor Dinkins. Ironically, however, it was David Dinkins who secured the funding for this increase when his administration enacted the Safe Streets/Safe City program. Perhaps counter-intuitive is the finding within Table 22:2 that under Mayor Dinkins, the funding for the five District Attorney's offices went up by nearly 32%, or close to three times the increase under Mayor Giuliani, which was less than 12%. Rudolph Giuliani, a former federal prosecutor, clearly took a much more frugal approach toward augmenting prosecutorial services than did David Dinkins. Probation expenses also grew at twice the rate under Mayor Dinkins than under Mayor Giuliani, 33% and 16% respectively.

However, one of the sharpest differences in priorities between the two mayors that fits their public images concerns spending for indigent defense services. Under David Dinkins, the money set aside to pay for lawyers for defendants too poor to hire private attorneys grew by nearly 36%, the highest rate of increase in spending for any component of the criminal justice system during his four years in office. During Mayor Giuliani's first administration, spending on defense services actually decreased by 10%. This reduction in defense services was primarily due to the severe budget cut which was imposed on the Legal Aid Society just after their staff attorneys went on strike to protest the raises that top management had bestowed upon its executive staff. In response to that brief work stoppage, Mayor Giuliani cut over $20 million from the Legal Aid Society's budget. Some of that money was used to fund alternative defense providers when Mayor Giuliani decided to create competition for the Legal Aid Society; he allocated taxpayer dollars to 11 private organizations to perform defense work which previously had been handled exclusively by the Legal Aid Society. However, total spending on defense services still decreased during Mayor Giuliani's first term. Overall, criminal justice spending increased by 19% under Mayor Dinkins compared to less than 12% under Mayor Giuliani, which is not a trend that many observers would have suspected.

Another obvious sign of the different priorities between the two mayors (aside from defense services and corrections) can be seen in social services and education spending. Spending on social services increased by 40% under David Dinkins but only by 5% under Rudolph Giuliani, a startling difference primarily due to the fact that between 1994 and 1997 staffing at these City agencies shrunk considerably. As for public schools, Mayor Dinkins increased spending on education by 25%, compared to just a 12% rise during Mayor Giuliani's first term.

Total spending for all City functions went up by 23% under David Dinkins but rose by less than half that rate, about 10%, under Rudolph Giuliani. The bottom line spending figures are a product of the more conservative fiscal policies adopted by Mayor Giuliani and of large revenue shortfalls (especially in 1994 and 1995) which forced him to curb spending growth. Under Mayor Dinkins, then, spending increases on education and social services far outpaced spending increases on criminal justice, even though criminal justice expenditures increased substantially. This was clearly the result of both his political priorities and his willingness to allow total City spending to grow. Mayor Giuliani's priorities were obviously totally different. He wanted to reign in the growth of governmental costs. Even though he increased spending on criminal justice less than Mayor Dinkins did, that additional allocation was twice as large as for social services (while under Mayor Dinkins, the social services increase was twice that for criminal justice); under Mayor Giuliani, education received only the same increase in budget as criminal justice (as opposed to twice the percentage increase under Mayor Dinkins).

CHANGES IN AGENCY EMPLOYEES

In addition to examining the budgets for governmental functions over time, it is also instructive to analyze headcounts, or the number of people working for a specific agency to carry out a governmental function. The reason for this is that many variables account for spending increases. While the main one is usually a growth in the number of personnel working in an agency, there are also added expenses due to salary hikes from collective bargaining agreements, rent increases, and service costs that are contracted out of government. Measuring headcounts gives a good approximation of the level of direct services provided by municipal government.

Table 22:3 tracks changes in employee headcounts for criminal justice, social services and education from 1979 to 1997.

The most obvious difference between this headcount table and the prior budget table is that the increases for all of the governmental functions are far less when examining changes in employees rather than changes in resources allocated to agencies. Again, this is because increased headcount is only one component of an expanding budget.

Interestingly, when headcount is examined during the period from 1979 to 1997 (see the last column of Table 22:3), criminal justice grew at almost three times the rate that education did (59% compared to 22%), as opposed to the identical 258% increase each function experienced in terms of budget expenditures. There are a few possible reasons for this seeming discrepancy. First, salaries for teachers (especially long time teachers) are high compared to other salaries, so the education budget can grow disproportionately with the addition of smaller numbers of staff. Second, non-staff costs for items such as textbooks, building maintenance and fuel are very high. Both these reasons would tend to inflate the education budget more than other budgets. However, in terms of the percentage increase in new staff added to criminal justice agencies and to the Board of Education between 1979 and 1997, the percentage increase in criminal justice far outweighs that for education. In fact, over 24,500 people were hired to work in criminal justice compared to 16,000 new staff for the school system. In this case, the headcount increases are more telling in terms of mayoral priorities than are budget figures.

Again, the Department of Correction experienced the largest increase in headcount, 219% (with the ranks of correction officers growing by 245%) of any other part of municipal government. In fact, the number of correction officers increased at nine times the rate of teachers. Prosecution was next with a 134% increase. The only function that did not grow during this period was social services, where the headcount stayed about the same from 1979 to 1997.

When the headcount figures from 1989 to 1997, the years of the Dinkins and Giuliani administrations, are examined, some other interesting trends emerge. First, although correction officers continued to increase, they did so at a much slower pace; meanwhile, the number of civilians working for the Department of Corrections began to decline significantly. This was primarily due to the fact that the Department was under tremendous pressure to limit spending even as the number of officers increased; the reductions came at the expense of the "less crucial" civilian staff. The other large decreases were in social services (down 20% from 1993 to 1997) and in the non-teaching staff of the Board of Education. The 20% drop in social services staff during the Giuliani administration resulted from a combination of factors: greater contracting out of services to non-governmental agencies, as well as a conscious policy of reducing headcount for general budget reduction purposes. As for the contraction of the non-teaching staff in the school system, which began in 1989, the Board, under pressure for a number of years to cut its "bloated bureaucracy" as some politicians have called it, reacted by imposing significant cuts of administration and support staff. The number of teachers continued to increase after 1989 but at a much slower pace than the increase in criminal justice personnel from 1989 to 1997.

Table 22-3:
EMPLOYEES WORKING IN CRIMINAL JUSTICE AGENCIES
AND OTHER FUNCTIONS
New York City, 1979 - 1997

FUNCTION	YEAR				PERCENT CHANGE			
	1978	1989	1993	1997	78-89	89-93	93-97	78-97
Police (1)	34,100	39,600	42,600	46,800	+16%	8%	10%	37%
Uniform	29,400	32,000	34,600	38,200	9	8	10	30
Civilian	4,700	7,600	8,000	8,600	62	5	8	89
Corrections	4,100	11,800	13,500	13,000	190	15	-4	219
Uniform	3,300	9,900	11,400	11,300	200	16	0	245
Civilian	800	1,900	2,200	1,600	147	13	-25	109
Probation	1,100	1,600	1,600	1,600	40	3	-4	34
Prosecution (2)	1,800	3,400	4,000	4,100	99	16	3	134
Juvenile Justice (3)	na	600	700	500	na	17	-17	na
Total Crj (4)	41,000	57,000	62,500	66,000	40	10	6	59
Social Services	23,000	29,200	28,800	23,100	27	-1	-20	0
Education	71,200	84,800	87,000	88,000	19	3	1	24
All City Employees	203,700	247,000	249,000	237,000	22%	1%	-5%	16%

Notes::
All headcounts are actual employment totals, as of June 30th of the fiscal year.
Headcounts are rounded off to the nearest 100.
Percents are rounded off to the nearest integer.
na= not available
 (1) Includes the Housing and Transit Police, until their merged with the NYPD in 1995.
 (2) Includes the 5 elected district attorneys and the appointed Special Narcotics Prosecutor.
 (3) The DJJ had its employees work overtime to make up for the declining headcount.
 (4) Doesn't include the DJJ workforce in 1978; also excludes lawyers contracted to serve indigents.

Source: Data provided by the Office of Management And Budget

Since many of the headcount trends changed during the 1990s, it is worth comparing headcount figures, as was done for budgets, for the administrations of David Dinkins and Rudolph Giuliani. (Refer back to Table 22-3 which compares the changes in headcounts for 1989 to 1993 and 1993 to 1997). Some interesting differences emerge between the two mayoral administrations and between some of the headcount trends versus budget trends.

Except for the NYPD, every criminal justice agency as well as education, social services and, in fact, the entire City headcount grew more slowly or was reduced during Mayor Giuliani's first term as compared to the Dinkins administration. As mentioned previously, however, the headcount growth in the number of sworn officers in the Police Department was due to the planned and budgeted growth which was part of David Dinkins' Safe Streets/Safe City program.

Corrections, whose headcount grew by 15% under Mayor Dinkins, was reduced by 4% under Mayor Giuliani (this reduction was primarily due to a significant decrease in the jail population during Rudolph Giuliani's first term). The five District Attorneys offices, which enjoyed almost a 16% growth in size under Mayor Dinkins grew at a dramatically slower rate, less than 3% under Mayor Giuliani. In fact, the total criminal justice headcount grew by close to 10% under David Dinkins as compared to less than 6% under Rudolph Giuliani. If the growth in the Police Department's uniform headcount is adjusted by attributing it to the Safe Streets/Safe City plan, there actually was no growth at all in the criminal justice headcount during Mayor Giuliani's first term.

Not surprisingly, in the area of social services, where headcounts declined slightly under Mayor Dinkins (down slightly more than 1%), a dramatically decreased headcount materialized under Mayor Giuliani, (a cut of 20%). In fact, the decrease in social services headcount of about 5,750 positions made up almost half of the total reduction of 11,900 municipal jobs which occurred during Mayor Giuliani's first term. The growth in employees of the Board of Education was just 1% during the first Giuliani administration compared to close to 3% under Mayor Dinkins. The entire City headcount which began declining slightly (about one half of one percent) during Mayor Dinkins' term, dropped at almost ten times that rate (down 5%) during Mayor Giuliani's first term.

When the proportion of total headcount devoted to criminal justice, social services and education is examined (see Table 22-4), the same trends noted earlier in the analysis of the budget become slightly more pronounced.

Table 22-4 shows that employment in criminal justice grew more substantially than in education, in terms of proportion of total City headcount. Additionally, the headcount for social service agencies actually declined as a proportion of all municipal jobs. Finally, the enormous increase in staffing correctional institutions is apparent from its share of total headcount jumping from 2% to close to 6% of all City workers. When examining workforce changes, the subtle shift of resources from social services to criminal justice, and especially to corrections, becomes more obvious. With criminal justice employment growing at a far greater rate than education (or any other governmental function), and with social service positions declining as a proportion of the total City headcount, it can be said that the justice system expanded at the expense of the social service safety net. Did this growth of the legal apparatus enhance public safety? The next section will demonstrate that it did not.

Table 22-4:
PERCENTAGE OF ALL MUNICIPAL EMPLOYEES
NEW YORK CITY, fiscal years 1978 - 1997

YEAR	1978	1997
FUNCTION		
Criminal Justice	20%	28%
Corrections	2	6
Social Services	12	10
Education	35	37
All Other	33%	25%

Notes: Percents are rounded off to the nearest integer.
Source: Data supplied by the New York City Office of Management and Budget

---

CHANGES IN WORKLOADS

Increases (or decreases) in resources can be the result of a myriad of factors. Resources can increase because an agency's workload increases (for example, more inmate admissions to the corrections system creates a need for more jail space and more officers, which in turn requires increased funding). Resource changes can also be the result of an administration's political priorities. For instance, the delivery of social services is clearly not as high a priority for the Giuliani administration as it was for the Dinkins'. The reduction in headcount for these agencies accompanied by the slow rate of growth of funds for social services during this administration was a reflection of that relatively low priority.

This section will examine the workload increases of agencies in the criminal justice system since 1978 in an attempt to see whether workload increases or decreases are responsible for the corresponding trends in their budget.

Changes In Arrests Made By The Police

The police are the engine that drives the criminal justice system. That is, the rest of the system reacts to the volume and type of arrests made by the police. Generally, the greater the number of arrests, the greater the number of prosecutions and indictments, which in turn cause more work for defense attorneys and courts, and a greater need for jail space and prison cells upstate (which are paid for by the Governor's budget).

Table 22:5 examines the growth in arrests, from 1978 to 1997. The table shows there has been a general upward trend in police arrest activity from 1978 (or more accurately, from 1980) to 1997. Except for a four year decline from 1989 to 1993, total arrests increased steadily over this period. This overall trend is mirrored in felony arrests through 1994. However, felony arrests have slowly but steadily declined from 1994 to 1997, as the number of serious crimes committed within city limits dropped sharply. Misdemeanor arrests decreased from 1987 to 1990, and then slowly increased from 1990 to 1993 and then soared from 1994 to 1997.

Table 22-5:
TOTAL ARRESTS
New York City, 1978 to 1997

TYPE OF ARREST	YEAR				PERCENT CHANGE			
	1978	1989	1993	1997	78-89	89-93	93-97	78-97
Misdemeanors	83,200	129,800	129,400	204,800	+56%	0%	58%	146%
Felonies	87,900	153,100	125,700	130,200	74	-18	4	48
All Arrests	171,100	282,900	255,100	335,000	65%	10%	31%	96%
Drug Felonies As % of Total (1)	9%	32%	31%	32%				

Notes: Arrests are rounded off to the nearest one hundred.
    Percent changes are rounded off to the nearest integer.
    (1) Percentage of all arrests that were on felony drug charges.
Source: DCJS Computerized Criminal History System

Clearly the greatest growth in police arrest activity (up 65%) took place during Edward Koch's three terms as mayor (1978-1989). That period of increasing workload was followed by a 10% decrease in total arrests during David Dinkins' term of office. This trend was dramatically reversed during Rudolph Giuliani's tenure with a big increase (31%) in total arrests brought about by a huge (58%) increase in misdemeanor arrests. In fact, the 31% increase in arrests during Mayor Giuliani's first four years is slightly less than half of what was achieved under 12 years of Mayor Koch (65%). Significantly, it was the dramatic increase in the number of felony arrests from 1978 to 1989 (74%) which changed the face of the criminal justice system. Ed Koch and his police department's reaction to the City's burgeoning crack epidemic was to make massive numbers of felony drug arrests. Since 1985, large numbers of felony drug arrests are the primary reason for the overall increase in total felony arrests up to the present. As Table 22-5 shows, drug felony arrests comprised less than one-tenth of all felony arrests at the start of the first Koch administration. By the time that David Dinkin's assumed office, felony arrests for selling drugs or possessing large quantities had more than tripled to about one-third of all arrests for serious offenses. That proportion of about one-third persisted throughout the 1990's. These arrests, as will be made clear later, caused an upsurge in the City's jail population. Misdemeanor arrests actually increased faster under Rudolph Giuliani's four years, 58%, than during the entire 12 years Ed Koch served as mayor, 56%. This increase can be attributed to the crackdown on minor quality of life infractions under Mayor Giuliani's direction. Clearly, arrests for minor offenses were not a high priority for the New York City police under Mayor Dinkins, who instead emphasized community problem solving police strategies.

The police department, it seems, is quite capable of increasing or decreasing the number of arrests it makes, based on policy priorities, deployment patterns, and anti-crime strategies. Therefore, the total system workload has little relationship to the actual number of police officers. Increases in police headcount do not explain increases in total arrests. Between 1978 and 1997, the number of police officers grew by almost 30% while the total number of arrests grew by over three times that rate (by 96%). From 1978 to 1989, the Koch years, arrests increased at 65.4% or more than seven times the 9% increase in the number of officers. From 1989 to 1993 (Dinkins), the number of officers grew by 8% compared to a 10% decline in arrests, and from 1993 to 1997 the number of officers grew by 10% but arrests increased by three times that much, 31%. Over the last two decades, the police have, at times, made arrests far in excess of any increases to the size of the police force, but they have also reduced the number of arrests even while the size of the force was increasing.

Changes In Indictments Secured By Prosecutors

One of the most important workload indicators for prosecutors, the courts, and the City jail and state prison system is the number of felony indictments secured annually. The number of accused felons indicted by grand juries determines the caseload of defendants that assistant district attorneys must prosecute and defense lawyers must represent. This court caseload in turn is one of the main determinants of the size of the inmate population that must be detained in City jails and that will eventually go to State prisons.

Table 22:6 illustrates the growth (and decline) of the number of annual indictments in New York City along with the annual percentage of felony cases which eventually resulted in an indictment.

Table 22-6:
FELONY INDICTMENTS
New York City, 1979 to 1997

	YEAR 1978	1989	1993	1997	PERCENT CHANGE 78-89	89-93	93-97	78-97
Felony Arrests	87,900	153,100	125,700	130,200	74%	-18%	4%	48%
Indictments	15,500	53,900	47,400	36,700	248	-12	-23	137
Percent Indicted	18	35	38	28				

Notes: Number of felony arrests and number of indictments are rounded off to the nearest one hundred.
Percents of felony arrests leading to indictment are rounded off to the nearest integer.
Source: DCJS Indictment Statistical System

A couple of notable trends are apparent from Table 22-6. First, the number of indictments climb steadily from 1978 to 1989, representing a 248% increase. From 1989 to 1997, however, felony indictments steadily declined in New York City, falling to 36,700 in 1997 (a 32% decrease). The decrease in indictments is partially the result of an overall decrease in felony arrests from 1989 to 1997 (down 15%). The other reason for the decline in indictments is the slipping percentage of felony cases which result in an indictment. This percentage rose from 18% in 1978 to 38% in 1993. That is, more than twice the proportion of felony arrests resulted in an indictment in 1993 compared to 1978, indicating that either the seriousness or gravity of felony arrests increased during that time period, or that prosecutors simply became more aggressive in trying to indict felony defendants. There can be little doubt that prosecutors were very intent on trying to indict drug felony arrestees during the late 1980s because the crack epidemic was being highly publicized during this time. In fact, from 1984 to 1990, the percentage of all felony arrests resulting in indictment rose from 27% in 1984 to 37% in 1990. However, the entire period of the 1990s has seen a dramatic decline in indicted felony cases far in excess of the proportionate decline in felony arrests. This is powerful evidence that there has been a huge decline in the actual amount of work that prosecutors, judges and defense attorneys perform in the Supreme Court (which processes indicted felonies - as opposed to the City's criminal courts which handle misdemeanors, where workloads have increased substantially). The decline in felony indictments is also evidence of a diminution in the seriousness of the felony arrests which have been made in the City over the last seven years. This may well be due to the emphasis on quality of life arrests as well as the significant declines in the number of reported felonies in the City.

Changes In The Jail Population

Whether examining budgets or headcount figures, it was evident that no component in the criminal justice system (nor other large governmental functions like social services and education) has increased as rapidly as the New York City Department of Correction. The reasons for this trend becomes obvious in Table 22-7.

Table 7:
SIZE OF THE CITY JAIL POPULATION
New York City, Fiscal Years 1980 -1997

FISCAL YEAR	1980	1989	1993	1997	PERCENT CHANGE 1980-89	89-93	93-97	80-97
Average Daily Population	8,500	17,400	19,300	19,200	+105%	11	1	126
Total System Admissions	48,100	120,000	106,900	133,300	150	11	25	177

Notes:: Populations and admissions are rounded off to the nearest one hundred.
1978 system admissions figures are not available. 1978 average daily population was 6,990.
Source: NYC DOC.

From fiscal year 1980 to 1997, the New York City jail system increased by 126% from an average daily population of 8,500 to around 19,200. Almost all of this increase, 105%, occurred between 1980 and 1989, during Ed Koch's tenure as mayor. The size of the system expanded by 11% under David Dinkins and remained stable under Mayor Giuliani. The City jail system grew most rapidly from 1988 through 1992. That is, the system expanded most rapidly during Mayor Dinkins' term, peaking at an annual average daily population of 21,400 in fiscal year 1992. Interestingly, when examining the year-to-year figures from 1993 to 1997, the size of the jail system has decreased in certain years by over 3,000 beds from the peak population during Mayor Dinkins' term of office. This trend continues up to the present with an inmate population hovering around 18,000. Given the decrease in indictments and fewer felony arrests (but many more "quality of life" misdemeanor arrests during the first Giuliani administration), the decreases in the jail population are understandable but are not something which many analysts would have predicted, given Mayor Giuliani's well-known conservative crime fighting agenda.

An extremely interesting trend illustrated in Table 22-7 is the relationship between the number of jail admissions and the average daily population over the years. During the period 1989 to 1993, the number of jail admissions rose by 11% and the average daily population expanded by the same amount. However, from 1993 to 1997, the number of jail admissions grew by 25% yet the daily population remained basically stable. This is due to the huge increase in misdemeanor arrests. More defendants charged with lesser crimes entered the detention facilities, but their lengths of stay were short. Thus, even though the sum total of admissions per year went up, the daily population remained about the same or even shrank a little as the proportion of people locked up for committing misdemeanors grew.

The explanation for the overall growth in inmates from 1978 to 1997 seems on its face to be relatively simple: as arrests and particularly felony arrests increase, so does the City's jail population. But this is only partly true. Felony arrests increased by 48%, total arrests by 96% and indictments by 137% from 1978 to 1997; but the City's jail population went up by 175%. Obviously there are other factors which determine the size of the City's jail population other than the volume of arrests or indictments. Prosecutorial plea negotiation policies and changes in sentencing severity are two key factors which have a huge impact in determining how many people go to jail and for how long.

One of the biggest factors influencing inmate populations, in addition to the number of arrests, is the length of stay of those awaiting trial who are housed in the City's jails. Because the City jail system is primarily a detainee system (that is, almost three quarters of all inmates are awaiting trial or their cases have not reached their final disposition), the longer defendants are detained, the larger the system must be.

In fact, the time spent by inmates awaiting felony trials has increased dramatically over the last eight years. From 1982 to 1989, the length of time it took New York City courts to dispose of felony cases actually shrunk by 32%, from an average of 153 days to 104 days. Since 1990, however, the average time until disposition has shot back up. What is especially puzzling about this pattern is that the court system actually disposed of felony cases faster from 1982 to 1989 even though indictments, the Supreme Court's main source of workload, increased by 92%. Since 1989, however, as indictments decreased by 32%, the time it took the courts to dispose of cases increased by 36% (as of 1997). As workload increased during the 1980s, the courts accomplished more work faster (in disposing of felony cases); as workload decreased during the 1990s, the courts accomplished less work and were slower in disposing of felony cases. These completely contradictory trends are one of the ongoing mysteries of the City's criminal justice system.

This paradox is more than simply an esoteric academic observation. The longer it takes the courts to dispose of cases, the more crowded the jails are (and the more facilities the City must build). If the courts disposed of felony cases today as fast as they did when there was significantly more work to do eight years ago, the New York City Department of Correction estimates it could save over $200 million annually by closing down jails which would become vacant as inmates left the system faster! The increasing length of stay in the 1990s is one of the reasons why the jail system increased in size from 1989 to 1993, even as total arrests, felony arrest and indictments all declined during this period.

Although the state prisons are not part of the City criminal justice system, it is worth examining how the number of convicted criminals the City sends to upstate prisons have changed since 1978. From 1978 to 1996, the number of criminals receiving state
sentences increased from 4,600 to nearly 14,500 (up 214%). However, since 1992, the City has sent fewer and fewer people to state prison every year, from 17,900 to 14,500 in 1996, a 19% decline. Given the City's recent decline in indictments and felony
arrests, this decrease is not surprising; however, is it not well known.

CHANGES IN OVERALL CRIME TRENDS

What, then, has happened to the reported rates of crime in New York City during this period of growing budgets, changing headcounts and changing workloads?

Over the last 20 years, total crime and violent crime rose from 1978 to 1981, then declined slightly from 1981 to 1985, and, beginning in 1986 started to climb steadily until they peaked in 1990. From 1978 to 1989, while Ed Koch was mayor, total index crimes increased by 25%, violent crimes by 38%, and murders by 27%. Since 1990, all reported street crimes and violent crimes in particular have declined, incredibly rapidly since 1994. Total crime and violent crime in New York City have fallen to their lowest levels in over 30 years.

One of the lesser known facts about these trends is that it was under David Dinkins that the City's crime rate first started its current remarkable decline. Though murders did remain at a high level during Mayor Dinkin's four years, total index crime reported to the NYPD took a downturn after years of steady increases, dropping by 16%, with violent crime dipping 9%. One of Mayor Dinkins' great frustrations is that he generally receives little credit for the City's declining crime rate since 1990. Given the impressive drops in every category of street crime during Mayor Giuliani's first term (reported index crimes down by 41%, violent crimes by 40%, and murders by 60%), this lack of public appreciation of Mayor Dinkins' accomplishments is not surprising. The fact that David Dinkins does not get recognition for crime rates beginning to slide during his years in office, or for expanding police and corrections, raises the question of how mayors come to the decision to enlarge the criminal justice system when resources are limited.

There are numerous reasons why a mayor would choose to spend more or less on any particular function of government. Mayors allocate funds based on workload, need, emergencies, unforeseen events, or personal political priorities. The last three mayors have come into office with different initial ideas about how much funding should be set aside for criminal justice, but during their terms they were confronted with unforeseen events that impacted workloads.

When Ed Koch became mayor in 1978, he probably never dreamed that the size of the jail system would triple under his three administrations. Although he can be labeled a "conservative" on law enforcement issues such as favoring long prison sentences and the death penalty (matters that are not under a mayor's control), Ed Koch probably had no preconceived notion that he would end up spending over $600 million more per year on jails in 1990 than in 1978. While spending on criminal justice probably would have increased during the 1980s anyway, the crack epidemic hit New York City hard starting in the middle of the decade. The use and sale of highly addictive rock cocaine led gangs to fight over its distribution and sale, and in the midst of this drug-related violence, police in the City increased felony drug arrests more than threefold from 1982 to 1989 (from 14,500 to 49,500). As a result, the jail system ballooned by over 12,000 beds during that same time. The response that Mayor Koch chose, to arrest large numbers of drug sellers and customers via police sweeps and buy and bust operations, reflected his law and order political philosophy. But this huge expansion would not have occurred to such an extent if there had not been a surge in illegal drug-taking.

David Dinkins, on the other hand, was labeled a "progressive" with political priorities that emphasized funding for child welfare services, health care, and public schools, and not criminal justice when he took over the helm of municipal government. He probably never intended that jails would be one of the fastest growing items in his City budget, nor that he would be responsible for one of the largest expansions ever of the NYPD. David Dinkins was not confronted by the sudden emergence a new problem such as the burgeoning crack epidemic that hit while Ed Koch was in office. However, shortly after taking office in 1990, he was met by a barrage of news media stories about murder and mayhem, culminating in a tabloid headline that beseeched him to take aggressive steps (Do Something Dave!). Under intense public and political pressure, he created the Safe Streets/Safe City plan which has added billions of dollars to the City's criminal justice budget since its inception in 1992 (it should be noted that Mayor Dinkins also included funding for drug education, prevention, and treatment programs). But the experience provides another example of a mayor being confronted with an unforeseen situation (in this case, largely created by the media) that compels him to accept policies he would not otherwise have chosen. There is no doubt that David Dinkins, given his political leanings, would have preferred to invest those scarce resources in programs for children. While both Mayors Koch and Dinkins reacted to different kinds of public events by significantly expanding the criminal justice system, it clearly pained David Dinkins much more than Ed Koch to do so.

Ironically, Rudolph Giuliani, who came into office with a reputation as a crime-fighter, has never been confronted with a situation analogous to the crack epidemic of the late 1980s or the series of screaming "do something" headlines of 1990. Without these external pressures or events, Rudy Giuliani has felt free to implement a variety of law enforcement strategies without significantly increasing the size of the City's criminal justice apparatus. If Mayor Dinkins is given credit for the planned and soundly funded expansion of the police force, there was no expansion of the system at all under Mayor Giuliani. Of course, if Rudolph Giuliani is confronted by a late 1990s equivalent of the crack epidemic, his policy choice might indeed be to increase the size of the criminal justice system. He might well act as the other mayors have done. The political pressure on any mayor to add police, prosecutors, and jail space during actual or perceived crime waves should not be underestimated. The City's recent experience of rapidly subsiding crime rates with minimally increased spending, however, has shown that the conditioned response of adding huge amounts of money to the criminal justice system in order to effectively quell criminal activity is both wrong and wasteful.

CONCLUSIONS:

Is there any overall lesson or conclusion to be drawn from examining the New York City criminal justice system's resources (financing and staffing), workloads and results (crime trends) after twenty years?

The completely counter-intuitive answer is that over the last 20 years, crime has increased the most when the City has increased spending the most; and crime has declined as City increases on criminal justice spending have slowed. During the three Koch administrations, the City increased criminal justice spending by 170% yet crime rose by 25%. During the Dinkins administration, criminal justice spending rose by 19% while crime declined by 16%. During the first Giuliani administration, spending only increased by 12% while total reported crime declined by 41%.

Clearly, to paint a simple relationship between spending and crime rates is misleading. On some level, it makes sense that as lawbreaking increases, a local government will spend more to combat disorder, and when illegal activities subside, the municipality will spend less. The lesson here is not that as spending decreases crime will decrease; nor is the lesson that as spending increases crime will decline. This is obviously not the case.

The crime problem is a complicated social phenomenon which is influenced by a host of factors including demographics, the health of the economy, the degree of social disorganization in communities, and the effectiveness of law enforcement strategies. There is no easy answer about how much resources are the right amount of money to spend in fighting crime. However, it is clear that it is absolutely not necessary to keep increasing the size of the criminal justice system in order to reduce crime. Nowhere is this lesson clearer than for the City's experience during the first four years of the Giuliani administration. The City experienced the lowest increase in criminal justice spending during this four year period compared to the prior 16 years. The City corrections system has shrunk in size, and the City courts send fewer people to state prison than they did before (a trend which started in 1992, before the dramatic downward drift in crime rates materialized). The police force has shown it can be more productive without hiring additional officers (as increases in arrests per officer attest).

Returning, then to the argument posed at the outset of this chapter, if the experiences of the last two decades prove anything, it is that more and more spending on the criminal justice system does not lead to greater public safety. Given the dramatic decreases in the City's crime rate, and the demonstrated ability to control crime with a declining rate of increased criminal justice spending and a declining incarceration rate, the City should move aggressively to severely limit further expansion of the criminal justice system, especially while there are such pressing needs in education and social services.